Windows NT® For Dumm

Important Windows NT TCP/IP Command Line Utilities

Each of these utilities performs some useful function; the "Help String" column shows how to get online help for syntax details on each command.

Name	Help String	Description
arp	arp /h	Displays and modifies the address translation table maintained by the TCP/IP address resolution protocol
ipconfig	ipconfig /?	Displays all current TCP/IP network configuration data
nbtstat	nbstat /h	Displays protocol statistics and current TCP/IP connections using NetBIOS over TCP/IP (NetBT)
netstat	netstat /h	Displays protocol statistics and current TCP/IP network connections
ping	ping	Verifies connections to local or remote computers (PING stands for Packet InterNet Groper; excellent IP troubleshooting tool)
route	route	Displays and manipulates network routing tables
tracert	tracert	Displays the route from your machine to a specified destination

Important Windows NT Net Commands

Each of these command line utilities performs some useful NetBIOS networking function; use Net Help to get general help on this command, or Net Help <command> to get help on a specific Net command.

Name	Description
Net Accounts	Provides command line tool to manage user accounts
Net Computer	Adds or deletes computers in a domain database
Net Help	Provides access to all Net command help files
Net Helpmsg	Explains Windows NT error messages
Net Print	Use this to view or control print jobs
Net Send	Sends messages to other computers or users on a network
Net Share	Display, create, or delete network shares
Net Use	Connect or disconnect a computer from a share, by name

...For Dummies®: Bestselling Book Series for Beginners

Windows NT® Server 4 For Dummies®

Windows NT Server 4.0 Administrative Utilities (Common)

You can access any of these programs by using the Start, Programs, Administrative Tools (Common) menus, or by typing in the name of the .EXE file below in the Run command.

Name	.EXE File	Description
Administrative Wizards	Wizmgr.exe	Easy way to access NT admin wizards
Backup	Ntbackup.exe	NT's built-in backup/restore utility
Disk Administrator	Windisk.exe	Use this to partition or format NT drives, and to manage mirror sets, duplexed drives, stripe sets, or volume sets
Event Viewer	Eventvwr.exe	Use this to investigate system, security, or application errors; alerts; or other events
License Manager	Llsmgr.exe	Manages and tracks Microsoft license usage throughout an organization
Network Client Administrator	Ncadmin.exe	Use this to build installable network clients for DOS or to copy client-based admin tools
Network Monitor	Netmon.exe	Use this to monitor network traffic and segment activity (install manually; not installed by default)
Performance Monitor	Perfmon.exe	Use this to monitor server performance from the CPU, to memory, to disk activity, network usage, and more
Remote Access Admin	rasman.exe	Use this to manage and monitor Windows NT's built-in Remote Access Server (RAS)
Server Manager	Srvmgr.exe	Use this to manage servers in a domain, and to add or remove NT machines from a domain
System Policy Editor	Poledit.exe	Use this to create and edit system policy files for users, groups, and computers
User Manager for Domains	Usrmgr.exe	Use this to manage user accounts, group memberships, and account policies
Windows NT Diagnostics	Winmsd.exe	Use this to document an NT system's configuration, hardware components, and settings

Cheat Sheet $2.95 value. Item 0524-6.
For more information about IDG Books, call 1-800-762-2974.

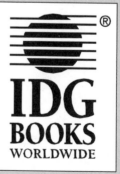

WINDOWS NT® SERVER 4 FOR DUMMIES®

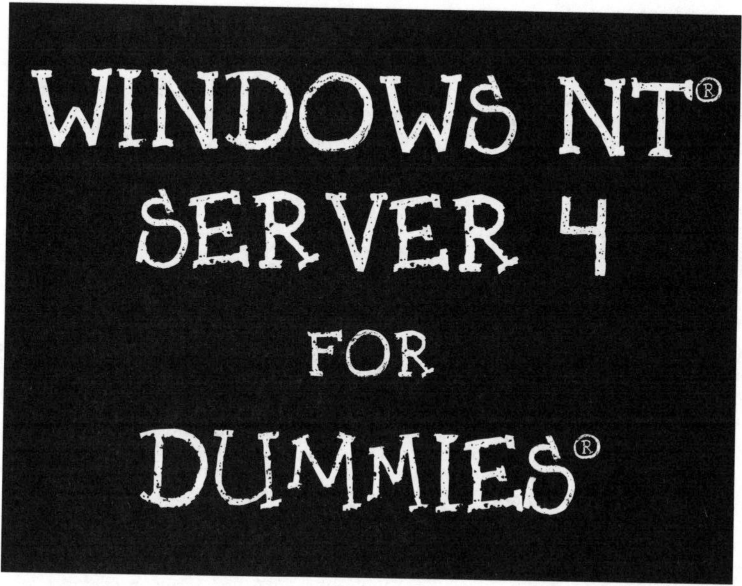

by Ed Tittel with Mary Madden & James Michael Stewart

IDG Books Worldwide, Inc.
An International Data Group Company

Foster City, CA ♦ Chicago, IL ♦ Indianapolis, IN ♦ New York, NY

Windows NT® Server 4 For Dummies®

Published by
IDG Books Worldwide, Inc.
An International Data Group Company
919 E. Hillsdale Blvd.
Suite 400
Foster City, CA 94404
www.idgbooks.com (IDG Books Worldwide Web site)
www.dummies.com (Dummies Press Web site)

Library of Congress Catalog Card No.: 99-60727

ISBN: 0-7645-0524-6

Printed in the United States of America

10 9 8 7 6 5 4 3 2

1B/QV/RR/ZZ/IN

Distributed in the United States by IDG Books Worldwide, Inc.

Distributed by CDG Books Canada Inc. for Canada; by Transworld Publishers Limited in the United Kingdom; by IDG Norge Books for Norway; by IDG Sweden Books for Sweden; by IDG Books Australia Publishing Corporation Pty. Ltd. for Australia and New Zealand; by TransQuest Publishers Pte Ltd. for Singapore, Malaysia, Thailand, Indonesia, and Hong Kong; by Gotop Information Inc. for Taiwan; by ICG Muse, Inc. for Japan; by Intersoft for South Africa; by Eyrolles for France; by International Thomson Publishing for Germany, Austria and Switzerland; by Distribuidora Cuspide for Argentina; by LR International for Brazil; by Galileo Libros for Chile; by Ediciones ZETA S.C.R. Ltda. for Peru; by WS Computer Publishing Corporation, Inc., for the Philippines; by Contemporanea de Ediciones for Venezuela; by Express Computer Distributors for the Caribbean and West Indies; by Micronesia Media Distributor, Inc. for Micronesia; by Chips Computadoras S.A. de C.V. for Mexico; by Editorial Norma de Panama S.A. for Panama; by American Bookshops for Finland.

For general information on IDG Books Worldwide's books in the U.S., please call our Consumer Customer Service department at 800-762-2974. For reseller information, including discounts and premium sales, please call our Reseller Customer Service department at 800-434-3422.

For information on where to purchase IDG Books Worldwide's books outside the U.S., please contact our International Sales department at 317-596-5530 or fax 317-596-5692.

For consumer information on foreign language translations, please contact our Customer Service department at 1-800-434-3422, fax 317-596-5692, or e-mail rights@idgbooks.com.

For information on licensing foreign or domestic rights, please phone +1-650-655-3109.

For sales inquiries and special prices for bulk quantities, please contact our Sales department at 650-655-3200 or write to the address above.

For information on using IDG Books Worldwide's books in the classroom or for ordering examination copies, please contact our Educational Sales department at 800-434-2086 or fax 317-596-5499.

For press review copies, author interviews, or other publicity information, please contact our Public Relations department at 650-655-3000 or fax 650-655-3299.

For authorization to photocopy items for corporate, personal, or educational use, please contact Copyright Clearance Center, 222 Rosewood Drive, Danvers, MA 01923, or fax 978-750-4470.

About the Authors

Ed Tittel is a grizzled veteran of the publishing game, with several hundred magazine articles and over 85 books to his credit. Ed has worked on five other *...For Dummies* books that vary from *HTML 4 For Dummies* (the fourth iteration on this subject, with Stephen N. James as his coauthor) to *Networking with NetWare For Dummies*, 4th edition (with James Gaskin and David Johnson), and other topics. Ed also presides over a small Austin, Texas–based consulting company, LANWrights, Inc., that specializes in network-oriented training, writing, and consulting. In his spare time, Ed likes to shoot pool, cook chicken stock, and harass his growing young Labrador pup, Blackie (or is it the other way 'round?). You can reach Ed via e-mail at `etittel@lanw.com` or on his Web page at `www.lanw.com/etbio.htm`.

Mary Madden is a freelance writer and consultant in the network and Internet arena. She co-authored *Windows NT Networking For Dummies* with Ed Tittel and Earl Follis, as well as other books and magazine publications. Mary currently spends most of her working time at Web design. Mary likes to surf the Net and play the happy householder in her spare time. You can contact Mary via e-mail at `mtml@flash.net`.

James Michael Stewart is a full-time writer who focuses on Windows NT and Internet topics. Most recently, he has worked on several titles in the *Exam Cram/Exam Prep* series for The Coriolis Group. Michael has worked on Windows NT 4 MCSE-level courseware and training materials for several years, including both print and online publications, plus classroom presentation of NT training materials. He has been an MCSE since 1997, focused on Windows NT 4.0. You can reach Michael via e-mail at `michael@lanw.com`, or on his Web page at `www.lanw.com/jmsbio.htm`.

ABOUT IDG BOOKS WORLDWIDE

Welcome to the world of IDG Books Worldwide.

IDG Books Worldwide, Inc., is a subsidiary of International Data Group, the world's largest publisher of computer-related information and the leading global provider of information services on information technology. IDG was founded more than 30 years ago by Patrick J. McGovern and now employs more than 9,000 people worldwide. IDG publishes more than 290 computer publications in over 75 countries. More than 90 million people read one or more IDG publications each month.

Launched in 1990, IDG Books Worldwide is today the #1 publisher of best-selling computer books in the United States. We are proud to have received eight awards from the Computer Press Association in recognition of editorial excellence and three from Computer Currents' First Annual Readers' Choice Awards. Our best-selling *...For Dummies®* series has more than 50 million copies in print with translations in 31 languages. IDG Books Worldwide, through a joint venture with IDG's Hi-Tech Beijing, became the first U.S. publisher to publish a computer book in the People's Republic of China. In record time, IDG Books Worldwide has become the first choice for millions of readers around the world who want to learn how to better manage their businesses.

Our mission is simple: Every one of our books is designed to bring extra value and skill-building instructions to the reader. Our books are written by experts who understand and care about our readers. The knowledge base of our editorial staff comes from years of experience in publishing, education, and journalism — experience we use to produce books to carry us into the new millennium. In short, we care about books, so we attract the best people. We devote special attention to details such as audience, interior design, use of icons, and illustrations. And because we use an efficient process of authoring, editing, and desktop publishing our books electronically, we can spend more time ensuring superior content and less time on the technicalities of making books.

You can count on our commitment to deliver high-quality books at competitive prices on topics you want to read about. At IDG Books Worldwide, we continue in the IDG tradition of delivering quality for more than 30 years. You'll find no better book on a subject than one from IDG Books Worldwide.

John Kilcullen
Chairman and CEO
IDG Books Worldwide, Inc.

Steven Berkowitz
President and Publisher
IDG Books Worldwide, Inc.

Eighth Annual Computer Press Awards 1992

Ninth Annual Computer Press Awards 1993

Tenth Annual Computer Press Awards 1994

Eleventh Annual Computer Press Awards 1995

IDG is the world's leading IT media, research and exposition company. Founded in 1964, IDG had 1997 revenues of $2.05 billion and has more than 9,000 employees worldwide. IDG offers the widest range of media options that reach IT buyers in 75 countries representing 95% of worldwide IT spending. IDG's diverse product and services portfolio spans six key areas including print publishing, online publishing, expositions and conferences, market research, education and training, and global marketing services. More than 90 million people read one or more of IDG's 290 magazines and newspapers, including IDG's leading global brands — Computerworld, PC World, Network World, Macworld and the Channel World family of publications. IDG Books Worldwide is one of the fastest-growing computer book publishers in the world, with more than 700 titles in 36 languages. The "...For Dummies®" series alone has more than 50 million copies in print. IDG offers online users the largest network of technology-specific Web sites around the world through IDG.net (http://www.idg.net), which comprises more than 225 targeted Web sites in 55 countries worldwide. International Data Corporation (IDC) is the world's largest provider of information technology data, analysis and consulting, with research centers in over 41 countries and more than 400 research analysts worldwide. IDG World Expo is a leading producer of more than 168 globally branded conferences and expositions in 35 countries including E3 (Electronic Entertainment Expo), Macworld Expo, ComNet, Windows World Expo, ICE (Internet Commerce Expo), Agenda, DEMO, and Spotlight. IDG's training subsidiary, ExecuTrain, is the world's largest computer training company, with more than 230 locations worldwide and 785 training courses. IDG Marketing Services helps industry-leading IT companies build international brand recognition by developing global integrated marketing programs via IDG's print, online and exposition products worldwide. Further information about the company can be found at www.idg.com.

1/24/99

Authors' Acknowledgments

We have too many people to thank for this book to fit them all on a single page, so we'll start by thanking everybody who helped on this project whom we don't call by name. We couldn't have done it without you!

Ed Tittel: As ever, I'm thankful to many people for making this book possible. To begin with, there's the crew at LANWrights, especially James Michael Stewart, my coauthor, and Mary Burmeister, who managed this project for us. Thanks also to Dawn Rader and Bill Brogden for making this the best place to work, bar none. Then, too, my other coauthor, Mary Madden, is due extra thanks for being such a good sport and for squeezing us into her busy schedule. Finally, I'd like to thank my family and friends, especially Tressa Riley, for making the world a better place to live.

Mary Madden: First, I'd like to thank Ed Tittel for inviting me to join this project and for handling so smoothly the pitfalls we encountered during its writing. Next, thanks to Mary Burmeister for taking my mangled text and making it readable. To Michael Stewart, thanks for all your great chapters in this book! I'd also like to thank the folks at IDG and the tech editor for the many valuable ideas they provided me. Finally, I'd like to thank my friends who put up with my crazy schedule while I worked on this book and who kept me laughing most of the time: Jim Huggans, Michael Spano, Mike Seaman, Nancy Starnes, Boots, JoAnne Holm, Sherif Ahmed, Mark Edwards, Cathy Gianaras, Nelda, and Broxey.

James Michael Stewart: Thanks to my boss and co-author, Ed Tittel, for including me in this book. To my parents, Dave and Sue, you are the best parents a guy could ever have. To Mark, every moment you are away, I learn how valuable friendship is. To HERbert, now that another little one is around the house, you are getting a bit snooty. And finally, as always, to Elvis — your memory lives on every night at Dallas because your death signifies the end of the drink specials!

As a triumvirate, we'd like to thank the many vendors who lent us hardware, software, and support during the research of this book, including Microsoft, O'Reilly, 3Com, and APC. We really must thank the outstanding editorial staff and contractors at IDG Books, including senior project editor Kyle Looper; technical reviewer Andy Simpson; copy editors Patricia Yuu Pan, Ted Cains, and Linda Stark; and editorial manager Leah Cameron. Thanks also go to production coordinators Shawn Aylsworth and Valery Bourke, and the fine team of proofreaders and page layout technicians.

Feel free to contact any or all of us in care of IDG Books Worldwide, 919 East Hillsdale Blvd., Suite 400, Foster City, CA, 94404. Check the "About the Authors" section for our e-mail addresses. Drop us a line sometime!

Publisher's Acknowledgments

We're proud of this book; please register your comments through our IDG Books Worldwide Online Registration Form located at `http://my2cents.dummies.com`.

Some of the people who helped bring this book to market include the following:

Acquisitions, Editorial, and Media Development

Senior Project Editor: Kyle Looper

Acquisitions Manager: Michael Kelly

Copy Editors: Patricia Yuu Pan, Ted Cains, Linda S. Stark

Technical Editor: Andy Simpson

Associate Permissions Editor: Carmen Krikorian

Editorial Manager: Leah P. Cameron

Media Development Manager: Heather Heath Dismore

Editorial Assistant: Beth Parlon

Indexer: Sharon Hilgenberg

Production

Project Coordinators: E. Shawn Aylsworth, Valery Bourke

Layout and Graphics: Linda M. Boyer, Kelly Hardesty, Angela F. Hunckler, Todd Klemme, Brent Savage, Kate Snell, Brian Torwelle

Proofreaders: Kelli Botta, Laura Bowman, Karen Sparrow, Ethel M. Winslow, Janet M. Withers

---

General and Administrative

IDG Books Worldwide, Inc.: John Kilcullen, CEO; Steven Berkowitz, President and Publisher

IDG Books Technology Publishing Group: Richard Swadley, Senior Vice President and Publisher; Walter Bruce III, Vice President and Associate Publisher; Joseph Wikert, Associate Publisher; Mary Bednarek, Branded Product Development Director; Mary Corder, Editorial Director; Barry Pruett, Publishing Manager; Michelle Baxter, Publishing Manager

IDG Books Consumer Publishing Group: Roland Elgey, Senior Vice President and Publisher; Kathleen A. Welton, Vice President and Publisher; Kevin Thornton, Acquisitions Manager; Kristin A. Cocks, Editorial Director

IDG Books Internet Publishing Group: Brenda McLaughlin, Senior Vice President and Publisher; Diane Graves Steele, Vice President and Associate Publisher; Sofia Marchant, Online Marketing Manager

IDG Books Production for Dummies Press: Debbie Stailey, Associate Director of Production; Cindy L. Phipps, Manager of Project Coordination, Production Proofreading, and Indexing; Tony Augsburger, Manager of Prepress, Reprints, and Systems; Laura Carpenter, Production Control Manager; Shelley Lea, Supervisor of Graphics and Design; Debbie J. Gates, Production Systems Specialist; Robert Springer, Supervisor of Proofreading; Kathie Schutte, Production Supervisor

Dummies Packaging and Book Design: Patty Page, Manager, Promotions Marketing

♦

The publisher would like to give special thanks to Patrick J. McGovern, without whom this book would not have been possible.

♦

Contents at a Glance

Cartoons at a Glance

By Rich Tennant

The 5th Wave
By Rich Tennant
System Integration at Disney World
"LOOK, I HAVE NO PROBLEM RUNNING MICKEY-MICROS AND PLUTO-PCs THROUGH A TINKERBELL BUS, BUT WE'RE NEVER GOING TO HAVE A HUEY-DEWEY-LOUIE-LAN ON A MINNIE-MINI WITHOUT SERIOUSLY UP-GRADING ALL OF OUR GOOFY SOFTWARE."

page 7

The 5th Wave
By Rich Tennant
OVENS
AT LAST!
4th GENERATION LANGUAGE TOASTERS
"WHY A 4GL TOASTER? I DON'T THINK YOU'D ASK THAT QUESTION IF YOU THOUGHT A MINUTE ABOUT HOW TO BALANCE THE MAXIMIZATION OF TOAST DEVELOPMENT PRODUCTIVITY AGAINST TOASTER RESOURCE UTILIZATION IN A MULTI-DINER ENVIRONMENT."

page 71

The 5th Wave
By Rich Tennant
"One of the first things you want to do before installing NT Server is fog the users to keep them calm during the procedure."

page 137

The 5th Wave
By Rich Tennant
"This is what happens when good networks go bad."

page 297

The 5th Wave
By Rich Tennant
"You the guy having trouble staying connected to the network?"

page 355

The 5th Wave
By Rich Tennant
"C'MON BRICKMAN, YOU KNOW AS WELL AS I DO THAT 'NOSE-SCANNING' IS OUR BEST DEFENSE AGAINST UNAUTHORIZED ACCESS TO PERSONAL FILES."

page 227

Fax: 978-546-7747 • E-mail: the5wave@tiac.net

Table of Contents

Part II: Putting Your Hardware in Place........................ 71

Introduction

Welcome to *Windows NT Server 4 For Dummies*, the book that helps anybody who's unfamiliar with Windows NT Server or networks in general, to find his or her way around a Windows NT Server–based network. In a wired world, networks provide the links that tie all of us together. Even if you're not using a network already, you will use one some day! This book tells you what's going on, in basic, straightforward terms.

Although a few fortunate individuals already may be acquainted with Windows NT Server and networks, a lot more of us are not only unfamiliar with networking, but may be downright scared of it. To those who may be worried about the prospect of facing new and difficult technologies, we say "Don't worry. Be happy." Using a network is not beyond anyone's wits or abilities — it's mostly a matter of using language that ordinary people can understand.

Ordinary folks are why this book talks about using Windows NT Server and networks in simple — and deliberately irreverent — terms. Nothing is too highfalutin to be mocked, nor too arcane to state in plain English. And when we do have to get technical, we'll warn you and make sure to define our terms, to boot.

This books aims to help you meet your needs. You'll find everything you need to know about Windows NT Server and networking in here, so you'll be able to find your way around — without having to learn lots of jargon or obtain an advanced degree in computer science along the way. We want you to *enjoy* yourself. If networking really is a "big deal" it's important that you be able to get the most out of it. We really want to help!

About This Book

This book is designed so that you can pick it up and start reading at any point — like you might read a reference book. In Parts I and II, networking basics are covered: concepts and terminology in Part I, and the design and implementation of networks in Part II. In Parts III through V, you'll find ample coverage of Windows NT Server and related networking topics. Part III covers installation and configuration of Windows NT Server, while Part IV covers its maintenance and management. Part V completes this picture with chapters on a variety of troubleshooting topics.

Each chapter is divided into freestanding sections, where each one relates to the chapter's major theme. For example, the chapter on installing network interface cards, or NICs, contains the following collection of information:

- A description of a network interface card and how it works
- The various PC buses for which NICs are available
- How to begin the installation process by documenting your current configuration
- How to insert a NIC into a PC
- How to configure a NIC once it's installed in your PC
- What to do when Plug and Play fails to live up to its promises
- Troubleshooting techniques to try when NIC installation doesn't work on the first (or second . . .) try

You don't have to memorize the contents of this book. Each section supplies just the facts you need to make networking with Windows NT Server easy to learn and use. On some occasions, however, you may want to work directly from the book to make sure you keep things straight.

How to Use This Book

This book works like a reference, so start with a topic that interests you. You can use the table of contents to identify general areas of interest or broad topics. The index, however, is your best tool for identifying detailed concepts, related topics, or particular Windows NT capabilities, tools, or controls.

After you find what you need, you can close the book and tackle whatever task you've set for yourself — without having to grapple with unrelated details. Of course, if you want additional information about your topic, you can check the cross-references. If you've never worked on a network before, it's a good idea to read Parts I and II in their entirety. Likewise, if you're new to Windows NT Server, you might want to read all of Parts III and IV. Otherwise, dig in wherever your fancy moves you!

When you need to type something at the keyboard, you'll see text that looks like this: **TYPE THIS**. You're expected to enter this text at the keyboard, then strike the Enter key. Because typing stuff can sometimes be confusing, we always try to describe what it is you're typing and why you need to type it.

This book occasionally suggests that you consult the Windows NT Server online help, printed manuals, the *Windows NT Server Resource Kit,* and even Microsoft's TechNet CD for additional information. In most cases, though, you find everything you need to know about a particular topic right here — except for some of the bizarre details that abound in Windows NT Server.

If there's a topic we don't cover in this book that you need to know more about, we suggest you look for a book on that subject in the *...For Dummies* series, published by IDG Books Worldwide. On the other hand, we also feel obligated to tell you that there's a whole world of Web information about Windows NT available on the Internet and that the Microsoft Web site at `www.microsoft.com/ntserver/` is not a bad place to start looking for such information.

Foolish Assumptions

We're going to climb out on a limb and make some potentially foolish assumptions about you, our gentle reader. You have or are thinking about getting a computer, a network, and at least one copy of Windows NT Server. You know what you want to do with these things. You might even be able to handle all these things yourself, if somebody could only show you how. Our goal with this book is to decrease your need for such a somebody, but we don't recommend telling him or her that out loud — at least, not until you've finished this book!

How This Book Is Organized

The book is divided into six major parts, each of which consists of three to five chapters. Each chapter covers a major topic, and is divided into sections, which discuss some particular issue or concern related to that topic. That's how things in this book are organized, but how you read it is up to you. Choose a topic, a section, a chapter, or a part — whatever strikes your fancy or suits your needs — and start reading. Any related information will be cross-referenced in the text to help guide you through the whole book.

Part I: Getting Grounded in Networking Basics

Part I covers basic networking concepts and terminology including basics of networked communications and what makes networks word — usually, some magical combination of hardware and software. If you're not familiar with networks, this part should come in handy. If you're already a seasoned networker, you can skip this part (and Part II). Look here for discussions about networking terms and concepts, such as client, server, protocol, and topology.

Part II: Putting Your Hardware in Place

Part II covers everything you need to know to build or extend a network, or simply to understand what's really happening on an existing network. It starts with coverage of network design and layout principles, and continues on to discuss how to install and configure network interface cards in a PC. After that, it examines the wiring that links network devices together and talks about how multiple networks can interconnect. Part II concludes with a review of all the software components you're likely to encounter on a Windows NT–based network and why you need them.

Part III: Revving Up Your Server

Part III tackles Windows NT Server head on, starting with its installation and configuration, plus the issues involved in installing and configuring network hardware specifically for Windows NT Server. It also covers how to install and manage print servers and services on a Windows NT–based network, how to handle TCP/IP addresses, and how to set up and manage domains and trust relationships in a Windows NT–based environment. This is where you figure out how to put the basic pieces of a network together by using Windows NT Server.

Part IV: Managing Your Network

Part IV picks up where Part III leaves off — that is, it talks about living with and managing a Windows NT–based network after the initial installation and configuration phase is over. It begins with a discussion of how to manage users and groups on an NT–based network, including profiles and policies, as well as local and global groups. Next, it moves on to cover how Windows NT controls access to NTFS files and directories, and to network-accessible file system resources called shares.

After a network's users, groups, and data assets are in place, rebuilding such a setup from scratch can be a real pain. That's where a backup comes in really handy, so Part IV continues on to cover the ins and outs of backing up and restoring a Windows NT Server machine, plus other aspects of fault tolerance. After that, a review of network security principles and practices should help to prepare you to protect your data from accidental loss and from would-be hackers and crackers.

Part V: Troubleshooting Network Snafus

Part V takes a long hard look at the common causes of trouble on Windows NT-based networks, and explores those areas that are most likely to fall prey to trouble. It begins with a look at some key Windows NT tools for troubleshooting systems then continues on to explore tips, tricks, and techniques for troubleshooting a Windows NT–based network.

After that, Part V moves on to explore common sources and solutions for printing problems, and concludes with a similar look at common sources and solutions for hardware-related difficulties on Windows NT machines. The idea is to identify common pitfalls and potholes and to help you get up, over, or around them without tearing out too much hair in the process. (At least one of your authors, who's as bald as an egg, has already done that for you, thank you very much!)

Part VI: The Part Of Tens

This part follows the grand tradition of the *...For Dummies* books, all of which include The Part of Tens. Here, you'll find lists of information, tips, tricks, and suggestions, all organized into short and convenient chapters. This supplemental information is designed to be both helpful and informative and is supplied at no extra charge.

Icons Used in This Book

The icons used in this book point you to important (and not so important) topics in the text.

This icon lets you know that you're about to encounter information that's important to understand if you really want to *get* what's going on with networking or with Windows NT Server. It may be painful at times, but you have to slog through it.

Ahoy there! This little icon lets you know when you can set sail for another part of the book for further, more detailed information on a particular subject.

Oh gee, we're getting so old that we can't recall what this one means. Maybe you should check one out and see if it's worth watching for!

This icon lets you know that you're about to be swamped in technical details. We include this information because we love it, not because we think you have to master it to use Windows NT Server or networks. If you aspire to nerdhood, you probably want to read it; if you're already a nerd, you'll want to write us about stuff we left out or other information we should put in!

This icon signals that helpful advice is at hand. We also use it when we offer insights that we hope make networking or Windows NT Server more interesting or easier. For example, whenever we include a shortcut that improves your productivity, it's usually marked with the Tip icon.

This icon means what it says — you'd better be careful with the information it conveys. Nine times out of ten it's warning you not to do something that can have nasty or painful consequences, as in accidentally wiping out the contents of an entire hard drive. Whoops!

Where to Go from Here

With this book at your side, you should be ready to wrestle with Windows NT Server and the networks it connects to. Find a subject, turn to its page, and you'll be ready to jam. Feel free to mark up this book, fill in the blanks, dog-ear the pages, and do anything else that might make a librarian queasy. The important things are to make good use of it and to enjoy yourself while you're at it.

The authors of *Windows NT Server 4 For Dummies* have built a comprehensive, electronic glossary of technical terms and jargon for the book to help you make sense of its contents when the occasional techno-term pops up in the text. In this glossary, you'll find flip, irreverent definitions and explanations at the click of a mouse. In fact, the electronic format makes it easier to look up these terms than by flipping pages in your book. For the inside scoop on the words that make our book work, check out the Web page at `www.dummies.com/ntserver4`. Be sure to take the opportunity to register your purchase online or to send the authors e-mail with feedback about your reading and learning experience.

Part I
Getting Grounded in Networking Basics

"LOOK, I HAVE NO PROBLEM RUNNING MICKEY-MICROS AND PLUTO-PCs THROUGH A TINKERBELL BUS, BUT WE'RE NEVER GOING TO HAVE A HUEY-DEWEY-LOUIE-LAN ON A MINNIE-MINI WITHOUT SERIOUSLY UPGRADING ALL OF OUR GOOFY SOFTWARE."

In this part . . .

In this opening part of the book, we provide background material about local-area networks, or LANs. We present the essentials: how computers communicate with one another, why that's a good idea, and what makes networks work. We also cover other vital concepts, including client/server networking; the rules of communication — called protocols — that computers use to exchange information; and the ways in which network wiring can be arranged — called network topologies.

Along the way, you discover all kinds of basic networking terminology and concepts that you may never have heard before (but which everyone will assume that you know when you work on or around a network).

Each chapter presents its material in small, easy-to-read sections. If information is really technical (mostly worth skipping — unless you're a glutton for punishment, in other words), it's clearly marked. Even so, we hope you find this information useful — and maybe, even worth a chuckle or two!

Chapter 1

Demystifying Network Mumbo-Jumbo

In This Chapter

- Understanding network hardware
- Recognizing the role of network software
- Making networks work
- Touring the parts of a network
- Recognizing when the network's up and running
- Sharing resources on a network
- Understanding trends in Windows NT networking

If you've ever used a telephone or watched cable TV, you've used a network, perhaps without even realizing it. Much of the world's modern communications infrastructure, including wired and wireless telephones, cable TV, and the Internet, depends on networks.

Windows NT Server also needs a network. Because a server's job is to provide file, print, and other services to clients across a network, using Windows NT Server without a network is like using a telephone that's not connected to anything. Although a telephone may have some value as a work of art, its true value comes from enabling you to connect and interact with other people. The same goes for Windows NT Server.

In this chapter, we introduce you to the various components that make up an NT Server network and briefly cover how each one works.

What's a Network?

A *network* is a collection of at least two computers that you link together in a way that enables them to communicate with each other. Most networks use electrical wires of some special kind to convey signals and data between computers. However, numerous types of networking media, including wireless broadcast technologies and fiber-optic cables, can support networked connections as well. In other words, you can get from "here" to "there" in many ways on modern networks!

The key ingredients to networking always include a physical connection of some type that permits computers to talk (and listen) using some type of medium. Even if your network medium is wireless, something must connect the computers to an antenna or similar device that allows your computers to receive and broadcast signals.

But more than hardware is involved in networking — although cables and connections are essential, without computer software to use these connections, they're purely decorative and can serve no useful purpose. In the sections that follow, you can find out a bit more about the necessary hardware and software that make networks work.

Hardware makes connections possible

First and foremost, networking requires working connections that enable computers to communicate with each other. Networking hardware makes connections between computers and a network happen and provides the medium (or media) across which information flows from sender to receiver.

A simplified view of networking

You can boil networking down to three essential requirements:

- **Connections** include the necessary hardware to connect a computer to a network, plus the cables (called the *network medium*) that ferry messages between computers. The hardware that attaches a computer to a network is called a *network interface*. In most cases, attaching a PC to a network requires inserting an adapter board called a *network interface card*, or *NIC*. Without a physical connection, a computer can't use the network.
- **Communications** define the rules that computers must follow to exchange and interpret information. Because one computer may run different software than another, the computers need a shared language that enable them to exchange messages and data. Without shared communications, computers can't exchange information, even though they may be attached by a common physical medium.
- **Services** are what computers talk about. In other words, services represent what computers do for each other, including sending or receiving files, messages, print jobs, and so on. Unless computers can perform services for each other across a network, a computer can't respond to requests from other computers, nor can it make requests to other computers.

Networking hardware covers a broad range of devices, many of which you may encounter on your own networks. In the first part of this book, we help you understand the roles and functions of the elements of a typical working network.

From the most basic of perspectives, computers need the following hardware to talk to each other on a typical network:

- A **Network Interface Card (NIC)** is plugged into a computer and attaches to a network cable (or other medium, if something else is being used). It handles turning computer bits into signals on the wire for outgoing stuff, and turning incoming signals into bits for incoming stuff.
- **Connectors** make it possible to attach the network medium to the network interface. For wireless media, connectors permit antennas or other broadcast emitters to be attached to interfaces. They bring all the separate pieces together, so to speak.
- **Cables** convey signals from sender to receiver, either using electrical signals for wire cables, light pulses for fiber-optic cable, or a variety of broadcast frequencies for wireless media.
- **Additional network devices** tie bigger and more complex networks together. These devices can range from relatively simple hubs used to interconnect interfaces on star-wired networks (Chapters 4 and 7), repeaters used to link individual cable segments (Chapter 7), and bridges, routers, and gateways. Suffice it to say, hardware plays an important role in networking, not just to attach computers to a network, but also to interconnect multiple networks, managing how and when data flows from network to network.

Networks need software, too!

Software enables a computer to access and use hardware, whether that hardware is used for networking-related functions or for other purposes.

By now, you should understand that hardware provides the necessary connections that make networking possible, and software supports the communications and services needed to access the hardware and the network to which it's attached.

Thus, many different kinds of software play a role in supporting networking abilities on modern computers. This software includes special-purpose programs called *device drivers,* which allow a computer to address a network interface and exchange data with that interface. The software collection also includes full-blown applications that can access data on a local computer or a server elsewhere on the network with equal aplomb. The software also includes a bunch of other stuff that sits between the small device drivers and full-blown applications.

Throughout this book, we show you how to recognize the various pieces of software involved in networking and how to best configure the software to work with Windows NT Server on a network.

Touring a Network's Facilities

When you take a tour of an average network, you discover many different types of equipment and a variety of related software. If you make an inventory of the different pieces of a network, you can use that list to figure out what's attached to your network, and what those devices do for your network.

The three faces of networking

Network software falls into one of three basic categories: *host/terminal*, *client/server*, and *peer-to-peer*. Each category reflects a certain type of networked communication.

- Host/terminal networks are usually based on an old-fashioned model for networking, even if they don't actually use old-fashioned equipment. In this network's original version, users access information using a device called a *terminal,* which consists of nothing more than a screen, a keyboard, and a network connection. All the software runs on a powerful computer called a *host* elsewhere on the network, and the terminal simply provides a way for users to access remote data and applications (which is why such devices are also known as *dumb terminals*). In more modern versions, PCs can act like terminals through the benefit of *terminal emulation software*, which the PC uses to access a host. The PC still provides some local smarts and access to local word-processing software, spreadsheets, and so on. Even though this represents "stone-age computing," lots of systems still work this way.
- A client/server network consists of a collection of smart machines. One or more of these machines acts as a *server* and has lots of storage space, a powerful processor, and networking software that enables it to handle requests for services from other machines. The other machines that interact with the server are called *clients.* Sometimes, client/server networks are also called *server-based networks* to emphasize the key role that the server plays. Windows NT Server provides the foundation of the client/server network that is the subject of this book, but Novell's NetWare and Banyan VINES are two other kinds of software that play similar roles on modern networks.
- On a peer-to-peer network, any machine that can be a client can also act as a server. Unlike client/server networks, no special-purpose machine acts as a server; on a peer-to-peer network, all machines are considered to be more or less alike in capability and in the services that they offer. If you use the built-in networking that's included in Windows NT Workstation, Windows 98, or Windows 95, you're already using peer-to-peer networking software.

You could refer to the equipment that hooks computers into a network, the cables or other networking media that ferry information between computers, and the hardware and software used to compose and control a network as the infrastructure that makes networking possible. You can also call the collection of connections, cables, interfaces, and other equipment the "glue," because these elements are what bind computers together into a working network.

A computer on every desktop

One of the primary advantages of using networks is that they take what you do at your desk — and we bet that you usually call it "work" — and permit you to interact with a network. This means you can access a file on a server as if it's part of your own disk drive, send a job to a printer elsewhere on the network as if it were hooked directly to your machine, and so on. That's why sharing resources remains the most highly touted benefit of networking, because networking connects your desktop to file stores, printers, applications, and information resources that would otherwise be inaccessible or too expensive to add to every desktop machine.

The terms *network client, desktop computer,* and *workstation* are all used more or less synonymously in network-speak. No matter what you call them, these machines are where users do the bulk of their work (and perhaps some play, at odd moments). One of the key goals that drives networking is to take all the desktops in an organization, whether they run DOS, Windows, UNIX, or the Macintosh OS, and interconnect them so they can communicate and share resources, such as large disk arrays, expensive color or laser printers, CD-ROM jukeboxes, or a high-speed connection to the Internet (all of which would be too expensive to connect to every desktop machine).

On most networks, the ratio of desktop machines to users is pretty close to one-to-one. In other words, each user has access to a workstation attached to the network, even if that user is not the only person who works on that machine. Because workstations are where requests for services originate, such machines are known as network clients, or more simply, as *clients*.

When you call such a machine a *workstation,* you emphasize its ability to support an individual user more or less independently. When you call such a machine a *client,* you focus on its connection to the network. Whatever you call it, it's a machine that sits on your desk that's connected to a network.

I'll be your server

Networking is all about obtaining access to shared services. Because networks are useless unless you can do something with them, access to services is what networking is all about.

On most modern networks, servers provide the capabilities necessary to obtain access to resources or to get things done. For example, when you send a print job to a networked printer, you can safely assume that, somewhere in the background, a print server is handling the job. Likewise, when you request a file from a network drive, a file server is probably involved. For every service, some type of server handles and responds to requests. Sometimes, a single server may provide many services; other times, a server may be dedicated to providing a single service.

The computers that provide services to clients are generically called *servers.* A server's job is to listen for requests from clients for whatever service or services it offers, and to satisfy any valid requests for its services. In fact, validating service requests is an important part of what servers do — you wouldn't want just anybody to be able to print out the salaries for all the workers in your company just because a user asks a print server to do so. You want that server to check that Bob is *allowed* to access that file before you let him print it! Throughout this book, you find out more about such validation, and other key aspects of what it takes for a server to provide services.

The ties that bind a network together

A common pathway must exist between any computer that requests services and any computer whose job it is to satisfy such requests. Just as you need a highway to drive from one city to another, you need a pathway over which your computer can send and receive data. On a network, that's the job of the media that ties all the various pieces together.

Look around and observe what types of cables and connections are in use. Get a sense for the structure of your network so you can tell which highways the users use — from the side roads that only the folks in the accounting or shipping departments use, to the main road that all users use.

When you observe how all these pieces work together — desktops, servers, and media, — you get a reasonably complete view of your network. Figure 1-1 depicts a simple network diagram that shows these purely physical elements of a network. Notice that clients (desktop machines) outnumber servers, and that the media ties all the pieces together. Networking follows the laws of supply and demand, so the more clients you have, the more (or bigger) servers you'll need — and the more work gets done!

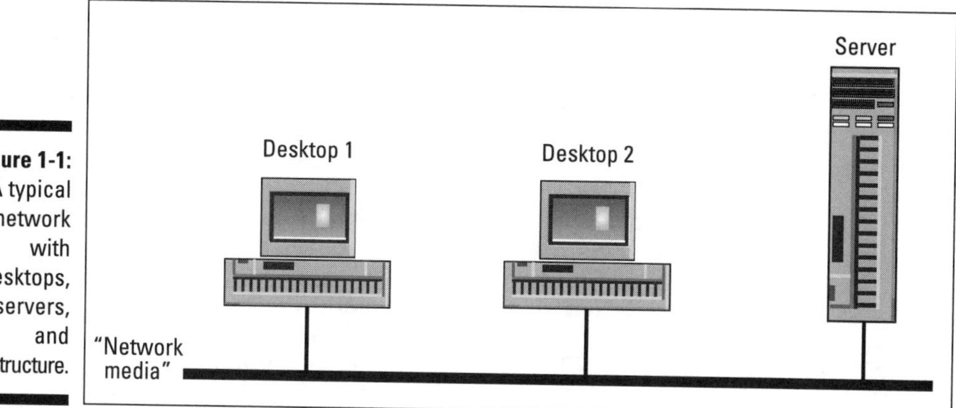

Figure 1-1: A typical network with desktops, servers, and infrastructure.

How Can You Tell That the Network's Working?

Figuring out whether the network is functioning is both easy and hard, and most observers, including novices and experts alike, agree that telling when a network's *not* working is easier than when it is! A client must know how to ask for services from the network and must state precisely what it's requesting. Likewise, a server must know how to recognize and evaluate incoming requests for its services and how to respond appropriately. Only then can a network work correctly. But understanding how this works means looking a little deeper into how clients state such requests and how servers satisfy them. In the following sections, we tell you more about the mechanics of this give and take.

Asking for services isn't asking for favors

Knowing how to ask for network services requires some ability to distinguish between what's available locally on a client machine and what's available remotely from the network. Determining what's local and what's remote is the key to handling network access correctly. This determination depends on specialized software to handle the job in the background, so users don't necessarily have to know the difference.

A computer's main control program is called its *operating system* because it defines the software environment that lets a computer operate and run the applications and system services that get things done on a machine. Most modern operating systems now include built-in networking capabilities to augment their control over local resources and devices.

Some of these modern operating systems are sometimes called *network operating systems* when they create network server environments. Their built-in networking capabilities include a broad range of network services as part and parcel of the underlying operating system. Windows NT Server certainly qualifies in this regard, because it offers a broad range of powerful and flexible networking capabilities.

Right out of the box, Windows NT understands the differences between local and remote resources. The same is true for most modern desktop operating systems, including Windows NT Workstation, Windows 98, Windows 95, the Mac OS, as well as that old (but still modern) war-horse, UNIX.

Within Windows NT, Windows 9*x*, Mac, and Unix operating systems, and through add-ons to DOS and Windows 3.*x*, a special piece of software known as a *redirector* keeps track of what's local and what's remote when users or applications request resources. The redirector takes generic requests for services and sends any that can't be satisfied locally to the appropriate service provider elsewhere on the network (in other words, to the appropriate server). Thus, if you ask for a file that resides on a server elsewhere on the network, the redirector hands your request off to that machine and makes sure the results of that request get delivered properly.

What services are available?

For a computer to use network services, the computer must know how to ask for them. That's what the *requester* does. But knowing what to ask for is as important as knowing how to ask. In most cases, applications supply the necessary information about the network services that they wish to access, either through information supplied from a requester or through knowledge built directly into the application itself.

Electronic mail programs and Web browsers represent good examples of applications with sophisticated, built-in networking capabilities. On the other hand, file system access tools, such as the Windows Explorer or My Computer, rely on the redirector to furnish them with views of (and access to) shared files and printers elsewhere on the network.

Please note that applications with built-in networking knowledge offer transparent access to network services because the applications know how to ask for services and, often, what to ask for on the user's behalf. This lets the user remain blissfully unaware of networking details and trivia. But file managers, printer controls, and other tools with access to both local and remote resources require users to be able to tell the difference between what's local and what's remote. In fact, such tools usually force users to request access to remote resources explicitly and directly.

Increasingly, finding out what services a network can provide is becoming more and more implicit, however. Windows 2000 (the planned successor to Windows NT 4.0) is expected to include a set of directory services that can catalog and describe the services that a network provides to its users. Likewise, Windows 2000 is purported to support a distributed file system that permits directories on multiple machines all around a network to appear as a single network drive to users, so that they don't have to worry about where individual files may reside.

Such sophisticated mechanisms should make it easier than ever before for users to request and access resources implicitly without having to know how to request the resources and determining where they reside. In the meantime, however, some explicit knowledge about such things remains necessary to use Windows NT's current networking capabilities.

It's All about Sharing Resources

The mechanics of requesting resources depend on having access to the right software tools that can determine when network requests are necessary. The software delivers the request to a server whose job is to listen for such requests and to satisfy all the legitimate ones. Ultimately, a server's job is to make resources available to all authorized users. This makes sharing possible and helps to explain the most powerful benefit of networking — namely, to provide a single place where multiple users can obtain controlled access to files, printers, scanners, data, applications, and more.

The secret to sharing is finding some way to make sure that everyone can obtain access to a shared resource. For example, for access to print services, a temporary storage space must hold incoming print jobs until their turn to be printed comes up. Thus, sharing a printer not only means providing access to the device itself, it also means keeping track of who's in line, providing a place where pending jobs can reside, and sometimes notifying users when a print job has completed successfully. All these mechanisms make sharing work and explain why servers are so important to any network.

Because servers bring services and data together in a single machine, servers provide a natural point of control and maintenance for the important stuff on a network, which is, of course, the stuff that everybody wants to share.

Trends in Windows Networking

As we write this chapter, Microsoft has just announced that it's discontinuing the use of Windows NT as a brand name and will refer to the next generation of this software as Windows 2000. This software will feature several types of servers, including Windows 2000 Server (which descends from Windows NT Server 4.0), Windows 2000 Advanced Server (which descends from Windows NT Server 4.0, Enterprise Edition), and Windows NT Datacenter Server (which is an entirely new, high-end Windows server operating system).

Based on early versions of the software and Microsoft's own announcements on the capabilities of Windows 2000, we see the following trends emerging for Windows networking as the next millenium approaches:

- **Use of Active Directory:** Active Directory is Microsoft's name for the directory services environment that Windows 2000 will support. Active directory should make it much easier for users to identify and access network resources and for applications to take advantage of such resources directly and automatically.
- **Access to Dynamic Disk Storage:** In Windows 2000, Microsoft plans to support a variety of sophisticated directory-sharing technologies. Dynamic Disk Storage will enable network administrators to define collections of files and directories gathered from multiple servers around a network and present them to users as if they all resided on a single network drive. This should make identifying and accessing shared files much easier.
- **Consistent Naming Services:** Part of locating resources on a network is knowing their names (or how to find them). Windows 2000 will use a single enhanced method to translate the human-intelligible names given to network resources into computer-intelligible network addresses, which should make managing and interacting with network resources simpler.
- **Web-Based Management Console:** Today, Windows NT Server includes a plethora of administrative tools, utilities, and facilities, all of which are required to install, configure, and maintain a Windows NT network. In Windows 2000, a single Microsoft Management Console (MMC) will play host to management tools (called MMC snap-ins) for all system services, resources, and facilities. The console promises to make Windows 2000's interface much simpler and its many capabilities more visually consistent, and therefore easier to learn and manage. In fact, this capability will work on any computer with a suitable Web browser (and an administrative password, of course).

When all these new capabilities are combined, the trends in Windows networking should be clear: easier, more straightforward access to network resources; simplified administration and management of such resources; and more sophisticated tools and technologies to describe, deliver, and control network resources. We can hardly wait!

Chapter 2

Understanding Client/Server Networks

In This Chapter

- Asking for services
- Providing services
- Scoping out a client/server conversation
- Networking the native way
- Adding on for networking capability
- Learning about the Microsoft Network (and other alternatives)
- Controlling network access
- Understanding Windows NT Server's network services

To a large extent, bringing Windows NT Server into a networking environment means buying into the client/server way of doing things. To help you understand the networking model that best explains the motivation for Windows NT Server, we explore the client/server model in greater detail in this chapter. Along the way, you discover more about the kinds of capabilities and services that really make client/server work and about the various ways that clients and servers interact on networks.

Clients Ask for Services

In Chapter 1, we explain that clients ask for services and that both hardware and software are necessary to make networking work on any computer. In this section, we take a closer look at the various pieces and parts involved in a client/server relationship to help you understand what actually happens when a client requests a service from a server.

At the most basic level, a client must have a network connection available to transmit a request for services. Likewise, the client must have the correct software installed to formulate a request and pass it on to the network, where a server can notice and respond to that request.

The client must have the following hardware:

- **Network Interface Card (NIC):** A NIC or other network adapter enables the computer to interact with the network. You must also configure the NIC properly to transmit signals onto the network medium and receive signals from the network medium.
- **Physical connection:** The link between the computer and the network must be working properly. Clients transmit outgoing signals and receive incoming signals through their connections to the network. Likewise, the network cabling itself — also known as the network medium — must be properly configured and interconnected for signals to get from one computer to another.

This takes care of the connections part in a three-part simple model for networking, which requires that connections, communications, and services all be available and working.

The software on the client computer handles the communications and services that are necessary for the network to operate. Here's a list of software that you normally find on a networked client computer, starting from the hardware level (or as close as software can get to hardware, anyway) and working up to the applications that request network services:

- **Network driver:** A special-purpose piece of software that enables a computer to send data from the computer's central processing unit (CPU) to the NIC when an outgoing message is ready to be sent. The network driver also forwards a request for immediate attention (called an *interrupt*) to the CPU when an incoming message arrives. You might say that the driver allows the PC to communicate with the NIC, which in turn communicates with the network.
- **Protocol stack:** The protocol stack is a collection of communications software that provides the kind of "shared language" (which we describe in Chapter 1) necessary for successful networking. The protocol stack governs which formats network messages can assume, and defines a set of rules for how to interpret their contents. Two computers must use the same protocol stack to communicate. We cover protocol stacks thoroughly in Chapter 3.
- **Redirector:** A redirector, or equivalent software, issues requests for remote resources or services to the protocol stack and receives the incoming replies from the protocol stack. With a redirector running in the background, applications don't need to be explicitly network-aware, because the redirector handles network connections.
- **Network-aware application:** Network-aware applications understand when service requests can be satisfied locally or must be satisfied remotely. In this case, a redirector may be present, but it may not necessarily handle certain kinds of network services (such as e-mail or Web-page access). However, the redirector may handle other kinds of

network services, such as providing access to a file stored elsewhere on the network that's applied as an attachment to an e-mail message. In such a case, the redirector handles grabbing a copy of that file across the network to attach it to the outgoing e-mail message.

When a client makes a request for a resource or service that requires access to the network, either the application (if it's network-aware) or a redirector (if the application isn't network-aware) formulates a formal request for a remote service. Satisfying the request may involve the transfer of a small amount of data (as when requesting a listing of a directory on a machine elsewhere on the network). But it may also involve transferring a large amount of data (as when sending a large file off to be printed or when copying a large file from the client machine to a server).

The request is ferried through the protocol stack that the client and server have in common. For short requests, a handful of short messages travel from the client and are reassembled and handled by the server. For large information transfers, the client breaks up a large file into hundreds or thousands of small information packages, each of which is shipped across the network separately and then reassembled on the receiving end.

The protocol stack talks to the driver to send little packages of data, called *frames* or *packets,* from the computer, through the NIC, across the network to its intended recipient (the server). On the receiving end, the same thing happens in reverse, with a few additional considerations that you find out about in the following section.

Servers Provide Services

In the previous section, we tell you that clients ask for services and that servers provide them. But what handling requests on the server side really means is that a special bit of software, called a *listener process,* runs continuously on the server and listens for requests for a particular service. When a request arrives, the listener process handles it as quickly as possible.

What usually happens on most server operating systems — including Windows NT Server — is that the listener process simply recognizes that a request has arrived. The listener process checks the identity and the associated permissions of the client, and if the client is who it says it is and has the correct permissions for the service, the listener process grants the request for service. It does so by creating a temporary process that exists just long enough to handle whatever service the client requests, after which the temporary process disappears. For example, a request for a particular file on a server would result in the creation of a temporary process (called an *execution thread* in Windows NT– speak) that exists just long enough to copy the requested file across the network. As soon as the copy completes, the temporary process goes poof!

Using a listener process that creates short-lived execution threads allows a server to handle large numbers of requests, because the listener process never stays busy for long handling individual requests. As soon as the listener process creates a thread to handle one request, it checks for other pending requests and handles them if necessary; otherwise, the listener process goes back to its job of listening for new incoming requests. Typically, a server has one or more listener processes for each service that the server supports.

Servers are largely demand-driven. That is, their job is to respond to requests for service from other sources. Only rarely must a server initiate activity independently. This "reactive mode" of server operation helps to explain why the client/server model is also known as a *request/response* or a *request/reply* architecture, in which clients make requests and servers respond or reply to them.

Other than the necessary listener processes and a set of service applications that actually perform services, servers need the same hardware components that clients do. Servers need one or more NICs with a working connection to the network to permit data to enter and leave the server.

On the software side, servers also need the following elements so their services can be available across the network:

- **Network drivers** to enable the server to communicate with its NIC. This software lurks in the background and exists only to tie the computer to the network interface card.
- **Protocol stacks** to send and receive messages across the network. This software also lurks in the background, and provides a common language shared with clients used to ferry information across the network.
- **Service application** that responds to requests for service and formulates replies to those requests. This software runs in the foreground and does the useful work; the service application includes the listener process, the temporary execution threads, and some kind of configuration and management console that allows it to be installed, configured, and altered as needs change. Typical service applications include things like database engines (SQL Server or Oracle), e-mail servers (Exchange), or mainframe gateways (SNA Server).

Most, if not all, software that resides on a server is network-aware, because delivering information across a network is a server's primary function.

A Client/Server Interchange

You may wonder what a conversation between a client and server looks like. Examining the exact formats that such a message exchange takes wouldn't do you much good. But the following sequence represents a pretty typical request to print a file on a network printer (in other words, through a print server) from a spreadsheet program:

1. **A user requests print services in the spreadsheet program by clicking the printer icon or by choosing File➪Print.**

   Assume that a network printer is set as the default printer for the designated print job.

2. **The spreadsheet program formats the spreadsheet and then builds an appropriate print file for the printer.**

   A print file includes the text and graphics that make up a file's contents, but also includes instructions on how (bold, italic, and so forth) and where (top, bottom, left, right) to place elements to be printed.

3. **The spreadsheet program sends the print file to the printer.**

4. **The local networking software (assume it's a Windows 98 redirector) recognizes that the printer is on the network and sends a print request to print that file to the print server.**

   The redirector accesses special name and network address information through a Windows networking service (called the Browse service, which talks to a browser server elsewhere on the network) to figure out where to send the print file.

5. **On the server side, the listener process recognizes and checks out the user's print request. We'll assume it's a legal request, so the listener process creates a temporary execution thread to handle delivery of the incoming print file packets from the client. This temporary thread tells the client to start sending the print file.**

6. **Having now obtained permission to start shipping the file, the protocol stack on the client chops the file up into small chunks called *packets* that are delivered to the temporary thread on the server.**

7. **The temporary thread on the server oversees delivery of the file and places it into a temporary holding area (called a *spool file*) where the print server stores all pending print jobs.**

   The print server places the job in the *print queue,* which stores the print jobs in the order in which they were received.

8. **When the print job reaches the head of the queue, the server creates another temporary thread that ships the job to the printer. In many cases, a different protocol is used to ship data from the server to the printer than the one the client used to ship data to the server in the first place.**

9. **In a final (and optional) step, the print server creates another temporary thread to notify the user that the print job has completed by sending a message to the client computer. Here, the same protocol used to transport the file from the client to the server will be used to send this message back to the client.**

What's worth noting here is that a type of conversation occurs between client and server. The client initiates this conversation when it asks for permission to print, and then sends the print job to the print server. The server takes over from there, storing the incoming print image file in its spool file, managing the queue, and then printing the file when its turn comes. The conversation ends when the server sends notification of job completion to the client.

Requests for other services, such as access to a database server, an e-mail server, or even a file server, are similar to the previous interchange. In such cases, the conversation usually ends when the server sends a data table, message, or file in reply to the client's initiating requests. This request/reply sequence is really what makes modern networks work.

Native Network Clients

Speaking historically, some of the ugliest problems with PCs have been networking related. Prior to the release of Windows for Workgroups in 1993, earlier Microsoft PC operating systems — primarily, Windows 1.*x,* 2.*x,* and 3.*x,* and all versions of DOS up to version 6.0 — included no built-in networking facilities.

Thus, to put a PC on a network, users not only had to deal with installing and configuring NICs and the driver software that makes them work. They also had to purchase or otherwise obtain networking protocol software and networking services software from other vendors. Because neither those users nor Microsoft provided any of these products, these products are called *third-party components*.

Suffice it to say, networking PCs before the days of built-in networking typically meant adding two or more third-party networking products to the mix of hardware and software components on each machine. Typically, one product was required to supply the protocol stack necessary for networked communications, and one or more other products were needed to access whatever services might use that protocol stack to do things across the network. For instance, you would buy a TCP/IP stack for your PC from Chameleon Software, then buy e-mail software from Qualcomm, and then tie it all together by guess and by gosh.

Starting with Windows for Workgroups, and then picking up in a major way with Windows 95 and Windows NT, Microsoft made networking a lot easier for ordinary mortals. They did so by providing built-in networking components as a part of the operating system itself. Although this made life hard for third-party vendors who had been making a good living from their protocol stacks and add-on services products, it definitely made using networks vastly simpler. It was especially appealing to users who wanted networking to be something you could "set and forget" rather than "set and regret" or "fret and reset!"

Today, Windows 98 and Windows NT include all the elements necessary for networking, from multiple types of protocol stacks to many different kinds of client and server capabilities. If you base your network entirely on Microsoft technologies or if the majority of your clients and servers use Microsoft technologies, handling networking is just like handling other parts of the Windows operating system. That is, you still have to know something about what you're doing (which is why you're reading this book, right?), but you don't have to be a rocket scientist to install, configure, and maintain the necessary protocol and service components.

In some compelling cases, however, you may have to mess with third-party networking components, as in days of yore. For example, your network may use a non-Microsoft server, such as NetWare, UNIX, or something else, to provide network services. Or perhaps the collection of built-in services delivered with Windows 98 or NT doesn't include something that you need, and you must add it to the mix yourself.

An example of a useful component that you may decide to add for yourself is NFS. On UNIX-dominated networks, the Network Filing System (NFS) plays the same role for sharing files that built-in file sharing plays on Microsoft networks. If you want to use this capability on Windows 98 or Windows NT, you'll have to buy it from a third-party vendor like Sun Microsystems (the inventor of NFS) or Intergraph (the purveyor of the fastest NFS implementation for Windows NT).

Since 1993, software vendors have come a long way in making their interfaces more Windows-like, making the process of installation and configuration more intuitive for administrators. Today, you can usually find Help files and Wizards to assist you when installing and configuring third-party components. Also, many third-party networks work by using Windows' own native networking facilities, with little or no alteration.

The critical issue in choosing between built-in Microsoft networking components and third-party alternatives (which we cover in detail in Chapters 3 and 8) is the kind of functionality your clients need. Certain client capabilities that third-party vendors offer may not work within the native Microsoft framework. If those third-party components don't work with the Microsoft components, you may have to weigh the requirements for this third-party functionality against the complexity of installing and configuring third-party networking software.

If requirements for third-party software are absolute or if their functionality is essential, you have no choice but to bite the bullet and face a possible configuration nightmare. For example, access to certain driver features in the NetWare client software that aren't supported in the Microsoft counterpart may force you to use Novell software, like it or not. Otherwise, you'd be better off sticking with native Microsoft client software.

Built-in Networking versus Add-ons

You may want to enable clients to access networking services that aren't built into the Microsoft Windows client software. Giving users access to this kind of functionality always requires additional software, such as the software necessary to access NFS. Although Windows 95, 98, and NT can support NFS, that support is not built into those operating systems. Thus, providing users with access to NFS requires obtaining, installing, and configuring additional software on their computers.

Adding new software to network clients is far less traumatic (and more common) than the situation in the previous section that involved changing out the Microsoft client software for Novell client software. As is the case when you install any application on a Windows operating system, the application must be compatible with the operating system, and you must install and configure it correctly. But software that uses only existing protocols and drivers on a Windows machine augments Windows' built-in capabilities, rather than replacing (or displacing) them. Thus, it's quite easy to add compatible products like Qualcomm's Eudora e-mail package, Ipswitch's WS_FTP Pro file transfer program, the Netscape Navigator Web browser, and many, many others to Windows 95, Windows 98, and Windows NT.

Nevertheless, many network administrators try to avoid adding unnecessary protocols and services to Windows machines. That's because each additional protocol and service consumes system resources, such as memory, CPU cycles, and disk space. Granted, they may not use much memory or CPU if they're never, or only seldom, used, but disk space is something they'll always consume!

One of the most profound ways to improve a Windows NT machine's performance is to eliminate unnecessary protocols and services, as well as the *bindings* that tie protocols and services together. Windows NT binds all protocols and services together by default, even when those bindings may not be necessary (or wanted). Thus, a bit of post-installation cleanup can improve performance, as well as remove unwanted software connections. This applies to both Windows NT Workstation and Windows NT Server (managing bindings is covered further in Chapter 8).

Adding third-party client applications or services to Windows machines is okay. This is especially true because most such software uses Windows built-in networking capabilities "under the hood."

Showing Off Your Network Component Collections

Modern Windows operating systems — by which we mean Windows 95, Windows 98, and Windows NT 4.0 — include support for two collections of client software for networking.

Both Windows 95 and Windows 98 refer to these collections as the

- Client for Microsoft Networks
- Client for NetWare Networks

These two client-software collections appear in Figure 2-1, which shows the Configuration tab in the Windows 98 Network Control Panel. Windows NT doesn't use the same terms; instead, in the Network Neighborhood display for a local network it refers to the Microsoft Windows Network and to the Novell NetWare Network. But either way, they're talking about the same things — two different sets of client software that provide access to two different sets of network resources.

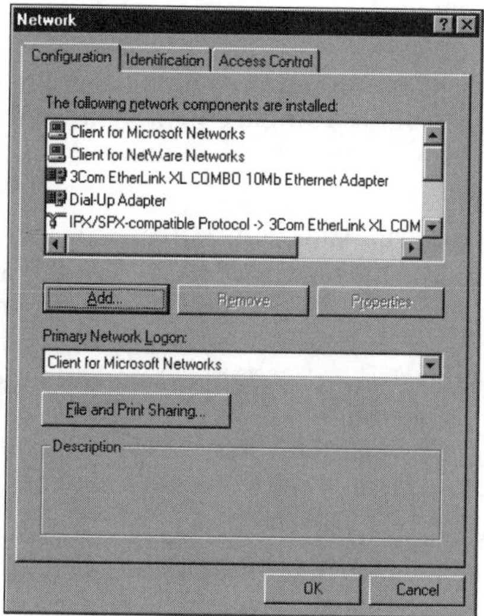

Figure 2-1: Windows 98 refers explicitly to a Client for Microsoft Networks and a Client for NetWare Networks as part of its network configuration; Windows NT is a little more oblique, but works the same way.

As the name suggests, the Client for Microsoft Networks includes the necessary components for a machine to function as a client on a Microsoft network. Likewise, the Client for NetWare Networks includes similar components needed to function as a NetWare network client. Additional software components come into play on Windows NT Server and on client machines that run Windows NT Workstation 4.0, Windows 98, or Windows 95, all of which we cover in Chapter 8.

Pondering the mysteries of the Microsoft Network

Even though Windows NT differs somewhat from Windows 95 and 98 in what it calls its networking software, all three of these operating systems contain both Microsoft- and Novell-specific collections of components. Windows NT calls these two collections the Microsoft Windows Network and the Novell NetWare Network, whereas Windows 95 and Windows 98 call them the Client for Microsoft Networks and the Client for NetWare Networks.

Thus, the Microsoft Network refers to the following collection of software components in all three operating systems:

- **Multiple Provider Router (MPR):** The MPR distributes requests for network services to the right type of *network provider,* which represents a specific type of network client environment (for Microsoft and Novell networks as per the preceding example). The MPR allows Windows 95, Windows 98, and Windows NT to support multiple simultaneous client connections. The MPR also defines a single common interface so applications can access features common to all networks through a single set of interface calls.
- **Microsoft Network Provider:** The Microsoft Network Provider defines an open interface that enables third-party vendors to integrate support for their networks. The Microsoft Network Provider also grants access to and management of network resources and components through common utilities, such as the Network Neighborhood and the Network applet in the Control Panel. The Microsoft Network Provider offers a single set of well-defined functions to browse servers, to connect to or disconnect from servers, and to interact with other network resources.
- **Installable File System Manager (IFSMGR):** This file system access facility integrates multiple file systems through a single interface. The IFSMGR also allows remote file system access requests to look exactly the same as local file system access requests in their structure and functions (they need differ only in how requested objects are addressed).

- **Client for Microsoft Networks Redirector:** This software component checks all application requests for resources, and hands off any requests for remote resources to the network interface, but passes requests for local resources to the local operating system.
- **NetBIOS interface:** This protocol interface defines a high-level request/response protocol that carries requests for remote resources (and their replies). In particular, the NetBIOS interface uses a special messaging protocol called Server Message Block (SMB), to carry requests from clients to servers, and responses to those requests from servers back to their originating clients.
- **Network protocols designed to support Microsoft's Network Device Interface Specification (version 3.1 or higher):** This refers to the built-in networking protocols for Windows operating systems that we discuss further in Chapter 3.
- **A generic NDIS Interface:** This programming convention defines a standard code interface to network adapters within Windows NT 4.0, 95, and 98 operating systems. It permits driver developers to interact with NICs using a well-known, well-documented set of program calls to move data from the computer to the NIC for outgoing messages, and from the NIC back to the computer for incoming messages.
- **A specific NDIS adapter driver:** This device driver translates generic network interface formats into formats specific to whatever NIC (or NICs) is installed in a Windows computer. (Note that only Windows NT supports multiple NICs in a single machine; neither Windows 95 nor Windows 98 offers this capability.)

Figure 2-2 shows this collection of Microsoft Network components and how the various components interact with an application that makes requests and the network that carries those requests to a server, and which delivers the corresponding replies to those requests. Please note that while Windows NT, 98, and 95 are all similarly constructed and use similar components, the details vary among these individual operating systems.

Noodling on the Novell Network

Even though component structure for the Client for NetWare Networks (see Figure 2-2) is similar to that for the Client for Microsoft Networks (which we cover in the previous section), the differences lie in specific NetWare-focused components that replace their Microsoft counterparts. At many steps along the way from the application to the NDIS driver, different components specific to NetWare are used instead.

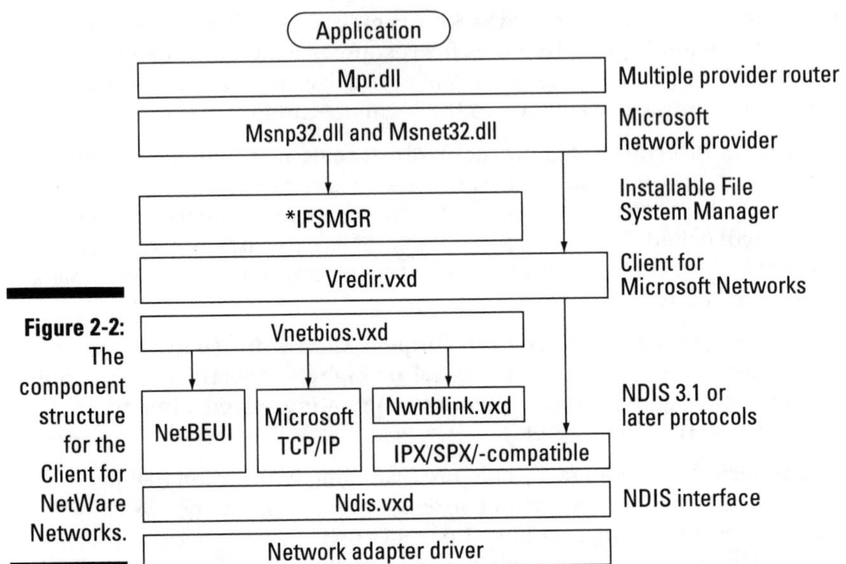

Figure 2-2: The component structure for the Client for NetWare Networks.

From top to bottom, the resulting collection of components is as follows:

- **Multiple Provider Router (MPR):** This software component is common to all network clients for Windows 95, Windows 98, and Windows NT. The MPR hands off network service requests to the appropriate network provider (it routes requests for Microsoft services to the Microsoft network provider, and requests for Novell services to the NetWare network provider).
- **A NetWare-compatible Network Provider:** This software component provides access to and management of NetWare-accessible network resources and components through common utilities, such as the Network Neighborhood and the Network Control Panel. Like its Microsoft counterpart, the NetWare-compatible Network provider offers a single set of well-defined functions to browse servers; to connect to or disconnect from servers; and to interact with other network resources.
- **Installable File System Manager (IFSMGR):** This file system access facility integrates multiple file systems through a single interface for consistent local and remote access to NetWare-based file and print resources when the Client for NetWare Networks is at work.
- **Client for NetWare Networks Redirector:** This software component hands off requests for remote resources to the NetWare network interface and passes requests for local resources to the local operating system.

- **One of several Network protocols:** Either IPX/SPX or TCP/IP could be used to access the network by the Client for NetWare Networks. At present, Microsoft thinks that the protocol most likely to be used here is its own IPX/SPX-compatible NWLink protocol. But because NetWare 5.0 now supports native TCP/IP, the indissoluble link between NetWare and IPX/SPX may soon be broken.
- **Generic NDIS Interface:** This device driver defines a standard interface to network adapters within Windows NT 4.0, 95, and 98 operating systems. The same interface works for both Microsoft and NetWare clients.
- **A specific NDIS adapter driver:** This device driver translates generic network interface formats into formats specific to whatever NIC (or NICs) is installed in a Windows computer. (Note that only Windows NT supports multiple NICs in a single machine; neither Windows 95 nor Windows 98 offer this capability.)

Please note the absence of a separate NetBIOS interface in this collection, which means that NetWare doesn't use NetBIOS-based names to navigate its networks. (For more information about NetBIOS and NetBIOS names please consult Chapter 8.)

The Client for NetWare Networks loses none of its NetBIOS capabilities even though there's no separate NetBIOS interface; applications still need NetBIOS support, and get it. Notice also that the multiple provider router (MPR), the installable file system, the protocols (except for the range of choices), and the NDIS components remain more or less the same for both Microsoft and NetWare clients.

Observing this component-based software structure, you might feel compelled to ask if mixing and matching software components from Novell and Microsoft is possible. Unfortunately, you must go all one way (Microsoft) or the other way (Novell) when putting network client software components in place on a Windows machine. No good comes of trying to meld the two!

You can run both Microsoft and NetWare clients side by side without difficulty, but you can't mix Novell components and Microsoft components willy-nilly on any Windows machine. Thus you can use Microsoft software to access both Windows NT servers and NetWare servers, or Novell software to access both Windows NT servers and NetWare servers. But you can't use Microsoft software to access Windows NT servers and NetWare software to access NetWare servers on the same machine.

Access Permissions and Controls

Part of each request that a client makes for a network resource includes the client's own identification. Another part names the resources that the client is requesting from the network. Clients normally use a password to access resources on a peer-to-peer network, which Microsoft calls *share-level access control* (because each password applies to a single shared resource).

In a Microsoft client/server network, the user's level of permissions governs that user's ability to access resources. In Microsoft-speak, *user-level access* means that when a user identifies him- or herself in a request for service, the user's account name helps to determine which requests the server can honor and which ones it must deny.

The server checks what resources the user has permission to access, and it also checks to see if the operation that the user requests is allowed. For example, Bob may be permitted to read a certain file, but he may not be able to write to or delete that file. If he requests a read operation, the request is permitted, but if he requests a write or delete operation, that request is denied.

Handling requests on a client/server network involves more work than may be immediately apparent, because a *security check* controls access and restrictions. Setting up permissions requires an understanding of which names to attach to resources, to the domains in which they reside, and to the users who state such requests. Much of what you find out in Chapters 8, 11–14, and especially Chapters 15 and 17 touch on these terms and concepts and should explain them to your heart's content.

Common (and Uncommon) NT-based Network Services

In the previous sections, we cover the request/response mechanism that handles all requests for network services and the ways in which responses occur. In this section, we explain what you can do within this structure. Thus, in no particular order (except alphabetical, that is), here's a laundry list of common services that you're likely to find on a Windows NT Server–based network. (You can examine a list of services on your Windows NT Server on the Services Tab in the Network applet or in the Services applet within Control Panel.)

- **Alerter:** Provides the ability to send alarms and alerts to specific recipients when events occur in Event Viewer, or thresholds are exceeded in Performance Monitor.
- **Computer Browser:** Manages the list of computer and resource names on a specific network, so that users can browse a list of what's out there (and available) in Network Neighborhood and other utilities.
- **Directory Replicator:** Provides a way for NT Server to generate copies of important files to other network machines, which may include other NT Servers, Workstations, or LAN Manager servers.
- **Messenger:** Provides a way for NT Server to deliver on-screen messages to designated recipients in response to explicit commands or to alarms and alerts.
- **Net Logon:** Handles user attempts to log on to the network and ferries information from a primary domain controller to all backup domain controllers within a single Windows NT domain.
- **NetBIOS Interface:** Handles name services and service requests that use NetBIOS protocols to ferry messages between a sender and a receiver.
- **Network DDE:** Allows dynamic updates to occur across a network. DDE (Dynamic Data Exchange) refers to a dynamic update technology used to propagate updates from one file or document to another when embedded objects in one document must reflect changes to that object in another document.
- **Network Monitor:** Permits tracking and graphing of network traffic on a single cable segment or into and out of a specific computer (where the Network Monitor agent is running).
- **NT LM Security Support Provider:** Provides a Windows NT security model that's compatible with LAN Manager (LM). This service handles encryption and delivery of logon requests that can't use the more modern Windows NT Challenge/Response protocol.
- **Plug and Play:** Promises more than it delivers; rather than making a Windows NT machine PnP (plug and play) compatible, it simply permits Windows NT to read configuration data from interface cards and other devices that include PnP-compatible BIOSes.
- **Remote Access Service:** Covers a whole range of RAS services that show up in the Services applet. RAS provides dial-in/dial-out communications services for up to 256 simultaneous connections on a single Windows NT Server.
- **Schedule:** Permits you to schedule activities or batch jobs against the system clock and run on demand. You may set up scheduled jobs to run only once or at regular intervals, depending on how you configure them.

- **Server:** Acts as the basic listener process for requests for service on a Windows NT Server (in fact, stopping the Server service is a good way to temporarily disable network access to a server). Although its name may suggest otherwise, this service is necessary on Windows NT Workstation machines and Windows NT Server machines alike.
- **Spooler:** Handles storage of files for pending print jobs; this is the service that manages the scheduling and retention of pending print jobs until their turn to print comes up.
- **Telephony Service:** Makes it possible for Windows NT to use the built-in Windows NT TAPI (Telephony Application Programming Interface) to access modems, telephones, ISDN, and xDSL devices through a standard dialer and telephone book interface. It is, therefore, also a key component of the RAS service.
- **Workstation:** Allows a Windows NT machine to issue requests for service. Although its name may suggest otherwise, this service is necessary on Windows NT Workstation machines and Windows NT Server machines alike.

Although this laundry list doesn't include every service in Windows NT Server, it should represent many of the services that you're likely to see running on most computers. Throughout this book, we give you a much better idea of what these and other services can do, how you must install and configure them, and what kinds of maintenance you have to give them.

Chapter 3

Matters of Protocol

In This Chapter

- Understanding what protocols do
- Networking rules of the road
- Moving data from hardware to applications, and vice versa
- Assembling the cast of protocols
- Toasting TCP/IP: the world's most popular protocol
- Introducing IPX/SPX and NWLink
- Understanding NetBIOS and NetBEUI
- Calling in the understudies: the "other" protocols

In this chapter, you examine the communications and messages that move around on networks. Here, we tell you more about what senders send and receivers receive, as you investigate the sets of rules — called *protocols* — that govern how computers exchange information across a network.

In essence, networked communications rely on a shared set of rules for exchanging information and for defining how data looks at the most basic level, such as how to present data digitally (or "What's a one, and what's a zero?"). These rules also dictate the formats for and meanings behind the addresses that indicate where "here" and "there" are on a network, along with lots of other critical information.

How Computers Talk to Each Other

Many of the ways that computers communicate and the ways that humans communicate have common elements. Take a phone call, for example:

- Phone calls use highly formulaic introductions to hook the right speakers together on each end of the connection ("Is this the Phlogiston residence? May I speak to Phil, please?"). Computers take a similar tack for network communications in that a sender often begins by asking the receiver if a conversation can begin, and only when permission is granted, does any actual exchange of data take place.

- Taking turns talking on the phone requires careful listening skills, and sensitivity to "open spaces" in the other party's talk, so that each party can speak when the opportunity presents itself. Computers have no intuition, so they exchange explicit signals when one party wants to switch from listening to talking. In fact, some communications techniques permit both parties to talk — and listen — at the same time!
- Ending a phone conversation can be a matter of mutual agreement, or it can involve well-known signals that one party wants to end the conversation. ("I have to let you go now" is a famous example of such a signal.) Likewise, computers also exchange signals to indicate that a network conversation is ready to end, and conclude by breaking their connection to each other.
- Humans also have coping skills to help them recognize unplanned endings to conversations, such as a failed cordless phone battery, driving beyond the edges of a cell boundary, or an outright connection failure. They also have the smarts to try again or give up, depending on whether they're satisfied their communication goals for the call. Computers are much more simple-minded; they wait until communications resume or a fixed interval of time — called a time-out period — elapses before recognizing that the connection is gone, and the conversation is over. Then, it's up to the application that initiated the conversation to decide whether it will try again, or give up.

Understanding the differences between human communications and computer communications can help you understand networking better. The biggest difference, it seems, is that humans can navigate by the seat of their pants far better than computers can.

Do what I mean, not what I say . . .

When humans communicate on the phone, what we say (or hear) is always interpreted and often misunderstood. What you think you said isn't always what another person thinks he or she heard. Human communication relies on shared rules and meanings, as well as a common frame of reference. Computers rely on these same elements to communicate; but because computers can't make judgment calls or use their intuition, these elements must be spelled out rigorously and completely. Computers can do only what they're programmed to do.

For computers to exchange data, every element in the data must be explicitly supplied. Computers can't pick up implications and hidden meanings. To communicate, computers have to begin with complete agreement about the following issues (as stated from the computer's point of view):

Standardizing the rules

Building a complete and consistent set of rules for computer communications is a time-consuming, nit-picky business that's entirely capable of driving most ordinary people bonkers. In the early days of the computer industry, individual companies or groups would put hordes of programmers to work building computer communications programs to solve specific, isolated problems.

But as time went on, programmers realized that this approach produced lots of unique ways for computers to communicate that worked only within the confines of small, isolated technical communities. Once the impetus to communicate spread farther, serious incompatibilities prevented these communities from exchanging data unless one community willingly gave up its unique way of communicating and adopted another's.

The U.S. Government played a key role in bringing order to this emerging network chaos. When the government tried to get computers from Company A to work with computers from Company Z, they quickly realized that they had a monster compatibility problem on their hands. A consensus soon emerged that a common set of rules for networking would make communications easier. Likewise, early network pioneers quickly learned that networking was difficult, if not downright impossible, when all players didn't adhere to the same set of rules.

If this tale had a storybook ending, it would be "Today, there's only one set of networking rules, which everyone uses wisely and well." Alas, that's not the case. Although the degree of networking chaos has substantially decreased, there are still many sets of mutually incompatible protocols in use on networks today, because hardware and software vendors try to stay on the "bleeding edge" by inventing more such rules as they boldly go where no network has gone before.

- What's my address? How do I learn my address? How do I learn other computers' addresses?
- How do I signal another computer to indicate that I'm ready to send (or receive) a message? That I'm busy? That I can wait if it's busy?

If you think about the telephone system, these issues are the same for both humans dialing a telephone handset and computers dialing a modem. In fact, these questions can be restated as follows:

- What's my phone number? How do I learn my phone number? How do I learn the phone numbers for other parties that I wish to reach?
- How do I place a call? How to I recognize a busy signal? How do I get the phone to keep dialing if the number I want to reach is busy? (Note also that the phone system handles busy signals and ring signals, so that both computers and humans can tell when a call is going through and when the party they're trying to reach is busy.)

These fundamental questions must be answered, and they represent just the beginning of a large and complex collection of details that have to be nailed down, codified, and implemented for computers to be able to communicate across a network. The answers to this entire collection of questions is the basis for a set of rules for computer communications; in fact, these rules represent the "rules of the road" — or protocols — for networking.

According to Protocol

The sets of networking rules that we talk about in the previous section are usually called *networking protocols* — but sometimes they're also called *networking standards, standard networking protocols,* and so on. Hopefully, you get the idea that these rules are shared by some group that wishes to be able to communicate amongst themselves, and define a common method for computers to communicate with each another. Any particular protocol defines a language, a structure, and a set of rules to permit such communications to take place.

A lot of work goes into defining a set of networking protocol, and even more work goes into building software to implement them. This is a mammoth undertaking, and the amount of work necessary to bring it off explains why users, software developers, and hardware manufacturers all find it convenient to stick to the protocols that fit their needs best.

In diplomacy, protocol establishes a rigid set of procedures and etiquette that representatives from sovereign governments must follow to prevent all-out war. For example, protocol helps explain why diplomats refer to screaming matches as "frank and earnest discussions" and to knotty disagreements as "constructive dialogs." Political doubletalk aside, the word *protocol* captures the flavor of rules for network communications quite nicely.

Geese come in gaggles, protocols come in suites

Although this book deals primarily with Windows NT Server and focuses on the Microsoft protocols, the set of protocols included with Windows NT represents only part of a large number of well-known and well-defined networking protocols. Microsoft does a good job of allowing multiple protocols to operate at the same time in Windows NT, including the government standard TCP/IP, Novell's IPX/SPX, as well as NetBIOS and NetBEUI (which were Microsoft's original — and only — protocols to begin with).

Upon examination of any networking implementation you're like to observe that protocols rarely, if ever, appear in the singular. Most networking protocols consist of a collection of specific message formats and rules for interaction, each with its own name and functions, rather than a single, monolithic collection of formats and rules. For that reason, protocols may also be called *protocol suites,* not because they like to lounge around on comfortable furniture, but because they travel in packs, like hyenas.

Raising the standards

One interesting thing about networking rules is that both vendors and standards groups call their protocols *standards.* Some vendors expend lots of effort talking about the difference between *de facto* and *de jure* standards. *De facto* means "It ain't official, but a lot of people use it, so we can call it a standard if we want to." *De jure* means "It's a standard because the ABC Association (a standards-setting body) has declared it such and has published this four-foot-high stack of documentation to prove it."

Behind the sometimes heated discussions about what is and isn't a standard lurks a control issue. Purists — including academicians, researchers, and techo-weenies — flatly assert that only a standards-setting group can be "objective and fair." Therefore, only the group can adequately select the very best that technology has to offer by putting it into their standard — thus making this the best of all possible standards.

The other heat source comes from vendors' desperate race to keep up with the marketplace and their customer's demands for better, faster, cheaper technology by struggling to get their products finished and out the door. "Of course, we have to control our technology," they say. "How else can we keep up?"

The objectivity, fairness, and leading-edge characteristics of most protocol standards may not be open to dispute, but establishing standards involves assembling groups of individuals who must agree on their contents. This takes time. Meanwhile, technology races ahead. (Nothing goes stale faster than leading-edge technology.)

It doesn't matter whether networking protocols are standards or not, whether *de facto* or *de jure.* The markets are where the action is. Vendors must involve themselves in all sides of the debate because they can't afford to miss any of the technology boats leaving port. Some astute vendors, including Microsoft, have published their "standards" and given customers and industry experts sufficient documentation to create workable networks and to keep up with the rapid pace of development.

Some standards bodies have also been wise enough to realize that a standard is a good thing only when it's widely used. These groups have been wise enough to let hardware and software vendors deal with the real-world issues involved in getting products to market. The winners in both camps are the most popular protocols. Microsoft's protocol selections for Windows NT (and its other versions of Windows) include the leading standard protocol, TCP/IP, and two widely used vendor protocol suites — IPX/SPX (which originated with Novell's NetWare) and NetBIOS/NetBEUI (which originated at IBM, but was enhanced in cooperation with Microsoft in the early 1980s).

A protocol's work is never done

If one key concept explains why protocols are necessary, it's that protocols handle the movement of information between the hardware on the network interface and the applications that access the network on a computer. The reason why one computer can't talk to another computer without both sharing a common set of protocols is that both sender and receiver need to be able to understand the other's operations, data formats, and delivery mechanisms. Without this common language, networking doesn't work.

Protocols fill in the gap between the network's hardware and its software. The programs that enable your computer to access the network must use a set of protocols. These protocols ferry data from applications all the way down to hardware, where a protocol says "send this message," to talk to the network. Going the other way, the protocol tells the hardware "give me the message," when the hardware indicates that an incoming message has arrived.

Most protocols are oblivious to the kind of network they're talking through. In most cases, protocols are unaware that the networking technology in use might be Ethernet, token-ring, or tutti-frutti. This indifference is possible because the part of the software that provides hardware access resides in a *device driver* for the network interface. The protocols themselves originate from other sources (in Windows NT, they reside in software components installed as part of the operating system, unless third-party components have been installed to displace these built-in components). Thus, when a protocol "talks to the network interface," it's really talking through the device driver to send data to the network or to receive data from the network.

Specific device drivers on a computer tell the protocol exactly how to talk to the network interface (or interfaces) in your machine. If you're lucky, you use a network-ready Intel or Alpha-based PC for NT Server (Microsoft supports both Intel 80486 processors and higher, plus the Compaq/DEC Alpha processors for Windows NT), which includes preinstalled networking abilities. Otherwise, you have to make sure that you install the proper network interface driver when you install Windows NT Server so that the machine can access the network.

As we explain in Chapter 2, some applications include built-in networking "smarts" through a special software interface. These *network-aware applications* are becoming increasingly common as networks become more widespread. Most of Microsoft's applications include some kind of network intelligence, but the amount of such brainpower varies according to the application's focus and capabilities. Other applications may use standard Windows application programming interfaces (APIs) and obtain network access anyway, totally unaware that the network is involved. This is where redirectors and other key system elements come into play. But whether an application is network-ready or uses system networking facilities, as soon as it accesses the network, it is using protocol software (and device drivers) on the system to accept incoming messages and to send outgoing messages.

The key to network access from applications and from a computer's operating system depends on access to a protocol suite. As we explain in Chapter 2, Windows NT includes all the components necessary to support both network-aware and network-oblivious applications, which makes Windows NT Server itself quite network-aware indeed. Even though applications (and the operating system) may make requests for network service, it's the protocols that do the dirty work of packaging up messages to be send across the network and then unpacking incoming messages into a readable form for incoming messages.

For other operating systems, such as Windows 95, Windows 98, UNIX, OS/2, and the Mac OS, built-in networking software also handles the network interface and the protocols and services that use it. DOS and older Windows 3.*x* versions, however, must use client networking software that Microsoft supplies with Windows NT Server (or some other alternative from a third party).

The Protocol Post Office

Most of the action that happens between applications and hardware consists of taking messages, breaking them down, and then stuffing them into envelopes as those messages move farther from the application and closer to the hardware. From the other direction — from hardware to application — the protocols unpack envelopes and stick individual pieces together to build a complete message. We hope that the resulting message is meaningful, but remember that the one immutable law of computing is GIGO — or "garbage in, garbage out."

Exploring a post office analogy here may be useful. The post office handles anything that has an address on it and sufficient postage to pay its way, as long as its conforms to the legal dimensions for a letter or a package. How is a letter delivered? It works something like this:

1. **You address a letter, stick on a stamp, and drop it in a mailbox.**
2. **The mail carrier picks up the letter.**
3. **The mail carrier delivers the letter to the local post office.**
4. **The mail sorters check the zip code and route the letter.**
5. **The letter is shipped to the post office that serves the destination zip code.**

6. **The mail sorters check the street address and route the letter to the appropriate mail carrier.**
7. **The mail carrier delivers the letter to the address and the recipient gets the letter.**

At least, that's the way it's *supposed* to work. The basic requirements for successful mail delivery are timely pickup, short transit time, and correct delivery. Factors that affect transit time and delivery are correct identification of and routing to the destination address, plus potential transportation delays between sender and receiver.

The similarity between networking protocols and the postal service lies in the ability to recognize addresses, to route messages from senders to receivers, and to provide delivery. The major difference is that the postal service, unlike networking protocols, doesn't care what's in the envelopes we send as long as they meet their size, weight, and materials restrictions. Networking protocols spend most of their time dealing with envelopes of varying sizes and kinds.

For example, suppose that you want to copy a 10MB file from your computer to another machine on your network. The file consists of a spreadsheet with some charts and graphics that include a sales forecast for the next quarter, so you want it to arrive quickly and correctly.

To use the post office (or what Net-heads call "snail mail"), you would copy the file to a floppy disk and mail it to the recipient. But that's not fast enough. Over the network, it gets there in about a minute and a half. While the file moves from your machine to the other, it's being chopped into lots of small packages to be sent, and reassembled into its original 10MB form upon receipt.

Size restriction — that is, the biggest chunk of data that can move across the networking medium in a single message — is only one reason that network messages are broken up and put into multiple envelopes. Handling addresses is another reason. In the post office example, the post office cares only about the destination zip code, whereas the delivering mail carrier cares only about the street address. Along the same lines, one protocol might care about only the name of the computer to which the file is to be shipped; at a lower level, however, the protocol needs to know where to direct the chunks of data moving from sender to receiver so that the file can be correctly reassembled upon delivery.

For senders, the protocol software spends most of its time taking things apart to send them accurately and completely. On the receiving end, the protocol software spends its time stripping off packaging information and putting things back together again. Both sender and receiver also exchange information during this process to monitor to accuracy and effectiveness of their communications and to determine if and when delivery is complete. Protocols also spend a lot of time keeping track of the quality and usability of network links.

In short, there's a lot more communication and activity involved in sending and receiving messages across a network than is required to route mail from the sending post office to the receiving one. But the mail analogy remains a pretty good explanation for how things work in general, ignoring the routine rooting around inside messages that protocols do, and the post office doesn't.

The Dance of the Seven Layers

Network protocols are grouped according to their functions, such as sending and receiving messages from the network interface, talking to the hardware, and making it possible for applications to do their things in a network environment, and talking to the software. Protocols are often called *protocol families* or protocol suites because they operate in groups.

This group organization involves stacking multiple layers of functionality, where software is associated with each layer. When the software that supports a particular network protocol loads on a computer, it's called a *protocol stack.* All computers on the network load all or part of the stack. They use the same parts of the stack, called *peer protocols,* when they communicate with each other as — you guessed it — *peers.*

The best-known collection of networking layers was developed as part of an open networking systems initiative in the 1980s called the Open Systems Interconnection (OSI) initiative. This model is known as the OSI Reference Model, because it defines a model that acts as a common frame of reference for understanding how networks work. Even though the OSI initiative never really achieved widespread adoption, the OSI Reference Model is a standard tool for explaining how network communications are structured and how they behave. The OSI Reference Model appears in Figure 3-1.

Other applications	Network aware applications
Operating system	
Redirector	
Protocols	
Interface driver	

Figure 3-1: The OSI Reference Model breaks networking protocols into seven layers.

The OSI Reference Model consists of seven layers, as follows (working from the bottom up):

- **Physical Layer:** This is the layer where the network hardware operates. Rules for this layer govern what kinds of connectors get used, what kinds of signaling techniques carry data across the network, what types of cables or other networking media that the physical, tangible part of the network can use. In some sense, this is the only part of the OSI Reference Model you can actually see and touch.
- **Data Link Layer:** This is the layer that handles communication with the network hardware, to convert the bits that computers use to represent data into equivalent signals needed to move data across the network for outbound messages, and to convert the signals for incoming messages into their equivalent bits. The Data Link layer is also where low-level hardware addresses for individual NICs and other devices are recognized and handled.
- **Network Layer:** This is the layer that handles routing of messages between senders and receivers, which means that it also handles translation between human-readable network addresses and computer-readable network addresses (which are not the same as the hardware addresses that the Data Link Layer handles). Each message that passes through this layer includes the sender's and the receiver's address to identify the parties involved. The network layer handles moving data from sender to receiver when they aren't both attached to the same cable segment.
- **Transport Layer:** This is the layer that handles chopping up large messages into so-called Protocol Data Units (or PDUs) to send them across a network, but also puts these PDUs back together to reconstitute the message upon receipt. The Transport Layer can also include data integrity checks by adding a bit pattern to each message based on a mathematical calculation before sending. This same calculation is repeated by the sender and the result compared to the value calculated before the data was sent. If the two values agree, the Transport Layer assumes that the transmission was accurate and correct; if they don't agree, the Transport Layer requests that the PDU be re-sent. This integrity function is optional in many cases, so that some Transport Layer protocols include an integrity check, while other such protocols don't.
- **Session Layer:** This is the layer that can set up ongoing network conversations, called sessions, between sender and receiver. This kind of ongoing connection makes it easier for computers to exchange large amounts of data, or to maintain an active connection when data will move regularly between the two parties to the session. Thus, the session layer handles session setup (which is just like dialing a phone),

session maintenance (which is just like having a phone conversation), and session termination or tear-down (which is just like ending a phone conversation, then hanging up the phone).

- **Presentation Layer:** This layer handles data conversion for network delivery. The assumption that drives this activity is that sender and receiver may not share a common set of data representations. So the presentation layer handles converting data from formats created by the sender into a generic format for network transit, and then converts that generic form into a format specific to the receiver upon delivery. This lets the programmers on both sides of the network connection assume generic formats for network data, and handle the details necessary to deliver that data to a specific client much more easily.
- **Application Layer:** This layer's name is something of a misnomer. It doesn't refer to the application or system service that seeks to send or receive data across the network. Rather, it refers to an interface layer between the protocol stack and such applications or system services. The Application Layer defines the methods by which applications or system services can request network access and by which they can obtain access to incoming data from the network.

Each of these layers functions more or less independently of the others. But the job of any given layer is to provide services for the layer above it, and to deliver data to the layer below it (or to send data to a receiver, at the Physical Layer). The encoding that a layer does on the sending side is decoded by the same layer on the receiving side. So the layered OSI model helps to emphasize that protocols on the sending end accept data from applications, convert that data into a generic form, manage conversations, prepare data to be sent across the network, handle data addressing and routing, and then convert that data into signals for transmission across the network. On the receiving end, that process is reversed: The protocols convert signals into data, figure out where that data is to be delivered, reconstitute incoming messages into their original containers, manage conversations, prepare the data for the client computer, and deliver that data to an application.

Some wags like to claim there's an eighth layer to the protocol stack, and that it's the most important layer of all. It's called the "Politics and Religion" layer, and jokingly refers to the organizational beliefs and requirements that drive network use. Even though there is no such layer in the OSI Reference Model, you'd be well-advised to keep this layer in mind any time you have to "sell" networking technology to upper management in your organization!

Common Windows NT Protocols (And More)

Just as diplomatic protocols grease the wheels of international relations, network protocols keep your network wheels turning. If you get to know these players, you may be able to gain more insight into how your network operates. You'll also be much better equipped to troubleshoot protocol-related problems.

The built-in Microsoft protocols include four protocol suites, plus support for an additional utility that Macintoshes can use to attach to Windows NT. Here are the core four in alphabetical order:

- **DLC (Data Link Control):** A printer and host access (terminal emulation) protocol.
- **IPX/SPX (Internetwork Packet Exchange/Sequenced Packet Exchange):** The NetWare core protocols, developed by Novell in the early 1980s.
- **NetBIOS/NetBEUI (Networked Basic Input-Output System/NetBIOS Enhanced User Interface):** A local-area protocol developed by IBM and refined by Microsoft; originally, the native protocols for LAN Manager and Windows NT. NetBIOS also works with IPX/SPX and TCP/IP, so don't be fooled into thinking that NetBIOS requires NetBEUI (it doesn't).
- **TCP/IP (Transmission Control Protocol/Internet Protocol):** A set of standard protocols and services developed at the behest of the U.S. Government in the 1970s and 1980s that's now the most widely used networking protocol in the world.

Windows NT Server also includes built-in support for AppleTalk, the networking protocol that's native to the Macintosh operating system. This add-in module (which isn't installed during Windows NT Server's initial setup) enables Mac users to access files, printers, and services on a Windows NT Server computer.

You can use any or all of these protocols on your network, which accounts for both the blessings and curses of NT networking. In the sections that follow, we tell you about each of these protocols and give you some guidance about when and why you may want to use one or more of them. Don't worry if the acronyms are unfamiliar or the terminology seems strange; concentrate on finding out how the protocols work to connect programs and services to your network (and your network's users). After you understand these concepts, you will know all the really important stuff.

Entering the acronym zone!

To set up and troubleshoot a Windows NT-based network, you need to understand what the various protocols do in order to make educated guesses about the kinds of problems each protocol may develop. When working with these protocols, you have to toss around awkward collections of letters (and sometimes numbers) with aplomb.

You should know which acronyms belong together and how the pieces of the various protocol stacks fit together. When things get weird — and we're sorry to report that they sometimes do — you must know about the Windows NT rogue's gallery of protocols so that you can run down the possible perpetrators.

Most protocol families are populated with abbreviations and acronyms. Take heart from this realization: Though familiarity may breed contempt, it will also enable you to navigate this complex bowl of alphabet soup!

DLC: Golden oldie

The Data Link Control (DLC) protocol is the oldest member of the group of Windows NT protocols. IBM developed DLC to connect token-ring based workstations to IBM mainframes and minicomputers. Printer manufacturers have adopted the protocol to connect remote (or so-called *network-attached*) printers to network print servers. You probably won't need DLC unless you use some kind of IBM host connection or an older network-attached printer (newer network-attached printers usually support TCP/IP-based print services, which makes more sense on networks that use TCP/IP).

DLC's primary use is to connect to mainframes and minicomputers through a gateway server. The workstation PC (the one on your desk) uses DLC to talk to the gateway, and the gateway translates that into IBM's Systems Network Architecture protocols, also known as SNA (or some other mainframe protocol), to a host computer.

Use DLC only if you must because it's a primitive, nonroutable protocol (this means a router can't forward DLC messages from one network to another). Its use is waning for both network printers and host connections, so you may be able to do without it altogether. Even the Hewlett Packard JetDirect printer interfaces now support both DLC and TCP/IP.

IPX/SPX: The original NetWare Protocols

Internetwork Packet Exchange (IPX), Sequenced Packet Exchange (SPX), and NetWare Core Protocol (NCP) are the original Novell NetWare protocols. IPX, SPX, and NCP, with more than 44 million regular users, are among the most widely used networking protocols in the world. You can use IPX with NetWare for a variety of operating systems, including DOS, Windows 3.*x*, Windows 95/98, Windows NT 4.0, Mac OS, OS/2, and some varieties of UNIX.

You normally need these protocols only if you have a NetWare 4.*x* or older server somewhere on your network. With its latest release of NetWare, version 5.0, Novell also provides native support for TCP/IP, so we expect usage of IPX/SPX to diminish over time. Please note that because Microsoft didn't want to pay Novell for the use of the IPX/SPX trade name, Microsoft refers to these protocols in Windows NT 4.0 as NWLink (short for NetWare Link) and in Windows 95/98 as the "IPX/SPX-compatible Protocol."

IPX/SPX is a reasonably well-behaved protocol with advanced routing capabilities. Therefore, you can use it on networks of all sizes, but using IPX/SPX typically means that you're using a NetWare 4.*x* server (or some older version) somewhere within your organization. You can wean yourself from this protocol over time, or do without it altogether, as your organization follows the inexorable trend to use TCP/IP, the protocol of the Internet (with which IPX/SPX is not compatible).

NetBIOS/NetBEUI: The original Microsoft protocols

IBM developed NetBIOS as a way to enable small groups of PCs to share files and printers efficiently. We treat NetBIOS differently from NetBEUI, because NetBIOS represents a widely used network application programming interface (API) and NetBEUI represents a specific set of networking protocols.

In fact, NetBIOS works over TCP/IP (where it's often called NBT, for NetBIOS over TCP/IP), as well as over IPX/SPX. Because NetBIOS provides access to some key services for Microsoft Networks, including name resolution, some version of NetBIOS is almost inevitably found on a Windows NT-based network. But because NetBIOS functions over all the major NT protocols, that protocol need not necessarily be NetBEUI.

Although Windows NT 4.0 and Windows 98 include refurbished 32-bit implementations of NetBEUI, and NetBEUI is built into many applications and networking products, NetBEUI has fallen out of use as the size and scope of networks have increased. Here's why: NetBEUI is a nonroutable protocol, which means it doesn't behave well on a large network interconnected by special devices called routers. It remains the fastest protocol and the easiest to install for small networks, which probably explains why Microsoft continues to include it with Windows NT (and its other modern Windows operating systems).

For networks of ten computers or fewer, NetBEUI is still a good choice, as long as you don't use TCP/IP for your Internet access. NetBEUI's simplicity, low overhead, and speed make it a good choice for small workgroups without incurring the complexity and management requirements inherent in TCP/IP. But even Microsoft recommends against using NetBEUI on networks with more than ten networking devices.

TCP/IP: The Internet suite

TCP/IP grew out of research funded by the Department of Defense (DoD) that began in the 1970s, when the feds realized that they needed some technology to help them link all their dissimilar computer systems together into a single network. The protocols are sometimes called the DoD protocols, because the DoD requires that all computers that it purchases be able to use these protocols. Likewise, they're also known as the Internet protocols, because they're the foundation upon which the Internet runs.

TCP/IP is actually an acronym for two members of the protocol suite: the Transmission Control Protocol (TCP) and the Internet Protocol (IP). According to Dr. Vinton Cerf, one of the Internet's founding technologists, over 500,000 networks are part of the Internet itself, but an equal number (or more) of private networks also use TCP/IP.

Given a global community of over 80 million users, TCP/IP is the most widely used of all the available networking protocols. TCP/IP is also deeply rooted in the UNIX community, due to its inclusion in the early-1980s public releases of the free Berkeley Software Distribution (BSD) of UNIX and its subsequent inclusion in the official AT&T/Bell Labs offering of UNIX shortly afterward.

Because TCP/IP was deliberately designed to enable dissimilar types of computers to interconnect and communicate, TCP/IP is available for probably more kinds of hardware than any other networking protocol. Thus, you shouldn't be surprised that nowadays most commercially available operating systems — including Windows, Mac OS, and UNIX — include built-in implementations of TCP/IP.

Because TCP/IP is the foundation for the Internet and the most widely used networking protocol, we consider it to be the default choice for most networks. Although learning and using TCP/IP can be a chore, it provides more functions and capabilities than any other protocol. Even Microsoft now recommends it as the best protocol to use with Windows NT Server.

Other protocol faces in the gallery

The following less common protocols may crop up on networks where you work:

- **AppleTalk:** The name of a set of protocols created by Apple Computer, whose Macintosh computer was one of the first mass-market computers to include built-in networking hardware and software. In most cases, where you have a Macintosh, you have some need for AppleTalk. Windows NT Server includes Services for Macintosh, which offer file and print access to Windows NT Sever to Macintosh clients.
- **ISO/OSI:** A nifty palindrome that stands for the International Standards Organization's Open Systems Interconnection protocol suite. OSI has never lived up to its original promise as a successor to TCP/IP. The few OSI protocols have gained some level of broad use in Europe, where they have established a foothold. OSI is out there in industry, government, academia, and business because many governments, including the U.S. government, require systems to be OSI-compliant.

  Like TCP/IP, OSI is available for a broad range of systems, from PCs to supercomputers. Most protocol stacks resemble the OSI Reference Model for networking, and this model remains the most enduring legacy of the effort that went into OSI networking in the 1980s. Numerous third-party ISO/OSI implementations are available for Windows NT, mostly from European companies, but Microsoft itself doesn't include these protocols with the operating system.
- **SNA:** This refers to IBM's Systems Network Architecture, its basic protocol suite for large-scale networking and mainframe access. Because SNA was a pioneering protocol, companies that invested heavily in mainframe technology have also usually invested in SNA. Many SNA networks are still in use, but the number is dropping because SNA is old, cumbersome, and expensive, and because TCP/IP is eating SNA's lunch, even on venerable mainframes. From a Windows NT perspective, the Windows NT BackOffice component called SNA Server offers a Windows NT-based SNA gateway to Microsoft Network clients.

The networking world includes hundreds of other protocol suites, each with its own collection of acronyms and special capabilities, but luckily you don't have to know all of them. If you haven't seen a certain protocol that you run on your network in this chapter, you probably know more about it than we do anyway!

Connection handling helps classify protocols

IP, IPX, and NetBEUI are *connectionless* protocols, and SPX and TCP are *connection oriented.* What does this mean? Why should you care?

All these protocols operate at lower levels. Earlier in this chapter, we tell you that the most important job of a lower-level protocol is to break up arbitrarily long messages into digestible chunks when sending data across a network and then put them back together when receiving data. These chunks, called *packets,* form the basic message unit for information moving across a network. These packets are further divided and stuffed into their envelopes by the access method in use. These envelopes are called *frames.* Look at it this way: Packets move up and down the protocol stack; frames dance across the wires.

Connectionless protocols work the same way as mailing letters through the postal service. You drop the letter into a mailbox and expect the post office to deliver it. You may never know if the letter actually gets there or not — unless it's a bill! IP, IPX, and NetBEUI provide no guarantee of delivery, and frames can arrive in any order.

Connection-oriented protocols, on the other hand, use a handshake to start communications, where the would-be sender asks the receiver if it can accept input before it starts sending. Once transmission is underway, connection-oriented protocols treat each message like sending a registered letter, where you get a return card to verify receipt of your letter. SPX and TCP packets are sequenced so that when they arrive they can be restored to their original order, which makes them more reliable. Connection-oriented protocols can also request redelivery or send error notices when packets are damaged or lost en route from sender to receiver.

IP and the other connectionless protocols are typically fast and require little overhead, but they're considered lightweight and unreliable. TCP and other connection-oriented protocols run more slowly than their connectionless counterparts because they keep track of what has been sent and received and because they monitor the status of the connection between sender and receiver. More record-keeping and data-check information is built into each packet, which raises overhead requirements but also increases reliability.

Hybrid Vigor: When Mixing Protocols Makes Sense

Sometimes, you may need to use more than one networking protocol on a single computer. This process may occasionally require you to go through some interesting contortions, but Windows NT Server is pretty accommodating about supporting multiple protocols simultaneously. In fact, you can run TCP/IP, IPX/SPX (NWLink), and NetBEUI on a single Windows NT Server machine on multiple network interface cards without too much hassle. The same is true of Windows 95/98.

Likewise, Macintoshes can run AppleTalk and TCP/IP together pretty easily, and UNIX can run as many protocol stacks together as you might need to obtain the range of network services necessary. A UNIX machine's protocol collection can include TCP/IP, NetBEUI, OSI, IPX, and more.

Chances are that your biggest problems in using multiple protocol stacks will crop up on older PCs running DOS or Windows 3.*x*, where the lack of built-in networking automatically increases the difficulty level of installing and using multiple protocols at the same time. Likewise, the limited memory management capabilities and lack of support for modern device drivers can make hybrid networking a real challenge.

What's What on Your Server?

Windows NT Server makes inspecting your system to see which protocols are installed incredibly easy. Just launch the Network Control Panel, and click the Protocols tab at the top of window. You see the result in Figure 3-2, which shows that we practice what we preached in this chapter by running only TCP/IP on our network.

The only protocols you have to worry about on your network are the ones that show up in this window (or the protocols that you know are supposed to show up but don't, as the case may sometimes be).

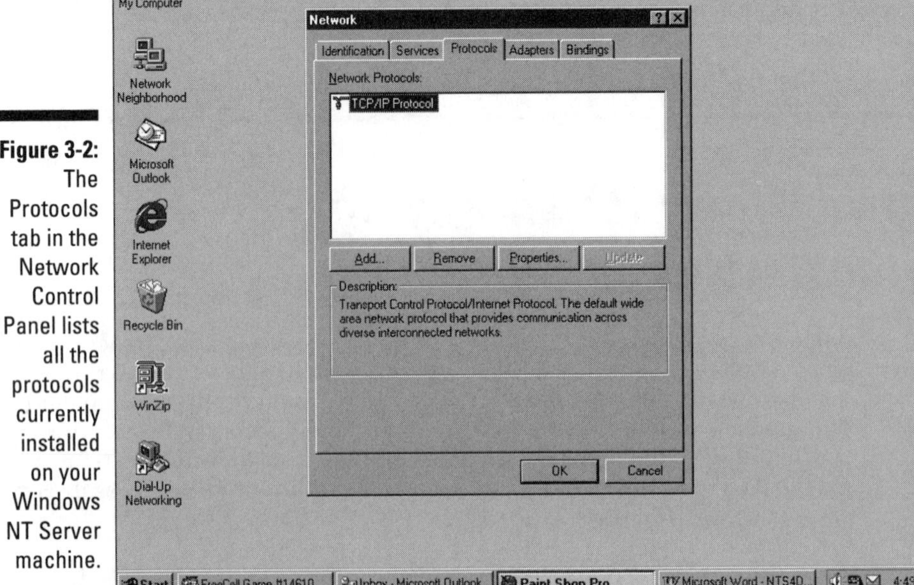

Figure 3-2: The Protocols tab in the Network Control Panel lists all the protocols currently installed on your Windows NT Server machine.

Chapter 4

My Kingdom for a Topology!

In This Chapter

- Drawing lines means creating a topology
- Understanding the three basic topologies: bus, star, and ring
- Combining multiple topologies and multiple instances
- Defining a network technology
- Understanding basic technologies: Ethernet, Token Ring, FDDI, and more . . .
- Making networks interconnect
- Using internetworking gear: of repeaters, bridges, routers, and . . .

When mathematicians get together, they enjoy nothing more than making up new terminology to bedevil the rest of us (maybe they don't want computer scientists to corner the market on bedeviling terminology). Mathematics is where the networking term *topology* originates; a topology describes the way that computers get wired together on a network. Beyond bedevilment, topologies provide a concise and accurate way to describe how a network's various pieces and parts can be brought together. In the first part of this chapter, we tell you all about the various topologies that you mix and match to create networks that operate efficiently.

But topologies don't tell the whole story about network design. You also have to consider the specific hardware you use and how that hardware interacts with other hardware — the *hardware implementation,* if you will.

Perhaps jealous of the mathematicians and their coining of cool terms, a group of computer scientists coined the term *network technologies* to identify the specific hardware and signaling methods used in a network. Perhaps jealous of *that* group of computer scientists, another group decided that it was more useful to think about the same hardware and signaling stuff by particular *access methods,* which concentrate on how the hardware gets permission to transmit onto the networking medium.

The second half of this chapter tells gives you the skinny on all specific hardware implementations, network technologies, and access methods that take a topology and make it into a real, working network.

Seeing a Topology for What It Really Is

Mathematically speaking, a topology represents some arrangement of lines between points in a graph. In a network, the word *topology* refers to the way that wires (lines) stretch between computers (nodes in a graph). So when you hear the word *topology* at a networking conference, what's being talked about is the arrangement of computers in a network.

Network wiring can be laid out in many ways. Figure 4-1 shows the two most common such layouts — the *star topology* and the *bus topology*. Another common layout, called a *ring topology,* uses a wiring pattern laid out in a circle, where the last computer in the ring links back to the first computer.

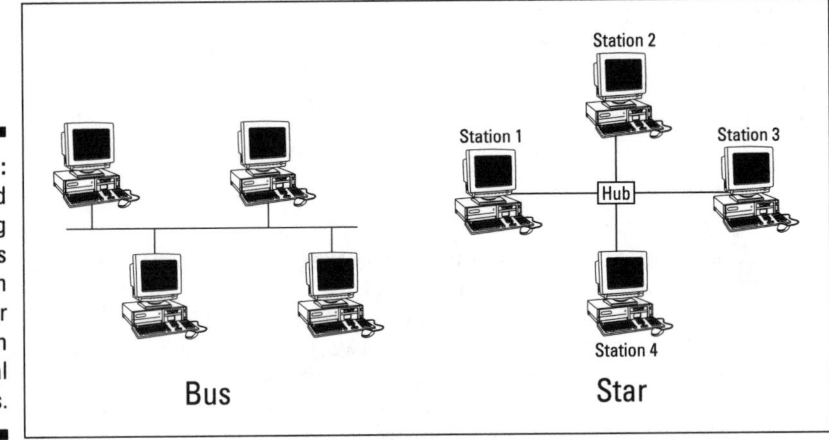

Figure 4-1: Star and bus wiring layouts often appear together on real networks.

Topologies can combine in all kinds of interesting ways. If you use a bus topology to link a number of separate stars together, you end up with a distributed-star network, which is also known as a hybrid network. Most real networks are hybrids of some kind, but most networks work better if you keep things simple.

A star is born

A star topology consists of separate wires that run from a central point (usually attached to a single device, called a hub; hubs are explained later in this section) to individual devices attached to the other end of each wire. A bus topology is a single cable to which all devices on a network (or on some part of a network, as is more often the case) are attached.

If you break a wire in a star topology, only one link is affected and everything else keeps working. But if you break a wire on a bus topology, everything connected to that bus loses the ability to access the network.

In a star topology, the hub at the center of the star acts as a relay for computers attached to its arms, like this:

1. The sending computer sends a chunk of data across the wire aimed at some destination computer.
2. The hub, positioned between sender and receiver, passes the message either to the destination computer — if it's attached to the same hub — or to some other hub or networking device, if it's not attached to the same hub.
3. The hub to which the destination computer is attached sends the message to the destination computer (assuming both sender and receiver are situated within a star topology — however, nothing prevents machines from communicating with each other across different topologies, as long as the right kinds of links are in place).

On a large network, the middle step might be repeated several times, as the data jumps from hub between sender and receiver, or from hub to bus to hub (and so on), until the data eventually reaches its destination computer.

Another one rides the bus

On a bus topology, every computer on the same wire sees every message that travels across that wire. If sender and receiver are on the same wire, called a *segment,* messages travel very quickly. If the sender and receiver are not on the same wire, a special message-forwarding computer, called a *bridge* or a *router,* passes the message from the sender's wire on toward the receiver's wire by copying the message and retransmitting that message.

The networking devices known as bridges and routers are discussed in more detail later in this chapter. For now, think of a bridge as a device that can forward information from one network to another based on MAC level addresses. A router, on the other hand, can route information from one network to another based on network addresses.

Just as you may need to forward a message through multiple hubs in a star topology, you can forward a message through multiple bridges or routers on a bus topology.

Ring around the network!

The other remaining major topology is called a ring topology. Real rings are built only seldom because they will fail completely in the event of a cable break. That's why networking technologies like the Fiber Distributed Data Interface, or FDDI, that use true ring topologies include dual cables and a fault tolerance scheme that permits the network to recover from the break of any single cable with little effect on network operations.

Truth to tell, most so-called ring topologies are really star- or bus-wired networks that impose a logical ring structure on the physical network, whatever its actual topology may be. Thus, you find that network technologies like ARCnet support logical rings atop star- or bus-wired networks, and other technologies like token ring that support logical rings atop star-wired networks (or distributed star-wired networks). This arrangement is shown in Figure 4-2.

TECHNICAL STUFF

Buses and rings are attractive because they keep track of who gets to send a message by circulating an electronic "permission form," also known as a *token,* around and around the network. Only a computer with possession of the token can transmit a message on the network, which completely eliminates any possibility that two computers might try to send a message at the same time. On average, every computer waits about the same amount of time for the token to come around, and thus, each computer has an equal shot at network access over time. This approach allows a network's available bandwidth to be used more fully before the network starts to slow down.

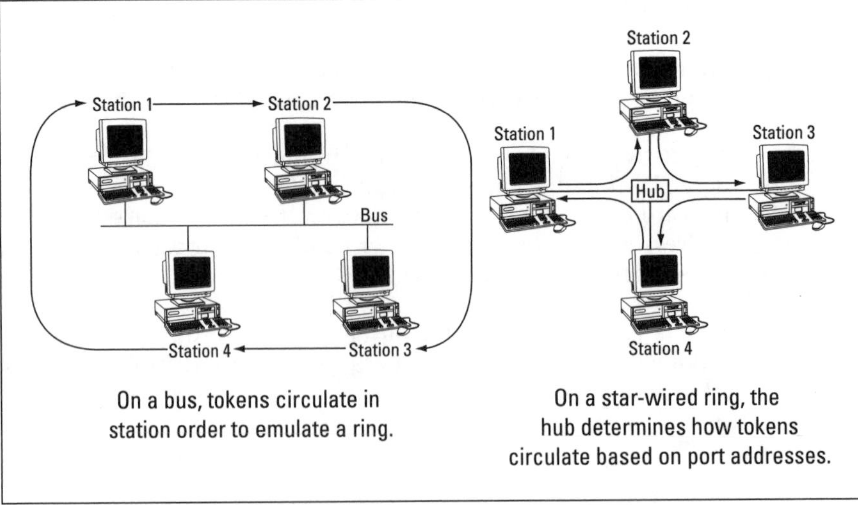
Station 1
Station 2
Bus
Station 4
Station 3
On a bus, tokens circulate in station order to emulate a ring.
Station 2
Station 1
Station 3
Hub
Station 4
On a star-wired ring, the hub determines how tokens circulate based on port addresses.

Figure 4-2: Physical stars or buses can support logical rings.

Logical versus physical

Networking topologies can be physical or logical. The physical topology of a token ring network is a star, but the way data is passed around from one computer to another is a ring. ARCnet can be a physical bus or star (or some combination of the two), but logically it's a ring. Not even Ethernet is exempt from this confusion. When Ethernet is wired as a bus, it acts like a bus; but when it's wired as a star, Ethernet still acts like a bus.

When thinking about networks, don't confuse a network's topology and the *networking technology* in use. The topology identifies the network's wiring scheme, plain and simple. The topology describes how communications can move around and among the computers and other devices on a network. The networking technology, sometimes called an *access method,* identifies how the network behaves and what kinds of interfaces and equipment it requires. The networking technology therefore also describes the network's physical characteristics in great detail, including:

- The network's electrical characteristics
- The type of signaling the network uses
- The type of connectors the network uses
- The types of interfaces and how they work together
- The maximum message size
- Everything else necessary to build a working environment

Topology deals with network layout; networking technology (or access method) deals with how a network operates. Put another way, a topology names the wiring scheme in use, and the networking technology defines what physical components you must buy to make those wires work.

Brand X Basics

All the many networking technologies available in today's marketplace can be broken down according to five categories. You can distinguish any one type of networking technology from another by answering all five of these questions:

A token of my esteem

Networks use sets of rules, called protocols, to communicate with one another. Some network technologies use tokens to control communications. Other network technologies opt for a free-for-all, in which any computer can send data any time the network's not already in use. Networks that send tokens are called token-passing networks. They use a token-passing protocol to control access to the networking media.

Following this protocol, computers must listen to the media to determine if it's in use (indicated by signals present on the media). If a computer wishes to transmit, listens, and doesn't hear any signals, it can go ahead and transmit right away. When another computer does the same thing at more or less the same time, data from one computer collides with data from another, and both computers must back off and try again.

Ethernet implements CSMA/CD (Ethernet) and while ARCnet and token ring implement token-passing protocols. The names that describe how the technologies access network media are called *access methods*. People often confuse topologies with networking technologies or access methods, but now that we've got this source of confusion straightened out, the details of the various networking technologies in this chapter should make more sense.

- What kind of access method, protocol, and topology does the network use?
- How does the network work?
- What are the network's technical pros and cons?
- What kinds of networking media does the network support?
- How business-friendly (cost, availability, reliability, and so on) is this network?

In the following sections, we ruminate over the pros and cons of the various networking technologies, just as you must do when you have to apply a particular technology to a particular topology with the goal of best serving the needs of your users.

Introducing the contestants

When you talk about networking technologies, you're talking about a specific type of hardware and associated driver software that, when added to a PC, can produce a working network connection. That is, of course, contingent on the right infrastructure — cables, connections, and ancillary equipment like bridges or routers — also being available.

For the purposes of this book, there are three networking technologies (but that's a tremendous oversimplification, as you'll learn later). These networking technologies are:

- Ethernet
- Token Ring
- Fiber Distributed Data Interface (FDDI)
- Other

Okay, you caught us sneaking in a fourth, catch-all entry (we almost called it miscellaneous) to give us the opportunity to say something about several of the multitude of other available (but less common) networking technologies that we choose not to cover in detail here. In fact, recent industry analyses indicate that it's about 75 percent likely that your network uses (or will use) one or more of the three networking technologies mentioned in the preceding list. Thus, even though we cover only a small number of such technologies in depth, we cover most networks, at least to some degree.

Into the Ethernet

Ethernet is the most well-known, widely used, versatile, and readily available networking technology today. As such things go, Ethernet has been around longer than most, since the mid-to-late 1970s. Ethernet was the brainchild of the Xerox Palo Alto Research Center (PARC) and later adopted by Digital, Intel, and Xerox (which is why the old-fashioned, 15-pin connectors for thickwire Ethernet are sometimes called DIX connectors). Ethernet has long been a "networking commodity" which means that plenty of vendors participate in this market, and that lots of options and choices for this technology are available.

Ethernet uses the CSMA/CD access method. The sidebar entitled "Ethernet: Network bumper cars" explains what this stuff means in everyday English, insofar as the subject allows — which isn't so very far, alas.

The easiest way to describe how CSMA/CD works is as follows: "Listen before sending. Listen while sending. If garbage happens, quit sending, and try again later."

Ethernet's strengths and weaknesses

Ethernet's strengths are as follows: It's robust and reliable, and it comes in a broad, affordable range of flavors. Ethernet's weaknesses include the inevitability of collisions and the more difficult troubleshooting techniques that a shared bus network requires. Ethernet's base speed of 10 Mbps is on the slow end for modern networks, but plenty of other higher-speed Ethernet implementations are now available (we give you the goods on these in Chapter 7).

Ethernet: Network bumper cars

The acronym that describes Ethernet's media access method is CSMA/CD, which stands for Carrier Sense Multiple Access with Collision Detect. Echoes are the auditory equivalent of a collision, and a collision means that you must repeat everything that was just said. The following list provides a definition for each term in this access method acronym:

- **Carrier Sense:** Everyone attached to the network is always listening to the wire, and no one is allowed to send while someone else is sending. When a message moves across the wire, an electrical signal called a *carrier* is used. By listening to the wire, you know when it's busy, because you *sense* the presence of an active signal.
- **Multiple Access:** Any device attached to the network can send a message whenever it wants, as long as no carrier is sensed at the time. This means multiple senders can (and sometimes do) begin sending at roughly the same time — when they think things are quiet — and that's why it's called *multiple access*.
- **Collision Detect:** If two or more senders begin transmitting at roughly the same time, sooner or later their messages run into each other, causing a *collision* to occur. Collisions are easy to recognize because they produce a garbage signal that is completely unlike a valid transmission. Ethernet hardware includes collision detection circuitry that immediately halts transmission when a collision is observed. When a collision occurs, each sender must wait a random amount of time before listening to wire and attempting to transmit again.

Ethernet does not perform as well for high-traffic applications or real-time delivery requirements (as for video and multimedia), and it does not degrade gracefully when extremely high traffic volumes occur on a network. In fact, Ethernet's CSMA/CD access method means that the effective ceiling on its bandwidth is between 56 and 60 percent of total bandwidth (or between 5.6 and 6.0 Mbps on a 10 Mbps Ethernet) because that's the level of use beyond which the increasing probability of collisions can result in network slowdowns or failures.

When planning for bandwidth consumption on an Ethernet network, use 55 percent of the available bandwidth (5.5 Mbps on a 10 Mbps network, 55 Mbps on a 100 Mbps network, and so on) as the ceiling for bandwidth on any network segment. If you plan to consume the entire bandwidth of Ethernet when designing a network, you'll be designing a network that's headed for trouble!

But there's no shortage of bandwidth available to Ethernet customers today. Most newer Ethernet NICs are so-called 10/100 designs, which means they can sense whether they're used on a 10 Mbps or a 100 Mbps Ethernet network, and set their speeds accordingly. And, as of late 1997, Gigabit Ethernet, with an astonishing 1,000 Mbps of total theoretical bandwidth, lifts the ceiling on network capacity to incredible heights, while retaining backward compatibility with other Ethernet implementations.

All the flavors of Ethernet

Ethernet comes in all the basic flavors; that is, Ethernet can run on any of the major media types — twisted pair, coaxial cable (multiple versions, in fact), and fiber optic — and works with both bus and star topologies. One unusual variant — 100BaseVG-AnyLAN — actually uses a different access method called demand priority that gives this implementation some interesting abilities (which we discuss in detail in Chapter 7).

Also, Ethernet devices that permit you to mix and match media are readily available, so you can use Ethernet to build networks of just about any size and for even the most hostile environments.

Getting down to business

Despite its age, Ethernet remains the most widespread and popular networking technology. Twisted-pair leads the pack for new Ethernet installations, but there's still a lot of coaxial cable out there. Fiber-based Ethernet is usually limited to networks in campus environments, where long distances and electrical interference issues are greatest, but it's also used in hostile environments (such as factory floors or engine rooms, where lots of heavy-duty equipment can create major interference) or for high-bandwidth applications, include both 100 Mbps and 1000 Mbps implementations.

The primary reasons for Ethernet's unshaken popularity are as follows:

- **Affordability:** Cabling is cheap, and interfaces range from $30 for bottom-dollar desktop NICs to less that $200 for reasonably powerful server NICs. Ethernet is not the cheapest of all available networking technologies, but it's darn close!
- **Freedom of choice:** Ethernet supports all kinds of media, numerous bandwidths, and lots of gear for building hybrid networks. In addition, a plethora of vendors offer hardware for Ethernet. If you have specialized needs for networking hardware or media, changes are good that an Ethernet variety that meets those needs is already available or on somebody's drawing board.

- **Experience:** Ethernet's longevity means that Ethernet-savvy individuals are easy to find. Also, lots of training and technical material on Ethernet makes expertise relatively easy to build.
- **Continuing innovation:** At 10 Mbps, the base Ethernet implementation is no screamer. But vendors make special high-speed network switches for Ethernet that can deliver the entire 10 Mbps to individual connections, and higher-speed Ethernet varieties are readily available, and widely used. As bandwidth demands increase, engineers have found ways to increase Ethernet's abilities to be able to keep up, as the recent standardization of Gigabit Ethernet as 802.3z already attests.

If you are tasked with building a new network and there are no compelling reasons to choose any particular networking technology, you should definitely choose Ethernet, because of all the reasons mentioned above!

Let's talk token ring

Token ring has gained a substantial foothold in the marketplace, although it hasn't been around in commercial form as long as Ethernet. Token ring is based on technology refined and originally marketed by IBM, so it is most commonly found in technology environments where IBM is entrenched. When personal computers started taking desktop space away from dumb terminals connected to IBM mainframes, IBM took action. They developed token ring as a way to tie all those new PCs into their mainframe computers.

Token ring uses a token-passing access method, a collection of individual point-to-point links between pairs of devices that are arranged in a circular, circulating pattern. *Point-to-point* means that one device is hooked directly to another; for token ring, that describes the connection between a computer and a hub, which may itself be attached to other hubs or computers. Although the devices used with token ring networks act like hubs, however, they are more properly known as multistation access units (MAUs) or controlled attachment units (CAUs).

Token ring is mathematically fair to everyone who participates, and it guarantees that the network isn't overwhelmed by traffic. Token ring is said to be fair because it constantly passes the right to transmit, in the form of a special message called a *token,* around the network. To send a message, a computer must wait until it obtains possession of the token. The token is not released until the message has been delivered (or until it's obvious that it can't be delivered). Everyone gets the same opportunity at using the token.

The easiest way to think about how token ring works is as follows; To send a message, first wait for the token. When the token comes by, if it's free, you can tack your message onto the token. When the token comes around again, strip off your message, and send the token to the next computer "downstream" around the ring.

Strengths and weaknesses of token ring

Token ring's strengths are equal opportunity for all devices and guaranteed delivery. Token ring works reliably and predictably, even when loaded to capacity. Token ring is available in two speeds: the slower (and older) version runs at 4 Mbps. This is 40 percent of the theoretical bandwidth for 10 Mbps Ethernet, but only slightly slower than Ethernet's effective speed.

The higher-speed (and newer) version of token ring runs at 16 Mbps, runs at 160 percent of Ethernet's theoretical bandwidth, but can handle three to four times as much data because it permits simultaneous use of multiple tokens and can use 100 percent of the total bandwidth. Waiting in the wings is a full-duplex implementation of token ring, which works much like switched Ethernet. For higher speeds, a 100 Mbps version of token ring is also under construction.

We hear you thinking: "If token ring is so great, why does anybody buy anything else?" Token ring has weaknesses that have less to do with technical considerations and more to do with inflexibility and expense. Token ring's major downside is that it requires expensive hub-like devices, called *multistation access units* (MAUs), and token ring requires that two strands of cable be run from each computer to each hub port (one for the outbound trip, the other for the return trip). These requirements add to token ring's expense and reduce the maximum distance possible between computers and hubs. Token ring is also more complicated and requires fancier connectors than Ethernet.

Many flavors of token ring

Token-ring implementations for twisted-pair and fiber-optic media are available, but twisted pair is the most common implementation by far and is the most likely medium when typing desktops to hubs. Fiber is the cable of choice for spanning longer distances and daisy-chaining MAUs (see the previous section for a description of MAUs). Only limited amounts of shielded twisted pair (STP) cabling are used on token ring networks. Because of individual cable length limitations and maximum ring-size limitations, cabling a token ring network takes more planning and number crunching that does cabling an Ethernet network.

Getting down to business

From a cost-benefit perspective, there's not enough upside in the reliability, fairness, and guaranteed performance of token ring to offset its higher costs. At present, token ring costs between 75 and 150 percent more than Ethernet without necessarily providing significant performance or reliability advantages.

Although there are two schools of thought on this issue — "Forget token ring. Ethernet rules." and "We're token-passing bigots. What's Ethernet?" — we're not about to climb out on either limb. If someone is giving away token ring at a price that's too good to pass up or if that's what your circumstances dictate that you must use — go ahead and use it. Token ring works just fine. We do not, however, recommend it as a technology of choice for starter networks, because of its expense and complexity.

Fabulous FDDI

The Fiber Distributed Data Interface (FDDI) supports moderate speeds of up to 100 Mbps and has the distinction of being one of the few true ring-wired network topologies around. FDDI was designed in the mid-1980s — at least 10 years after Ethernet and token ring — to provide a high-speed, token-passing network technology. A newer version, called FDDI II, is now available that adds support for video, image, and voice data to conventional network traffic. You needn't pay attention to whether new devices are FDDI I or II, though, because all new FDDI equipment is FDDI II, and nobody pays much attention to those Roman numerals anyhow.

FDDI was originally designed as a kind of superhighway for network data, to tie individual networks together. FDDI's bandwidth is 100 Mbps, which puts it in the middle of the speed rankings for networks that appear in Figure 4-3. This figure includes all the various technologies we mention in this chapter, so that you can get an idea of how the individual options stack up.

One of FDDI's best applications is as a network backbone. Just as your backbone ties your skeleton together, and carries your nervous system to the brain, a network backbone provides a special-purpose high-speed link to tie multiple networks together. All FDDI networks aren't backbones, however, nor does every network backbone use FDDI. It just happens that FDDI's ability to span a 100 kilometer ring makes it unusually well-suited for large campus environments.

FDDI uses a token-passing access method. FDDI cable uses a real ring topology, but consists of two rings. One ring transmits messages clockwise, the other transmits messages counterclockwise. If either ring fails, the other automatically takes over as a backup. Better still, if both rings get cut in the same place — watch out for guys with backhoes on your campus! — the two rings automatically splice together to form a ring that's twice the length of the original ring, but still able to function.

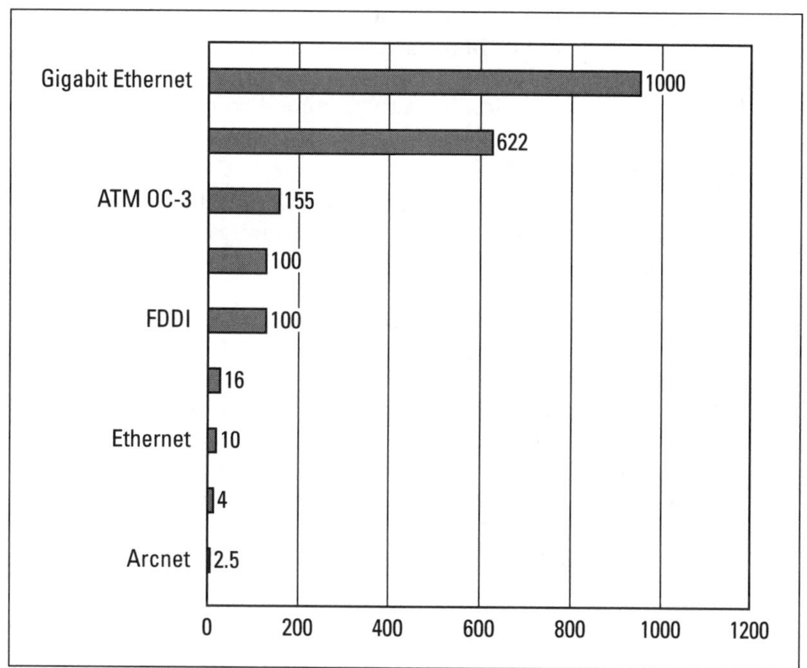

Figure 4-3: Ranking the speed of networking technologies

Although FDDI functions well as a network that interconnects other networks, it can also be used as a LAN technology to hook computers together. At present, however, its expense makes FDDI more likely to be used as a campus backbone. The gradual introduction of higher-speed backbone technologies (like Gigabit Ethernet) should spell the gradual phaseout of FDDI over the next 10 years as backbone bandwidth requirements continue to escalate.

Strengths and weaknesses

FDDI's biggest advantage is reach, now that its 100 Mbps speed is no longer such a big deal. FDDI can support rings as big as 100 km in circumference (that's about 62 miles for non-metric types). FDDI can support as many as 500 active devices on a single ring, which is more than the other networking technologies we discuss in detail in this chapter.

On the downside, FDDI requires fiber-optic cables for runs of any length. There's a CDDI (where *C* stands for copper) but it doesn't support cable runs longer than 75 feet, so it's impractical except for workstation connections.

Cost is another negative for FDDI. Fiber optic cables are more expensive to buy and install, and FDDI NICs cost between $700 and $1,800 each. FDDI looks good primarily where campus backbones are concerned, and Gigabit Ethernet is not an option (or a requirement) right now.

Getting down to business

For widespread use, FDDI is caught between its high expense and its relatively modest bandwidth. This puts it squarely in a niche, aimed at campus networking situations.

Not many operations are yet willing to shoulder the burden of running fiber everywhere. Even so, Gigabit Ethernet and FDDI should cost more or less the same over the next two to four years. Think about it: Gigabit Ethernet delivers ten times the bandwidth at the same price as FDDI, with built-in Ethernet compatibility. FDDI maxes out at 100 Mbps and requires special equipment to link to Ethernet networks. Not much of a choice is required here, if you ask us! We expect Gigabit Ethernet to win the backbone contest hands-down, even for the kinds of large campus networks that appear to require FDDI today.

What other networking technologies are there?

If you have to ask "What else is there," you're probably wondering why this book fails to mention your networking technology of choice. We hate to be the bearer of sad tidings, but if you're not using either Ethernet, Token Ring, or FDDI, you may be networking too hard (or at least, networking the hard way). Sorry.

In fact, hundreds of other kinds of networking technologies are in use today. At least one such technology exists for every letter in the alphabet from A for ARCnet to X for XDSL. But exotic networking technologies can be a problem for Windows NT Server too. If you're using an exotic networking technology, make sure that NT Server works with that stuff before you spend any money on the software.

The good news is that Windows NT runs over a reasonable subset of networking technologies. The bad news is that you'll have to do some research to find out if what you're using is one of the technologies that NT runs on. Worse yet, you'll have to work harder to do basic stuff that less exotic networking technologies take for granted, and you may have to pass on some sophisticated capabilities as well, such as network attached printers and other peripheral devices.

One rising star in the area of high-speed networking is ATM, an abbreviation for asynchronous transfer mode. In the last couple of years, several companies have begun to offer LAN equipment built around ATM. Long-distance telephone companies already use ATM implementations that run at 155 (OC-3) and 622 (OC-12) Mbps, and current ATM specifications also support speeds of 1.2 (OC-24) and 2.4 (OC-48) gigabits per second (Gbps) as well.

ATM is a fast-switching technology that requires a hub-like switching device and network interfaces for each computer. You can expect to spend at least $2,000 per workstation (including allocated switch and fiber optic cable costs) to bring ATM to your computers. That probably explains why it, too, remains far more popular as a backbone technology than as a way to interconnect computers.

The best way to find out what's what is go online and seek out the collective wisdom that's so readily available. You can check in on any of Microsoft's Usenet NT-focused news groups through `msnews.microsoft.com`, visit MSN, or drop in on any of the numerous NT-focused mailing lists and ask: "Does my (fill in the name of your networking technology here) work with NT Server?" If you don't have access to online information resources, ask around. With so many users worldwide, you shouldn't have to look far to find somebody who can help you.

About Ancillary Equipment

Numerous networking devices besides computers may sometimes be required to help you build networks, especially when those networks grow beyond the confines of a simple workgroup of 20 users or fewer. Without dwelling too much on their features and more sophisticated functions, here is a set of devices that you will find available for most major networking technologies (or that incorporate interfaces based on such technologies) that you can use to extend or interconnect existing networks:

- **Repeater:** A repeater is a simple networking device that copies incoming signals from one connection, restores them to their original form, and then resends them out on one or more other connections (called ports). The notion behind the name, of course, is that this device "repeats" exactly what — and everything that — it "hears." Repeaters can link only media segments that use the same networking technology together, but those segments can be of different media types. Repeaters operate at the Physical Layer of the OSI model (the OSI model is explained in Chapter 3).

  Use repeaters when you reach the limits of the cable lengths that a given networking technology will support. They permit you to extend your networks further than they could otherwise go. Please note also that networking technologies also have rules about the maximum number of repeaters that may be situated between any sender and any receiver on a network.

- **Bridge:** A bridge is a networking device that examines the addresses of incoming network traffic and only copies incoming messages to other network segments if their destinations may be reached through (or on) those segments. The notion behind the name is that these devices act as semi-intelligent links between networks and can check low-level hardware addresses to decide what may pass from one network segment to another. Bridges operate at the Data Link layer of the OSI model (at the MAC sublayer, in fact; the OSI model is explained in Chapter 3 of this book).

Bridges can not only link media segments for the same networking technologies together, but so-called "translation bridges" can interconnect network segments that use different networking technologies. (Linking FDDI and Ethernet is a common example.) The protocols on both sides of the device must remain the same, however.

Use bridges when your network includes nonroutable protocols like NetBEUI or DLC and such traffic must be forwarded from one network segment to another. Note that some routers (next item) include bridging functions, and that hybrid devices called brouters (item after next) can perform both bridging and routing functions.

- **Router:** A router is a sophisticated networking device that can read and resolve network addresses from incoming traffic. Routers can perform all kinds of interesting functions on such data, including filtering incoming data by address, managing multiple protocols with ease, blocking and allowing not just certain types of protocols, but also certain ranges of addresses associated with certain protocols, and more. Routers operate at the Network Layer of the OSI model. (This model is explained in detail in Chapter 3 of this book.)

  Routers can interconnect dissimilar networking technologies and can even reformat data for transmission on an outgoing port whose technology differs from that of the incoming port. The most common case here is where 16 Mbps token ring and Ethernet may be linked together. Because token ring supports much larger message units than does Ethernet, a router may have to break a single token ring message up into as many as 44 equivalent Ethernet messages.

Routers are what make it possible for two separate networks to function independently yet still exchange information when they must. Routers make phenomena like the Internet possible and have played a critical role in its growth. Use routers when you seek to operate and control your own network(s), but when connectivity to other networks is also required.

- **Brouter:** A brouter combines the functions of a bridge and a router. That is, it acts like a bridge for nonroutable protocols, and like a router for routable protocols. Brouters are most commonly used on networks where both kinds of protocols are in use. They are also used when a local network requires bridging of nonroutable protocols, but access to the Internet or some other public network requires routing of routable protocols. Brouters operate at both the Data Link and Network Layers of the OSI model. (This model is explained in Chapter 3 of this book.)

- **Gateway:** A gateway is a device that can translate application information from one kind of environment to make sense to another kind of environment. Typical examples include e-mail gateways, which may translate between Microsoft Exchange native formats and the native e-mail format for the Internet, known as the Simple Mail Transfer Protocol (SMTP) and vice-versa.

  Other gateways can translate between dissimilar protocol suites, such as SNA and TCP/IP. Still others provide support for moving data between other dissimilar applications of the same type, such as database management or transaction processing systems. Gateways operate primarily at the upper layers of the OSI model (which is explained in Chapter 3 of this book), but primarily at the Application and Presentation layers.

As you climb this set of ancillary networking devices their sophistication and abilities increase, while their speed and overall handling capacity decline. That's because each step up this ladder involves increased processing and data-handling capabilities, which takes time and programming smarts, and therefore lowers the overall capabilities of the devices.

You often find items at the lower end of this ladder — such as repeaters and bridges — sold in the form of simple "black boxes" that are more or less ready to plug in and use. Routers and brouters, on the other hand, are usually special purpose, high-powered, high-speed computers that can accept two or more interface cards (one for each connection that you will want to make to this device).

Windows NT itself includes reasonably powerful built-in routing abilities, and additional software (Routing and Remote Access Services, or RRAS, Proxy Server, and so forth) can be added to Winodws NT to greatly enhance its abilities in this area. Gateways, on the other hand, usually occupy a general-purpose computer, but are also normally dedicated to performing only that job.

Mixing and Matching Network Technologies

Networks can mix and match topologies within the confines of a single networking technology with ease, but interconnecting different networking technologies requires more sophisticated equipment. Here is a brief rundown of interconnecting issues:

- **Interconnecting different media within a particular networking technology:** Most vendors offer simple devices (that is, repeaters and bridges) to interconnect network segments that use different types of media, such as twisted pair (10BaseT) and coaxial (10Base2) cable for Ethernet, for instance. Windows NT Server itself can handle multiple network interfaces, each with a different media type as well.
- **Interconnecting different networking technologies within a network:** As long as the protocols stay the same, routers or brouters can handle the job, such as interconnecting Token Ring and Ethernet segments. Likewise, Windows NT Server's own built-in routing capabilities allow it to function as a low-end router and interconnect different network technologies with ease. It just can't do those things as quickly as a special-purpose, high-end router like those from Cisco Systems, Bay Networks, and so forth.
- **Interconnecting fundamentally different protocols or applications:** Gateways really shine when fundamentally different protocols or applications must exchange information. This involves considerably more effort and intelligence than the lower-level services that these other devices provide. But gateways must also be sensitive to many more nuances and levels of functionality that those other devices, so this probably explains why they're more prone to problems than other choices as well.

In its TCP/IP settings, Windows NT asks for the address of a gateway. This term is used in a different sense than what we've been discussing here. In that case, the term gateway is synonymous with router and, in fact, points to a device that can forward packets not directed to the local cable segment for delivery to the outside world. Be sure to keep this in mind when you configure TCP/IP for Windows NT!

Part II

Putting Your Hardware in Place

The 5th Wave **By Rich Tennant**

"WHY A 4GL TOASTER? I DON'T THINK YOU'D ASK THAT QUESTION IF YOU THOUGHT A MINUTE ABOUT HOW TO BALANCE THE MAXIMIZATION OF TOAST DEVELOPMENT PRODUCTIVITY AGAINST TOASTER RESOURCE UTILIZATION IN A MULTI-DINER ENVIRONMENT."

In this part . . .

Having covered basic networking terminology and concepts in Part I, we try to cover something more tangible here in Part II — namely, the bits and pieces of equipment and cabling so necessary to the proper operation of any network.

To begin, you determine the basic principles of network layout and design, as you seek to translate networking concepts into a working network. After that, you tackle the ins and outs of network interface cards, or NICs as they're more usually known. With cards in place in your computers, the cables that tie them together come next. Finally, we cover the essential software elements that let your computers talk to the network, and the network talk to your computers.

Along the way, you figure out how to build a new network or extend an old one, and how to take stock of an existing network. You also bring the parts of a network together to create a harmonious whole rather than a hodge-podge of odds and ends. The goal here is to help you understand who the players are and how to make them function as a gung-ho team.

Chapter 5

Designing a Network

In This Chapter

- Turning design ideas into working networks
- Mastering network design fundamentals
- Situating servers and other network devices
- Checking your design to make sure it breaks no rules
- Using logical principles to organize your network
- Mapping your network
- Keeping up with changes

Whether you're constructing a network in its entirety or simply renovating a piece of an existing network, the basic approach is the same. You begin by planning what you wish to accomplish and gathering the ingredients necessary to realize your plans, and then you execute those plans according to whatever blueprint you devise. You also have to bring all the pieces together, to apply solid organizational principle to your network, and to document what you add (and what you find already in place) on your network.

Analyzing Your Requirements

Whenever you set forth on a network project, you should begin by analyzing your requirements. If you're building a network from scratch, this phase can take weeks or even months of effort; if you're simply extending or repairing an existing network, planning may take a day or less of your time.

Whatever the scope of your project, your plan should contain the following components:

- **A brief statement of your overall objectives, plus a more lengthy statement of requirements that addresses: what applications and services users need to access; estimates of user-to-server bandwidth requirements; and estimates of server-to-server bandwidth requirements (where applicable).** For example: *The new XYZ Inc. network will provide 60 users with access to Windows NT file and print services, plus access to a SQL server sales and inventory database. Each user will require no more than 1 Mbps bandwidth, and there are no prime time server-to-server bandwidth requirements, because all backups are scheduled for after-hours and weekends.*
- **A complete list of all the elements that you must purchase or otherwise acquire to meet those objectives.** For example: *The Accounting, Manufacturing, and Sales servers will act as routers to link two network segments of 10 users each together, for a total of 6 user segments based on 10 Mbps Ethernet. The three servers will be connected using a 100 Mpbs Ethernet backbone using 100BaseT. We will purchase 6 16-port 10/100 Ethernet hubs (one per user segment) to leave room for growth, and three two-CPU 450 MHz Intel Celeron Pentium II servers machines, each with 256 MB RAM and 18 GB of disk space. The Accounting Server will have an 80 GB DLT tape drive attached, so we can back all three servers up across the backbone.*
- **A description of the role each element will play on the network, the location of each element on the network, the configuration of each element, and the point in time during the installation process when you plan to add each element to the network.** You should use a map or a set of plans to guide you in placing cables, computers, and other components, and a timeline to indicate the order that you have to install everything. For example: *The Accounting Server will handle users from the Accounting and Purchasing departments; the Manufacturing Server will handle users from the Manufacturing and Engineering departments; the Sales Server will handle users from Administration, and from the Sales and Marketing departments. All servers, the backbone, and all hubs will be installed when the company is closed between December 23 and January 4. The network should be operational when normal business operations resume after New Year's.* The map of the proposed network is shown in Figure 5-1.
- **A test plan that describes how you plan to test individual elements, individual cable segments, and the entire network to make sure everything functions properly after you finish the installation.** For example: *The three servers will be installed first and tested individually the weekend before the Christmas break. On December 23 and 24, the 100 Mbps backbone will be installed. On December 28, the backbone will be tested. Next, the hubs will be installed and tested on December 28 and 29. On December 30, workstations on all existing 10 Mbps cable segments will be connected to the new 10/100 hubs and tested individually. From December 31 to January 2, automated testing software will exercise the entire network. On January 3, a network technician will visit our site with Bob, the site administrator, and any last minute changes, repairs, or adjustments will be performed. Thus, we believe the network will be ready for use on Monday, January 4.*

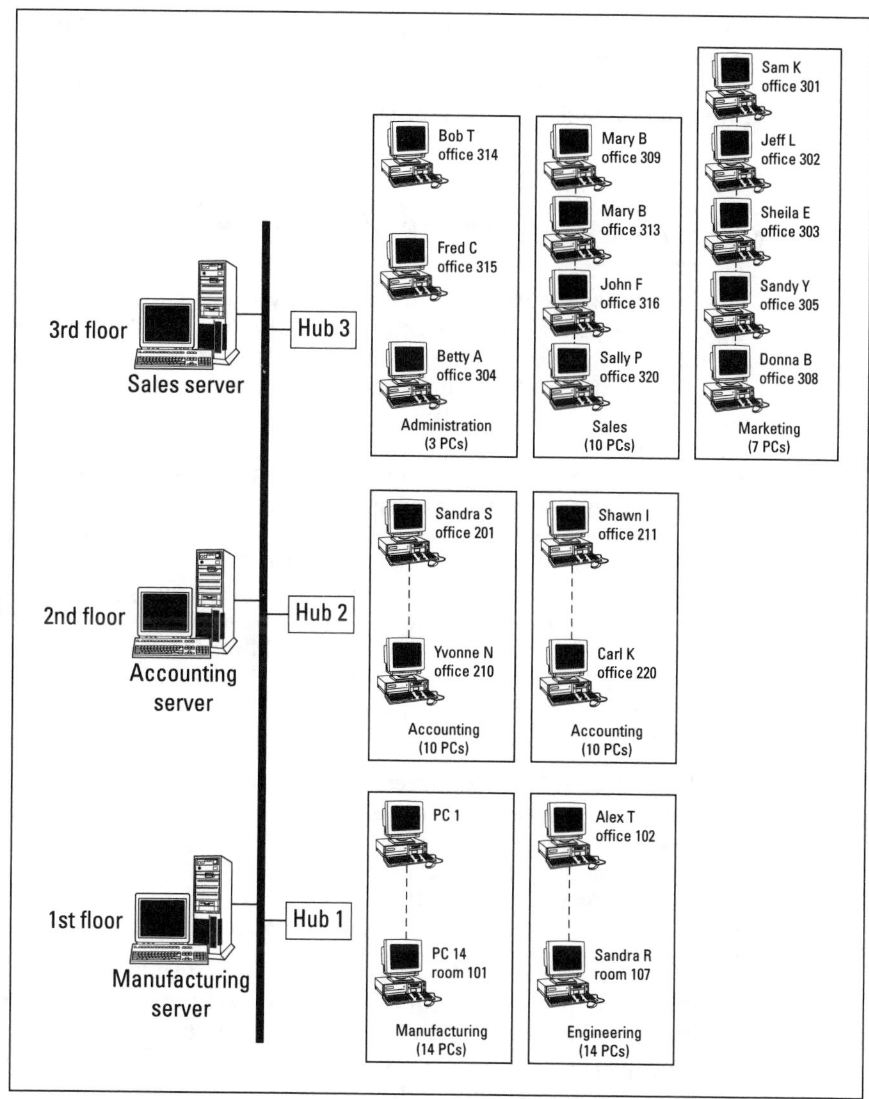

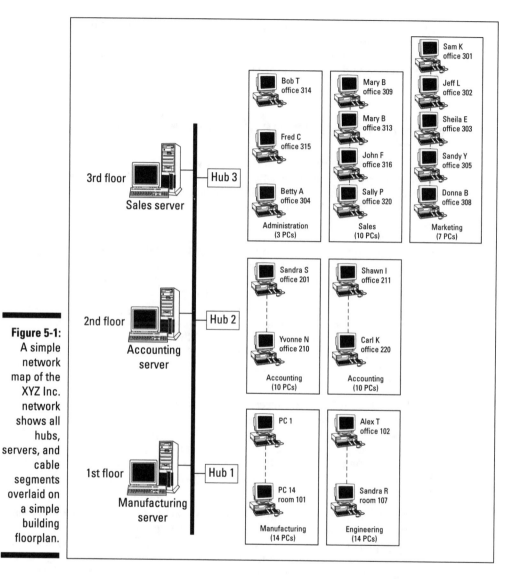

Figure 5-1: A simple network map of the XYZ Inc. network shows all hubs, servers, and cable segments overlaid on a simple building floorplan.

This plan can help you to decide where you must place key network elements — such as servers, hubs, and other networking devices. More importantly, the plan can also help you determine what kind of networking technology and bandwidth you need to deploy to meet your objectives. Since most businesses work on a budget, building a plan will also help you make sure you won't try to spend more than you're allowed to, or to incorporate more exotic technologies than you can afford.

Your network implementation plan should also help you evaluate your current network backbone or to plan a new one, to be able to carry all the traffic that normally comes together on these critical network segments. (We discuss backbones in more detail at the end of Chapter 7.)

The (Very) Basics of Network Design

The set of possible implementations that you can choose from when designing a network are almost innumerable. To help you distinguish among what's improbable, what's possible, what's feasible, and what's recommended. Here's a set of guidelines that should be of great help when designing a network to meet your needs:

- **Select a networking technology:** When adding on to or expanding an existing network, this decision is easy — it simply requires picking something identical to or compatible with whatever you're using. For new networks, you need to analyze the kinds of applications and services that users require in order to select an appropriate technology. For ordinary office work (e-mail, word processing, spreadsheets, basic database access, and so on) 10 Mbps Ethernet works well; for high-traffic or real-time applications like CAD, imaging, video conferencing, voice over network, and so on, 100 Mbps to the desktop makes more sense.

- **Stay close to the resources:** When designing a network, the smartest thing you can do is minimize the distance between users and the resources they most commonly use. This applies to printers (so that users can get easy access to output), servers (so that cable runs needn't be too long), and other services (such as fax machines, scanners, copiers, and so on) that users must access to do their jobs.
- **Build an online work environment:** When designing a network, you must also take into account current working patterns and arrangements in your offices. If accounting and purchasing must work together all the time, perhaps they also need to share a server. This also applies to the kind of network you build: For small companies, centralized control and tight security may get in workers' ways; in large companies, centralized control and tight security are the norm. You must serve the communities that currently exist in your organization and use the network to help users communicate and be productive wherever possible.
- **Arrange servers, hubs, and other key resources:** The places where wiring congregates — namely at punchdown blocks, wiring centers, and equipment rooms (or closets) — sometimes dictates where certain equipment must be placed. Be sure to check the distance between those locations and the areas where workers reside. In most cases,

offices are designed to support cabling from a centrally located wiring center or equipment room for groups of offices. If that's not the case in your workspace, you may have to add new equipment rooms and wiring centers or move workers to bring them closer to existing facilities. Either of these solutions takes time and costs serious money, so be sure to get your management involved in deciding which options make the most sense and how your organization will handle these changes.

For more information on key wiring equipment, and how to figure out where it's located, please consult *Networking For Dummies*, 3rd Edition, by Doug Lowe, IDG Books Worldwide, 1998. ISBN 0-7645-0346-4. It describes these critical networking components and how to find them in your workplace.

- **Build better backbones:** Depending on your choice of networking technology, you will probably want to arrange your network to include a special highway for data to travel across when multiple network cables come together. This can happen between servers, as with the XYZ Inc. example that appears at the beginning of this chapter. Such portions of the network are called backbones.

  A backbone can be something as simple as a so-called *collapsed backbone,* where a high-speed switch links multiple cable segments together (and the switch provides a single high-speed connection between all cable segments). Or a backbone can be as complex as a *staged backbone,* where intermediate segments jump from normal 10 Mbps Ethernet to switched Ethernet or 100 Mbps Ethernet at the server (as in the XYZ Inc. example mentioned at the beginning of this chapter). More complex backbones might even include a segment of Gigabit Ethernet on the innermost segment where traffic is heaviest.

- **Plan for growth:** When planning your network, design at least 30 percent spare, unused capacity into your system. This spare capacity should include network ports (unused ports on hubs), unused network cables in offices and cableways, and bandwidth on individual network segments. That way, you can grow within your current environment for a while without having to redesign your network on a regular basis. If your annual growth rate exceeds 30 percent, obviously you want to design at least one year's planned growth into your network, if not one year's planned growth *plus* 30 percent.

- **Work within the system:** As you discover when you start deploying a network in any organization, networks have a political side as well as a technical one. When you plan a network, you should work within your system in at least two ways: First, you want to make sure management knows about and approves of what you plan. Second, you want to make sure that you handle the work, contracts, purchases, and so on within the rules and regulations of your organization. If you neglect either of these guidelines, the only thing you'll learn how to network is trouble!

- **Check your design:** After you put your network design down on paper, review that design against what you know about the networking technologies it uses. Be especially careful to check the maximum cable lengths, maximum number of devices per segment, and maximum number of cable segments and devices between any two ends of the network against the rules that apply to the technologies you plan to use. You don't want to build a network that tries to break these rules, because if you do, you network may not work. Or worse, it may work for a while and then quit working, as you add new users or devices to the network. If you check your work before your build, you won't try to build something that can't work or that's inherently prone to trouble.
- **Ask for a sanity check:** Because you've put a network design down on paper and checked your work, you should also solicit input from one or more networking experts. Redesigning a network is always easier while it's still in the planning stages; you don't want to have to fix a flawed design after you've set it up. The more qualified advice you can get before you start building, the better off you'll be in the long run. In fact, this advice is worth paying for, because it can save you a world of hurt (or your job, for that matter).

Although this list of network design principles is by no means exhaustive, it should lead you down the pathway of designing a network that works best for your organization. Because these guidelines consider work patterns, politics, and organizational rules, as well as technology, the resulting network should serve your organization well for more than just technical reasons.

Situating Servers, Hubs, and Other Network Devices

After your plan is in place, you need to purchase the necessary equipment, cables, connectors, and so on and start deploying the components that make a network work. When you start situating key network equipment — including servers, hubs, routers, and so on — you need to make some important decisions about where to put them.

For small organizations of 25 people or less, using separate locked facilities to store hubs and servers may not make sense. Small organizations tend to be more informal and are less likely to have the kind of budget that supports a full-time information systems (IS) staff. In these circumstances, you usually want to situate your networking gear along with all your other gear — out in the open with other equipment for easy access to one and all. But if you do put them in the open, you'll want to make sure that only users with valid passwords can log onto such equipment. Otherwise, locking it up is highly recommended.

Larger organizations tend to be more concerned about security and control, and, therefore, they usually situate key networking components in locked equipment rooms and in locked wiring closets or wiring centers at various locations around their offices. Because the equipment has to be close to the wiring, it's not uncommon for servers to reside in wiring closets along with punchdown blocks, hubs, and other networking equipment.

Only authorized personnel should be permitted to access these facilities, and only authorized personnel can add users or equipment to the network, usually within a system of regularly scheduled updates or maintenance. In office buildings, for example, this usually means one or two wiring closets or equipment rooms per floor, where only authorized personnel have keys or access codes to get them into these rooms.

Pick the approach to situating your servers that makes sense for your organization, and stick with it. If you're going to follow rules for placing equipment, share those rules with employees so that they know what's going on. In fact, formulating a security policy for most networks is a smart move, and you should regularly explain that policy to your employees in detail. (For more information on this subject, see Chapter 17.)

Most small- to medium-sized companies — such as the fictitious XYZ Inc. mentioned at the beginning of this chapter — put their servers into small locked rooms at each end of those floors they occupy in an office building. This keeps the distances between users' desktops and the wiring centers acceptably low, and puts their servers alongside the punchdown blocks and hubs they use to manage their wiring. This approach also provides controlled access to the equipment and software that makes their networks work in a small number of closely managed locations. Finally, it addresses the need for adequate ventilation and power control that hubs and servers require for proper operation, but which most wiring closets do not offer.

Check Your Work as You Go

Normally, you install cable and equipment at the same time you build a network. You may run your own cables for your network and perform all equipment installation and configuration yourself, you may contract both the cable and equipment installation out to third parties, or you may pick some point between these two extremes. Whichever way you go, somewhere along the way, you'll be ready to put the finished pieces of your network together.

When it comes to installing cabling of any kind, your authors highly recommend that you use experienced cable installers with good references. The company that owns or operates your office building may even require a licensed cable installer to perform any such installation work. Here's why this is a good idea:

- Adhering to building and fire codes is mandatory, but it can also be tricky; calling on an experience professional is a good way to stay out of trouble.
- Cable placement and routing is sensitive; a trained professional knows how to avoid potential trouble spots and will always test their work to make sure the network will behave properly.
- High-speed networks are much more finicky and prone to installation difficulties than lower-speed networks. The faster you want your network to go, the better off you'll be if you leave the cabling to a professional.

We strongly advise that you bring a network up in small, manageable pieces. If you're installing multiple cable segments, bring up individual cable segments one at a time and test them to make sure each one works before hooking them all together. Likewise, if you're installing a backbone or a server cluster, test individual components separately before trying them out en masse.

When you install equipment, apply the same principles. After you install and configure a machine, check it by itself to make sure it works before attaching it to a network. This is as appropriate for hubs and routers as it is for server and desktop computers.

Our suggestions on piecewise checking and gradually increasing the complexity of your network comes from experience. We learned the hard way that throwing everything together all at once can cause problems that are simply too hard to troubleshoot because you have to deal with too many unknown elements.

At each step along the way toward building or extending a network, check your work. Fix problems as they arise, and you'll make steady progress toward the kind of well-run, well-organized network that you want to build!

Keeping in Touch with Your Organization's Needs

After you build a network, you may be tempted to rest for a while to enjoy your success. After all, you've earned it, right? However, while you certainly should pat yourself on the back, you must also realize that the real work begins as soon as users start using a network (or a new portion of an existing network). If you're responsible for a network, this not only means keeping things running for the moment, but also keeping them running — and running well — over time.

While the network you build or extend may meet your users' needs at first, any network's ability to continue to meet users' needs is going to diminish over time. Growth, technology change, and new applications and services almost guarantee that nothing stays the same for long in the workplace — this includes your network as well as the systems and services that the network delivers to your users.

Therefore, you need to conduct regular reviews of how well your network meets users' needs. In small or slow-growing organizations, you may have to review the network only once a year. But in large or fast-growing organizations, you should review the network on a quarterly basis.

Your network review should include at least these three elements:

- **Traffic analysis and usage review:** You can conduct this yourself by using the built-in Windows NT Server tools and facilities and third-party software tools. The idea is to take a snapshot of your network during ordinary-load, light-load, and peak-load conditions. If any of these loads starts to approach the boundaries of what the current design can reasonably support, you should start planning to extend and expand your network again.
- **User interviews:** You can do this on a one-on-one basis with selected users in your organization or hold meetings with individual workgroups and departments. The idea is to give employees a chance to share with you their observations, gripes, and wishes regarding the network. This can give you a great opportunity to not only gauge user satisfaction and networking knowledge, but to determine if you should give employees additional training on how to make more effective use of the network.
- **Management review:** You should meet with management regularly as well to find out what they're planning and what future information processing needs they're considering, as well as to gauge their impressions of and beliefs about the network, as you report your findings from the previous two bullets to them.

If you perform these reviews and keep in touch with upcoming changes and requirements, you can keep your network and your organization more tightly synchronized than if you neglect them. Planning for change and growth is extremely important on modern networks, because they're becoming critical business tools that organizations depend on to get their work done. If you take a proactive approach and plan for the future, you can stay ahead of the curve!

Mapping Your Network

Earlier in this chapter, we've introduced you to most of the basic principles involved in designing and building a network. You should also have a good idea about how networks should work. But as you spend more time around networks, you may realize that what they *do* isn't nearly as important as what you *know* about what they do.

Whether you wrestle with networks only occasionally or all the time, you soon discover that there's nothing like a network map to help you find and keep track of things on the network.

It's more than just a map!

Calling the collection of data that describes your network a map may not do the concept justice. A network map is more than a drawing that indicates where things are on your network — but creating such a drawing is an excellent way to start building a network map. The reasons why a network map is more than a mere depiction of a network is because it should include the following elements:

- A list of all computers on your network, with supporting documentation
- A list of all networking equipment — including servers and hubs, plus any repeaters, bridges, routers, and so on — with supporting documentation
- A list of all printers and all other specialized equipment on the network, such as scanners, fax machines, and so forth, with supporting documentation
- Lines to indicate where cables run and where junctions, taps, and other media-related elements are located

Formalizing your network map

Because a network map is so important and such a powerful tool, pause right here and start one immediately. Be prepared to spend some time and energy on this project, because most of the data that makes up a network map is naturally scattered all over the place.

Building a detailed network map is a worthwhile investment. It will pay for itself many times over as you come to depend on it. At worst, you discover more about your network than you ever wanted to know (but not more than you'll ever *need* to know). At best, you get to know your network so well that it will unlikely throw you any curve balls — and you may even find some things to tweak and tune while building the map.

Start at the beginning

Getting your hands on a set of your building's architectural drawings or engineering plans can help a great deal. If you can find them, go to an architect's supply vendor and make copies of these plans that you can mark up and use as a base map. (Most plans are created using an old-fashioned, ammonia-based copying system called *blue-line*. You can copy even large-sized plans for less than $25 per plan.)

If a professional cabling outfit installed your network, you should be able to get a copy of its cabling plans, which work even better than architectural drawings or engineering plans because they probably already show where the cable is laid and how much of it you've got. This is another good reason why "do it yourself" may not be the best way to cable your network.

If no such plans are available, you can sketch a room-by-room layout on rectangular grid paper (such as an engineering pad) to make it easy to draw to scale. Be sure to mark the location of machines, approximate locations for cable runs, and so on.

Put it on the map

Anything that merits attention or costs money is worth recording on your map. You don't need to go into great detail about each and every connector or note the exact length of every cable (approximate lengths to within a meter or so are useful, however). Indicate every major cable run, every computer, and every piece of gear attached to the network.

You probably won't have enough room to write all this information on the map itself. Therefore, you should key information to a machine or cable name and record the actual details in a file on your computer. Or if you prefer to do things your own way, that's fine — just make sure you know how to find later on what you've recorded. Whatever scheme you adopt, use it religiously. In addition, make some brief notes about how your scheme works, so that somebody else can use your map if you're not available to explain it.

Building a network inventory

The information you gather while producing a network map creates a detailed inventory of what's on your network and where everything is located. Unfortunately, you quickly find out that this is *a lot* of information.

To make keeping an inventory easier for yourself (and anyone who must follow in your footsteps), build a template or form that you can fill out for each item on the network. This approach forces you to collect consistent information — and makes delegating information gathering to others much easier. Your inventory should include all of the following information for each computer on the network:

- **The hardware configuration for each machine:** This should include a list of all interfaces and their settings, information about installed RAM and drives, and the make and model of the keyboard, display, and so on. If you can find out who sold you the equipment, write that down, too.

  Keeping track of equipment is typically the accounting department's responsibility. Check with them for a copy of your company's capital assets or a depreciable items inventory (if available). This kind of documentation normally includes serial numbers and other identification for hardware on the network. If no one in you company has gathered such information, you should collect it yourself. It's valuable.
- **The software configuration for each machine:** This should include listings of configuration files, operating system data (including version number, most recent Service Pack applied, and so on), as well as a list of programs and versions installed on the machine.
- **The network configuration for each machine:** This should include the make and model of the NIC, plus a list of driver files with names, version numbers, dates, and sizes. (You can capture a directory to a file easily on Windows operating systems and use this as the basis for this information.)

In addition to information on each computer, your inventory should also include the following information:

- **A list of other equipment, such as hubs, routers, printers, and so on:** Include the manufacturer, model, make, and serial number for each piece of equipment. If the equipment includes memory modules, disk drives, or plug-in interface cards, get information about them, too. If the equipment uses software or firmware, record the name, version, release date, and any other information you can garner about such items.
- **A list of all the cable segments on the network:** Give each segment a unique name or number, and associate your records with whatever kind of identifier you use for those segments. Record the type and make of cable, its length, locations of its ends, and any significant connections or intermediate locations that you may have to visit some time in the future.
- **A list of all the vendors who've worked on your network or its machines:** Include names and phone numbers of contacts at each operation. This can be a valuable resource for technical support and troubleshooting. Over time, you want to add the names and phone numbers of tech support or other individuals at these organizations who prove to be knowledgeable and helpful.

Essentially, the information you gather while creating and maintaining a network map forms a database of everything anyone needs to know about your network. To improve access to and usability of this data, you may want to consider storing the text data for your network map in an honest-to-goodness database engine. If this is too labor-intensive, a file- or paper-based approach works, but takes more effort to maintain over time. Whatever method of recording data for your map you use, be sure to keep your inventory complete and up-to-date.

Keeping up with changes

One thing that you can always be sure about when it comes to networks: They're always changing. You map is only as good as the information it contains. And the map only remains useful if that information is an accurate reflection of the real network in your organization.

Whenever anything changes on your network, make updating the map and its associated database a priority. Sitting down and checking your map is much less work than walking around and looking at the real objects that the map shows. If the map is current, you can keep on top of things from the comfort of your office. If it's out of date, you'd better start walking!

Chapter 6

Installing Network Interface Cards

In This Chapter

- Understanding your NIC
- Catching the bus
- Choosing advanced NIC features
- Configuring your NICs
- Checking your work
- Dealing with device drivers
- Troubleshooting NIC problems

Buckle up, because it's time to hook the network up to your prospective Windows NT Server, in preparation for putting that sucker to work!

For most PCs, whether they run Windows NT Server or some other operating system, the network interface (or interfaces, if a machine has more than one network connection) come in the form of network interface cards, known affectionately as NIC. For the uninitiated, NIC is pronounced "nick" just like what sometimes happens when you're shaving. NICs provide the essential link between the network medium and a computer that needs to access the network.

In this chapter, you find out about the basic types, functions, and capabilities of NICs, and how to pick the right kind to use in your server. Along the way, you have a chance to pick up lots of tips and tricks about setting up these all-important components correctly the first time, every time.

What's in a NIC?

A typical NIC is an add-in card that's configured to work inside your PC. Its role is to work both sides of the network connection, as follows:

- The NIC plugs into your computer's bus or a special adapter slot so it can talk to the CPU, and the CPU can talk to it. This capability essentially defines a NIC's most important role — namely, its ability to permit a computer to access the network medium and vice-versa.
- A NIC's accommodation for a network connection (where the medium plugs in) requires an external connector to enable the network medium to connect to the NIC in some form or fashion. Some NICs include more than one connector, so if you change your network or your mind, you don't have to throw out the old to put in the new.
- Your networking technology determines the details of how the NIC accesses the network medium. There are NICs for Ethernet, token ring, FDDI, and so on. Unlike connectors, adapters don't normally support more than one networking technology.

Figure 6-1 shows all the important connections on a NIC, including the bus connector (which makes the NIC and the CPU accessible to one another) and the media interface (which makes the NIC and the networking medium accessible to each other as well). Media connectors vary with the networking technology and physical media in use. By learning to recognize what you've got, you can select the NIC (or NICs) that's right for your network.

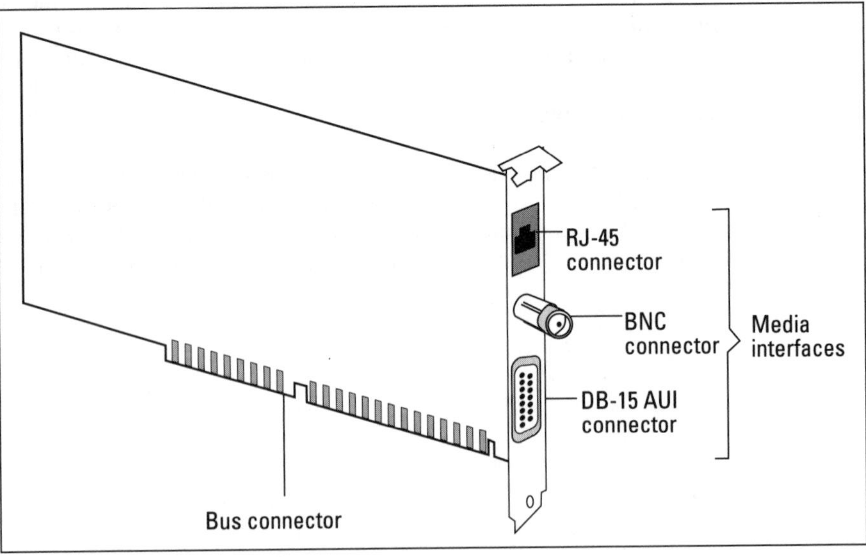

Figure 6-1: The NIC creates a bridge between your computer and the network.

Figure 6-1 shows a so-called three-way combo card for Ethernet, with an RJ-45 connector for twisted-pair (10BaseT), a BNC connector for thinwire (10Base2), and a AUI connector for thickwire (10Base5). If this sounds like so much gibberish, don't worry — you can explore exactly what all this gobbledegook means in Chapter 7.

Not all NICS come in the form of adapter cards that plug into a bus inside your computer. Some laptops, portables, and other machines can't accommodate standard internal interfaces like conventional desktop PCs usually can. For these machines, you can attach an external network interface, called a *parallel-port connector,* that does the same job as a conventional NIC. Figure 6-2 shows a parallel-port connector from both front and back.

Especially for laptops, you can often install PC Card adapters (formerly known as PCMCIA, or Personal Computer Memory Card International Association, adapters) according to your networking whims. PC Cards look a lot like fat credit cards, and are about the same size. You slide them into and out of your computer's PC Card slot. Laptops sometimes require an NIC PC Card for a network connection in the office and a modem for remote access to network resources when the laptop owner is away from the office. Windows NT supports a mechanism known as "hardware profiles" that makes it easy to set up multiple hardware configurations for such machines (for more information, check out Chapter 9).

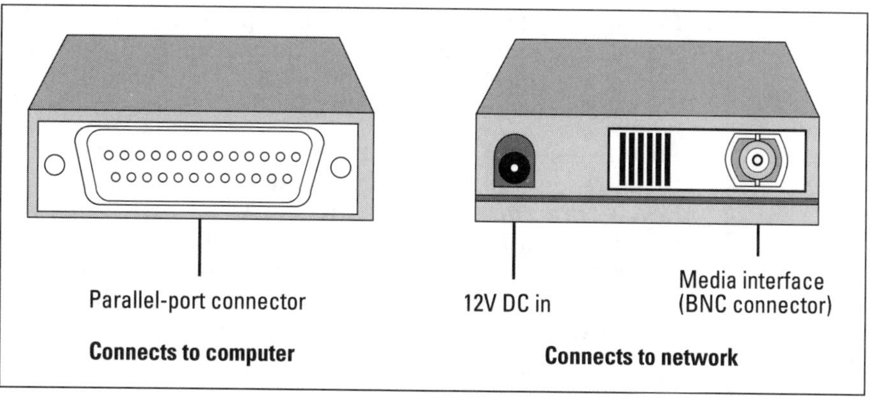

Figure 6-2: An external network interface is a NIC that attaches outside your computer.

Catching the Bus: ISA, EISA, MCA, or PCI?

If your computer is a PC, you have to match its NIC (or NICs) to whatever internal bus (or buses) have open slots. In this section, we introduce information about a variety of buses that you may find in your PCs, and we offer tips about which ones are better than others.

Because Windows NT Server's primary job is to handle network service requests, you want to install the fastest, most capable NIC(s) that can work with your PC. You can then expect the best possible performance for all clients on your network!

The business end of a NIC plugs into a PC bus and is called an *edge connector.* You can recognize the types of interfaces that your computer includes by looking at a computer's bus slots. Likewise, looking at your NIC can tell you what kind of bus it's made for. Figure 6-3 shows the four types of buses covered in this section, with their respective edge connectors.

NICs come in a variety of flavors that generally correspond to the bus architectures that have found their way into and out of vogue since the 1980s. Here is a brief list of these architectures:

- **ISA:** Industry Standard Architecture (pronounced "ice-ah") describes the bus that most PCs have used since IBM introduced the PC/AT in 1985. ISA is still the most common PC bus, so it may be an option that you must consider for your NT Server machine.
- **EISA:** Extended ISA, (pronounced "eesa") which is fairly difficult to find today, represented an attempt to extend the capabilities of the ISA bus. EISA is *backward compatible* with ISA, which means that you can plug an ISA card into an EISA slot and it will work fine in spite of the fact that the cards have slightly different edge connectors (refer to Figure 6-3). Although EISA cards provide higher performance than ISA cards and were designed specifically for servers, EISA never really caught on.
- **MCA:** The Micro Channel Architecture is a 32-bit bus developed by IBM, with most of the same advantages as ISA and EISA: higher-speed and a broader, 32-bit data path. If you have a Micro Channel PC, you must buy Micro Channel NICs to go with it, because MCA is a replacement bus, not necessarily an expansion bus. Micro Channel's main advantage is that you can usually plug in an NIC and it handles its own configuration itself. This convenience does not come cheap, however — MCA cards still cost more than most other cards. Micro Channel buses are rare today except in high-end IBM machines such as RISC workstations or AS/400 minicomputers.

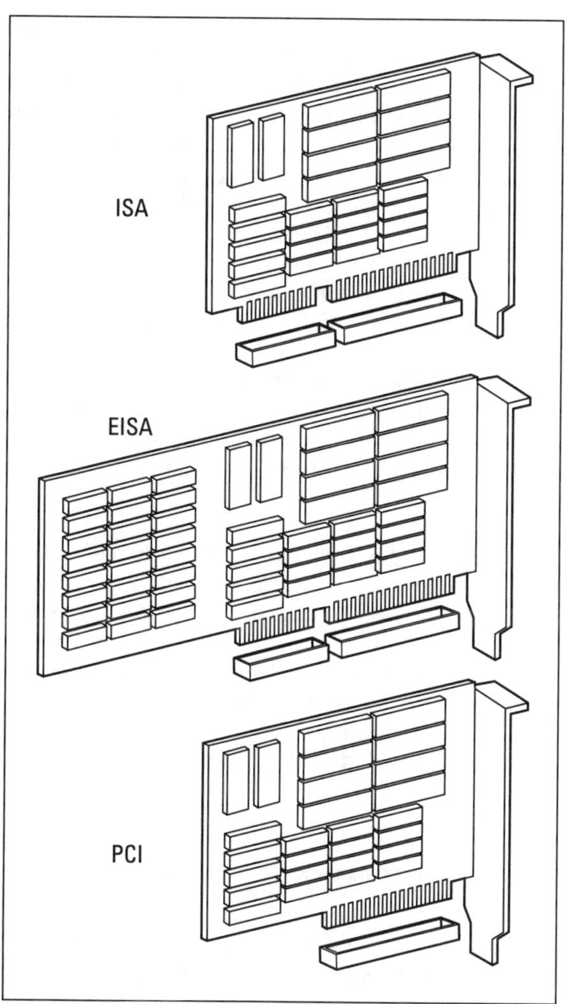

Figure 6-3: PC buses and their connectors are made to match up perfectly.

- **VLB:** VESA Local Bus is a 32-bit bus technology that runs at speeds up to 66 MHz. A VLB slot uses one 32-bit Micro Channel Architecture (MCA) slot plus a standard ISA, EISA, or MCA. This allows manufacturers to design boards that use the local bus or the standard bus at the same time. VLB supports a bus management technique known as *bus mastering,* which enables the board to take control of the bus and frees the CPU to handle other tasks, thereby speeding up overall system performance. Because of VLB's dependence on Micro Channel Architecture, VLB has become a thing of the past.

- **PCI:** The peripheral component interconnect, developed by Intel, provides a high-speed data path between the CPU and up to ten peripherals while coexisting with ISA or EISA (like other expansion buses). Like VLB, PCI supports bus mastering to free up the CPU. With PCI, you plug ISA and/or EISA boards into their usual slots, and plug high-speed PCI controllers into PCI slots. PCI supports 32- and 64-bit implementations, with clock speeds up to 100 MHz and data transfer rates up to 132 megabytes per second. It's no wonder that PCI has more or less won the bus wars and that it has become the high-speed local PC bus of choice. PCI offers the best performance for peripheral adapter cards, and when it comes to server NICs, that's the name of the game!

High-speed buses such as EISA and PCI are great and emerging standards like FireWire (IEEE 1394) and Fibre Channel are even better because high-speed buses meet a server's need for speed in spades. On the other hand, you don't always have the money or open slots to use a high-speed connection, so do the best you can.

We feel PCI is the way to go today because it's already widely available and supported in Windows NT 4.0. When Microsoft ships Windows 2000, PCI may no longer stand out as the king of the NIC performance hill. But right now, PCI's the best (and only real) game in town when it comes to providing high performance and advanced features. That's why we recommend spending the money required to get the fastest PCI NIC for the networking technology of your choice: You can use PCI to make your NT Server as fast at networking as it can be, which is highly desirable on a network server.

Choosing High-Performance NICs

Certain built-in NIC features can affect network performance significantly. Poor NIC performance hurts doubly on a server, because it limits access to its services for everyone. In fact, on those networks where all users share a common medium, such as Ethernet, a slow NIC on any computer on a single cable segment decreases available bandwidth for all network users as long as that slow NIC stays busy.

When selecting a NIC for a Windows NT Server computer, start by identifying the network media and the connector that the card must fit. This means recognizing what type of network technology is in use and deciding what type of connector the NIC must provide. After covering these basics, you must consider numerous other NIC options that can boost a card's speed and data-handling. Because server performance is critical, by exploiting all NIC options available, you improve your network's overall performance.

Here is a select set of NIC options to look for in a card bound for use in a Windows NT Server machine (you may not be able to find a NIC that supports all of these, but try for as many as you can find — and afford):

- **Bus mastering:** Enables a NIC to control a computer's bus to initiate and manage data transfers to and from the computer's RAM. Bus mastering thus permits the CPU to focus on other tasks. It offers the biggest performance boost of any of the items mentioned here, and can increase network performance from 20 to 70 percent. Bus mastering cards cost more than other NICs, but are essential for server use.
- **Direct Memory Access (DMA):** Enables NICs to transfer data directly from on-board RAM buffers into a computer's main RAM without requiring the CPU's involvement in the data transfer. DMA can boost NIC performance by as much as 20 to 25 percent.
- **On-board coprocessors:** CPUs built into a NIC itself; they enable NICs to process data without involving the CPU. Most modern NICs include coprocessors to boost network performance, so it's hard to estimate their overall contribution to performance improvements.
- **RAM buffering:** Incorporates additional RAM on a NIC to provide storage space for incoming and outgoing data. Extra buffering boosts network performance because it enables a NIC to process data as fast as possible, without having to pause to empty and refill its buffers.
- **Shared adapter memory:** Causes a NIC's buffers to map directly into computer RAM addresses. This fools the computer into thinking that it's writing to its own memory, when it's really accessing a NIC's buffers. In other words, the computer treats a NIC's RAM as if it were its own.
- **Shared system memory:** Reverses the preceding item, and enables an on-board NIC processor to write to an area in the computer's RAM as if it were NIC buffer space. This enables a NIC to treat computer RAM as its own, and may be preferable to shared adapter memory because it permits a NIC to manage memory, and frees the CPU for other tasks.

As network traffic loads go up, the value of these options follows suit. When selecting a NIC for your server, purchase the fastest NIC you can afford. In such cases, invest in a 32-bit, bus-mastering NIC that uses either shared adapter or shared system memory and includes added buffer space.

Avoid Trouble: Get Off to a Good Start

Before you start mucking around inside your PC, be prepared. Messing with your system is one of the few things that can flat-out kill a computer — or you! If you take some preventive steps at the outset, you can ward off all kinds of trouble, and probably get back to work more quickly.

NIC installation maneuvers can turn out in one of two ways. With luck, your brand-new NIC will be safely ensconced in your PC, doing exactly what it's supposed to do. Otherwise, it will be back in its original packaging, ready to be exchanged for whatever it is that you now know you *really* need!

Here are some other tips that should improve your installation experience:

- **Unplug any PC before your open it up:** Electricity is your friend, but there's no reason to get up close and personal with it. *Never, never, never* open a PC that's plugged into a wall socket. This mistake can get you or your machine (or both) fried. This is, technically speaking, not a good thing.
- **If you can't go forward, make sure you can go back:** It can sometimes happen after you install an NIC that you turn on the computer, and get a big, fat, resounding nothing! The worst case of all may require sending the computer to a professional for repair. In the not-so-bad (and more common) case, if you take out the new stuff, and reverse any software changes you've made, you're back where you started.

  Reverse software changes, you ask? This brings us to a crucial preemptive step that you must always take before fiddling with hardware. *Before* you start messing around, back up any system that will be affected. Backing up confers two vital benefits. First, assuming the worst happens and a DOA computer results, you can install your backup on another similarly configured machine and keep working until the original computer gets back from the shop. Second, if the new installation doesn't work, you can use the backup to restore the machine to the pristine state it presumably enjoyed before you mucked it up.

  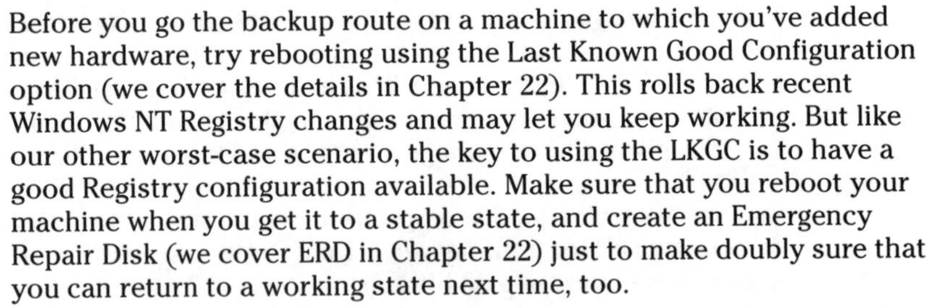

  Before you go the backup route on a machine to which you've added new hardware, try rebooting using the Last Known Good Configuration option (we cover the details in Chapter 22). This rolls back recent Windows NT Registry changes and may let you keep working. But like our other worst-case scenario, the key to using the LKGC is to have a good Registry configuration available. Make sure that you reboot your machine when you get it to a stable state, and create an Emergency Repair Disk (we cover ERD in Chapter 22) just to make doubly sure that you can return to a working state next time, too.
- **Figure out what you're dealing with:** A PC can act like a minefield when adding another interface to an already jam-packed machine. If you don't have an inventory of what's installed, and related configuration data, make a list of what's installed and the settings for each item. This makes quick work of installation and may head off configuration anxiety before it can strike. Time may be money, but remember: It always takes longer to do it over than to do it right to start with.

There's a peachy DOS utility called the Microsoft Diagnostic Utility (MSD.EXE) and an equally nifty NT utility called the Windows NT Diagnostics (also known as Winmsd.exe) — available from the Administrative Tools (Common) menu. Each of these utilities can tell you things about your PC's configuration that come in handy when you install a NIC.

- **Give yourself room to maneuver:** Clear some work space for yourself. Find some small paper cups or other small containers to hold screws and connectors. If you're really going to take things apart, label what goes where to help eliminate guesswork during reassembly. Also, make sure that you have the right tools for the job. Go to a computer store and get one of those $50 to $100 general-purpose computer toolkits that come in those nifty zip-up cases. (We got a peach of a kit like this from Jensen Tools at `www.jensentools.com/` on the Web.)

You build up static as you walk across carpets or move around in dry conditions. Therefore, always carry NICs in their anti-static wrappers and ground yourself before you put your hands in a machine or handle computer hardware. To dissipate static buildup, use anti-static wristbands or heel-caps.

- **Learn the lay of your LAN:** You will eventually connect any installed NIC to a network. Part of the configuration drill is knowing the names and addresses of other servers, users, and networks around you. Before you start, read the installation requirements provided by the NIC's manufacturer and go over any of the details that you need to supply during installation. This heads off any needs to stop part-way through the process to dig up missing information. Invest the ounce of prevention that helps avoid expensive, time-consuming cures!

Beware the Golden Fingers!

Reading motherboard or adapter manuals from offshore manufacturers gives you a unique opportunity to decipher the bizarre forms that written English can sometimes take in the hands of non-native speakers. For example, one Taiwanese company describes an edge connector (the part of the NIC that plugs into a PC's bus slot) as "golden fingers."

Even if those fingers are brass rather than gold, make sure they're firmly seated and fully connected when you plug a NIC into an empty bus slot. That is, make sure the edge connector is hidden from view and that the network interface on the side of the card is well-positioned in the cutout on the back of your PC case. Don't jam the edge connector into the computer's bus socket; rock it carefully if you must. Too much force can peel the golden fingers away; if that happens, you need a replacement card.

You should also screw the metal tab into place, using the screw that attached the placeholder before you removed it. Figure 6-4 shows the placeholder with the screw notch.

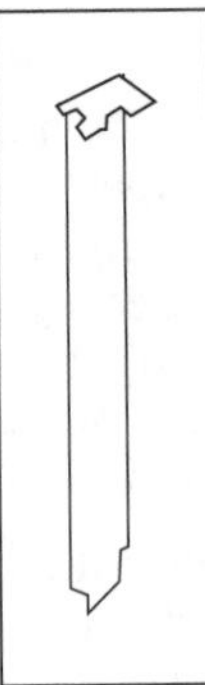

Figure 6-4: Empty slots are closed off by placeholders; they keep dust and dirt out of your PC case.

Two things are worth noting about PC placeholders:

- Be careful with the little screw that holds the placeholder in position. If you drop a screw, you can usually get it to show itself more readily by picking up the PC case and rocking it back and forth gently. *Never* use a magnetized screwdriver to pick up a screw you've dropped; otherwise, you computer's data may become screwy.
- Be sure to put the placeholder in a toolbox or spare-parts drawer so that you can find it again later. If you must ever remove the NIC (or any other card) from your PC, you'll need the placeholder to close the case up again. Some cases use odd-sized placeholders, so life will be simpler if you can find the right placeholder when you need it.

NIC Configuration Details

Configuring a NIC requires making all the right hardware selections and choosing appropriate software settings. Windows NT 4.0 is probably the last version of NT in which you need to worry about such details, because Microsoft promises that Windows 2000 will finally be Plug and Play compatible (this means that NICs should more or less configure themselves). But for now, you must deal with numerous different settings and make sure that the right configuration information is furnished to the NIC's software drivers.

NICcus interruptus

Activity on a network can occur at any time. To receive incoming data and handle outgoing traffic, the NIC must be able to signal the CPU or the bus (for incoming traffic) and vice-versa (for outgoing traffic).

The most common way to handle such activity is to reserve an interrupt request line (IRQ) for a NIC's use. PCs typically support from 15 to 23 IRQs, numbered 0 through 15 or 23, depending on the number of interrupt controllers installed. Interfaces use IRQs to signal activity. Each NIC must have its own assigned IRQ value in a range that the card itself can handle.

These variables help explain why mapping a PC's configuration is a good idea. Your mission, whether you like it or not, is to find an IRQ that no other adapter is using and that your new NIC can accept. If such an IRQ is not available, you must alter another card to free up a usable IRQ. For PCI NICs, this exercise is not so difficult, because PCI handles IRQs itself.

Setting IRQs usually means making software settings, setting DIP switches (DIP stands for dual-in line package), or moving jumpers. The software stuff is self-documenting, but we explain how to work with the latter two elements in the next sections.

DIPsy doodles

Most *DIP switches,* which are really banks of individual switches, indicate which way is on or off. If you can't tell, and the manual doesn't help, call the vendor's tech support department right away. They know the answer and this will save you unnecessary and potentially dangerous guessing and experimentation. Figure 6-5 shows a typical DIP switch. Here again, DIP switches are an ISA thing; you won't find them on PCI NICs.

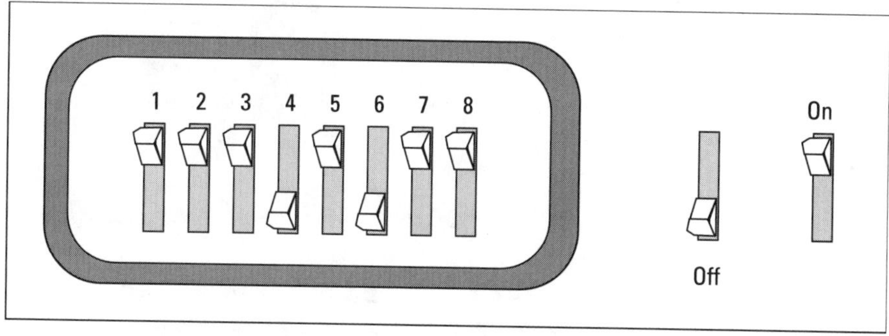

Figure 6-5: DIP switches and jumper blocks often control a NIC's various settings.

Jumping jiminy!

Jumper blocks are made of two rows of adjacent pins that are connected with teeny-tiny connectors called *jumpers* (see Figure 6-6). The pins are usually numbered, with designations that start with J followed by a number (for example, J6).

Sliding a jumper over both pins turns a jumper on. To turn a numbered pin set off, remove the jumper from both pins and slide it over one of the two pins so that it sticks out from the pin block (as in the middle position in Figure 6-6). Often when you set IRQs with jumpers, you insert one jumper for an entire block of pins. The pin set you jump selects the chosen IRQ. In that case, make sure that the jumper is firmly seated on both pins.

Defaults, dear Brutus

Before you worry overmuch about DIP switches or jumpers, check the NIC manual to find out where the factory set the IRQ by default. If this default setting is not in use, you can stick with that default and do nothing else. Consider it a blessing when this happens!

Any I/O port in a storm

Each card in a system has a unique I/O port address, with certain addresses reserved for certain interfaces, especially video cards. NICs are quite choosy, and can normally get an I/O port address assigned from a reserved range of addresses. This address is generally handled by software, or by a DIP switch setting, on most NICs because of the broad range of possible settings.

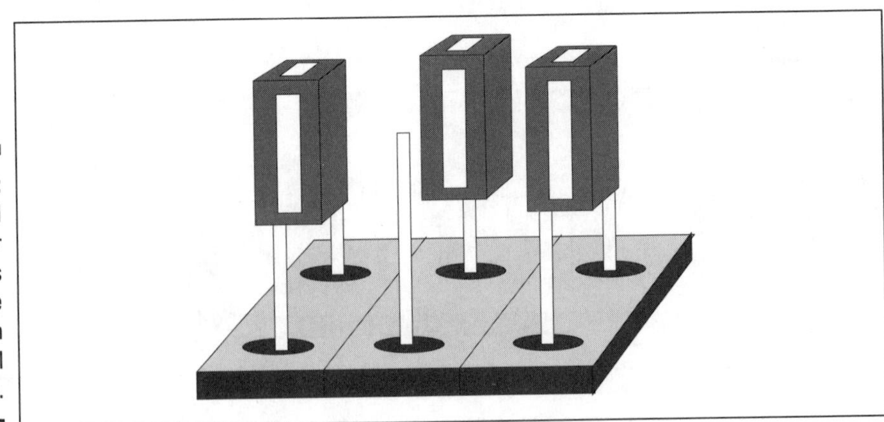

Figure 6-6: A typical jumper block has multiple pins, with individual jumpers.

I/O ports exist to let a computer read from or write to memory that belongs to an interface. When an interrupt is signaled, it tells the computer to read from, or write to, an I/O port. The information written to, or read from, the I/O port's address is copied across the bus between the NIC and the CPU.

Direct access: Setting DMA

Some NICs use a technique called directory-memory access (DMA) to move information between the NIC and the CPU. The result is fast copying of information from the computer's memory to the NIC, and vice-versa. This technique has become less necessary (and less common) as computers and equipment have become faster.

DMA matches up two areas of memory: one on the computer and another on the NIC. Writing to the memory area on the computer automatically copies data to the NIC, and vice versa. *Setting a DMA address* means finding an unoccupied DMA memory block to assign to your NIC. Again, your earlier research on what settings are already occupied can help you avoid conflicts. Choose an unoccupied block and make the right NIC settings to match it. If you encounter a conflict, you'll have to figure out some way to resolve it. Remember to check your defaults here, too.

Running the bases: The MemBase setting

NICs contain their own RAM, called buffer space, to provide working room to store information coming on and off the network. This buffer space must be assigned an equivalent region in the PC's memory.

Just as with IRQs and DMA, this setting must be unique. Watch out for potential address conflicts and steer around them. If software doesn't do the job automatically, you usually use jumpers to set the base memory address (MemBase) for your NIC. Common settings for network cards include C000h, D000h, and D800h.

If a NIC card is on the Hardware Compatibility List (HCL), a possible configuration is probably listed as well, so you don't have to figure everything out without help. But you do have to choose basic elements even in the Windows NT environment — including the IRQ and sometimes the base I/O address and the DMA settings. Also, be sure to check your NIC's installation software before you install Windows NT: Even today, many NICs include only DOS installation software. Therefore, you'll need to install the card under DOS and then install Windows NT (which will probably detect and preserve the card's configuration on its own). Phew!

In the Driver's Seat

After you install NIC hardware, you need to deal with device driver software. If your NIC is of recent vintage, the drivers on the disk that's included with the card actually may be worth using.

In that case — which we rank right up there with your chances of winning the lottery — you can load the disk, run an installation program, supply a few values here and there, and be ready to roll. If you're not that lucky, you'll have to chase down drivers on your own.

Our advice: Always determine the latest and greatest drivers for your NICs before you start installing them. Ask for help in the following order:

1. From the company that sold you the NIC.
2. From the vendor that built the card.
3. On the Internet. Use your favorite search engine to search for the NIC by vendor and model. This usually produces usable information, if not usable software.

Cabling Up to the NIC

Okay, the software's installed and the hardware is plugged in. All that's left is cabling the NIC to the network. For modular technologies, such as twisted-pair Ethernet or token ring, that means inserting the LAN cable's modular connector into the receptacle on the NIC. For other technologies, it means hooking up a T-connector or a transceiver cable from the LAN to your NIC. Whichever option applies to your circumstances, make sure that the connection is tight and the NIC is seated solidly in its slot. Then you're ready to fire it up!

Looking for Trouble in All the Right Places

You've navigated through a maze of potential address conflicts and have set your NIC to steer clear of all shoals. The software's installed, so everything should work, right? Well, sometimes it does (loud cheers and much laughter) and sometimes it doesn't (serious grinding and gnashing of teeth). You find out that things don't work in one of three ways:

- **Your PC doesn't boot:** This one is obvious. When you're unable to boot, it's time to start undoing what you just did. First, restore the system to its state before you started messing around. (You *do* have a backup, right?) If that works, you know that the NIC is the problem. Seek out some help from one of our recommended sources. If your system still doesn't work when you're back to square one, you have bigger problems. Time to visit the repair shop!
- **Your PC boots, but doesn't load the drivers:** The most common reasons that drivers fail to load are as follows:
  - **Loose connections:** Make sure that the wire is tight and properly seated on the NIC, and make sure it's plugged into something on the other end.
  - **Installation problems:** Make sure that the drivers are in the right directory, and that this directory is referenced in your bootup file or defined in your PATH statement. Because Windows NT actively searches your hard drive for drivers (as long as your NIC is on the HCL), this normally won't be a problem for NT machines.
  - **Conflict!** You may have missed something and introduced a conflict. Try all your other stuff; it's a dead giveaway if something else has quit working also. Time to return to square one and recheck all system settings. Something somewhere is squirrely, so be extra careful!

  The good news here is that such a problem is most likely to result from a loose connection or a configuration boo-boo. If it's not one of those, it may be time for a visit to the repair shop!
- **Your PC boots partway, but hangs on a blue screen:** Sometimes, Windows NT will start booting, but hang up on a solid blue screen filled with white text that starts with an error code. This condition is known as the "blue screen of death" (aka BSOD) to Windows NT aficianados.

  When the BSOD appears during installation, it's usually related to some kind of hardware driver problem. If it happens right after you install a NIC, but Windows NT has booted before, guess what? The NIC driver you just installed is not working properly and will have to be replaced with a working one. Make sure you've got the latest and greatest driver from the NIC vendor. If in doubt, send some e-mail or call tech support. If this problem occurs during an initial installation of Windows NT, it may not be clear what's causing the problem. If that's the case, consult Chapter 21, which deals with Windows NT boot problems, or Chapter 22, which covers installation and configuration tips.

- **You try to use the network and it fails to respond:** This is a subtle variant on NIC driver problems and usually results from one or more of the same causes. You're treated to an extra layer of mystery here, though, because the conflict may result from another application rather than a driver problem. Or the network may be stymied by an incorrect NIC setting, an incorrect network configuration, or an invalid login sequence (that is, the software works okay but you're telling it to do the wrong stuff). You must work your way through a careful process of elimination to find an answer. Good luck, and take lots of breaks. Remember, you can always ask for help!

After you've made it over any humps and can communicate with the network, you're ready to get to work. Or, if you're a fledgling network administrator, you'll have the pleasure of helping someone else get to work for the first time. Either way, you'll have pushed the networking wave another machine ahead!

Chapter 7

Linkin' Networks, Not Logs

In This Chapter

- Finding a happy networking medium
- Picking from the many flavors of Ethernet
- Examining the network backbone
- Choosing between a network and an internetwork
- Linking WANs
- Planning for success

Buying computers does not a network make! You have to connect computers so that they can communicate. Several ways for setting up communications among computers are available; which one you choose depends on your budget and bandwidth requirements. Okay, so most of it depends on your budget!

Transmission media is a fancy term used to describe cabling and atmospheric transmission. The media provide the means by which computers talk to one another across a network. In fact, computers can communicate through the airwaves by using broadcast transmissions, through the wiring in a building, or across a campus. Linking long-haul or Internet connections to local networks means almost no limit to what your network can access!

In this chapter, we examine different methods for interconnecting a network using cable and other media. You find out which media are appropriate for desktop connectivity and which media are appropriate for server-to-server activity. You also discover more about network anatomy as we tackle two ticklish subjects — namely, backbones and WAN (wide area network) links.

Find the Happy Network Medium

A happy network medium has nothing whatsoever to do with a content TV psychic. Rather, finding the right network medium means implementing network cabling that won't cause bottlenecks on your network.

Depending on whether you're building a network from the ground up, you may need to take a different approach to evaluating cabling options for your network:

- If you stepped into a job where a LAN is already in place, cabling is probably in place, too. Evaluating the type, capabilities, and usability of an inherited network is almost always a good idea. That way, you can decide whether you can live with what you've got, or whether some changes might be in the wind. You may find, for example, that old cabling causes so many difficulties that you're better off replacing or upgrading it. We've actually popped out ceiling tiles and found badly spliced cables hidden from easy view.
- If you're planning a brand-new network, one of your planning concerns is to determine your cabling needs. Try to determine your network cabling needs *before* ordering equipment for your network, because you can often order computers and peripherals with appropriate NICs preinstalled and preconfigured (of course, NICs are preinstalled and preconfigured on an existing network, but then your choices have been made for you). The more work you can save yourself, the better you'll like it!
- If you employ a contractor to handle your cabling maintenance, don't assume that every old cable is replaced if it's not completely up to snuff. A contractor may choose to reuse substandard cables to save on material costs. Without proper wiring, your network may be in constant trouble (or it may not even work at all).

If you work with a cable contractor, require the contractor to test each network cable, and insist that the contractor provide those test results for your inspection. In fact, many companies hire one contractor to install cables and another to test them. By doing so, they ensure that the common tendency to overlook errors or potential sources of problems on a network can be avoided — plus, it never hurts to get a second opinion.

The most common cabling technology for LANs is *baseband cable,* which is cable set up for baseband transmission. For this reason, we concentrate on baseband cable in this book. Check out the sidebar entitled "Choosing the pipes for your network plumbing" for a description of baseband transmission and how it differs from broadband transmission.

If you know what to look for, the name of a particular type of cable can tell you a great deal about its transmission properties. Cable notation breaks down as follows:

- The speed of the Ethernet in Mbps
- The cable's technology — broadband or baseband
- The cable's rated distance, in hundreds of meters, or the type of cable — twisted pair or fiber optic

Choosing the pipes for your network plumbing

The wiring on a network is like the plumbing in a house. Just as pipes are the pathways through which your water flows to and from your plumbing fixtures, a network's wiring is the means through which computers transmit data using electric signals. The amount of data that computers can move through such a plumbing system at any one time depends on the size of the pipes installed. The larger the pipes, the more data computers can send.

You can think of a network's *bandwidth* as the size of a network's pipes. Bandwidth represents a range of usable frequencies and is measured in hertz (Hz). The higher the hertz rating for a networking medium, the higher its available bandwidth is. Higher bandwidth translates into bigger pipes to carry the data. However, just because you have big pipes, doesn't mean you always get to carry what you expect. Throughput is the actual amount of data flowing through the pipes.

Different types of cabling are rated for different amounts of data flow at different distances. Remember, however, that even if a pipe is large enough to handle all the water you send through it, that pipe can still get clogged. So although a given amount of data can theoretically flow through a cable, in the real world, you may see less data flow than the maximum bandwidth indicates. In the same way that lime and rust deposits can restrict the water flow in pipes, noise, crosstalk, electromagnetic interference (EMI), and other network maladies can degrade the actual performance of your cable. *Throughput,* commonly measured in bits per second (bps), describes the actual amount of data that's flowing through a cable at any one time.

If you take one pipe and divide it into little pipes, you've just reinvented the concept of *broadband transmission* (in which multiple transmissions at different frequencies use the same networking medium simultaneously). If the pipe is kept whole instead of subdivided, you end up with the concept of *baseband transmission* (in which the entire bandwidth is used to carry only one set of frequencies and one transmission at a time).

Whew! Got all that? Maybe it's time to call Roto-Rooter!

For example, 10Base5 stands for [10 Mbps] [baseband] [5 x 100 meters = 500 meters]. So from the name alone, you can tell that the baseband cable's Ethernet is rated to handle up to 10 Mbps on a segment up to 500 meters long.

Any time you see a T or an F in a cable term, replace that letter with *twisted pair* or *fiber optic,* respectively. For example, the term *10BaseT* means baseband cable's Ethernet is rated at up to 10 Mbps using twisted-pair cables. Likewise, 10BaseF means the same thing, except that it uses fiber-optic cables.

Cabling ain't that difficult

Wiring and cables come in all sizes and shapes. Each type of cable has associated distance limitations. Each type also has different price tags, transmission characteristics, and so forth. Some of the more common types of cable you encounter on modern networks include twisted pair, coaxial, and fiber optic.

Twisted-pair cable: TP is not a tent

Twisted-pair wiring comes in two flavors: unshielded twisted pair (UTP) and shielded twisted pair (STP). To explain shielded versus unshielded wiring in the simplest terms possible, STP incorporates a foil or wire braid surrounding its wires, which are twisted together in pairs; UTP doesn't.

UTP

You've probably been exposed to UTP (unshielded twisted pair) cable if you have any kind of phone system in your organization. You may have even seen such cabling inside the walls of your home, if you watched the contractors build it. A UTP cable consists of pairs of copper wires that have plastic jackets encasing each wire. The pairs are twisted together, and the entire cable is enclosed by an outer jacket. Figure 7-1 depicts a cross-section of a typical UTP cable. The twists in the cable are important because they improve the transmission characteristics of the wires involved and make them more resistant to interference. This puts a whole new twist on twisted pair!

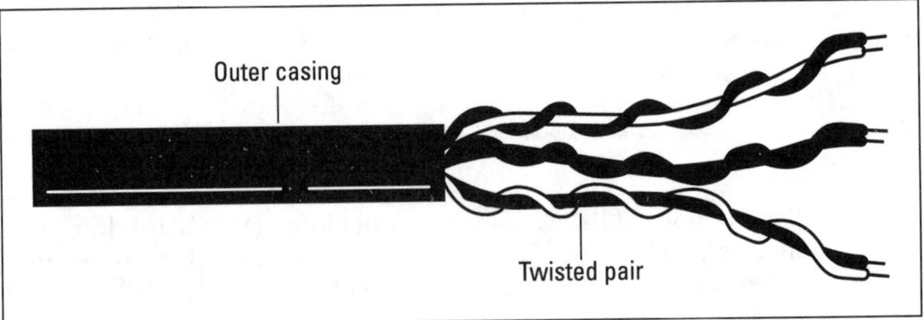

Figure 7-1: Come on baby, let's do the twist!

Notice that the U in UTP means *unshielded.* That notation is included because another type of twisted-pair cable is shielded — STP (shielded twisted pair). The difference is that STP includes an extra layer of shielding around the twisted wires. Both types of cable are used in modern networks, but UTP is more common because STP is more expensive. You find out more about STP later in this section.

Voice-grade UTP (CAT 1 and 2 — see the following paragraph for all the skinny on CAT) is the kind of cable you find in your home and in most phone systems. Voice-grade UTP cable is designed to carry voice signals and is quite inexpensive. Some organizations find that they have extra phone wire already pulled and terminated in offices, so they use this cable for their networking needs. The problem is that voice-grade UTP is not designed to carry data. If you have a small LAN that doesn't carry much traffic, this cable may work. But if you're building a mighty network with huge database applications, you won't find voice-grade UTP acceptable. You need to install UTP cable with a higher CAT rating.

What's a CAT rating? *CAT* stands for *category.* The Electronic Industries Association (EIA) placed ratings on UTP cable based on how fast a cable can transmit data. Here's the current roster of CAT ratings that you can find in use in the workplace:

- **CAT 1 and 2:** Use only for voice and low-speed data.
- **CAT 3:** Use for data speeds up to 16 Mbps.
- **CAT 4:** Use for data speeds up to 20 Mbps.
- **CAT 5:** Use for data speeds up to 100 Mbps.
- **CAT 5 Enhanced:** Use for data speeds up to 200 Mbps.
- **CAT 6:** Use for data speeds up to 600 Mbps.

CAT 6 cable is different from its CAT 1–5 counterparts. Each pair is wrapped in foil shielding, and then all the pairs are again wrapped in another layer of foil shielding. All this extra shielding is what helps to protect this cable from noise and other disturbances. The only question we have left is: "Why is CAT 6 called UTP if the cable has shielding?" Some questions just must go unanswered!

If you already have UTP cable in place on your network and you're not sure how it's rated, call in a cable contractor to test your cables to tell you what you've got installed.

If you plan to install CAT 5 cable for your network, make sure that the connectors used from one end of the network to the other are also rated CAT 5. If you follow whatever connection your computer makes on the network through the wall and so on, you find numerous components along the way, including *wall plates, punchdown blocks, patch panels,* and more. All these must be rated CAT 5 for the network to function properly.

UTP cable is cheaper and more widespread than STP, but it has a few minor foibles that you may not like. Because it's unshielded, UTP is prone to interference from external sources, such as fluorescent lighting. It's not unusual to pop ceiling tiles and find UTP cables strung over light fixtures or near elevators. This placement can lead to network interference; therefore, you should be careful how and where you place your cables.

Another cost factor for twisted-pair cable is that it requires you to connect workstations through a hub. You can buy simple eight-port hubs for under $100, so added cost may become a consideration if you are planning a large network. On the plus side, so-called *smart hubs* can be advantageous on a network because they can actually help you manage your cabling — but those smarts show up on the price tags for such equipment. At the very least, less expensive hubs always have blinking lights that can tell you which ports are active and when data is transmitting or not.

STP: High performance for Token Ring networks

STP, shielded twisted pair, adds an extra layer of shielding around its twisted pairs. This shielding is a wire mesh that sits between individual pairs and the outer jacket. STP can transmit data at speeds of up to 155 Mbps across spans of up to 100 meters, but such implementations are atypical (and quite expensive). Normally, you find 4–16 Mbps Token Ring network implementations based on STP (but sometimes, on UTP as well).

10BaseT

You hear quite a bit about 10BaseT in your networking travels. It's a star topology that uses hubs connected with twisted-pair cable and is an Ethernet standard rated for a transmission speed of 10 Mbps and can use CAT 3 UTP. You can install CAT 5 for 10BaseT implementations to prepare for higher bandwidths, such as 100BaseT. The following list tells you what you would need to construct a 10BaseT network starting from the device to the computer room:

- **NICs:** Ethernet NICs with RJ-45 connections
- **Cable:** CAT 3-5 UTP from NIC to transceiver (if external transceiver)
- **Transceiver:** Can be external or onboard the NIC
- **Cable:** CAT 3-5 UTP from transceiver (or NIC) to wall
- **Wall plate:** With RJ-45 sockets
- **Cabling in wall:** CAT 3-5 UTP
- **Punchdown block:** Incoming UTP wires brought here and with a tool are beaten down into a block of wires.
- **Cable:** CAT 3-5 UTP from punchdown block to patch panel
- **Cable:** CAT 3-5 UTP patch cable from patch panel to 10BaseT hub

The following list points out some limitations you must follow when implementing 10BaseT:

- **Distance:** From network device to hub, cable runs cannot exceed 100 meters.
- **Nodes:** Cannot use more than 1,024 nodes on a network without subdividing that networking and adding a repeating device between the divisions.
- **Hubs:** You may not plug more than 12 additional hubs into a main hub to increase the total number of network devices accessible.

The most predictable places to find STP implementations are on older Token Ring and LocalTalk networks or in older IBM mainframe environments. IBM is Token Ring's original designer and it still makes and sells Token Ring parts. That's why most "Big Blue" shops use Token Ring networks.

STP cable may require electrical grounding, and it's not much fun to install. STP cable is thick and inflexible, which makes it much harder to route and handle than UTP. STP's connectors are bothersome and don't always plug in easily either. STP cable is expensive, so unless you require the higher bandwidth that STP can deliver, you might do better to stick with UTP to simplify your network's installation and to keep costs down.

Coaxial (coax) cable

Coaxial cable, also called *coax,* is another popular transmission media for both old and new networks. Most networks used coaxial cable exclusively before UTP became popular in the mid-1980s. Initially, only thick coaxial cable (which we like to call "frozen yellow garden hose") was available. Thick coax is quite cumbersome to handle and a real pain in the neck to install. Imagine pulling frozen garden hose through the ceiling and then having to connect transceivers to that cable! Maybe frozen garden hose is easier, after all. . . .

Coaxial cable incorporates two layers of insulation. Beginning in the middle of the cable and spanning outward, the cable has a copper wire that is surrounded by a foam insulator, which is surrounded by a wire mesh conductor that is then surrounded by an outer jacket of insulation. This jacket, in turn, is surrounded by a plastic casing, called *cladding.* Figure 7-2 shows a cross section of a well-dressed piece of coaxial cable.

The way you determine cost for the different types of coaxial cable is simple. The larger a cable's diameter, the more it costs. In this case, bigger is not necessarily better, but it's more expensive. Table 7-1 shows various coax cable ratings based on the U.S. Government's Radio Grade (RG) cable specifications.

Table 7-1 Coax Cable Classifications

Classification	*Name*	*Ohms*	*Use*
RG-8 and RG-11	Thicknet	50	Thick Ethernet
RG-58	Thinnet	50	Thin Ethernet
RG-59	Broadband	75	Cable television
RG-62	ARCNet	93	ARCNet

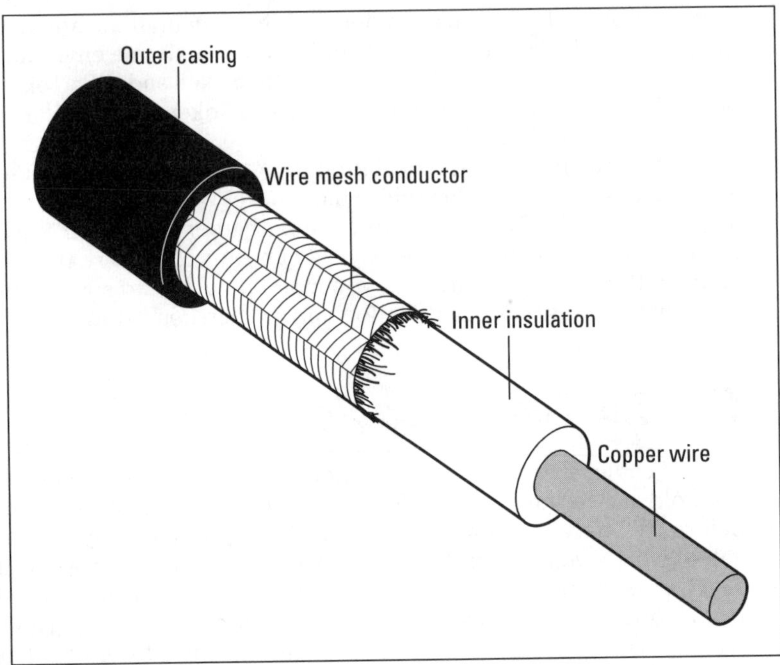

Figure 7-2: An inside view of coax cable.

You probably noticed that we slipped in some new terms in Table 7-1, such as Thicknet and Thinnet. These are just different classifications of coaxial cable, and we describe them in more detail in the following section, because they're implemented frequently in smaller organizations.

The cost of coax cable is directly proportional to its diameter. The thicker the diameter of the cable, the more it costs, and consequently, its equipment also costs more.

10Base2 (Thinnet)

Thinnet goes by some aliases, such as RG-58, CheaperNet, Thinwire, and 10Base2. Remember that 10Base2 means that this cable is rated at 10 Mbps and can span a distance of 185 meters (okay, so they didn't want to put the notation of 10Base1.85) without any repeating devices. It's a thinner type of coax cable (thus the names Thinwire and Thinnet) and is quite popular because it's cheap (hence the name, CheaperNet)!

Thinnet is flexible and easy to work with because it's quite thin. You find a lot of Thinnet coax in smaller organizations that have only one floor or suite of offices because it costs less than CAT 5 UTP and STP and doesn't require any dedicated connecting devices, such as hubs.

Because 10Base2 cable is thicker than UTP, it requires funny-shaped connectors that you've probably seen in Radio Shack but didn't recognize. These connectors are called British Naval Connectors (BNCs) or T-connectors. The latter name is descriptive of this connector's shape, as shown in Figure 7-3. The top part of the "T" interconnects cable segments, and the bottom of the "T" attaches the cable to a computer's NIC. In addition, 10Base2 requires terminating resistors at each end of a cable segment, one end of which is often grounded.

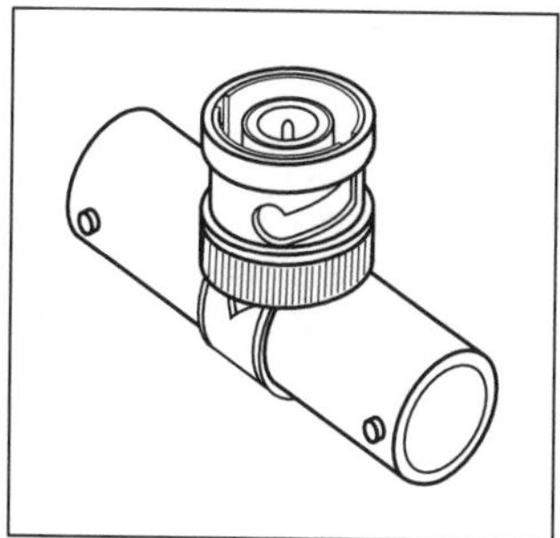

Figure 7-3: The BNC is also known as a T-connector because of its distinctive shape.

So how do you connect computers and devices to a network using 10Base2? First, picture a straight line with devices attached to it. 10Base2 is a *bus topology* (see Chapter 4), so it extends in a straight line where each device on the network attaches between two cable segments, as shown in Figure 7-4. Devices hook up to the network through the bottom of a T-connector that plugs into the NIC on the back of each computer.

Install terminating resistors on the unused sides of the T-connectors at each end of the network.

When installing a 10Base2 network, you must be aware of the number of devices that an individual cable segment can support and how far such a segment of cable can reach. Table 7-2 lays out key information that you need to review before installing a 10Base2 network or when checking out somebody else's installation.

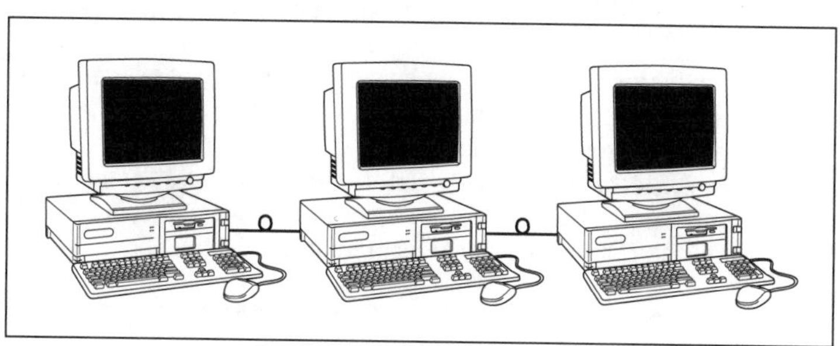

Figure 7-4: Network attachment between two cable segments.

Table 7-2 10Base2 Limitations

	Trunk Segment	*Entire Network*
Max length	607 feet	3,035 feet
Max nodes	30	1,024
Min node distance	20 inches	20 inches
Max # repeaters	n/a	4
Max # segments	n/a	5

10Base5 (Thicknet)

10Base5 is a thicker coaxial cable and is, therefore, more expensive than 10Base2. It's also less pliable and subject to more stringent bend radius restrictions (in English, this means that if you bend it sharply, the cable doesn't work properly). If you can visualize trying to poke a little hole into a frozen garden hose, you quickly realize that you need some sort of special clamping or tapping device to get through the thick layer.

To connect network devices to 10Base5 coax, special mechanical devices called *vampire taps* are required — instead of the T-connectors that 10Base2 uses. The tap clamps onto the coax cable and penetrates through the coax to its inner conductor. You must use devices called *transceivers* (an abbreviation for transmitter/receiver) to convert a digital signal from the computer into an electrical signal on the wire, and vice versa.

Packing up your trunk

A *trunk,* or network segment, consists of an entire cable segment on a network that spans from one repeating device to another, or to which individual computers may be attached. In 10Base2, a trunk may only span 607 feet and may have no more than 30 devices attached. Also, each device on a trunk must be spaced at least 20 inches from the next device.

You may not use a single unbroken cable segment that's more than 300 feet long. That means you must have at least three devices on a segment that spans 607 feet. If you ignore these restrictions, the network is likely to experience difficulties. You can, however, add repeating devices to network trunks and, therefore, extend the length of your network.

Repeating devices take an incoming signal from the network, strip out the noise, amplify the signal, and pass the data onto the next segment of the network. In 10Base2, though, even if you use repeaters, the network's maximum span has physical limitations. The total network span cannot exceed more than 3,035 feet, and you cannot (theoretically) place more than 1,024 devices on a single 10Base2 internetwork across all cable segments (practically, experiments indicate that the real limit is more like 900 devices).

10Base5 uses external transceivers and can support transceiver cables up to 50 feet long, which permits the 10Base5 cable to act as a kind of backbone, and the transceiver cables to extend to desktop machines. This arrangement makes routing the frozen yellow garden hose quite a bit easier, because it doesn't have to snake its way from computer to computer as does 10Base2.

A typical 10Base5 cable layout is depicted in Figure 7-5. This kind of arrangement also explains why 10Base5 cable is primarily used for network backbones or on older networks that haven't been upgraded since their original installations (usually in the 1970s or early 1980s, when this cable represented the only available Ethernet technology).

Table 7-3 lists the distance and nodal limitations on 10Base5 networking.

Table 7-3 — 10Base5 Limitations

	Trunk Segment	*Entire Network*
Max length	1,640 feet	8,200 feet
Max nodes	100	1,024
Min node distance	8 feet	8 feet
Max # repeaters	n/a	4
Max # segments	n/a	5

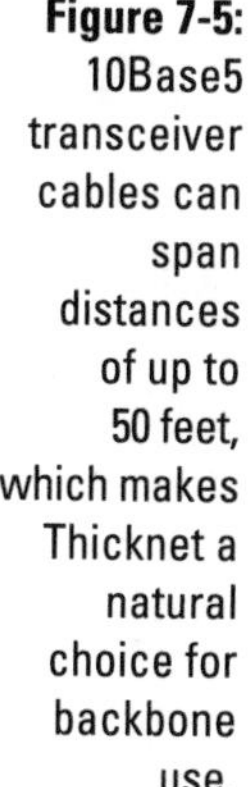

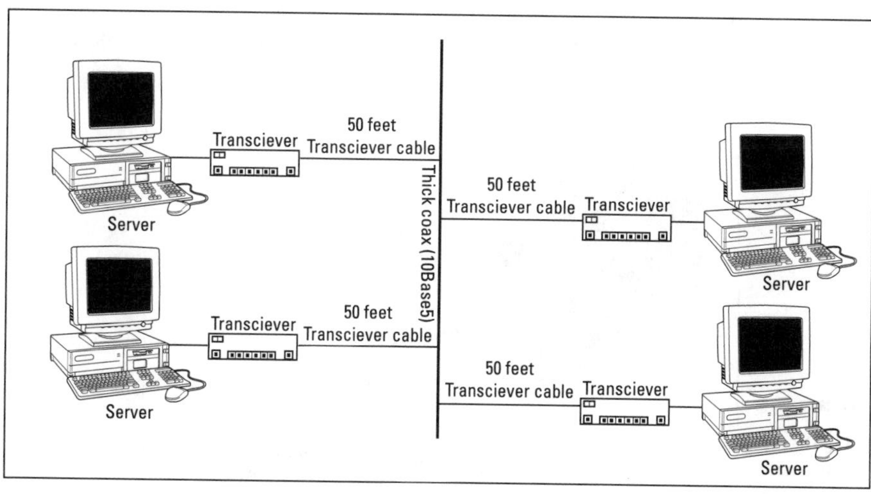

Figure 7-5: 10Base5 transceiver cables can span distances of up to 50 feet, which makes Thicknet a natural choice for backbone use.

Although 10Base5 permits five cable segments to be tied together, it's interesting to note that only three of those cables can contain network devices. This limitation is known as the 5-4-3 rule in Ethernet: On any path from one terminator to another on a network, up to five cable segments may be joined by up to four repeating devices, but only three of those cable segments may be populated with more than two devices.

If you have a small network and a restricted budget, coax can be a good choice, but because of expense factors and ease of installation, Thinwire is invariably a better choice for such installations than Thickwire. You may, however, decide to mix these two cable types if the distance limitations of Thinwire don't permit your cables to span sufficient distance.

You can purchase ready-made cables of different lengths to speed your network installation. Otherwise, you have to purchase special crimping tools and build these cables yourself. If you decide to build your own, spend the extra $200 or so to buy a low-cost cable tester to make sure your cables are put together properly. You can find tools like cable scanners, Time Domain Reflectometers (TDRs), and crimping tools, along with white papers and cabling specs at `www.microtest.com` — Microtest is the most popular vendor in cabling equipment today.

Fiber-optic cable

Fiber-optic cable is different from twisted-pair and coax cable because it uses light signals instead of electrical signals to transmit data. Looking at the layout of the cable, it appears similar, but it has a glass or plastic fiber as its inner conductor instead of a copper wire like you see in the others. Figure 7-6 shows you what the inside of a fiber-optic cable looks like.

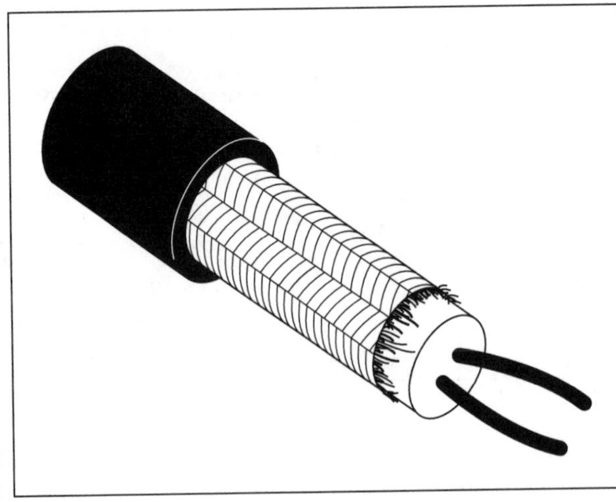

Figure 7-6: An inside view of fiber-optic cable.

Notice in Figure 7-6 that the inner glass core is surrounded by a cylinder of glassy material called *cladding*. Surrounding the cladding is a plastic jacket, and the entire cable has another strong jacket around it. The outer jacket is designed to be thick enough to protect the inner fiber from being broken when the cable is handled (with care, that is).

Although it has a higher price tag than its metallic counterparts, fiber-optic cable can also handle greater bandwidth, which means that it can transfer more data over longer distances. Fiber-optic cable is largely immune to EMI and other sources of noise that affect electrically conductive cables. One factor that adds to the expense of fiber-optic cable is the care that's required during installation. A knowledgeable technician must carefully polish each glass fiber with specialized tools and then add special connectors to the cable.

You often find fiber-optic cable installed between buildings in campus environments or between floors in a building. Very rarely do you see fiber pulled to the desktop because of the expense involved — you must use fiber-optic NICs, and two cables must be attached to each workstation because one cable is used to transmit outbound signals, while the other one is used to receive inbound signals.

In some special cases, such as hospitals, it's necessary to run fiber-optic cable to some desktops because X-ray and MRI equipment can interfere with electrical cables. Additionally, the bandwidth requirements for medical imaging equipment can be so extreme that conventional electrical cables can't handle the traffic involved. Though the appetite for bandwidth is always rising, don't expect your desktop to have a "high-fiber diet" any time soon!

For light signals to pass through a fiber-optic cable, a transmitter must be attached to one end of the cable and a receiver to the other end of the cable (that's why two cables are necessary to permit any single device to both send and receive signals). On the transmitting end, an *injection laser diode* (ILD) or a *light-emitting diode* (LED) sends light pulses down the cable. These light pulses are reflected within the glass core and bounce against the mirror-like cladding through the length of the cable until they reach a *photo diode receiver* at the cable's other end. Notice that data flows only in one direction. The receiver converts incoming light pulses into electrical signals and passes the data to the NIC.

Because of the way that light pulses travel through fiber-optic cable, it's important to note that splicing two such cables together requires great care so that the cable's signal-carrying capabilities are not reduced. Otherwise, a light pulse may arrive at the splice but may not make it through to the other end of the cable. We call this situation a bad splice, but your users will call it much worse names!

Fiber-optic cable is the most expensive cable we've described thus far, but it offers the highest bandwidth and the most room for future bandwidth growth.

A final note about cabling

If you're going to install cable yourself instead of hiring a cable contractor, here are a few final notes we'd like to share with you:

- Obtain a copy of the blueprints for your building or floor and make sure that all the electrical devices and outlets are clearly marked on the copy. This map assists you in placing cable away from electrical devices or motors that can interfere with your network. You don't want to install cable near elevator motors, transformers, or other heavy-duty electrical devices (unless you're using fiber-optic cable; even then you must protect it from potential sources of damage and wear and tear).
- Obtain all relevant local, state, and federal building code regulations and make sure that your plans conform to such ordinances. You want to evaluate these requirements before making any cable purchases because some codes require you to purchase plenum-rated, fire-retardant cable. Other codes require you to use plenum-rated cable only when you run cable through locations that are likely to catch fire rapidly. In any case, it behooves you to know the rules that apply before you purchase and install a network.

  Plenums are the air handling spaces in between the ceiling of one floor and the floor of the floor above where cable is often strung. Fires spread more rapidly in these areas because air carries the fire rapidly, so plenum-rated cable is often required to keep fire and smoke from spreading through a building.
- Determine which parts of the network you are able to build and maintain on your own and which parts you must subcontract. For example, if you have the time and inclination to build cables and also have the time to troubleshoot the network when those cables don't work, so be it. We recommend that you buy as much prefabricated cable as possible and only make your own cables when you absolutely must. Why? Because companies that make cables do it all the time, and they are good at it. If you only make cables for your network occasionally, you may introduce problems.
- Try to hire a contractor to install the cable for your LAN. The wiring is your network's infrastructure. If it's not installed properly, wiring can cause endless network snafus. Wiring contractors should provide you with bids, install the cabling, label all cables, test and certify all cables, and provide you with final documentation. You're responsible to keep them on track. Don't assume that a contractor will follow local ordinances unless you require them to. Put your expectations in writing and keep tabs on their work.

Upping the Bandwidth Ante

As organizations have come to depend on LANs and WANs, they've placed more applications and information on their networks. Speedy retrieval of such information becomes critical to such organizations. This retrieval is where the need for additional bandwidth often makes itself felt.

Conventional text-only documents don't normally put too much strain on a network. But today, data often takes the form of audio, video, graphics, multimedia, and other complex types. Such files or data streams tend to be much larger than plain text files and often impose delivery deadlines on networks. If this scenario is hard to picture, think how frustrating it is when the audio track and the video track get out of synch on your TV, and then multiply this frustration by several orders of magnitude. Then think about what delivering time-sensitive audio, video, or multimedia data across a network really requires. . . .

In fact, such complex forms of data can easily consume the entire bandwidth of an ordinary 10 Mbps network while servicing only one or two users' demands. That's why an increasing emphasis on building networks with greater bandwidth capacities is emerging in the workplace. The added bandwidth is increasingly necessary to handle more complex types of data traversing the network and to prepare the infrastructure to deal with emerging applications, such as network teleconferencing, network telephony, collaborative development, and all kinds of other gee-whiz technologies now under construction.

That's why we feel compelled to tell you about some of the cabling alternatives available for today's networks that just might be able to accommodate tomorrow's bandwidth needs. Please read the sidebars for the full picture, if you really want to understand what's out there!

100 megabit Ethernet

Two flavors of 100 Mbps Ethernet are available today, each with its own particular access method: CSMA/CD (which means Carrier Sense Multiple Access/Collision Detection and it's discussed in detail in Chapter 4) and demand priority (as described later in this chapter). When proposals for 100 Mbps were solicited, two factions emerged: one that used the same CSMA/CD access method as used in conventional Ethernet (the resulting specification is now known as Fast Ethernet or 100BaseT), and another that used a demand priority access method (now known as 100BaseVG-AnyLAN).

Both factions put proposals forward to implement their approaches. Curiously, both proposals were ultimately accepted as standards, but each one fell under different IEEE committees. Today, the Fast Ethernet standard falls under the 802.3 standards family, but the 100BaseVG-AnyLAN standard falls under the IEEE 802.12 standards family.

100BaseT is similar to 10BaseT except that it has a higher bandwidth. When implementing 100BaseT, you must use equipment designed to support 100BaseT throughout your network, but otherwise, designing and building networks is pretty much the same (albeit quite a bit faster) as for 10BaseT. It's even possible to mix and match 10BaseT and 100BaseT technologies on a single network, but you need to include hubs that have 10 Mbps and 100 Mbps capability to bring these two worlds (10 Mbps and 100 Mbps Ethernet) together.

100BaseVG-AnyLAN offers the same bandwidth as 100BaseT but uses four pairs of wires instead of two pairs in each cable. Doubling the number of pairs enables a different access method, called *demand priority,* to control access to the network medium. In addition, 100BaseVG-AnyLAN permits devices on the network to receive and transmit at the same time (that's one reason why the number of pairs in the cable is doubled).

100BaseVG-AnyLAN hubs help to manage the demand priority scheme and provide arbitration services when multiple requests for network access occur at more or less the same time. When using the CSMA/CD access method, workstations listen before sending, and they transmit as soon as they recognize that the medium is not in use. This arrangement leads to collisions when two or more stations begin to broadcast at more or less the same time, especially as network utilization increases. But when a demand priority device wants to transmit data across the network, it signals the hub, and the hub determines when that device may access the network. This setup eliminates collisions and permits networks to function at higher utilization rates than CSMA/CD permits.

On the down side, networking equipment and cabling for 100BaseVG-AnyLAN is more expensive than that for 100BaseT, even though it offers better performance. Perhaps that's why 100BaseT has proven more popular in the marketplace than has 100BaseVG-AnyLAN.

Gigabit Ethernet

You're probably wondering what you can implement on your network when you start running out of bandwidth using 100-megabit technology. From there, the next step up is to gigabit Ethernet. Although gigabit Ethernet technologies are currently available, they're not yet in broad use. But because the need for speed will never decrease, we want to give you a taste of this technology so that you can salivate over it — even if it's unlikely to show up in your office any time soon.

To begin with, you must understand that gigabit Ethernet is not a networking solution for the desktop (in fact, no conventional PC or other desktop machine can come close to saturating a gigabit Ethernet network). Rather, gigabit Ethernet currently functions primarily as a backbone technology, especially in large networks where certain pathways must carry huge amounts of traffic. Ideally, gigabit Ethernet helps to boost server to server communications and permits ultra-fast data transfers between switches on a network backbone.

Gigabit Ethernet uses the CSMA/CD access method and the same frame size and formats as conventional Ethernet. Therefore, you can integrate this technology into existing Ethernet networks easily, and you don't need to buy new protocol analyzers, network management software, and so forth.

To jump on the gigabit Ethernet bandwagon, the devices you need to add to your network include:

- Suitable NICs and connectors for your servers
- Proper cables (fiber-optic, in most cases; though twisted pair options are under development)
- Upgrades to those routers and switches that must handle gigabit Ethernet traffic

In some cases, this new emerging standard may require that you replace certain pieces of equipment; but for modern routers and switches, this new emerging standard may require only new EPROM chips and upgrades for certain interface cards. Eventually, as the price of the technology drops, you might even consider adding gigabit Ethernet interfaces into your high-end workstations. This probably won't be necessary for a few more years, however.

The Gigabit Ethernet Alliance offers a terrific white paper on this technology. You can download it from: `www.gigabit-ethernet.org/`. It gives a great overview of gigabit Ethernet and describes what kinds of applications demand this kind of network speed.

Network Chiropractic: All about Backbones

At two points in this chapter, you can read about technologies that are suited for *network backbones* — this term applies to both 10Base5 and gigabit Ethernet. If networks have backbones, do they also have hip bones and tailbones? How about it?

Actually, the term *backbone* has a specific meaning in networking. It's a particular cable segment that ties other cable segments together, or that provides a high-speed link to accommodate high network traffic on cable segments where large quantities of traffic aggregate. If you think about this situation for a minute and take a quick look at Figure 7-7, you should begin to understand that saying "a cable segment that ties other cable segments together" and "a cable segment where large quantities of traffic aggregate" are two ways of saying the same thing.

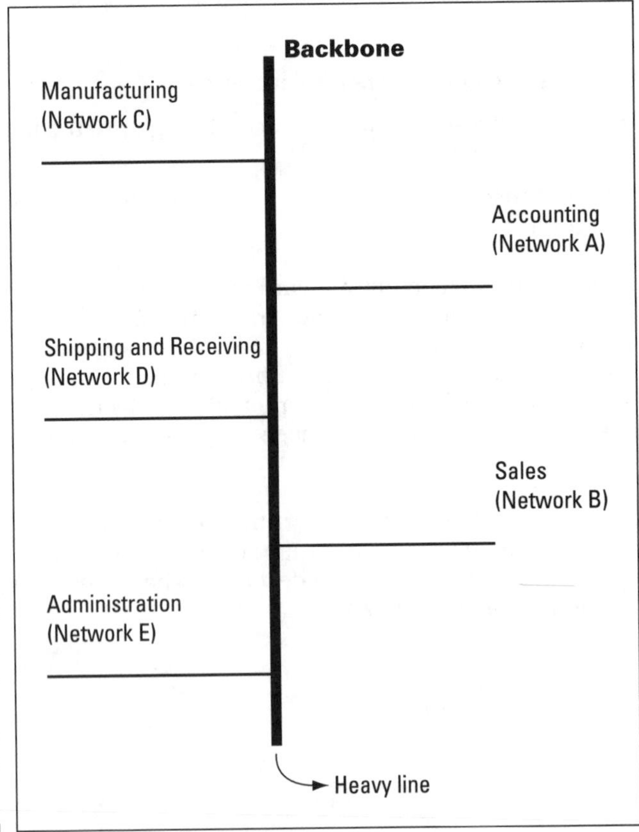

Figure 7-7: A backbone ties all the pieces of a network together.

Simply put, a backbone provides a link that ties many other cables together. As the demand for network bandwidth goes up for individual users, the amount of traffic that backbones must carry multiplies accordingly. Just as a human backbone holds the body together and carries the central nervous system to the brain, a network backbone ties all its pieces together. Backbones also often provide links to outside resources like the Internet or access to massive centralized data collections, such as mainframe databases and their ilk.

Many Networks or an Internetwork?

Another subtlety of networking has to do with the relationship between individual cable segments and the network that encompasses all of them. For historical reasons too tedious to relate, the term *network* is often used to describe only those devices that attach to a single cable segment.

This circumscribed interpretation of the word *network* made it necessary to invent the term *internetwork.* An internetwork is what happens when some devices (such as repeaters, bridges, routers, and gateways) are attached to two or more cable segments to create a "network of networks." In internetworks, information from one cable segment can flow through one or more of those devices to move from one cable segment to another. The mother of all internetworks, of course, is the world-wide Internet itself, which is a network of more networks than you (or we) want to think about for too long.

When you're dealing with technical talk about networks, be sure that you understand what the word network means in the context of whatever discussion is underway. In most cases, it doesn't matter that what may commonly be referred to as a network is really an internetwork, but when it does matter, it matters a lot. So pay attention!

Linking for the Long Haul

Just as talk about backbones leads to talk about the Internet, talking about networks of networks leads inevitably to talk about WANs. In days of yore, only companies with deep pockets could afford to worry about WAN links, because they were quite expensive. But these days, with high bandwidth connections to ISPs (Internet Service Providers) becoming increasingly common, many small- to medium-sized outfits now have to worry about linking their internetworks to other networks through a variety of long-haul digital links.

The many flavors of WAN links

WAN links span a huge range of functionality, bandwidth, and associated costs and include a broad range of technologies. These days, Windows NT Server does a pretty good job of supporting all kinds of WAN links because of its multiprotocol and router support, including:

- **ISDN (Integrated Services Digital Network):** This relatively low-speed digital link connects through the telephone system, giving it nearly global reach. Windows NT Server includes built-in drivers for a variety of ISDN interfaces and supports a broad range of ISDN-based bandwidths. Normal ISDN connections occur through a so-called BRI (basic rate interface) and support one or two 64 Kbps data channels for a maximum bandwidth of 128 Kbps. Monthly costs for a typical ISDN connection vary from a low of $100 a month to as high as $500 a month in some markets. Some ISDN rates accumulate on a per minute basis, so be sure to check with your local telecomm company.
- **xDSL (Digital Subscriber Loop):** This term describes a higher-bandwidth technology that also uses conventional phone lines to handle digital data. Windows NT Server didn't ship with xDSL drivers, but most xDSL PC devices ship with suitable drivers for use with the Windows NT 4 operating system. Most conventional xDSL devices offer bandwidth that ranges from 256 Kbps to as high as 1.544 Mbps. xDSL costs are still unclear in many markets, but it looks like they'll be competitive with ISDN.
- **Cable modems:** Cable modems use CATV coaxial cables to send and receive network data. Although cable modems are not broadly available in all markets, most metropolitan areas serviced by national cable TV companies, such as Time Warner or Cox Communications, are piloting cable modem implementations. Cable modems usually offer high bandwidth downstream (up to 1.544 Mbps for incoming data) but less bandwidth upstream (up to 512 Kbps for outgoing data). Cable modems are way cheap and can cost as little as $40 a month (but the medium is shared, unlike all the other alternatives mentioned here, so more users means less individual bandwidth).
- **T1/E1 or T3/E3:** These terms represent the most common high-end digital services for medium-sized companies and larger. T1/T3 describes two classes of digital service available in North America; E1/E3 describes two similar classes of service available in Europe and elsewhere in the world. Bandwidth for T1 is 1.544 Mbps; for T3 it's 45 Mbps; for E1 it's 2.048 Mbps; and for E3 it's 34.368 Mbps. All these services cost at least $1,000 a month and use expensive equipment. T3/E3 costs upwards of $20,000 a month in most markets.

For most Windows NT Server-based networks, understanding how to connect to your local ISP is all the WAN linking you'll ever need to do. For most situations, this means T1 or slower technologies. For these circumstances, NT Server can perform creditably as a router, or it can work admirably with an external routing device to help you make the outside connections your network needs.

Chapter 8

If You Build It, They Will Come!

In This Chapter

- Determining what network clients need
- Examining the client for Microsoft Networks
- Making the NetWare connection
- Making clients work for a living
- Living with your choices

Working across a network gives users the capability to access resources not available on their local computers. The capabilities to share files, printers, and other resources stand out as a network's most important advantages. (Well, they are if you discount enhanced communication and reduced hardware, software, and Internet connection costs.) To access all these shared network resources, you must connect your users to the network, which requires client computers. After you create a network, your users will use the client computers to access the shared network resources. Thus, if you build it, they will come!

A *client* is simply any computer with the ability to communicate over a network. Some clients are as powerful as the servers hosting the network, whereas others are so featureless that they can do little more than send a simple file to a printer or transfer a file from a local drive to a network drive (or vice versa).

In this chapter, you find out what a client is and what your choices for clients are — whether you're participating in a Microsoft network or a hybrid network (that is, one combining Microsoft and Novell NetWare components) or even using a Microsoft client on a non-Microsoft network.

What All Good Network Clients Need . . .

A *network client* is simply a computer. You do have a few other requirements, but you start, at least, with an ordinary computer. Both your home PC and a $10,000 workstation can communicate with a network, and both require the same type of elements to accomplish the task.

You need to add four key elements, or *components,* to a computer to transform it from a stand-alone system to a network participant — a client. The following list describes these components:

- **Network interface card (NIC):** *NICs* provide a physical connection between your computer and the network so that your computer can transmit and receive communication signals. For the particulars on choosing and installing NICs in your network, check out Chapter 6.
- **Interface drivers:** These small programs enable the computer to communicate with the NIC. *Interface driver* software usually comes with the NIC, and you can also download the software from the manufacturer's Web site. See Chapter 6 for more information on drivers.
- **Protocol stack:** A *protocol stack* is a type of software that defines, prescribes, controls, and regulates data over networks. You can think of a protocol as a language, and computers must speak the same language for communication to occur. The same is true for clients and servers on a network. Without a common protocol, you can't exchange data. See Chapter 3 for more information about making the correct protocol choice.
- **Client software:** In a Windows NT network, *client software* is a driver-like tool that the client computer uses to join the network. The client software talks with the authentication-services system on the network, requesting network access by proving to the network controller that you're a valid participant. Older client software (or client software for less-capable operating systems) does little more than help you send a name and password to the network controller. Modern clients do a bit more: They also control whether the actual computer has valid access; they look for user profiles (customized desktop/operating system environments); they enforce policies (imposing security restrictions by preventing access to programs, drivers, or hardware); and they reconnect network resources (such as mapped drives and network printers). See Chapter 2 for more information on client software.

With all four components in place (the NIC, interface drivers, protocol stacks, and client software) your computer can connect to, communicate with, and participate in a network. In the following sections we take a look at a few of the clients available from Microsoft for connecting with Microsoft networks and other networks.

The Client for Microsoft Networks

The *Client for Microsoft Networks* is both the general term and the specific name of the client that Microsoft provides for connecting Windows NT networks and Microsoft operating systems (including a fairly successful little OS known as Windows). You can use the Client for Microsoft Networks driver-utility combo to implement network capabilities onto older client operating systems, such as DOS and Windows 3.*x*, or to fine-tune the existing network support for newer operating systems, such as Windows 9*x* and Windows NT Workstation.

Doing it for DOS

DOS, more affectionately called *MS-DOS*, is the first and oldest operating system that Microsoft distributed. In fact, Bill Gates himself helped write the code for this way back when he was just another geek who couldn't get a date. *DOS* stands for *D*isk *O*perating *S*ystem and it provides the base-level machine instructions that enable hardware to respond to user requests for resources. In the DOS environment, the only resources are those of local drives — basically, hard drives and floppies — and locally attached printers. (CD-ROMs came years after DOS but Microsoft eventually added support for CD-ROMs to DOS.) If you didn't have a peripheral attached locally, you were SOL (silly, orange, laughable).

DOS doesn't include NIC drivers, protocols, or a network client in its repertoire so, without additional specialized software, a DOS computer can't participate in a network. Fortunately, this specialized software is available: The Microsoft Network Client version 3.0 for MS-DOS is the client software that you use to connect MS-DOS machines to a Microsoft network. You can pull this utility off the Windows NT 4.0 Server distribution CD from the \Clients\Msclient directory. You must jump through several hoops to configure the network properties, but the README.TXT file provides enough documentation to accomplish the task.

Microsoft Network Client version 3.0 for MS-DOS adds NIC drivers, protocol support, and basic client capabilities to a DOS workstation. By using this tool, you can access drive shares (that is, network drives) and shared printers. One problem: DOS limits you to filenames that comply with the DOS 8.3 naming scheme, which means that you can access from DOS only those network resources with a share name of eight (8) characters or less (and without any spaces) and an extension of three (3) characters. Unlike long file names (LFNs), sharenames do not have 8.3 equivalents. If you name a share with a nine-character name, it's not accessible to MS-DOS clients.

After you install it, the client software loads the NIC and protocol drivers into memory during bootup. The system then attempts to contact an authentication server on the network. If communication is possible, you see a prompt for a logon name and a password. After you successfully complete the logon, you can access the network. The process is that simple!

Back to Windows 3.x, once more with feeling

Windows 3.*x*, Microsoft's GUI operating system of the late '80s, failed to include network capabilities. Just as you do with DOS, you need additional software and drivers to gain network access for a Windows 3.*x* system. Fortunately, Windows 3.*x* uses the same tool that DOS uses to access the network. The Microsoft Network Client version 3.0 for MS-DOS tool works with Windows 3.*x* because Microsoft built Windows on top of DOS. You can, therefore, think of Windows 3.*x* as a DOS application or even as an interface enhancement rather than as a full-fledged operating system.

Using the DOS network client with Windows 3.*x* requires following these few extra steps:

1. **Install Microsoft Network Client version 3.0 for MS-DOS with the full redirector. (Don't worry about the full redirector now; it's just a choice you can make during setup).**

   Installation instructions are included in the README.TXT file included with the client as well as in Chapter 16 of the Windows NT Server Resource Kit's Networking Guide.

2. **Start network access by typing** NET START FULL **at the command line.**
3. **Open the Change System Settings dialog box from the Windows Setup utility in the Main program group and then change the Network setting to** `Microsoft Network (or 100% compatible)`.

This procedure enables Windows 3.*x* to communicate over a DOS-level network link.

Windows for Workgroups — when 3.x just isn't enough

Microsoft released a network-capable version of Windows with the release of Windows for Workgroups (WfW), or Windows 3.11. Essentially, WfW is the same operating system as Windows 3.*x*, except that it includes native support for NICs, protocols, and network clients. Therefore, anyone can easily attach a WfW computer to a network or connect multiple WfW systems together to create a peer network.

The Windows NT Server 4.0 distribution CD includes an update to make WfW more compatible with the network capabilities of Windows NT. You can find the update files in \Client\Update.wfw. You simply copy these files over their older versions in the \Windows\System directory. The Windows NT Server CD also includes a 32-bit TCP/IP protocol stack for WfW.

Windows 95/98 Options

In 1995, Microsoft released a completely revised and updated version of their extremely popular GUI operating system — Windows 95. Then, in 1998, Microsoft released another major improvement — yep, you guessed it: Windows 98. These two desktop operating systems are currently the top choices for use as network clients. They include native support for networking, are easy to use, and, more important, they almost fully configure themselves. Other than your needing to provide a few key addresses or names, the networking subsystem can self-install. (Everyone bow to the god of Plug and Play.)

Since 1995, working with any Microsoft operating system released prior to Windows 95 is almost pointless. You have only the following two reasons to even consider using MS-DOS, Windows 3.*x*, or WfW:

- The hardware you're working with doesn't meet the minimum Windows 95 requirements: a 386DX CPU, 4 MB RAM, a VGA monitor, and 55 MB of free disk space.
- A required application doesn't operate on Windows 95.

If you're working with a DOS, Windows 3.*x*, or WfW client and neither of these reasons applies, you should upgrade to Windows 95.

Using Windows 95 or 98 as a network client clearly shows the distinction between the various network components. Figure 8-1 shows the Network applet from Windows 98. Notice how distinctly the network components appear on-screen: NIC drivers (adapters), protocols, and clients all appear on separate lines and have their own unique icons.

The networking systems of Windows 95 and Windows 98 are very similar. In fact, most of the interfaces are the same. The only significant differences are that Window 98 includes more versatility, component drivers, and reliability; and it uses more disk space and memory.

The Client for Microsoft Networks is installed on Windows 95 and Windows 98 in the same manner. Open the Network applet, click Add, select Client from the list, click OK, then locate and select Client for Microsoft Networks. Then, finally, click OK. You'll be prompted for the path to the distribution files. That's it.

After you install the Client for Microsoft Networks, you must configure it. Choose Start⇨Settings⇨Control Panel and double-click the Network icon. On the Configuration tab of the Network dialog box that appears, select Client for Microsoft Networks from the list, click the Properties button to display the Properties dialog box, as shown in Figure 8-2, and configure the following items:

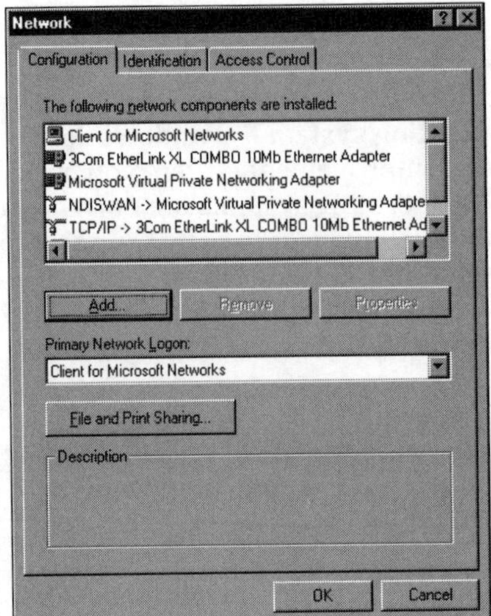

Figure 8-1: The Network applet from Windows 98.

- Select the Logon to Windows NT Domain check box and enter the domain name in the text box beside it. (For more information on domain names see Chapter 13.)
- Select type of network logon: Quick (logon only) or Logon and restore network connections.

Windows 95 includes a selection for a Primary Network Logon. This selection drop-down list box defines which network the system uses to authenticate the user/system while booting/logging in. After you install the Client for Microsoft Networks, you can select it in this field.

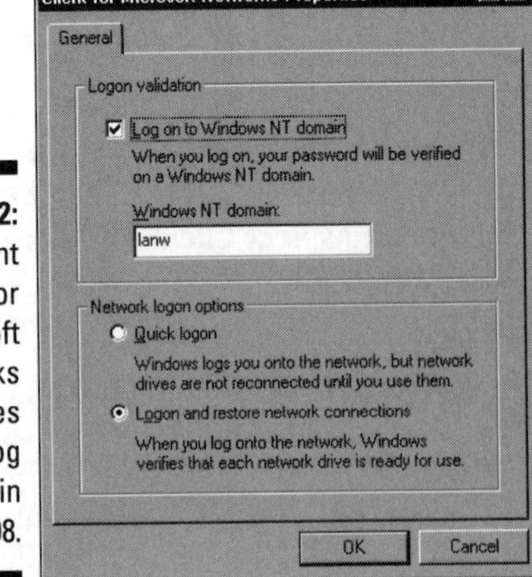

Figure 8-2: The Client for Microsoft Networks Properties dialog box in Windows 98.

Unlike previous operating systems, Windows 95/98 isn't limited to a single network type. In fact, a Windows 95/98 system can be a member of a Microsoft and a NetWare network at the same time. You must choose one as the primary, but both networks are still accessible. To configure such a system, you must use the Microsoft provided clients for each network.

Windows NT rules the roost!

The best client for a Microsoft network in a Windows NT Server-hosted domain is a Windows NT Workstation client. The Client for Microsoft Networks is built directly into the underlying structure of Windows NT Workstation. NT Workstation is designed to maximize network communications.

Furthermore, unlike previous operating systems, Windows NT Workstation actually becomes a member of a Windows NT Server-hosted domain. The inclusion of the client in the domain makes limiting access to network resources to authorized computers a much easier task. In environments where security is critical, Windows NT Workstation clients pay off in spades. Windows NT Workstation has many of the same capabilities as Windows NT Server and, with a few Microsoft supplied add-ons, nearly all of the administration tools are available on NT Workstation.

The Network interface of Windows NT is even more divided or separated than that of Windows 95/98. As shown in Figure 8-3, the Network applet has a tabbed page for each network component (that is, adapters and protocols). This setup offers you fine-grained control over the configuration and operational settings for each component of the network infrastructure. In addition, Windows NT Workstation is more adept at using multiple NICs, protocols, and clients at the same time!

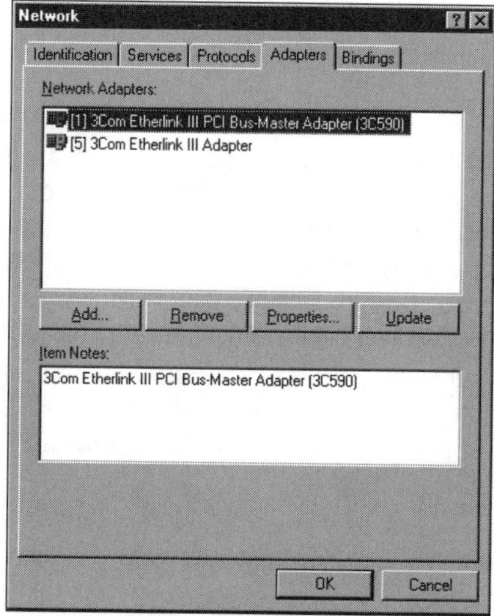

Figure 8-3: The Network applet from Windows NT Workstation.

Making the NetWare Connection

NetWare is a widespread network type. Until Microsoft developed and deployed Windows NT, NetWare was the leader in the network operating system industry. But even with Windows NT sweeping the globe, NetWare remains highly entrenched in many situations. Numerous organizations that use NetWare are creating hybrid networks instead of transforming completely to NT. Clients, therefore, need to connect to both Microsoft and NetWare networks in such situations.

Just as you do with Microsoft networks, you want to steer clear of older NetWare clients. Although connecting MS-DOS, Windows 3.*x*, and WfW clients to NetWare networks is possible, doing so usually isn't worth the hassle. Whenever and wherever possible, deploy Windows 95/98 or Windows NT Workstation clients to connect to NetWare networks.

Microsoft's client for Novell networks

Microsoft developed clients that you can use to connect their operating systems to NetWare networks. These clients are typically known as *Microsoft Client for Novell Networks* or *Microsoft Client for NetWare Networks*.

In Windows 95/98, you install the NetWare client as a distinct networking component, just as you do the Microsoft client. After you install it, you need to configure the Microsoft Client for NetWare Networks for your particular network configuration. This process includes defining the preferred server (the server that you use for authentication), the first drive letter to use for mapping NetWare network drives, and whether to enable logon script processing. If NetWare is your primary network, you want to set the Primary Network Logon to Microsoft Client for NetWare Networks.

On Windows NT Workstation, the Microsoft Client for NetWare Networks is known as *CSNW (Client Services for NetWare)*. This service is the client utility that enables an NT Workstation computer to participate in a NetWare network. You install the utility on the Services tab of the Network applet (click the Add button and select it from the list). After you install the client, you configure it based on the type of NetWare servers present. If you use NetWare 3.12 or earlier servers, you define a preferred server. If you use NetWare 4.*x* or newer servers, you define a default tree and context. CSNW works with NetWare 4.*x* and higher systems that have bindery emulation enabled or that are using *NDS (Novell Directory Service)*.

Novell's alternative client software

Novell has developed clients for Microsoft clients so that you can connect them to NetWare networks. These clients typically fall under the heading of *Novell Clients for NetWare Networks* and are available from Novell on the intraNetWare Client Suite CD and the NetWare 5 CD. The CDs contain client software for Novell BorderManager, intraNetWare, and NetWare environments for DOS, Windows 3.*x*, Windows 95, Windows NT, OS/2, and Mac OS clients in English, Portuguese, French, Italian, German, and Spanish.

Why use the Novell client instead of the Microsoft client for NetWare connectivity? Well, you should use the Novell client if you don't want to connect to both NetWare and Microsoft networks at the same time and if the Microsoft client doesn't offer you the capabilities that you need to access NetWare-hosted resources, functions, or capabilities. The Novell client enables all NetWare functions, whereas the Microsoft client has some limitations (for example, not supporting all the DOS-based NetWare utilities).

If you're using Windows 95/98 as a NetWare client, you have the following three client choices from Novell:

- **Novell Client for Windows 95/98:** This client is a protected-mode, 32-bit client that supports NetWare 4.*x* and higher and NDS.
- **NetWare VLM:** This client is a real-mode, 16-bit client that supports NetWare 3.*x* and 4.*x* and also includes NDS support.
- **NetWare NETX client:** This client is a real-mode, 16-bit client that supports NetWare 2.*x* through NetWare 4.*x* (with bindery emulation).

If you plan to use any of the Novell clients, visit the Novell Web site at `www.novell.com` for more information.

Making Clients Work for a Living

Just because you think you have all the right components doesn't always guarantee that your network connection is going to function on the first try. More often than not, you need to change settings several times and perform multiple reboots before you get everything just right. (You usually forget to make all the necessary settings the first time around rather than experience an actual problem with the client software or networking components.)

You need to deal with each network component — NIC, driver, protocol, and client — on an individual basis. The following sections cover troubleshooting steps for each component.

Note: The troubleshooting steps that we describe in the following sections assume that the network is actually functioning. If other clients can't access to the network, the problem is probably not with the clients but with the network itself or with the servers hosting the network. If the steps that we describe in the following sections don't remedy the problem, you need to look for problems external to the client. After you solve those external problems, return to the client for further testing.

De-infesting NICs

NIC troubleshooting is a hardware-level activity. Hardware troubleshooting involves understanding the hardware and software environment in use and the capabilities of the NIC device.

First, ensure that all the connections are firm and secure. Doing so may involve opening the computer case and reseating the NIC. You also want to inspect the connecting edges for damage on the NIC and/or the motherboard. Next, verify that all other physical connections inside the computer are firm and correctly seated. After you close the case, check that all cables (not just the network cable) are firmly attached and undamaged. Replace any sharply bent, frayed, or broken cables.

Next, compare the resource settings of the device with the available free resources of the computer. This process involves the IRQ, I/O port, DMA, and memory in use. You can obtain this information through the System Information utility in Windows 95/98 or the Windows NT Diagnostics in Windows NT. You may want to view the resource availability readings without the NIC in the computer. After you determine what settings are available, you need to consult the NIC's documentation to see whether you can configure it to use the free resources. If not, you may need to remove or alter the configuration of other cards to release resources that the NIC can used. Depending on the NIC, you may need to make manual jumper or dip-switch changes on the card itself, use a utility to set the NIC BIOS level settings, or just have Plug and Play make the resource settings automatically.

If these two operations don't result in a functioning NIC, you need to determine whether the NIC itself is defective or the motherboard is problematic. Doing so involves testing the NIC to a different bus slot, using a different NIC in the suspect bus slot, and testing the NIC in another computer. If either the NIC or motherboard is defective, get a replacement or get it repaired. You need to discuss this procedure with your hardware supplier.

THE CHAPEL IN MARLBORO May 20, 2007

CELEBRATION OF OUR FAITH
9:00 A.M. and 10:15 A.M.

Prelude

Welcome and Greeting

O God Our Help in Ages Past
Friend of God
Praise to the Lord the Almighty
In Christ Alone
Days of Elijah

Offering – Choir Special
Worthy, Faithful, and Righteous

Interview with Judy Elder

Sermon Scripture
Romans 5: 1-2

Sermon – Pastor Joel Cochran

Closing Invitation
My Jesus I Love Thee #364

Benediction

Fun for Kids

6:00 P.M.

This Evening!

Guests — We are glad you are worshiping with us at The Chapel today! Two attended nurseries are available for infants and 1-year-old children during both morning services. Children's classes and youth groups meet at 9:00 A.M. Adult church school classes meet at 9:00 or 10:15 A.M. A list of classes, times, and room locations is available at the information desk in the main foyer. During the school year, children in K-5th grades attend the 10:15 worship service and are dismissed to JAM Sessions before the scripture reading. Pre-school classes are available for children during the entire 10:15 service.

Weekly Schedule

BIBLE STUDY/PRAYER

- **Prayer Groups** meet at 8:00 A.M. each Sunday morning. Men meet in the Safe Harbor exercise room. Women meet in Safe Harbor room #1.
- **Prayer Group** meets at 1:00 P.M. Wednesdays in the conference room. All prayer warriors welcome.
- **Men's Bible Study** at 7:00 P.M. Mondays. Direct questions to Dale at 330-877-6109.
- **Men's Bible Study** Tuesdays at 6:00 A.M. at Frontier Restaurant, Hartville.
- **Men's Bible Studies** Fridays at 6:45 A.M. at Arabica in Hartville, and Fridays at 7:00 A.M. at Luna's in Alliance.
- **Women's Bible Study** Tuesday, 9:00 –11:00 A.M. in The Source.

SPORTS

- **Every Monday, Wednesday, and Thursday** from 6:00 – 9:00 P.M. the weight room is open and someone is available to give instructions on how to use the equipment to develop an individualized exercise program. Direct questions to Matt McLouth at 330-935-0132 ext. 1-228.
- **The Safe Harbor Walking Path** is open, starting at the south-west corner of the parking lot. Part of the path goes through the parking lot, which is marked by painted footprints.

SPECIAL GROUPS

- **Grief Share** meets in Safe Harbor Room #3 at 6:00 P.M. Sundays. Contact Jim Justice Sr. at 330-606-6617.
- **Jolly Pilgrims** (ages 50+) meet for a lunch and program on the second Tuesday of each month at 11:45 A.M. in room #7.

Please submit announcements to Linda by 9:00 A.M. on the Wednesday before the Sunday on which you wish them to appear in the bulletin.

CHILDREN

- **JAM Sessions** during the 10:15 A.M. sermon, Sundays
- **We Be JAMmin'** for kids K- 5th grade, 6:00 to 7:00 P.M. Sundays in Safe Harbor gym is over until September. **Come celebrate tonight at the JAM Festival!**

MUSIC

- **Orchestra Rehearsal** 4:30 P.M. Sundays in the Sanctuary.
- **Worship Team Rehearsal** 7:00 P.M. Tuesdays
- **Choir Rehearsal** 6:45 P.M. Wednesdays in the Sanctuary.
- **Drama Team Rehearsal** Thursdays. Contact Rick Bowers for information.

YOUTH

- **High School Church School** taught by Matt McLouth meets at 9:00 A.M. Sundays in The Source.
- **Controlled Chaos** meets from 6:00 - 8:00 P.M. Sundays in The Source.
- **Middle School Church School** taught by Aaron Long meets at 9:00 A.M. Sundays in room #7.
- **Youth Group** meets from 6:00 - 7:30 P.M. Sundays in room #7.
- **Youth Ministry and Service Teams** 7:00 P.M. Wednesdays in The Source.

Check www.marlboro-chapel.org for weekly calendar updates, information, activities, and recent sermons as MP3 podcasts.

COMING UP...

- **Baby and Child Dedication** will be held on **Sunday, June 3rd** in either service. If you have a child or baby to dedicate to the Lord, please call and notify the church office.

- **NEST Community Bible Study for Women** will begin on **Thursday, June 7th** at 7:00 P.M. The study will be *Believing God: Experiencing a Fresh Explosion of Faith* by Beth Moore. Cost is $20. Call Jennifer Forrest at (330) 829-9173 or Lou Mills at (330) 877-6238 with questions.

- **Graduates:** If you or someone you know is graduating from either high school or college, please inform the church office by May 27th. We want to recognize you for your accomplishments on **Sunday, June 10th**.

- **Tears to Joy** Bible Study will soon begin again. Please keep checking the bulletin for start up dates.

- **A Swiss Steak Dinner,** sit down or carry-out available, will be held Saturday, June 30th from 4:30 – 7:30 P.M. This will be a fundraiser for our High School Youth who are going to Mississippi through "Adventures in Missions" this summer. Tickets go on sale beginning June 3rd in the church narthex.

EARLYBIRD REGISTRATION!

Sunday MAY 20

Register at the table in the north hallway in the A.M. or at the JAMfest in the P.M.
Receive your official VBS t-shirt.

Adults — Please sign up to supply cookies!
We need 2,000 of them!

I can teach a JAM Session once each month...

(during the entire 10:15 A.M. service)

- ❑ 2-year-olds
- ❑ 3-year-olds
- ❑ 4&5-year-olds

(during the 10:15 A.M. sermon, approx. 40 min.)

- ❑ kindergarten ❑ Grades 2-3
- ❑ Grade 1 ❑ Grades 4-5

I prefer teaching on the...

- ❑ 1st Sunday ❑ 2nd Sunday
- ❑ 3rd Sunday ❑ 4th Sunday
- ❑ I have no preference.

NAME________________________ PHONE ________________

Complete and return to the information desk or to an usher. Thank You!

ANNOUNCEMENTS. . .

Thank you to all whom have been saving aluminum cans and/or money for the homeless children in Bransk, Russia. From January 1st to April 30th we saved 843 pounds of cans, plus gifts that added up to $445, which gave us a total of $910. Thank you, Larry Mattes and Dave Whitsett.

Nursery Helpers Needed – We are looking for ladies and/or couples willing to serve in the nursery beginning June 1st. This involves a one-year commitment one hour a month. Please contact Jan Lucas at (330) 935-2521.

Bonds available; A participant in our last Bond Program needs to sell her portion of bonds, preferably to someone in our congregation. If you would be interested, please contact Jerry Mort at (330) 935-0132, ext. 1-237.

Calling all veterans! If you have a photograph of yourself in uniform, please share it with us for our Memorial Day bulletin. Either scan the photo (at least 150 dpi) and e-mail as an attachment to serenacochran@ameritech.net or leave a print in the envelope provided at the information desk and we will scan it and return it to the envelope on June 10th. Be sure to include your name and military branch.

MILITARY PERSONNEL: Adult Ministries desires the names and addresses of ALL MILITARY PERSONNEL that are immediate family members here at The Chapel so that they may send cards and care packages. Please call the church office and leave this information with either Linda or Jackie.

Prayer requests: If you would like to request prayer from Chapel intercessors, you may e-mail Chris Bailey at Im4Christ316@aol.com.

Visit the Library now highlighting well-known author, Tim LaHaye or check out a video of a previous church service you may have missed. Remember all items must be checked out with the librarian. Hours: **Sunday 8:30 to 11:45 A.M.**

Alliance Pregnancy Center is experiencing a shortage of boys' and girls' baby clothes, sizes 12mos. – 2T. Maternity clothes, baby wipes, baby toiletries, diaper bags, formula, baby food, and cribs are also needed at this time.

OUR CHURCH FAMILY...

Please remember those from our church family who have been in the hospital or who have been ill. A card, friendly phone call, or visit would be greatly appreciated.

- **Grady Paul Eldridge** is recuperating at home from a broken hip.
- **Dolores (Dodie) Reed** is in St. Thomas Hospital, room #708 with a fractured knee.

Dear Chapel Family, we would like to thank you for all of your support in the passing of our father, Robert Bixler. Your cards, visits and meals meant so much. We feel blessed to be a part of the Chapel family. In Christ's Love, Jerry and Bonnie Bixler and family.

Men's Softball Schedules
All Saturday Games
Questions – Call Pastor Jason
330-935-0132 ext. 1224

	BLUE TEAM	RED TEAM
May 19	7:00 p.m.	4:30 & 5:45 p.m.
June 2	5:45 & 7:00 p.m.	7:00 p.m.
June 9	7:00 p.m.	5:45 p.m.
June 23	4:30 & 7:00 p.m.	4:30 & 5:45 p.m.
July 7	4:30 & 7:00 p.m.	4:30 & 5:45 p.m.
July 14	5:45 & 7:00 p.m.	4:30 & 5:45 p.m.
July 21	5:45 & 7:00 p.m.	4:30 p.m.

FINANCIAL REPORT

Tithes & Offerings for the week of May 13th:
$14,402.46 ($18,154.00 needed per week)
Tithes & Offerings year to date:
$310,518.01 ($344,926.00 budgeted YTD)

The Endowment Fund of The Chapel in Marlboro exists to support special projects, as selected by the Board of Trustees. Are you interested in contributing to this important fund by remembering The Chapel in your will? Contact **Jerry Mort** at 330-935-0132, ext. 1-237.

The Chapel exists to...

Present Christ to the lost.
Unite in celebrative worship,
Restore wholeness
Provide meaningful friendships and
Opportunities for
Service, while
Equipping people for ministry and a life of
PURPOSE!

We believe that true happiness and a worthwhile life can only be realized through faith in Jesus Christ. Every worship service and activity of this church is designed to help you live life to the fullest. If you are a new-comer with no church home, we invite you to make The Chapel yours!

The Chapel in Marlboro fulfills its purpose by leading believers to maturity through evangelism, instruction, service, fellowship, and worship.

Our Ten-Fold Vision is...

...To strive for excellence in all endeavors;
...To be a church where all are welcomed;
...To establish people in the truth of the Bible, thus producing disciples of Jesus Christ;
...To have knowledgeable and compassionate pastoral staff who can and do help people;
...To encourage participation by all members in ministry (meeting the needs of others in Jesus' Name);
...To present the "good news" of God's salvation, offered through the Lord Jesus Christ frequently, if not weekly;
...To encourage the development of small groups, where people may experience real friendship and personal growth;
...To have a world mindset; a desire to minister beyond the walls of the church to other countries and people groups;
...To continually develop the acreage and facilities for community and spiritual ministry;
...To glorify God in all that we do.

Our Present Strategy

The pastors of the church are constantly evaluating ministry to assure that the purposes, mission, and vision of the church are being fulfilled. Occasionally, a ministry comes to fulfillment and needs to be terminated, while new ones need to be started and others need maintenance. The past two years have been focused on property development and sports/recreation ministry. Emphasis now will turn toward special teaching sessions and small group formation for adults. The next session, *Addiction Busters*, is scheduled for Saturday, July 7th, 8:30 A.M. in The Source.

THE CHAPEL IN MARLBORO

8700 Edison Street N.E. (State Route 619) Marlboro-Louisville, Ohio 44641
Phone 330-935-0132 FAX 330-935-0700

Web site www.marlboro-chapel.org E-mail Chapelinmarlboro@rrbiznet.com

After-hour Emergencies – 888-9PASTOR or 888-972-7867 Heartline – 330-935-0505

Women's Ministry Information – 330-935-0132 – ext. 1-237 FACES (Fine Arts Community Enrichment School) – ext. 1-237

STAFF OFFICE EXTENSIONS:

Rev. Joel Cochran, *Senior Pastor* – ext. 1-225
Rob Cochran, *Adult Ministries* – ext. 1-229
Jason Shelton, *Sports* – ext. 1-224
Aaron Long, *Middle School* – ext. 1-229
Zita Patton, *Christian Education Secretary* – ext. 1-227
Jerry Mort, *Administration* – ext. 1-237
Andy Grubbs, *Worship* – ext. 1-231
Matt McLouth, *High School* – ext. 1-228
Linda Balzer, *Secretary* – ext. 1-220

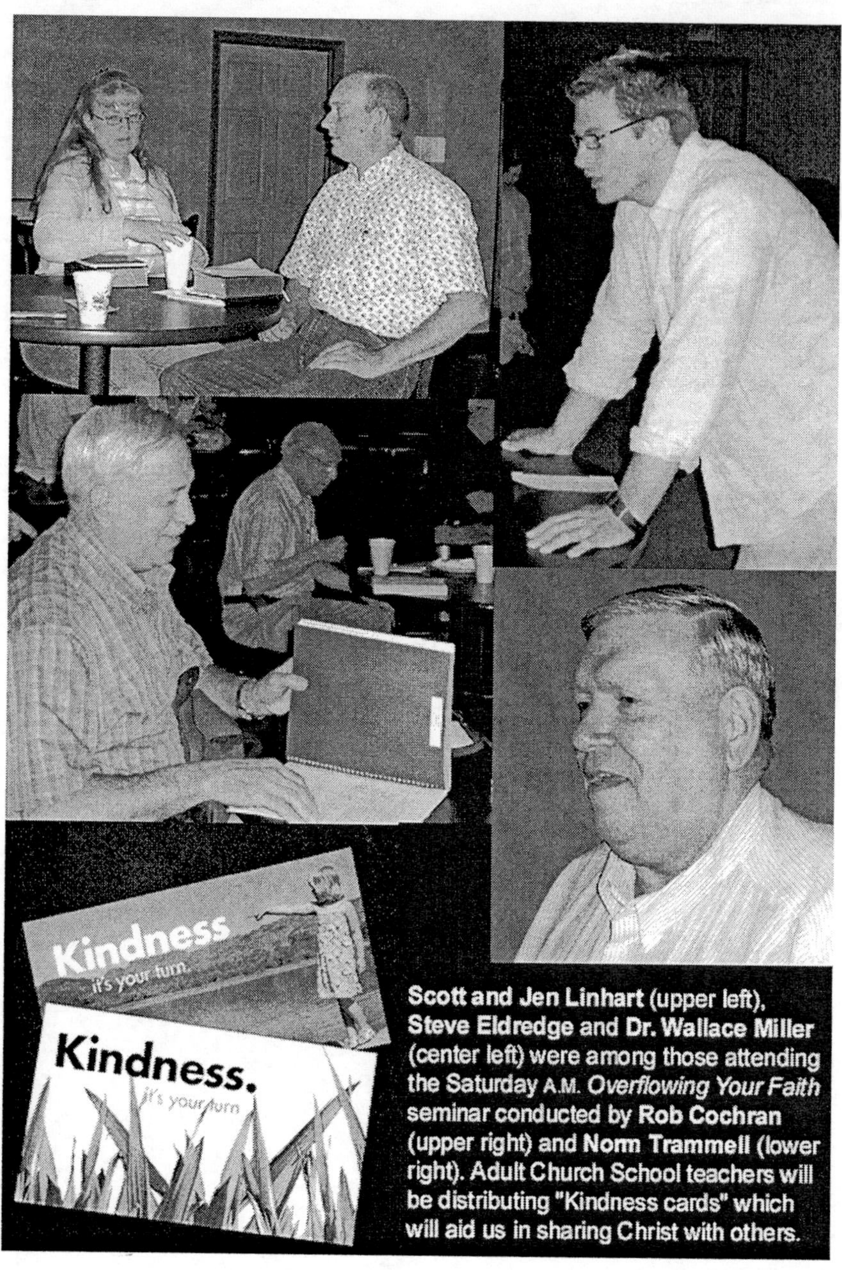

Scott and Jen Linhart (upper left), **Steve Eldredge** and **Dr. Wallace Miller** (center left) were among those attending the Saturday A.M. *Overflowing Your Faith* seminar conducted by **Rob Cochran** (upper right) and **Norm Trammell** (lower right). Adult Church School teachers will be distributing "Kindness cards" which will aid us in sharing Christ with others.

Driving me lazy

If the driver for the NIC is at fault, you have only one solution — replace the driver. You can do so in any of several ways (although, depending on the operating system, driver type, and manufacturer, not all these options may be available). Select one or more of the following techniques:

- Remove the driver completely and then reinstall it from the original OS distribution disks, from the original driver disk that came with the NIC, or from an updated distribution (which you can usually download from the Internet). Typically, you remove the driver through the same interface in which you installed the driver or through the Device Manager of Windows 95/98.
- Update the driver from the original OS distribution disks, from the original driver disk that ships with the NIC, or from an updated distribution (which you can usually download from the Internet). Typically, you update the driver through the Device Manager of Windows 95/98 or the Network applet of Windows NT.
- If you can't remove the driver or perform an update, reinstall the driver from the original OS distribution disks, from the original driver disk that ships with the NIC, or from an updated distribution (which you can usually download from the Internet).
- Double-check that you're using the correct driver version for the NIC and the OS in use.

If these actions fail to resolve a driver-related problem, you need to contact the NIC/driver vendor for further resolution options.

Protocols, schmotocols

You perform Protocol troubleshooting in one of two areas: Either you reinstall the protocol or you change the configuration settings. Reinstalling a protocol is similar to reinstalling a NIC driver, as we describe in the preceding section: You need to remove/reinstall, update, or install over the existing protocols from the original OS distribution files or from updated files from the OS manufacturer or a compatible release from a different vendor. (We highly recommended that you stick with the Microsoft versions of protocols for Microsoft products to ensure compatibility and to qualify for Microsoft technical support.)

If the protocol itself is functioning correctly but network communication is still not possible, you need to verify the protocol's configuration settings. (NetBEUI doesn't have any user configurable settings. Only Macintosh clients use AppleTalk, so we don't discuss it here.)

TCP/IP Settings

TCP/IP is the protocol that you use most commonly and, unfortunately, also is the most complicated to configure. You need to verify each of the following items on your client:

- **IP Address:** This address is the unique identifier for each client. You must not duplicate it within the same network. Verify that the assigned IP address is correct for the subnet in use. Furthermore, the IP address can be automatically assigned if a *DHCP* (*D*ynamic *H*ost *C*onfiguration *P*rotocol) server is in use. (***Note:*** DHCP enables a small block of IP addresses to support a larger number of clients if those clients are not all powered up at one time.)
- **Subnet mask:** This mask is the logical element that you use to divide a network into subnets. A subnet divides a network based on IP addresses. Individual computers can't communicate outside their own subnet without a gateway machine or a router. The subnet mask is automatically assigned if a DHCP server is in use.
- **Default Gateway:** This item is the IP address of a gateway machine (a multihomed server) or a router, which are used to transmit communications from one subnet to another.
- **DNS:** This item is the IP address of a *DNS*, or *D*omain *N*ame *S*erver, which you use to resolve domain names (such as `www.microsoft.com`) into an IP address. (See Chapter 12 for more information on DNS.)
- **WINS Server:** This item is the IP address of a *WINS* (*W*indows *I*nternet *N*ame *S*ervice), which you use to resolve NetBIOS names (such as SERVER12 or ACCT12-3) into an IP address. (See Chapter 12 for more information on WINS.)

After you make any changes to the TCP/IP settings, even if the system doesn't prompt you to do so, always reboot your system. This reboot ensures that the new settings go into use and clears any information or configuration based on the previous settings.

IPX/SPX Settings

IPX/SPX is the protocol that people most commonly associate with NetWare networks. You find IPX/SPX and compatible protocols on many non-NetWare or hybrid networks. Microsoft supports a compatible protocol that it calls NWLink, which you can use in a pure Microsoft network or in one with NetWare members. In any case, IPX/SPX is a very easy protocol to troubleshoot. Just as with TCP/IP (and any protocol for that matter), if the protocol is defective, you need to reinstall it.

The only configuration setting you need to work with is the frame type. Several versions of IPX/SPX are in use that are slightly different from each other. The default setting of the frame type is Auto. The Auto setting attempts to determine the frame type already in use on the network and then puts the discovered frame type into use on the client. This procedure, however, is useful only in a network environment that uses only a single frame type. If multiple frame types are in use or you want to manually set the frame type, you have the following options:

- Ethernet 802.2 (which NetWare 3.12 and 4.0 servers use by default)
- Ethernet 802.3 (which NetWare 3.11 servers use by default)
- Ethernet II
- Token Ring
- Token Ring SNAP

See Chapter 4 for more information on the various topologies.

After you make any changes to the IPX/SPX settings, even if the system doesn't prompt you to do so, always reboot your system. This reboot ensures that the new settings go into use and clears any information or configuration based on the previous settings.

When all else fails

Client troubleshooting is simply verifying that you configured the network authentication and connection information correctly. For clients on Microsoft networks, double-check the domain/workgroup name. For clients on NetWare networks, double-check the preferred server or directory tree. In rare cases, you need to remove and reinstall the client.

Living with Your Choices

The network itself, your budget, the capabilities you require, and the software you're using often are what determine your choice for a client. These parameters define the hardware, the operating system, and, ultimately, the network components that you need to use to establish network communications. After you install and deploy a computer as a network client, the work of maintaining the client has just begun.

You must maintain vigilance for security alerts, product updates, system patches, or other issues. Just because a client works correctly today doesn't ensure that it's always going to operate correctly. As your network evolves, your clients must adapt to the changes. This adaptation can mean upgrades to the hardware, installing new operating systems, applying patches to correct problems, or reconfiguring network clients or services.

The best places to obtain more information about Microsoft-related issues are the TechNet CD (`www.microsoft.com/technet/`), Microsoft's online support knowledge base (`support.microsoft.com/`), the Microsoft Web site (`www.microsoft.com/`), and Microsoft's public NNTP news server (`msnews.microsoft.com`).

Part III

Revving Up Your Server

"One of the first things you want to do before installing NT Server is fog the users to keep them calm during the procedure."

In this part . . .

When the networking basics are taken care of, you can jump headlong into the embrace of Windows NT Server, and that's just what this part of the book is all about. It begins with coverage of the installation and configuration of Windows NT Server and continues with the details of configuring protocols and settings for network hardware in a Windows NT environment. Next, you tackle installing, configuring, and managing printers and print services with Windows NT Server. Following this exercise in hard copy, you tackle the mysteries of TCP/IP addressing and configuration, and then conclude with a rousing chorus on Windows NT domains and trust relationships.

In short, Part III takes you through everything you need to know to install Windows NT Server, and how to use it to set up and deliver basic network services to your users. While some of the more exotic and interesting services are not covered here, what is included will get your network up and running without too much muss or fuss.

Along the way, you find out how to build your network around Windows NT, including basic system and network configuration, printing, and domain access and use. You also discover how to configure Windows NT Server to deliver the goods across your network, be it for file or print services.

Chapter 9

Installing Your Server Software

In This Chapter

- Upgrading or installing from scratch?
- Looking under the hood
- Using the Windows NT install utilities
- Installing Windows NT Server, step-by-step
- Troubleshooting snafus
- Automating installations

Windows NT Server 4.0 is easy to install and takes little time, especially if you plan ahead. By following our suggestions in this chapter, we hope that you can avoid some common installation problems, many of which relate to lack of correct equipment. If not, we provide a troubleshooting section to smooth out any ruffles you encounter along the way.

Upgrade or New Install?

Whether you're installing Windows NT Server 4 for the first time or you're upgrading from a previous version, planning can help ensure a smooth installation.

Upgrade, as the term implies, means that you currently have a version of Windows NT Server installed and you want to upgrade it to a later version. We strongly recommend that you begin by backing up all the data on any machine that you plan to upgrade. (We cover backups in Chapter 16.) Although you can upgrade to Windows NT 4 without losing current data, hardware and software sometimes have minds of their own and can foul up things. A smidgen of prevention can save you some real heartache!

If you're installing Windows NT for the first time, you need to make some decisions about how you're going to set up the server before you install the software. You have the following three basic ways to install Windows NT:

- **CD-ROM:** This type of installation requires that you have a computer with a network interface card (NIC) installed. We focus on this type of installation in this chapter.
- **Across the network:** This type of installation requires that the computer is attached to the network and that an install image of the CD-ROM files is available on a network share elsewhere on the network.
- **Automated install:** This type of installation requires you to input installation information into a data file that you can then merge into a script file for execution.

Checking the list

We offer the following pre-installation list to help you gather the information and equipment that you need for your setup. Windows NT's Setup program doesn't require all the items that we list in the following sections during installation, but we like to have everything handy whenever we install so that we don't need to run around looking for things during the actual process.

Manuals

The following is a list of books that you may want to have within arm's reach (although, of course, this book is the most important!):

- **Windows NT Server 4 manuals:** The manuals you receive with Windows NT Server 4.
- **Computer hardware manuals:** The manuals for the machine on which you plan to install Windows NT Server 4.
- **DOS manuals:** You need these if you don't know how to create a DOS partition using the FDISK utility. (A DOS partition is where you will load DOS drivers and other information.)
- **Modem manual (optional):** Grab this manual only if you plan to install one or more modems on this server.

Software

Make sure that you have the following software handy so you don't find yourself hunting around halfway through the installation:

- **Windows NT Server 4 CD-ROM:** This disc is the CD-ROM that ships with Windows NT Server. You need the CD key from the yellow sticker on the back of the jewel case.
- **Windows NT Server 4 Service Pack CD-ROM:** Although you can always download the latest Service Pack from Microsoft's Web site, it's quite voluminous. Applying the Service Pack from a CD-ROM is much more efficient — if you can lay your hands on one.
- **DOS disks:** The latest version of DOS, including the FDISK utility that you need to install a small FAT partition.
- **Blank formatted floppy disk:** At the end of the installation, you create an emergency repair disk, also called an ERD.
- **NIC driver:** Windows NT Setup should find the NIC in the server, but keep a floppy with the necessary drivers at hand in case it doesn't.
- **Small Computer System Interface SCSI drivers:** Windows NT Setup should recognize all SCSI devices if they're listed in the HCL. Keep these handy, just in case.

Hardware

Of course, setting up Windows NT Server 4 also requires some hardware, particularly the following:

- **Computer:** You must have this item to install Windows NT! Make sure that it includes a mouse, and we recommend at least a Pentium processor.
- **RAM:** The more memory that you can afford, the better. We like at least 64MB.
- **CD-ROM drive:** If you're installing Windows NT from a CD-ROM, you need this item installed. Later model computers allow this drive to participate in the boot sequence and this allows you to start your Windows NT installation directly from the CD.
- **Hard Disk:** We like to see at least 4GB of disk storage space.
- **Modem:** If this server connects to the Internet or provides access to remote users, a modem (either internal or external) is one way to provide this connection. We prefer a 56KB modem.
- **Cables:** Depending on what components you install, you may need modem cables, satin telephone cables, power cords, monitor cables, and more.

Information

You need to make several choices as you go through the setup routine. You're better off if you already have an idea of what you're going to answer before you begin the install. Consider the items in the following list:

- **SETUP.TXT file:** The Windows NT Server installation CD provides this file, which you find in the \i386 subdirectory, for some last-minute information and installation details gathered too late to include in the printed manuals. Check there for a lot of good information.
- **FAT/NTFS:** *NTFS* is the Windows NT native file system and is much more secure than FAT. We recommend that you create only a small FAT partition (200MB) by using the DOS FDISK utility and format the remainder of your hard disk as NTFS. Doing so allows you to load drivers and other components onto your system for emergency use if the system crashes. You can partition the hard disk with any operating system of your choice; we find DOS efficient for what we need to do while troubleshooting.
- **Licensing:** You need to know how you purchased your Windows NT and client licenses, because the Windows NT Setup program asks you whether you want per-seat or per-server licensing.
- **Computer Name:** Each computer needs a unique name that you can identify easily on the network.
- **Domain Name:** If this computer is a Primary Domain Controller (PDC), you must create a domain name. If this computer joins a current domain, you're best off connecting this computer to a network with access to that domain. Keep the domain name handy.
- **Primary Domain Controller, Backup Domain Controller, Server:** If this computer isn't a PDC, is it a Backup Domain Controller (BDC) or simply a stand-alone server? (See Chapter 13 for more information on PDCs and BDCs.)
- **Protocols:** Determine what protocols this computer uses (or will use) to communicate. If you're planning to use TCP/IP, refer to Chapter 12 for more details about that protocol. Decide whether you must configure TCP/IP manually or automatically through a DHCP server. If this server connects to the Internet, make sure that you have a valid IP address.
- **Remote connectivity options:** Does this server connect to the Internet or host a Web server? If so, you can install Internet Information Server (IIS) to provide Web services and Remote Access Services (RAS) for the connectivity. RAS can also enable your users or customers to dial into the network. You can always install RAS and IIS later. In either case, you need either an analog or digital phone line. It's helpful to know the phone number to the phone line so you can test the connection.

What's Under the Hood?

Before installing Windows NT Server 4, whether just upgrading or performing a new install, you need to know Microsoft's minimum hardware requirements. If your server doesn't match these requirements at the barest minimum, your installation can halt midway and leave you stuck. Microsoft goes easy on its minimum requirements, so we provide some more realistic numbers to match real-world needs. If you follow Microsoft's numbers, you can expect to end up with a "doo-dah" server that lacks the "zip-a-dee" part. Table 9-1 shows a comparison between Microsoft's numbers and our real-world numbers.

Table 9-1 Minimum Requirements: Microsoft versus Dummies

Item	*Microsoft Says:*	*Real-World Says:*
Processor	Intel 486	Pentium or better
RAM	16MB	64MB or better
Monitor	VGA	SVGA or better
NIC	One	One (at least 32 bit)
CD-ROM	None	12X or better
Hard disk	124MB	250MB or better*
Floppy disk	3.5" or 5.25"	3.5" high density

**Note: 250MB is only what's recommended to just install the Windows NT operating system. You must factor in items such as application software that you add to this Windows NT Server. For most small to medium sized offices, plan to start out with 4GB hard disk space, but chunk out 250MB of this for the Windows NT Server operating system.*

You can squeak by with Microsoft's minimums, but many of your server's capabilities end up terribly slow or intractable. Although DOS supports low-resolution monitors, for example, because of Windows NT Server's graphical user interface (GUI), you want to use a higher-resolution monitor (SVGA or better). More is better in many cases (disk space, RAM, processor power, and so on); buy as much as your budget permits so that you don't need to upgrade too soon.

Take a trip to Microsoft's Web site, particularly the Windows NT Server pages at www.microsoft.com/ntserver. There you can find white papers and Frequently Asked Questions (FAQs) that answer common questions to many issues, such as licensing, minimum requirements, upgrades, and more. If you don't find enough answers there, head to www.ntfaq.com for a searchable Windows NT FAQ site.

Windows NT utilities aplenty

Utilities abound for Windows NT because of its popularity. No single operating system can do everything that users want. Programmers and others adept at computing typically develop small scripts or programs to perform functions that the basic operating system doesn't include. You can find many of these utilities, especially installation tools, on the Internet at popular Windows NT Web sites, such as `windowsnt.miningco.com`, `www.windowsntmag.com` or `www.bhs.com`.

Microsoft sells a Windows NT Server Resource Kit for each version of Windows NT Server. You can purchase this kit on the Internet or at a bookstore. The package includes utilities for installation, file management, troubleshooting, and planning purposes. The following list of installation tools gives a good notion of what comes with this kit:

- **Domain Planner:** A planning guide for those organizations that require a complex domain structure.
- **NTCARD40.HLP:** Information and configuration help for NICs, SCSI adapters, and sound cards.
- **NTDETECT.CHK:** A special version of NTDETECT.COM that provides information about your machine during bootup.
- **SETUPMGR.EXE:** A tool that helps with unattended Windows NT installation using text-based answer files.
- **SYSDIFF.EXE:** A tool that provides a method to upgrade machines with new operating systems and applications. It takes a snapshot of a model machine and applies changes to other machines.
- **WNTIPCFG.EXE:** A graphical configuration utility for IP.

Another important item to check is whether your server appears on Microsoft's Hardware Compatibility List (HCL). Microsoft's test lab spends its time testing products for compatibility with Windows NT. Obtaining Microsoft lab certification means that an organization can display Microsoft's logo on its product or products. Similarly, Microsoft places listings for certified products in its HCL.

Selecting a network server from the ones listed in the HCL helps to ensure the smoothest installation possible, because you know Microsoft has already tested and certified that product. Certifying products for the HCL is an ongoing task at Microsoft, and the company provides an updated listing every month on its Web site (at `www.microsoft.com/ntserver`) or its FTP site (at `ftp://microsoft.com/bussys/winnt/winnt_docs/hcl`). You also can find an entire HCL in the Windows NT product manuals, but it's obviously not current because it shipped with the product in August 1996.

If you inherit a server and don't know much about its internals, use the Hardware Query Tool (HQT) for Windows 4.0 utility (see Chapter 22 for more on hardware analysis). It runs as a DOS batch file on a server and determines whether its equipment is HCL-compatible. This utility resides in the \support\hqtools subdirectory. Run this utility to see what items on your server the HCL lists; then go to Microsoft's Web site (at `www.microsoft.com`). Use the Search button to locate the searchable HCL and check your system components.

Installing Windows NT Server, Step-by-Step

In this section, you walk through an entire Windows NT 4.0 Server installation, screen by screen. We don't have enough space in this book to present screens for every possible type of installation, so we provide instructions on how to install Windows NT 4.0 Server from a CD-ROM. We divide this coverage into sections to make it easier to read and digest.

Preparing the server

The first major task in getting the software onto a Windows NT Server is to make the server ready for the process. Generally, these are the issues you must resolve before traveling into the Windows NT Server installation process proper, so follow these steps:

1. **Create a 200MB DOS partition using the DOS FDISK utility.**

   Note: You may not need to perform this step if the Windows NT installation program runs from your CD-ROM drive without additional drivers loaded. If you can start the Windows NT Installation program from your boot floppies, or from your CD-ROM, skip this step.

   Then, if Setup doesn't recognize your CD-ROM drive, you can load the drivers on this partition and start the Windows NT installation from here or insert the Setup floppy #1 and reboot the computer. If your CD-ROM drive still isn't recognized, you'll need to go back to step one and create the FAT partition with DOS and load the appropriate CD-ROM drivers.

2. **Install the NIC in the server.**

   Don't close the server's case — you may need to adjust that card's settings.

3. **[Optional] Install the modem into the server if you need an internal modem and want to connect this server to external sources such as the Internet.**

Starting Windows NT — DOS-based setup

There are several different ways to install Windows NT Server.

- **Floppy boot disks:** Windows NT ships with three boot diskettes and a CD-ROM. You can install Windows NT beginning with the three installation disks and Windows NT will prompt you for the CD. The installation floppies load CD-ROM drivers so when you're asked to insert the CD, hopefully the Windows NT drivers will recognize your drive. If not, you have to load the CD drivers for your model manually.
- **CD-ROM boot installation:** If your computer permits the CD-ROM drive to participate in the boot sequence, and you have the file AUTORUN on the Windows NT Installation CD, you can boot the installation program from the CD and omit the use of the floppies.
- **Across the network installation:** You can perform this if you have the Windows NT installation files available from some other computer on the network.

There are three Windows NT installation diskettes labeled: Setup Disk 1, 2, and 3. Each disk has a corresponding zero length file named Disk101, Disk102, and Disk103. When you build these disks from the CD-ROM, you can tell which of the three disks you have by examining a directory of those disks and looking for the zero length file.

- Disk 101 contains the kernel, HAL, ntdetect.com, and others.
- Disk102 contains drivers, system files, .dll files, system32 folder, server service file, and others.
- Disk103 contains many more drivers and system files.

The following steps begin the Windows NT installation process. Here, you see only the Windows NT DOS-based setup. Windows NT loads drivers, copies the Windows NT install files, and prompts for basic information before it uses the GUI interface. Follow these steps to perform an installation using a bootable CD-ROM server: (If you don't have that type of server, start with Setup Disk #1 and reboot your server. Follow the prompts until Setup asks you to load the CD.)

1. **Insert the Windows NT Server 4.0 CD-ROM into the drive and reboot the computer.**
2. **From the \i386 subdirectory, execute the WINNT file.**

   Note that if your server automatically recognizes the CD-ROM drive upon boot, you will not have to complete this step since the boot sequence will find an AUTORUN file and load Setup automatically.

   The Windows NT Server 4 setup screen appears.

3. **Select the Windows NT Setup option and press Enter.**

   Go get yourself a cup of coffee as Setup copies files to the hard disk (which takes a few minutes). After Setup finishes, it prompts you to restart the computer to continue installation.

4. **Click the Restart Computer button to restart.**

   Setup reboots, loading all sorts of drivers in the process (specifically, we hope, the drivers that can recognize all your system components), along with a nice, blue background. Setup then presents you with a Welcome to Setup screen with four options.

5. **Select the second option, To Set Up Windows NT Now, press Enter, and then press Enter to continue.**

   Setup goes about the process of detecting your fixed drives. At the end of this process, Setup displays the message `Setup Has Recognized The Following Mass Storage Devices` and presents a list of what it found. Here is where it detects IDE, SCSI, and CD-ROM drives. If your devices don't appear on the list, you need to add them at this point. You need to add a driver for each device not on the list, because Windows NT hasn't recognized them and requires you to supply them. If everything looks okay, press the Enter key to go to the next step.

6. **Press the Page Down key to reach the bottom of the lengthy licensing agreement message (after reading the legalese, of course) and then press the F8 key to tell Setup that you read the agreement and accept it.**

   If this server already has Windows NT installed, Setup detects the previous installation and presents you with the following message. If the installation is a new one, you don't see this message.

   ```
   Setup has found Windows NT on your hard disk in the
         directory shown below.
   C:\WINNT "Windows NT Server Version 3.51"

   Setup recommends upgrading this Windows NT installation
         to Microsoft Windows NT Version 4.0. Upgrading
         will preserve user account and security informa-
         tion, user preferences, and other configuration
         information.
   -To upgrade Windows NT in the directory shown above,
         press ENTER
   -To cancel upgrade and install a fresh copy of Windows
         NT, press N
   ```

   Setup then presents a list of hardware and software components that it found on your system and asks you whether that list is correct. (We've yet to find a case where this list is incorrect.)

7. **If the list is correct for your computer, highlight the option for The Above List Matches My Computer and then press Enter; if the list is incorrect, supply Setup with the correct information.**

   Setup presents you with a partition information screen similar to the one that follows. This screen shows information about your hard disk. Remember that we formatted a 200MB DOS FAT drive that you see as an existing drive in the following information. If you didn't format the 200MB drive above, you can create it here along with another partition for NTFS.

   ```
   The list below shows existing partitions and spaces
         available for creating new partitions.

   Use the UP and DOWN ARROW keys to move the highlight to
         an item in the list.
   -To install Windows NT Server on the highlighted parti-
         tion or unpartitioned space, press ENTER.
   -To create a partition in the unpartitioned space,
         press C.
   -To delete the highlighted partition, press D.

   2247 MB Disk 0 at ID 0 on bus 0
   200 MB IDE/ESDI Disk (2047 MB free)
   Unpartitioned space
   ```

8. **Highlight the Unpartitioned Space line and press C.**

   Doing so tells Setup to create a new partition for Windows NT.

9. **Tell Setup what type of file system you want.**

   You can choose Format the Partition Using the FAT File System or Format the Partition Using the NTFS File System. (You want to Select NTFS because you already have a 200MB DOS FAT partition.) Setup tells you to wait while it formats this new partition.

   Setup is now ready to copy the necessary Windows NT files to your hard disk and presents a screen asking whether you want to install the files in the \WINNT subdirectory. This directory is the default directory for Windows NT installations. We like to keep this default because other items you install later look for this directory. Doing so doesn't mean that you can't point other applications and Windows NT utilities to a new directory if you choose; we just prefer not to stray from defaults unless a program forces us to do so.

10. **Press the ENTER key to accept the \WINNT directory or type a new directory name if you must.**

   Windows NT Setup provides lots of default suggestions, including directory placement, VGA settings, and more. The more defaults that you accept during installation, the better are your chances of a smooth installation. Most options you can change later. We like to get through the entire installation first and then tweak settings later.

11. **After Setup asks whether you want it to perform a secondary exhaustive examination of your hard disk, you can safely select the ESC option to skip this examination.**

    We never find a second exam necessary, unless we encounter disk problems. Setup copies the necessary files to your hard disk and then tells you that this portion of Setup is complete and to reboot the server.

12. **Take out all floppies and CD-ROMs you have in the machine and reboot.**

    Setup actually reboots the machine twice. The first time that it reboots, it converts the new disk partition to NTFS. Then it reboots again and resumes installation. Until now, you've seen blue, text-based Setup screens. As Setup itself reappears, it takes the form of a GUI wizard that guides you through the remainder of the installation process. Continue to Step 1 of the following section to continue the installation.

Setup's GUI wizard: Gathering info about your computer

After you complete the DOS portion of the setup, the GUI wizard loads, which provides you with a guide through installation from this point forward. The wizard tells you that it's going to break up the rest of the installation into three phases: gathering information about your computer, installing Windows NT Networking, and finishing Setup. Follow these steps:

1. **On the GUI wizard screen, click the Next button to continue.**

   Setup asks you to enter your name and organization's name.

2. **Enter the information that Setup requests and then click the Next button to continue.**

   Setup's next screen shows you what you just entered and asks you to verify that the information you typed is correct.

3. **If your info is correct, click the Next button again to continue to the next screen; if not, make any necessary changes and then click Next button to continue.**

   Setup requires that you enter the CD key now. This step is Microsoft's way to protect itself against software piracy. This number appears on the yellow sticker on the jewel case for the Windows NT Server 4.0 CD.

4. **Enter the CD key number and click the Next button.**

   We find that writing the CD key on the top of the CD-ROM (where the label is) with a fine-point permanent marker is a handy reminder. Whenever you install Windows NT with that disc, you need only to look on the disc for the key. Otherwise, you must remember to bring the jewel case. Don't write that number on the bottom of the CD, however, because that's where Windows NT itself resides.

Setup next presents a Licensing Mode screen, where you select the radio button for Per Seat Licensing or Per Server Licensing. Check your purchase order to verify what license you purchased before marking this selection. *Per Seat licensing* is typically for use on enterprise networks and *Per Server licensing* on small networks. Be aware that you may change from Per Server licensing to Per Seat licensing only once, so you must consider this installation option carefully before continuing.

5. **Select either the Per Seat Licensing or Per Server Licensing radio button, as appropriate for your situation, and click the Next button to continue.**

6. **Enter a name for the computer, per Setup's prompt, and click the Next button.**

   (This name must be unique on your network.) We prefer that this name also be descriptive of its function (for example, *FS2West* for "file server 2, West wing"). Setup then asks you to select a server type, as the following text shows:

```
Server Type

Please select a type for this server

        -Primary Domain Controller
        -Backup Domain Controller
        -Stand-alone Server
```

7. **Mark the appropriate server type selection and click the Next button.**

   Setup permits only one PDC per domain. If you designate a machine as a PDC and want to make this machine a stand-alone server later, you must reinstall Windows NT on that machine. Consider carefully what type of server you want this machine to be to avoid reinstallation.

8. **Enter an Administrator password for the Windows NT Server, per Setup's prompt.**

   The Administrator password must be 14 characters or shorter. This password is the one that you use to log onto the file server's console either locally or remotely. Write this password down until you memorize it. You can always change it later.

9. **After you enter the password, type it again for confirmation and click the Next button.**

   Setup presents you with a yes/no option to create an ERD. We think that the ERD is valuable — but not right now. We prefer to wait until installation is complete, after we add everything, and then to create this disk.

10. **Choose No for now and click the Next button.**

    From the screen containing the following messages, Setup asks you which components you want to install on this server. Setup marks certain components for install by default, and you may select or deselect any option. We like to install what we can at this point rather than return later to reinstall options. Windows Messaging is handy if you plan to use MS Exchange, and it requires only 4.6MB of disk space. You can leave the Games deselected if you're not inclined to play games at work.

    One additional note: We like to deselect and then reselect those options that are already marked so that we can verify that all components within that selection are included. If you deselect and then select the Accessories option, for example, and you look in the right window pane, you should see a note that 13 of 13 components are selected. This process just ensures that all options within the Accessories component are installed.

    ```
    Select Components
    X Accessibility Options
    X Accessories
    X Communications
      Games
    X Multimedia
      Windows Messaging
    ```

11. **Select or deselect the default components on this screen to match what components you want installed on your server and click the Next button.**

Wait! You're not finished yet! There's still one more phase to complete on the installation, then you can take a break!

Setup's GUI Wizard: Installing Windows NT Networking

In this part of the installation process, you add information about the networking components in your server including domain information, NIC information, and more. Follow these steps:

1. **Click the Next button to start the Installing Windows NT Networking portion of your installation.**

   Setup asks you how you plan to connect this server to the network, as shown in the following text message.

   ```
   Windows NT needs to know how this computer should par-
         ticipate on the network.

    Wired to the network
    Your computer is connected to the network with an ISDN
         adapter or Network adapter

    Remote Access to the network
    Your computer uses a modem to remotely connect to the
         network
   ```

2. **Select the Wired to the Network option and click the Next button.**

   Setup asks whether you want to install Windows NT's Internet Information Server (IIS).

3. **If you plan to use this server on an intranet, or to support Web services on this server, select this option and click the Next button if you want to use Microsoft's IIS product.**

   Later, Setup enables you to choose which of the Internet services (Gopher, FTP, WWW, and more) that you want to install.

   Setup now needs to know what kind of NIC you have installed in this server. It can find out by performing a search to detect the NIC for you, or you can enter this information manually. We like to give Setup the first crack, because it's less work for us!

4. **Click the Start Search button.**

   If your NIC is listed in the HCL, Windows NT should find it and provide its drivers so that you needn't do anything manually. If Setup detects your NIC, it shows that information to you. If it doesn't, you must manually indicate which NIC is in the server by clicking the Select from List button. If the server includes more than one NIC, repeat this process for each NIC and click the Next button.

   Setup now needs to know which protocols this server needs. It gives you three choices: TCP/IP protocol, NWLink IPX/SPX Compatible Transport protocol, and NetBEUI protocol. If the server has more than one NIC, you can assign different protocols to each NIC or you can install all protocols on one NIC. If the server communicates with NetWare devices by using IPX, you need to select the NWLink option. We like to start by selecting the TCP/IP protocol because we use TCP/IP as our primary protocol.

5. **Select the correct protocol option for your server and click the Next button.**

   Setup now presents you with a list of services that it can install on this computer, as the following message screen lists. We like to install all the services listed because Windows NT can be finicky if you try to add a service later on. In fact, some services depend on other services loading first, so if you don't install them now, you can find them quite complicated to add later. We even needed to reinstall Windows NT because we *didn't* load one of these services. Make sure that you select all the necessary options (everything that the following text message lists). If you didn't elect to install IIS, however, you don't see it on this list. We don't need to add additional services, but you can browse them to see which ones aren't installed yet.

   ```
   Listed below are the services that will be installed by
          the system. You may add to this list by clicking
          the Select from list option.
   Microsoft Internet Information Server 2.0
   RPC Configuration
   NetBIOS Interface
   Workstation
   Server
   ```

6. **Select the services that you want Setup to install and click the Next button.**

   Setup now tells you that it's ready to complete this phase of the install by adding the networking components you selected.

7. **Click the Next button unless you want to edit your previous choices in which case you click the Back button and make any corrections.**

   You now see Setup copying NIC drivers; if it needs IRQ numbers and DMA settings, it asks you to enter that information on-screen. If you used the HQT tool we mentioned earlier in the section entitled "What's Under the Hood," you can glean the information that Setup needs from its report.

   Setup installs whatever protocols you selected. If you chose TCP/IP, it requests a TCP/IP address for this machine. If a DHCP server on the network automatically assigns IP addresses, you can provide Setup with this information. If you don't, Setup asks you to input an IP address manually. For most servers, manual entry is necessary, because address changes make servers too hard to identify on a network. Click the No button to the Setup prompt "Do you wish to use DHCP services" and see the following tip for an explanation why.

We prefer to say no (click the No button) to the Setup prompt "Do you wish to use DHCP services" during the installation process because we can specify this information later. If you tell Setup to use a DHCP server to assign an IP address and Setup can't find that server, you end up troubleshooting something else during your Windows NT install. You can enter a dummy IP address during installation and then change it later if you want.

If you followed our advice in the previous tip, Setup next presents a tabbed window similar to the one shown in Figure 9-1. The TCP/IP configuration window opens on the IP Address tab. Setup selects the Specify an IP Address option by default if you selected No to the DHCP server earlier. Here is where you must enter an IP address for this server manually.

8. **If you already know the IP address information, enter it now; if not, use a dummy address, as long as it's valid.**

   You must enter a valid subnet mask along with this IP address.

9. **If you know the DNS server information, the IP gateway address, and WINS server address, click on those respective tabs and enter that information now.**

   If you don't know this information, you can add it after the installation is complete. Click the Next button when you're done.

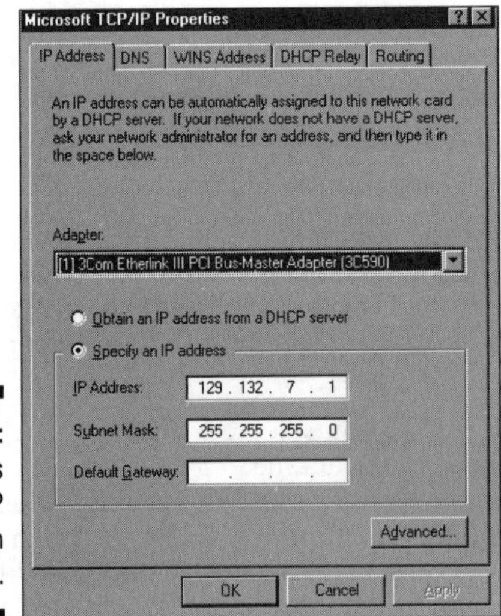

Figure 9-1: Setup's TCP/IP information screen.

Setup binds whatever protocols you specify to the NICs and services and presents you with a list that indicates how you may find information on this server. We don't like to rearrange the order at this time. Again, the more defaults you accept during installation, the fewer problems you encounter in tweaking Windows NT before initial installation is complete.

10. **Click the Next button to continue.**

    Setup now gives you the opportunity to revise any of your previous choices.

11. **Click the Next button again if you don't need to make any revisions to your previous choices or the Back button if you do.**

    If you told Setup that this machine is a PDC earlier, you must provide a name for the domain now. Setup already knows the computer name for this server because you assigned that earlier. Chapter 13 covers domains in detail.

12. **Type in the domain name and click the Next button to continue.**

    Setup is ready to complete this phase of the installation by installing the networking components you chose and configured.

13. **Click the Finish button to go on to the next Setup phase.**

Setup's GUI Wizard: Finishing setup

If you chose to install IIS earlier, Setup asks you to configure IIS components, as the following message screen shows. As you select each component, Setup tells you the subdirectory in which it plans to install that component. We prefer to install all services at this time because we can delete them later. Installing services now and deleting them later is easier than adding services later. Notice that none of these components takes up much disk space, so you don't need to worry about disk space at this time.

```
Internet Information Server 2.0 Installation

     Internet Service Manager
     World Wide Web Services
     WWW Services Examples
     Internet Service Manager (HTML)
     Gopher Service
     FTP Service
     ODBC Drivers & Administration
```

To finish your installation, follow these steps:

1. **Mark those components that you want to configure and then click OK.**

   If you know now, for example, that this server doesn't need FTP services, you can deselect that choice here. Setup creates subdirectories for these services if those directories don't yet exist and then asks you if you want to change those subdirectories. We always like to accept the default subdirectories that Setup presents whenever possible.

   After you click OK, Setup begins to install the IIS options you select and provides you with informational messages along the way or asks you to input more information. If you select Gopher, for example, Setup prompts you to configure it further after installation through the Control Panel. You don't need to do anything but click the OK button on this message. If it's installing the ODBC drivers (assuming that you selected that option), Setup stops to ask you to highlight specific ODBC drivers. At this time, the only option available is the SQL server ODBC, so you highlight that option and click the OK button.

2. **Take whatever action Setup prompts you to do and click OK to continue with the installation.**

   Setup next presents a date and time screen so that you can set these elements on this server, as shown in Figure 9-2.

3. **Use the down arrow to scroll down and highlight your local time zone and then specify whether you want this server to automatically change its time for Daylight Savings by marking the box next to that option.**

   This step is handy, because by setting the time now, you don't need to remember to set the time after DST kicks in.

4. **Click on the Date tab and add the correct date to this server and click the Close button.**

   Setup now wants to test and install this server's display adapter.

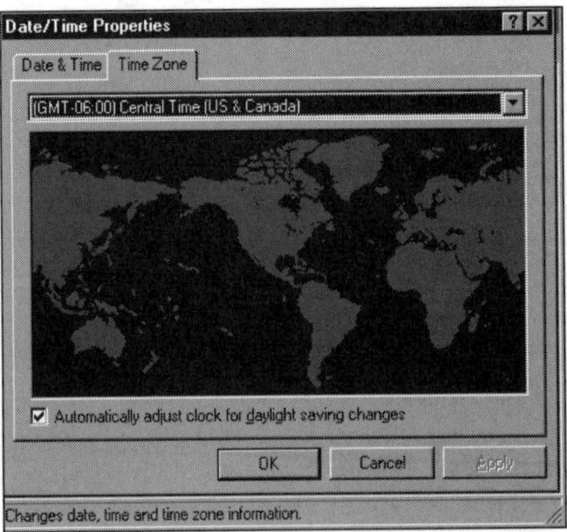

Figure 9-2: Setup's Date and Time Zone screen.

5. **Click the Test button to test the video settings.**

   You'll see a screen with all sorts of colors and lines on it, and after about five seconds, Setup will come back and ask you if you saw the screen okay. Many people forget to hit the Test button, and Setup doesn't move on until you test the video settings.

6. **Select the appropriate settings and click the OK button after you finish.**

   Unless you have a specific monitor, you're best off just selecting the VGA settings for now until you're sure the entire installation completes. You can always add other video drivers later. If you introduce something that doesn't work, you may not know whether the fault's that of the driver or whether something's wrong with the installation.

Finished! Setup now tells you that it needs to restart your computer. After it reboots, you need to enter the Administrator's password you chose. Phew!

Copying the \i386 subdirectory from both your Windows NT Server 4.0 CD-ROM and your Service Pack disc to your newly installed server makes drivers and other resources immediately available to you should you want to add services and resources later. If you don't take this recommended step, you must insert the CD-ROMs every time that you want to add resources or services to that machine.

P.S. Post-Installation Needs

After you finish the basic installation, you've simply defined a basic server. You need to dress it up with things such as users, groups, applications, services, and printers, as we describe in the following sections. We also present some additional fixes and preventative items to install and create should your server ever crash or attract unwanted bugs.

Windows NT Service Packs

Microsoft supplies Service Packs to fix bugs in its software for most of its products. After Microsoft first releases a product or a new version to the general public, no Service Packs are available. Users soon begin sending bug reports, however, and Microsoft engineers fix those bugs. Every now and then, Microsoft gathers up these changes and places the related fixes into Service Packs for each product. Service Packs are cumulative; if you install Service Pack 4 (SP4), you needn't apply SP1, SP2, or SP3.

The fixes in these Service Packs are designed to get rid of the bugs in your system and tide you over until Microsoft releases a new version of its product. If you install Windows NT Server 3.51, for example, you apply Microsoft's Windows NT Server SP1 for Windows NT Server 3.51 after it becomes available. Then, as SP2 becomes available, you apply that fix to your Windows NT 3.51 Server . . . and so on. Note that the Service Packs are cumulative, so if you just now install Windows NT 3.51, you would only need to apply SP5 since that is the most current at the time of this writing. After you install Windows NT 4.0, you start over but apply each new Service Pack for Windows NT 4.0 as it becomes available (SP1 then SP2 and so on).

After you complete a basic Windows NT installation, you need to apply the latest Service Pack to this installation to help avoid known bugs. If you have the Service Pack available on a CD-ROM, that's great! As you install Windows NT, Setup enables a feature called *autorun* for you. Thereafter, any time that you insert a CD-ROM into the server, Windows NT automatically opens the installation screen for that product. All you need to do is insert the Service Pack CD and click the option on the left that says "Install Service Pack 4" to install it from the pop-up browser screen. This option calls the spsetup.bat file and installs the Service Pack 4. If you don't have the Service Pack on disc, download it from Microsoft's Web site (at `www.microsoft.com`). It's a large file, so download it while the Internet's not busy and you have some time to burn.

You may have to install the Service Pack each time you install a new component or service on Windows NT. That's because you're installing the component using software and drivers from the Windows NT Installation CD-ROM which may contain older versions of like files than the Service Pack CD. So, if you install something new on your Windows NT Server and it doesn't function properly, reapply the Service Pack and then retry.

Emergency Repair Disk

We suggest, too, that you create the ERD that we talk about in the section "Setup's GUI wizard: Gathering info about your computer," earlier in this chapter. After you complete your installation, with all your options selected, is a good time to build an ERD.

To begin with, you need a blank, formatted floppy disk. You find the repair disk utility in the \WINNT\SYSTEM32 subdirectory. Click the RDISK application and select the option for creating a disk. Later, if your system crashes, Windows NT can use this disk to try to rebuild your system. Each time you update your Windows NT Server with new software, Service Packs, or configuration changes, you always want to update your ERD.

If Installations Go South . . .

We hope you have a smooth installation, but you may encounter some problems. If so, you can look to this section.

- **CD-ROM problems:** The entire Windows NT installation ships on a CD-ROM, so if you can't read the CD, you can't install Windows NT (unless you're installing over a network). CD-ROMs are similar to music records in that one little scratch or speck of dust on the surface can cause problems. The CD may be okay, on the other hand, but the drive isn't functioning correctly or Windows NT doesn't recognize the drive. We hope that your drive appears on the HCL. To determine whether the drive or the CD isn't functioning, take the CD to another CD-ROM drive and see whether you can read it there. After you determine which element is the culprit, you can replace either one and retry your installation.
- **Hardware problems:** If Windows NT Setup doesn't recognize a server's hardware, it's likely to stop. Make sure that the machine's hardware appears in the HCL and that you configured all devices correctly. If you have more than one SCSI device, for example, make sure that they are chained correctly.
- **Blue screen of death:** Sometimes Setup simply crashes and gives you a blue screen; other times, it gives you a display of error codes that only a propeller head could understand. By itself, the blue screen simply means that you must reboot. If you get a fancy stop screen, however, you can look at the first few lines to determine the error code. Using this number, you can look up the error message in the error-message manual. Stops typically occur if a driver problem occurs; if you look beyond the first few lines of the error message screen, it tells you which drivers were loaded at the time the crash occurred. A good idea is to write the first few lines of the stop screen down before attempting to reboot. If you're feeling really nerdy, run the WinDbg utility that you find on the installation CD-ROM under \Support\Debug — but you must connect the malfunctioning server to another server to transmit and view the debugging information.
- **Connectivity problems:** Installing a machine as a BDC to join an existing domain requires that the existing PDC be visible to Setup. Check to make sure that you typed the domain name correctly. One character off and Setup can't find it. Be sure that all network links leading to the PDC are up and that the PDC is online.
- **Dependency problems:** Some services in Windows NT depend on other services loading correctly. If service A doesn't load, service B doesn't work, and you get error messages if service B is set to automatically start at bootup. If a NIC doesn't install correctly, for example, all services that use that NIC fail to start as well. Your first order of

business, therefore, is to get the NIC functioning correctly. If you get this far in the installation process, you can view the Error Log (Start⇨Programs⇨Administrative Tools⇨Event Viewer) to see which service did not start and then work your way from there.

- **Script file errors:** The Windows NT automated install program is not forgiving if you mistype a script. If a script stops midway and the Windows NT Setup program asks you for manual input, you entered something incorrectly. Check the input file to look for transposed letters or anything else that may be out of place. Scripts expect to feed the computer exactly what you put in the script file. If you don't enter the right information, Setup doesn't receive the information it expects.

- **SETUP.TXT file:** If you encounter driver problems or other problems missing from the preceding list, obtain and read this file to see whether some late-breaking news that Microsoft couldn't get into the manuals may have affected your installation. The file resides in the \i386 subdirectory.

About Automated Installation

Windows NT includes an unattended installation feature that enables you to install Windows NT without keyboard interaction. You need only to start the process and walk away. Unattended installation uses a script file that pipes in information and keyboard strokes from a data file that you compose in advance. If you already know all the answers to the questions that the install program asks, you can answer these questions and place them in a data file. You can use more than one data file for different types of installation.

Unattended installation is great for organizations that install Windows NT over and over on identical machines with the same hardware configurations. Large enterprise networks that include remote offices can also take advantage of unattended installation, because home office administrators can customize script files and transmit them to a remote office. The caveat here is that you must test the script files thoroughly in the central office for accuracy; otherwise, the folks in the remote office may soon be screaming for help!

Chapter 10

Configuring the Network Hardware (Blech!)

In This Chapter

- Plugging ain't playing
- Making hardware work
- Driving to town — understanding drivers
- Doing it with DOS
- Checking to make sure everything works
- Mediating hardware conflicts
- Building the basic toolkit

Seems that the hardest part of setting up a computer system is getting all the hardware to cooperate with each other. Just as you get one device working, another quits working. When you begin to understand some of the internal workings of Windows NT Server and what it requires of hardware devices, the task of setting up hardware becomes a little less daunting. In this chapter, you figure out device settings and resources, discover where the potential problems may exist, and find out how to avoid hardware conflicts.

There's No Plug and Play Here, Man!

Plug and Play allows you to install devices and resources on a computer without conflict. The way it works is that a computer contains a Plug and Play Basic Input Output System (BIOS) and a Plug and Play operating system (OS). Any time Plug and Play hardware or resources are installed on a computer, they are automatically configured so that no conflict arises between IRQs (interrupt requests), memory, and other configuration issues. Thus, the catchy title: "Plug" for plug the device in, "and Play," meaning your device is ready to go.

Windows NT Server does not support Plug and Play. You can install a driver named PNPISA.INF (found on the Windows NT Installation CD, in the directory /DRIVLIB/PNPISA/I386) to detect Plug and Play resources in your server, but don't call Microsoft if you want any support for this. Microsoft doesn't support this on Windows NT Server, so you're on your own if it doesn't work properly. To install the driver, just right-click on the PNPISA.INF file.

Installing this driver sets some Registry values located in:
`HKEY_LOCAL_MACHINE\SYSTEM\CurrentControlSet\Services\pnpisa\Enum\`

We don't like to install unsupported equipment or drivers on our Windows NT Server. Instead, we prefer to look at the Hardware Compatibility List (HCL) and install only those listed components. If you're installing a server at home that no one will use, by all means, tinker around with the Plug and Play driver. However, if you are setting up this server for an organization, we recommend that you don't implement the Plug and Play driver. Even though it might work, it might not when you least expect it.

Getting All Your Hardware to Play Nicely Together

Just imagine: Everything on the server is running smoothly, and you add one device. Suddenly, the server craters or just one device or port stops working. You might install a NIC and all of a sudden, the serial port stops working, which happens to be the port you use to connect to the Internet. Consequently, you have to spend eight hours trying to get the serial port to work, and in the meantime, your users can't dial in or use the network. Nothing can be more frustrating. To avoid such a scenario, try to install your new devices during non-working hours. We like to see all installations done on a weekend, and preferably, on a test server first.

Before you install a device, research that device and find out if any known bugs are associated with it. The known bugs possibly are cured by simply installing the latest Windows NT Service Pack or by installing a newer driver for the device. If you have this information ahead of time and have downloaded the necessary drivers or Service Packs, you can avoid having to download any drivers when your server is torn open. You can perform searches on Internet search engines, such as `www.yahoo.com` and `www.search.com`, with keywords that denote the new device you plan to purchase and install. You can also join a mailing list ahead of time, such as WINNT-L on the Internet (`www.liszt.com`), and post a question like `I'm about to purchase and install XX device and I would like to know if there are any known bugs associated with this device.`

What's in a mailing list and newsgroup?

Internet mailing lists are found on just about every topic you can think of. New ones form every day, and we find the computer-related mailing lists extremely useful. So what are mailing lists and how do they work? Essentially, mailing lists consist of a group of people with a common interest who post questions and answer questions on a given topic. Mailing lists are so called because you must first sign up or subscribe to the list. Once you belong to the list, you can read all the mail sent to you and also post a related question to the entire mailing list. This means that everyone on the list will see your question.

Mailing lists are global and, usually, computer-related lists have quite a roster of members. If you belong to one that has 3,000 members, chances are that at least one of those 3,000 people will provide you with a solution or answer to most of your questions and problems. Sometimes you might get three answers to one question with different approaches to solving your problem. You are essentially tapping into the knowledge of all the people on the list who may have done what you're trying to do already.

You can turn to a couple of places that list Internet mailing lists: `www.liszt.com` and `www.onelist.com`. In fact, at the latter site, you can create and moderate your own list for free. So, if you don't find the list you're looking for, create one and invite people to join.

Newsgroups are similar to mailing lists in that you are tapping into the knowledge of people around the world. The mechanics are slightly different, however, because you must have a news reader program (which comes with most popular browsers), and your ISP must support that program. Following are a couple of good newsgroups for you to start out with, and you can join others as you become more familiar with how they work:

- `comp.os.ms-windows.net.setup.misc`
- `microsoft.public.windowsnt.setup`

Visit `www.ntfaq.com` and read through the frequently asked question (FAQ) information provided to gain valuable information on various Windows NT topics. John Savill, who maintains the site, spends two hours a day keeping this up-to-date. For example, on John's site you learn that there's a tool on the Windows NT Server Installation CD that allows you to test SCSI devices. He tells you where on the CD to look for this tool, and which manufacturers it supports.

Sometimes you can employ a few tricks to get things to work, and if you don't do research ahead of time, you may spend extra hours you don't have in order to solve problems.

Buy smart

Most people have a tendency to buy cheaper equipment for your workstations to save money, but we like to buy smart on the server. *Buying smart* means that you should spend a little more money on the server components and buy name-brand equipment. For example, a mouse is something that you are going to use on the server for everything. Pay a little more ($10) and get the Microsoft mouse and you'll have mouse activity as soon as you install the server. The monitor is also something you'll use a lot. Buy a monitor from a well-known vendor and it's sure to be on the Hardware Compatibility List (HCL).

As for the actual server's motherboard and CPU, we like both Compaq and HP servers because they are very dependable servers that have been in the networking arena for quite some time to have a proven track record. Dell is coming into the forefront quickly as a server with a good track record. Compaq has the longest record working as a server for Microsoft and therefore has great technical support along with a helpful Web site.

Keep in mind that servers are different machines than the regular desktop machine. You need a server built for expansion, such as HP's Netservers and Compaq's Proliants and Prosignias. These servers have slots so your server can expand with more disk controllers, memory, and CPUs. And, last but not least, these servers ship with CD-ROM drives able to boot your Windows NT Installation CD automatically without having to use the floppies.

If you have operations globally, you want to pick a computer company that is also global.

Understand the hardware

Don't install equipment, devices, or drivers on the server before understanding its basic operation and knowing how to undo something. For example, it's possible to install a video driver and then reboot the server, and not be able to see anything on the monitor. This situation can be scary, but if you know ahead of time that you can back out of this by choosing the standard VGA option at boot time, you can install new drivers with confidence.

Windows NT registers all devices and drivers in the Control Panel⇨Devices section. Browsing through this area helps you learn what Windows NT is loading for drivers for specific devices. Sometimes, Windows NT loads the wrong driver, and you have to manually unload one and load another. This predicament is common, for example, with the EIDE hard drives.

You can change resource settings for any device using Windows Diagnostics (Start⇨Programs⇨Administrative Tools⇨Windows NT Diagnostics). If you load the Plug and Play driver and then set a lot of resource settings manually, some of the Plug and Play devices may not work properly. This is because Windows NT is trying to set resources and you may be overriding them with your settings. Try not to change configurations if you don't have to.

The following sections cover the most important devices you need to familiarize yourself with on the server.

CD-ROM drives

CD-ROM drives can be IDE, EIDE, or SCSI. What's interesting here, however, is that although you might install an IDE CD-ROM drive, you can still find it in the SCSI devices listing in Control Panel, as shown in Figure 10-1. If you select one from the HCL, Windows NT should recognize it because its installation program loads drivers for SCSI, EIDE, and IDE at boot time. Some drives don't have drivers yet, so you can load the Windows NT generic driver. Chances are, though, that not all of the functionality of the drive will be available.

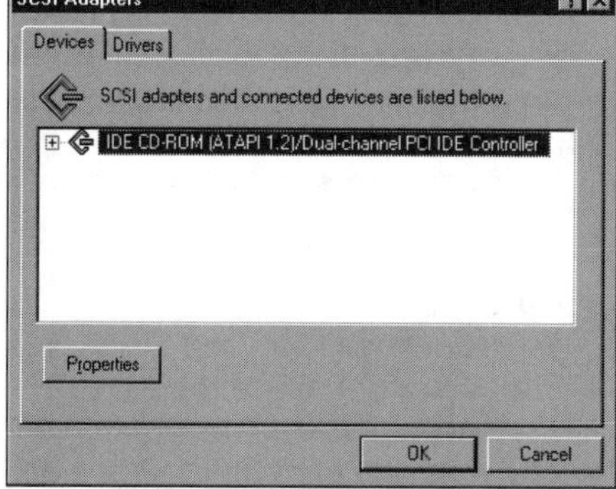

Figure 10-1: Viewing the NT CD-ROM devices.

Hard drives

Hard drives can be IDE, EIDE, or SCSI. Sometimes you try to load a hard disk that is EIDE and Windows NT gets a little confused and loads the IDE driver (ATAPI.SYS) instead. In cases where Windows NT messes up, you have to go unload the wrong driver and reload the correct one in the Devices section of Control Panel.

Not only can you install hard drives in your system, but you can also configure them several different ways using the Windows NT Disk Administrator utility in the Administrative Tools. Here you can create partitions, mirror drives, and create stripe sets.

When you divide a physical hard drive into separate logical drives, you *partition* the hard drive. You may be familiar with this concept from being able to have C and D drives on a local workstation. Although you only have one physical drive, logically it appears as two or three or however many partitions you create. When you add a file system, such as NTFS or FAT, to one of the partitions, it becomes a *volume*. You can allow volumes to span across multiple partitions and you can group those partitions into one volume set. So if you have one physical drive that you create two partitions on, then install NTFS on one partition, and FAT on the other, you end up with two volumes. Each associated volume gets assigned a drive letter designation, such as C:, D:, or E:. If you have three partitions, and you install FAT on partition #1, NTFS on partition #2, and NTFS on partition #3, you end up with three volumes.

Depending on the type of disks you install, you can add fault tolerance to your system by *mirroring* or *striping* (with parity) the drives. These techniques are levels of Redundant Array of Inexpensive Disks (RAID), which is supported in Windows NT Server, but only levels 0 (striping no parity), 1 (disk mirroring), and 5 (stripe with parity).

Mirroring a drive (RAID level 1) is really taking two drives and attaching them to one disk channel. Everything that is written to Disk A is also written to Disk B. If Disk A fails, Disk B can take over until Disk A can be rebuilt. Obviously, because there are two drives to write to, write activity takes longer. However, because there are two drives to retrieve information from, read activity can occur faster if multiple heads are present to perform multiple reads at one time. Mirroring requires twice the disk space of whatever amount you need.

The drawback of mirroring is that if the disk channel fails, then both of the mirrored drives connected to the disk channel will fail at the same time. To prevent this sort of failure, another layer of fault tolerance can be added called *duplexing,* in which you place the disks on two separate channels. You can mirror these drives across the different channels to have disk mirroring and disk duplexing at the same time, providing protection against both disk crash and disk channel failures.

Striping with parity (RAID level 5) allows you to have a number of disks and to spread *parity* information across all the disks. If one of the disks crashes, the system can rebuild the information on the disk using the parity information on the other remaining disks. For example, if you install four disks and place them all in a stripe set with parity, then data is written to the disks in stripes across three of the four disks; and parity information, from which the data can be reconstructed, is stored on the fourth disk. The data is written to the disks (striped across) starting from disk 1 and going to disk 4. This continues in this fashion and then goes back to disk 1 to start again. In each cycle, the parity information is stored on a different disk. In other words, all the parity information is not stored on one particular disk.

Striping with parity doesn't require double the disk space like mirroring does, and it can be just as effective. It does take up the equivalent of one disk though. If you have four drives, 25 percent of the total disk space will be used to contain the parity information.

Striping with no parity (RAID level 0) is similar to RAID level 5, but no parity information is written to reconstruct the drives should one fail. The problem with this approach is that there is no fault tolerance built in. If one drive fails, you lose all of the data since it can't be reconstructed. We don't recommend you use this RAID level.

There are differences between software RAID handling and hardware RAID handling (hardware array controllers). When you perform software RAID (the server handles everything), you chew up processor cycles. If you implement hardware array controllers, the process of striping and calculation of parity information can be offloaded to the controllers.

You can find more information about RAID and performance factors by doing a search on the Internet with the keyword "RAID." You can also visit sites like Adaptec (`www.adaptec.com`) and search their site for white papers and detailed information.

Video adapter/monitor

Windows NT has a standard VGA driver that it loads at boot time. This driver should be sufficient for most of your needs in viewing the network. We don't like to allow Windows NT to try to detect the video card because sometimes it hangs the installation if it detects improperly. Instead, we prefer to leave it at VGA until after the installation and then change settings if we want to. You can view and change information about the server's video under Control Panel⇨Display⇨Settings, as shown in Figure 10-2.

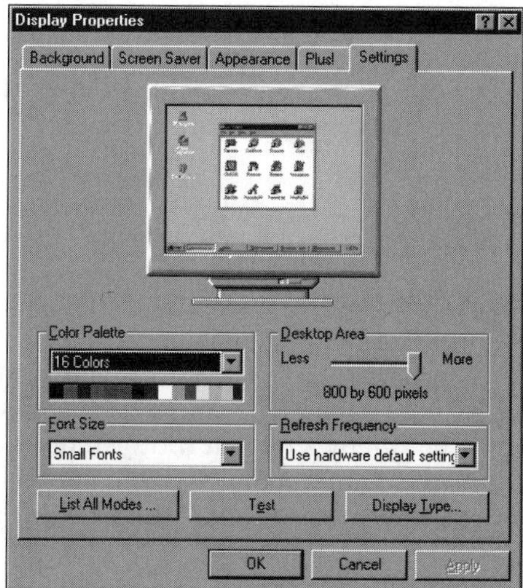

Figure 10-2: Viewing or changing the Windows NT display properties.

If you have Windows NT 3.51 video drivers, don't use them on Windows NT 4 because Microsoft reprogrammed this area and chances are you'll crash your server. We recommend that you always obtain updated drivers, but in this case — we insist.

Memory

Memory can foul you up because you can buy cards that have bad chips on them, plus you can configure your memory so that it causes problems. Always have spare memory cards, or at least know where to get them. If more than one device is loaded into the same memory location, you get memory errors. Always check the memory listing to see what devices are loading and where, as shown in Figure 10-3.

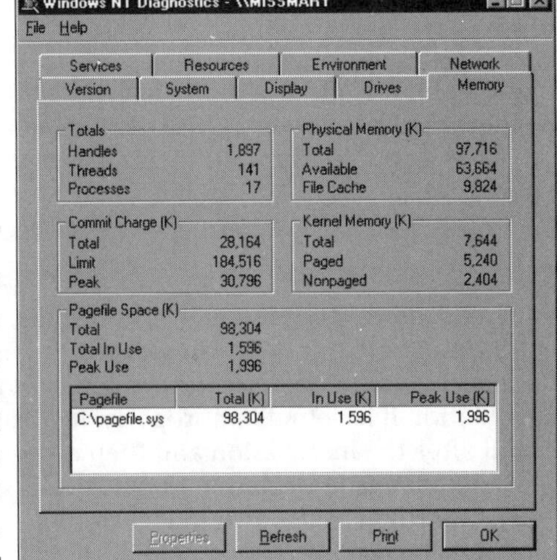

Figure 10-3: Viewing information about devices loaded in memory.

At the end of this chapter, in the "Essential Installation Toolkit" section, we discuss some memory debugging tools you can download from Microsoft's Web site to poke further into your memory.

Understanding the installation process behind the scenes

Figure out what Windows NT is doing when it's installing components, or itself, and you can find ways to determine what's not working properly. For example, if you attempt to install Windows NT but the system hangs when it tries to determine what hardware is in the box, you might spend hours swapping out parts to figure out which one doesn't work. However, you can make your life easier if you know that Windows NT uses a program called NTDETECT and that you can create a version of NTDETECT that steps through each component it's trying to detect and provide information to you.

Follow these steps to create a version of NTDETECT so that you can watch the process as it occurs:

1. **Use the Windows NT Server installation floppy #1.**

   This is the first floppy disk of three that ships with Windows NT and, optionally, Windows NT allows you to build these disks if you lose them. If you haven't created these disks yet, see the section titled "The Essential Installation Toolkit," Step 2, in this chapter, for more information.

2. **Copy \support\NTDETECT.CHK from the Windows NT Installation CD to your floppy disk and name it NTDETECT.COM.**

3. **Put the floppy in Drive A of the server and reboot it. As Windows NT boots and performs the detection process, it displays the information for you.**

You also should know how to interrupt the installation process while Windows NT is detecting system components. For example, you may want to manually install SCSI drivers during the installation process. You can do this by pressing the F6 key when Windows NT displays the message "Setup is inspecting your hardware."

Once you understand the processes that occur on this system and how they occur, you can make adjustments and changes a lot easier. If you can afford to, get a spare system and play around with it. Hit all sorts of keys and find out what they do. Try to crash the test system and then fix it.

Drivers Wanted (How to Find 'em and Grab 'em)

A *driver* is a small software program designed to translate instructions from the operating system into a format that peripherals can understand. Peripherals typically don't operate properly without a driver because the operating system speaks one language, and peripherals talk their own language. For example, installing a printer on a network without installing the corresponding printer driver is unusual. You can find generic drivers for most devices and when you don't have the device's specific driver, sometimes the generic driver will operate the peripheral. Using the generic driver, however, may prevent you from getting some of the bells and whistles from the device.

You obtain the latest drivers for devices and resources from one of two locations: Microsoft Web site (`www.microsoft.com`) or the manufacturer's Web site. If you install only devices listed on the HCL, then you're likely to find the device driver on the Windows NT Server 4 Installation CD. This driver, however, may not be the latest driver available. We recommend that you visit both Microsoft's Web site and the manufacturer's Web site to verify that you have the latest driver, because updated drivers fix bugs that exist in previous versions of the drivers.

When you download a driver, you want to be sure that you grab the Windows NT driver and not another operating system's driver. Windows NT is very specific about the drivers it uses. For example, if you download the Windows 95/98 driver and try to install it on your Windows NT computer, it won't work. Remember that the driver translates information between the operating system and the device or resource. So, if you load the driver for Windows 95/98, the driver is expecting instructions in a Windows 95/98 format, not Windows NT.

First, Do It with DOS

Encountering difficulty in getting Windows NT to recognize a device isn't uncommon. We find it helpful in these cases to install the device on DOS to see if the device is even functioning. DOS is much more forgiving than Windows NT when it comes to recognizing devices. Remember though that you'll need the DOS driver for this device, not the Windows NT driver.

Checking Your Work

After you get everything installed, you can look at all of the settings for your devices and system resources to see if there are any conflicts. Figure 10-4 is a screenshot of the Windows NT Diagnostic tool found under Administrative Tools. You can gain all kinds of information from this tool regarding your system's IRQ and memory usage, and more.

Mediating Hardware Conflicts

Because Plug and Play isn't supported by Windows NT, you have to manage hardware resources yourself. Having more than two devices conflict with one another when you install them is possible, so in this section you discover the most common items you need to know about to avoid such conflict: IRQ, Base I/O, Direct Memory Access (DMA), and serial and parallel (COM and LPT) ports.

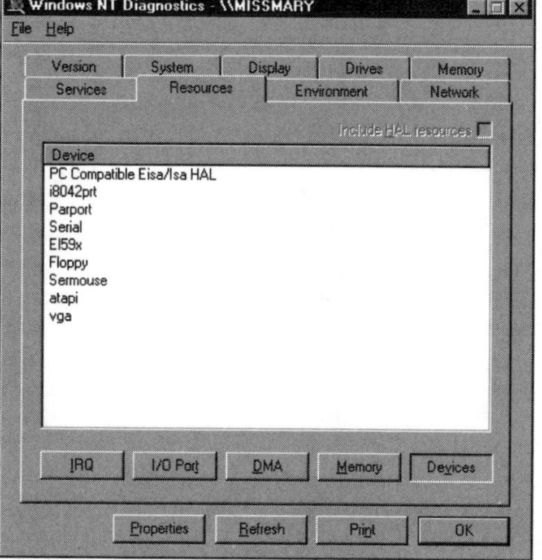

Figure 10-4: A screenshot showing the Windows NT display of system resources.

Interrupt requests (IRQs)

Devices and resources in a computer need a way to notify the processor when they have data to transmit or just need attention. They do this by using an *interrupt,* which essentially tells the processor, "Hey man, I need your attention." When you plug a board into a slot on the computer's motherboard, there is a connection between the slot and the processor known as the *interrupt line.* The device sends its message through this channel to the processor.

Devices are assigned IRQ numbers, which must be unique. Each time a device needs attention, it sends its associated IRQ information to the processor so the CPU knows which device needs attention. If you have two devices assigned the same IRQ number, then when the processor sees the interrupt, it doesn't know which device needs attention.

Some devices, such as NICs, have buffer areas for data. If a NIC sends an interrupt to the CPU and the CPU does not process or move that data to another area of memory, the data can drop off into never-never land.

When you first install a device and find that something else doesn't work, there's a good chance that the device you just installed is grabbing an IRQ that another device uses. Sometimes IRQs are manually set with jumpers on boards or dip switches, so you need to be careful when you plug boards in. Windows NT allows you to manage your device settings, as shown in Figure 10-5.

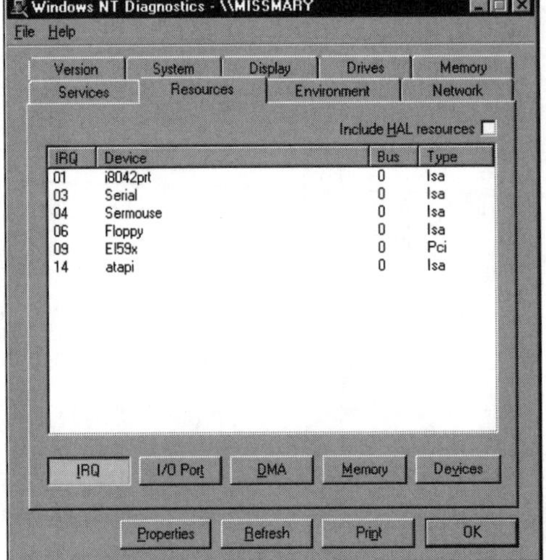

Figure 10-5: Viewing IRQ information for devices using the Windows NT Diagnostics Tool.

Direct memory access (DMA)

Direct memory access (DMA) is a chip located on the motherboard that moves data from a card (for example, NIC) to the main memory instead of the CPU performing the task. This process frees up the CPU to perform its processing tasks while the DMA chip handles the movement of data. The card still notifies the CPU, in the form of an interrupt, that it has data to be moved. The CPU then notifies the DMA chip to go do the work.

Now, you can do something special with DMA. You can place a DMA chip directly on a card and allow the card to move data directly to and from memory without calling on the CPU. Some NICs are designed with DMA chips on them. This is called *bus mastering* and it's supported in Windows NT if you have at least Service Pack 3 installed, but you may have to enable it with the \support\utils\i386\DMACHECK.EXE utility found on the Service Pack CD. You can find more information about using this utility from Microsoft's Knowledge Base article: `support.microsoft.com/support/kb/articles/q191/7/74.asp`.

Base I/O (input/output) address

Devices that hold data, such as NICs, need address space so that other devices and the CPU know where that data is. This address is known as the *Base I/O address.* The problem comes when two devices are trying to use the same address space in memory. When the CPU goes to get some expected data, it finds garbage instead. Your job is to look at the devices and make sure that none of these addresses conflict. You can do this with the Windows NT Diagnostics Tool in Administrative Tools, as shown in Figure 10-6.

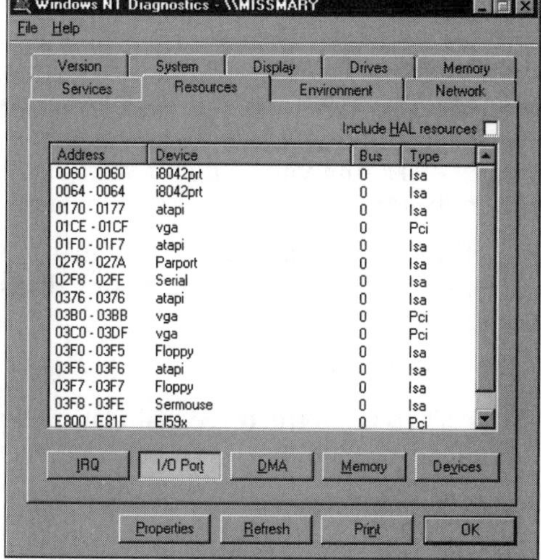

Figure 10-6: Viewing the Windows NT Diagnostics Base I/O addresses on a system.

Serial and parallel ports (COM & LPT)

Ports are the receptacles on the back of the computer where you plug in peripherals and devices. Some ports come built in like the parallel and serial ports, and some you add by plugging cards into the motherboard. You can even add extra serial and parallel ports if you like.

Many parallel ports for LPT1 have factory defaults set to IRQ 7. If you attempt to load another device using this IRQ, you get unexpected results. Some NIC cards come preset to IRQ 3, which is commonly used for serial ports. You want to take a look at all your devices if you encounter a problem and change any settings to unused ones.

The Essential Installation Toolkit

If you have your tool bag ready, we discuss some items we think you may want to include in your bag of tricks.

We keep the following tools handy for all occasions:

- **Set of bootable DOS floppies.** Even if you have just Windows 95, we've always found these DOS floppies to be helpful when you need to boot a machine and remove partitions. On your floppies, have a copy of FDISK.EXE (for creating, removing, or adding partitions), DELPAR.EXE (for deleting partitions), and DELTREE.EXE (for cleaning up after partial installs or disk problems).

- **Set of bootable Windows NT floppies.** In case your CD-ROM is not recognized as bootable by Windows NT or your machine for some reason, you can build bootable floppies for Windows NT that you can create during the installation process or separately. Windows NT ships with three bootable floppies, but if you lose them, you can build them. This process builds three disks that you can boot your machine with and load the appropriate drivers so Windows NT will install properly.

  To build these floppies, insert your Windows NT Installation CD-ROM into your server and have three blank formatted floppy disks available. Then follow these steps:

  1. **Start⇨Run \i386\winnt32 /ox.**

     This tells Windows NT to build the three installation floppies and will prompt you to insert each floppy as it copies files.

  2. **Insert each floppy when prompted.**

- **Generic Windows NT boot floppy.** There are times when you need to boot your Windows NT machine with all generic drivers just to get it to boot. To find out more about how to do this, please turn to Chapter 24 for the details.

- **Windows NT–related CDs.** Always keep the Windows NT Server 4 installation CD and latest Windows NT Server 4 Service Pack handy. We like to write the CD-Key on the CDs themselves with an unerasable marker because we always seem to lose the jewel cases that contains the CD-Keys on the back of them.

- **Driver diskettes.** Any device or resource you plug into your network has a corresponding driver. Although many of these drivers are found on the Windows NT Server Installation CD, they might not be the latest. As you add drivers to your network, keep a copy of them on a set of disks that you keep together.

- **Windows NT OEM Support Tools.** Download these diagnostic tools for free from Microsoft's site: `ftp://ftp.microsoft.com/bussys/winnt/winnt-public/tools/OEMSupportTools/OEMTools.exe`. This 5MB file is not for the faint of heart. It includes the following tools:

  - **Kernel debugger:** Good for examining the dumps reported when the system crashes.
  - **Kernel memory space analyzer:** Another dump tool for poking into kernel memory problems.
  - **Pool enhancements:** Memory pool tools.

Chapter 11
Printing on the Network

In This Chapter

- Printing the Windows NT way
- Meeting the Printers Folder
- Adding a (networked) print device
- Sharing print device access
- Managing Windows NT-based print devices
- Teeing off with the right print device driver
- Preventing print device problems

Next to not being able to access network resources, nothing freaks your users out more than not being able to print out their work. We bet you can't find a network administrator who can say that he or she hasn't struggled with print devices (such as laser printers) at one time or another. We think Microsoft designed Windows NT with a good model for printing and, in this chapter, you'll find out the specifics on how to set up print devices on your network and how to avoid some common problems.

Throughout this chapter, we use the Microsoft terminology "print device" and "printer," which may be confusing in the real world. Microsoft defines "print device" as the physical printer, such as an HP LaserJet 4Si and they define "printer" as the spooler. We use their terms here to be technically accurate. However, if this is your first time working with Windows NT, this may be confusing.

Windows NT Has a Print Model

Windows NT Server's print scheme has these five basic pieces as you trace a path from the user to the print device:

- **Print users:** Print users are the folks who want to send print jobs to a print device that's either located on the network or attached to their workstation. To actually print, users must have a *print device driver* installed on their workstation. The only exception to this rule occurs when printing on a Windows NT network from a workstation with the Windows NT Workstation operating system. In this special case, print users don't need drivers at their workstations because they can use the drivers installed on the Windows NT Server. That is, for all Windows NT Workstations on the network, you install one print device driver on the server and you're done. Windows NT Server and Windows NT Workstation do the rest for you — how nice!
- **Print jobs:** Print jobs are files that are formatted at the workstation by an application and a print device driver, and submitted for output on a local or network print device. If the print device is local (attached to the workstation), then the output is printed. If a network print device and print server are involved, then the output is sent (spooled) to a queue on the print server until a print device is available to service the request.
- **Print servers:** Print servers are computers that manage the network print devices attached to them. A print server can be any computer located on a network that has a print device attached and runs some flavor of a Microsoft operating system, such as Windows NT Server, Windows NT Workstation, Windows 95, or Windows 98. (Even a user workstation can function as a print server — although we don't like this approach because it typically brings traffic to the user's workstation.) When users submit print jobs, the print server stores the job in a queue for the print device and then polls the print device to check for its availability. If the print device is available, the print server pulls the next job out of the queue and sends it to the print device.

  Any network administrator or user with appropriate access rights can manage print servers from anywhere on the network. By default in Windows NT, anyone that's a member of the following groups can manage print servers: Print Operators, Server Operators, and Administrators.
- **Print queues:** Print queues are hard disk locations where spooled files wait in line for their turn to be printed. Each print device has at least one corresponding queue (though additional queues are possible), and as users submit print jobs, the jobs go into the queue to be printed. You define a queue for a print device when you add the print device in the Printers folder and assign it a name. Print jobs enter the queues on a first-come, first-serve basis.

  Only someone with access to manage queues (Administrators, Print Operators, and Server Operators) can alter the printing order of a print queue. You can assign users on your network to manage the print queues for you. Windows NT has a built-in group called Print Operators, and you can add users to this group to give them the proper access rights for the task by choosing Start⇨Programs⇨Adminstrative Tools⇨User Manager.

Giving users print-queue management rights may be seen as political if you don't make the assignments properly. Some folks may accuse others of playing favorites when print jobs are rearranged in the queue. We've seen this happen a lot. Try to pick people who are neutral, and your life will be easier!

- **Print devices:** Print devices are physical devices, such as HP laser printers. You can walk up to them and touch them. Print devices can be attached locally to a workstation or server, or directly to the network.
- **Printers:** Printers are also referred to as logical printers. Logical print assignments aren't something you can touch, but are assignments made so printing is easier for the user. Check out the following sections for descriptions of the differences between logical print assignments and physical print devices.

Physical print devices

We call print devices *physical print devices* because you can walk up to these devices and touch them. Print devices such as lasers, plotters, ink jets, and bubble jets fall into this category. You can attach a physical print device locally to a workstation, server, print server, or directly to the network (as shown in Figure 11-1).

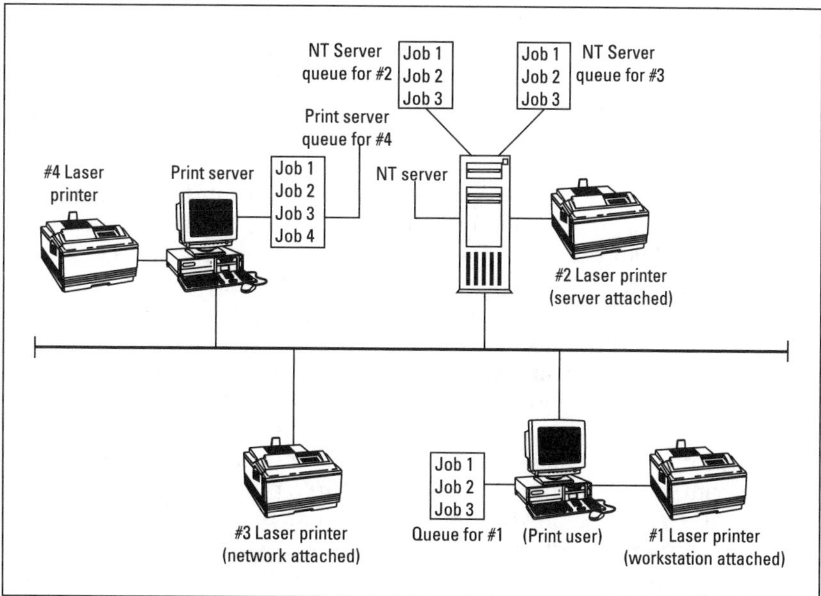

Figure 11-1: A network showing different methods to connect print devices on a network.

A print server is just a network-attached workstation that services print jobs — so, technically, we could lump workstations and print servers in the same category. We list them separately in this case because we want to distinguish between a workstation where a user sits and a dedicated print server workstation located somewhere on the network.

Logical print devices

A *logical printer* isn't really a print device at all — it exists intangibly, only in the form of a Windows NT definition. It's sort of like a name that Windows NT uses to identify a physical print device (or a group of physical print devices, as you see later in this section). Each time you define a print device and its properties in Windows NT, the operating system assigns a logical printer definition to the physical print device so that it knows to which physical print device you want to send your jobs.

When you first install a print device, a one-to-one correlation exists between the physical print device and the logical definition. However, you can expand the use of logical printer assignments to allow for one logical printer to serve as the definition for several physical print devices. This use is known as *print device pooling,* and you set it up through print device properties by adding ports to the print device's definition.

You need not be too concerned about defining logical printers unless you intend to pool the print devices. This happens whenever you attach a print device to the server (as explained later in the section "Attaching print devices to servers"). Just understand that Windows NT correlates a logical printer definition to one or more physical print devices attached to your network.

For example, you're likely to have several print devices connected to your network, and all or many of them may be of the same type, such as HP4MV. If you don't define a logical printer definition for Windows NT, how will it know which HP4MV print device to send your jobs to? You could be running all around the building looking for your expense report! Defining a logical printer definition keeps order in your world. You could name one logical printer *2FLWest,* and you would know that your report is sent to the HP4MV on the second floor of the West wing of your building.

Another bit of magic that logical printers can help you with is balancing print jobs. Suppose that you have three physical laser print devices (A, B, and C) located on your network in close proximity. If a user chooses to send a print job to printer A while printer A is working on a large print job, a lot of time and resources could be wasted if printers C happened to be sitting idle.

You can help your users in this regard by setting up one logical printer definition and assigning it several different physical print devices to print to. Your users then print to the one logical printer, and it figures out which physical print device is available. This takes the decision making and worrying from the user and places it in the hands of the logical printer. The only caveat here is avoiding too much distance between print devices. Try to make sure that all physical print devices are in the same general area so your users don't have to run around the building looking for their printouts.

When setting up logical printers to service more than one physical print device, the physical print devices must be identical. The only change you can make is to properties such as bin number and paper size of each print device.

Conversely, you can assign several logical printers to service one physical print device. You want to do this if users are printing special items, such as envelopes. Define one logical printer to print to the envelope bin on the physical print device and define another logical printer to print letter-size paper on the same print device. If you name the logical printers something descriptive, then the users will know where the print device is and what type of function it performs. For example, naming two logical printers *2FLWestEnv* and *2FLWest* tells the user that 2FLWestEnv is on the second floor of the West wing and it prints envelopes, whereas the other is a normal print device on the second floor of the West wing. Both logical printers actually service the same physical print device, but they may print to different bins on the print device, or one may pause the print device between pages, and so on.

Here, you don't need to do anything other than define separate print devices that all print to the same port.

Server Side Installation

Before you set up clients to print on your network, first make sure to go to the server and install all the print device definitions, drivers, and hardware, and then go to the client side. Doing so ensures that when you finally get to the user's workstation, you can submit a test print job right away because all the components are in place. If you start at the user's side first, you have to go back later to test.

Meet the printer folder

Nearly everything you want to do with print devices can be found on the server in the Printers folder in the Control Panel (more quickly available by choosing Start⇨Settings⇨Printers). We say *nearly* everything because the print device drivers are stored outside of the print devices folder (most of the drivers are found on Windows NT Server's CD-ROM).

Upon installing Windows NT Server for the first time, the Printers folder contains only an Add Printer icon to guide you through a physical print device (or logical printer) installation. Each time you install a new print device by clicking the Add Printer icon (we cover installation later in this chapter), Windows NT assigns it a separate folder in the Printers folder, as shown in Figure 11-2.

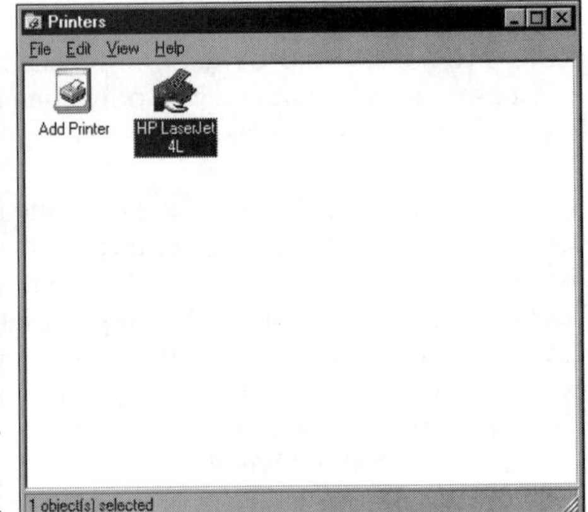

Figure 11-2: The NT Printers folder showing an installed print device plus the Add Printer icon.

Any time you want to do something to this print device, such as share it so that others can see it on the network, you come to this Printers folder location and right-click on the particular print device. Next, select Properties from the pull-down list and you see a window with tabs. You make all of the changes to the particular print device in the print device's Properties dialog box, so take some time to familiarize yourself with the settings that are available. The following sections describe adjustments that are available from this important starting point.

Adding a (networked) printer

In an ideal world, your network and users would allow you to set up one type of print device in one manner (all laser print devices of the same make and model with NICs, and so on); however, in the real world, things don't pan out like that. Therefore, the engineers at Microsoft designed Windows NT Server to give you four options to attach print devices to your network: print server, Windows NT Server, workstation, or networked as shown in Figure 11-1.

In the following sections, we show you the four different approaches to installing print devices on your network. Although all of the approaches are different, three of the four installations are very similar; they're just performed on different machines. For example, the steps for installing print devices attached to networks and for installing print devices attached to workstations are very similar. Both machines have a print device hooked up to their local ports, and they both share print devices on the network.

Attaching print devices to servers

You may find a need to attach a print device directly to your server. We don't like this method unless your organization can't afford to spare a machine as a print server. Why? Because any time you attach a device to a file server, you run the risk that it may get hosed and crash the server. We've seen this happen often, so we advise against attaching a print device to your server whenever possible. If you're on a tight budget, however, you may need to use this configuration.

To attach a print device to a Windows NT Server, you need a print device, a cable, the Windows NT Server installation CD (if you didn't copy it to your server's hard disk), a Windows NT Server, and any print device drivers for clients you want to install for automatic download to the client.

Connect the print device directly to one of the ports on the server (for example, LPT1) and install the print device on this machine in its Printers folder by choosing Start⇨Settings⇨Printers. Then follow these steps:

1. **Double-click on the Add Printer icon, which invokes the Add Printer Setup Wizard, select My Computer (local print device), and click Next.**
2. **Select the port you attached this print device to (such as LPT1) and click Next.**
3. **In the left window, highlight the print device manufacturer; in the right window, highlight the model of the print device. Click Next.**

   If you don't see your print device listed here, it means you have to provide the Add Printer Setup Wizard with the driver. Click the Have Disk button and point the wizard to the location and path where the driver resides.
4. **Type a name for this print device and click Next.**
5. **Type in a share name for this print device, then choose which client operating systems will access the print device. Click Next.**

   The share name is the name that your users will see when they print to this print device so make it meaningful (for example, 2ndFLWestEnv). Also, you need to have the operating system print drivers handy to install (see Step 7), so that Windows NT Server can automatically download the drivers to the clients.
6. **Decide whether you want to print a test page at this time (we like to wait until the end) and click Finish.**

   Setup copies files from Windows NT's installation CD to this Windows NT Server's hard disk.

7. **When Setup pauses to ask you for the location and path of the client operating system drivers you selected in Step 5 (if any), type in the path information and click OK.**

   You can select Skip File if you experience problems with this and come back later. Setup shows you the customizable print device's properties. See the section "Managing Windows NT–based Printers" later in this chapter for further information.

8. **Click the Ports Tab to define the port that this print device is connected to (for example, LPT1).**

If you are familiar with setting up print devices on Windows 95/98, then you probably whipped through the previous steps quickly because the print device setups are similar. At this point, you have set up the following:

- **One basic logical printer that points to one physical print device on a Windows NT Server:** We say basic because you haven't customized any options for this print device yet, such as paper bins, dots per inch, and separator pages. You probably weren't aware that as you defined this physical print device, you also assigned it a logical printer. Remember that there's a one-to-one correlation between the two each time you install a physical device and define it unless you add more physical devices.
- **A print queue for this print device:** Even though you weren't aware that you did this, Windows NT does this for you when you when you define the print device. To view the queue, double-click on the print device icon. You won't see anything in the queue just yet.
- **Shared access to this print device by everyone on the network:** When you define a share name on the network for a print device, Windows NT defaults to everyone having access to this print device unless you change the default.

You can have multiple logical printers pointing to one physical print device. If you wanted to assign another logical printer that services this physical print device, you would repeat the previous steps but assign a new computer and share name. You can assign different print device properties for this physical print device for each logical printer you define. Each logical printer you define here requires 30–40KB of space in the Registry.

Attaching print devices to print servers

In the preceding section, we show you how to hook up a print device to a Windows NT Server so that your Windows NT Server functions as a print server on your network along with its other duties. To help manage the load on the server, you can offload this printing task to another computer on your network called a print server.

The print server is another computer on your network with a print device attached that you set up to manage print spooling, print queues, and jobs. We like this method because it frees up the Windows NT Server to perform other tasks. When your clients print to the print server, they bypass the Windows NT Server and send print jobs directly to the print server.

You can install any Microsoft operating system that you like on the computer. We recommend at least Windows 9*x*, but we prefer Windows NT Workstation because you can download the print drivers directly to the client workstations from the print server automatically with no intervention on your part. This means you don't have to install drivers manually on each of the client workstations.

After you've installed a computer and operating system, repeat Steps 1–8 from the "Attaching print devices to servers" section if you're using a Windows NT Workstation as the operating system. If you're using Windows 9*x*, repeat the same steps but exclude the downloadable print device drivers from Steps 5 and 7. Instead, you have to go to each client and install the corresponding print device drivers.

Attaching networked print devices to print servers

Some print devices, such as HP laser print devices, are neat because you plug a NIC into them and they're almost ready to be placed anywhere on your network where there is an electrical outlet and an available network connection. We say *almost* ready because you have to install the Data Link Control (DLC) protocol on the print server's Control Panel Network icon (Start⇨Settings⇨Control Panel⇨Network) for this to work or have the TCP/IP protocol installed.

To install the DLC protocol:

1. **Double-click on the Network icon.**
2. **Click the Protocols tab and then click the Add button.**
3. **Scroll down until you see the DLC protocol, select it, and click OK.**

The first challenge that you face is finding the print device on the network when you set it up on the print server. The trick to tracking down the print device is to connect the print device to the network and perform a print device self-test so you can find the MAC address of that print device. The self-test spits out a sheet of paper that provides the code, so you should bring the output with you to the print server so that you can match the address.

For example, you can install a Hewlett-Packard laser print device by first adding a print device of that type in the print server's Printers folder (choose Start⇨Settings⇨Printers) and then double-clicking the Add Printer icon to bring up the Setup Wizard. Then follow these steps:

1. **Select My Computer (local print device) and click Next.**
2. **Click Add Port.**
3. **Select the Hewlett-Packard Network Port in the Print Destination box and click OK.**
4. **Type the name of the print device in the Name text, hit the Tab key, and hit your refresh button.**
5. **Choose the print device's matching MAC address in the Card Address area and click OK.**
6. **At the printer ports dialog box, click Close.**
7. **In the Available Ports window, mark your networked print device with a check and click Next.**

From there, just define the information for this print device like any other. Be sure to give this print device a unique share name so other users on the network can see it.

Note that you can perform the previous steps without the print device being attached to the network, but you have to type in the yucky Card Address. Otherwise, the print device can't be found on the network.

Attaching print devices to a workstation

Some users may have print devices on their desktop that you want to make available on the network to other users. Attaching a print device to a workstation is the method that's the least desirable because it involves users going to another user's workstation to pick up their print jobs. This can cause a disruption in workflow to the user who's unfortunate enough to have the print device on his or her desk. However, in smaller organizations where budgets are tight, this method is used.

You must go to the user's workstation desktop and share that print device on the network. You can restrict access to that share so the entire organization isn't permitted to print there. Where do you find all this? In the Printers folder (Start⇨Settings⇨Printers for Windows 95/98 users) on the user's desktop, of course! Right-click on the Add Printer icon if no print device is installed and choose the print device to be a local print device connected to LPT1 and assign it a name. If a print device is already defined, then right-click on the print device icon and select Properties to give this print device a share name. After you share the print device on the network, other users can see it.

However, this method causes the user's workstation to manage the printing process. You can define this workstation-attached print device on your Windows NT Server so it will manage the print process. Here's how:

1. **Go to the user's computer desktop and define a share for this print device, but limit access to the username of "NTServer."**
2. **Mosey back over to the Windows NT Server.**
3. **Add a user named "NTServer" in User Manager (Start⇨Programs⇨Administrative Tools⇨User Manager).**
4. **Double-click Add Printer in the Printers folder.**
5. **Follow the same steps as in the "Attaching print devices to servers" section earlier in this chapter, except you make the following changes:**
    - Click on the Add Printer icon and choose the networked print device instead of the locally attached print device (My Computer).
    - When you select the port, choose the share name you gave the print device on the client's desktop.
    - Give this print device a new share name that the rest of the users on the network will see.

Unless you are tight on money, we don't recommend that you use this method. It can cause aggravation for the user who has to share the print device with other people on the network and can disrupt that user's work environment. Use this method only if your budget doesn't allow one of the other methods.

Sharing Printer Access

After you've installed a print device on your network (as we explain in the preceding sections), the next step is to create a share on the network for that print device. (Refer to Chapter 15 for more details on Windows NT network shares.) Until you share a print device, your users can't see it on the network. You can share a print device easily by using the Printers folder (Start⇨Settings⇨Printers). Right-click on the print device you want to share and select Sharing from the menu options. Doing so opens up the Sharing tab. Select the Share radio button and type a descriptive share name (for example, 2ndFlWest). Click OK and you're done!

When you share a print device, it's available to everyone on the network by default. You must specifically restrict groups or users from accessing the print device if that's what you want.

If you have MS-DOS based clients on your network, make sure that your share names for print devices are only eight characters long.

Client-Side Installation

The final step in setting up networked printing is generally to set up the print devices on the client side. Fortunately, not much is required in this process. Everything you need will be on the Windows NT Server, the print server, or the user's Printers folder on their desktop, depending on which operating system they use.

If the client operating system is Windows NT Workstation, you only need to add the print device in the Printers folder (Add Printer) and select networked print device. The reason is because the print device is actually attached to another computer somewhere on the network, not local to this workstation. For the port, use the Browse option and find the share name of the print device you want to print to. That's it!

Remember that Windows NT Server and Windows NT Workstation work together so Windows NT Server provides the print drivers dynamically for Windows NT Workstation clients.

If your clients have Windows 95/98 and your clients are printing to a Windows NT Server, and you've installed the various client operating system drivers at the server, then you simply add the print device in the Printers folder (Add Printer) and select it as a networked print device. When you select the port as the share name of the networked print device, Windows NT Server automatically downloads the drivers.

Managing Windows NT–based Printers

You can view and perform some management of your print servers, queues, and print devices from anywhere on the network, including your Windows NT Server. So, from one location, you can view what's going on with all of the print devices on your network. The only thing you can't do remotely is install something on the print device itself, such as memory or cables. But you knew that already! The following list includes some issues to keep in mind as you manage print devices:

- **Disk space on server:** If you set up spooling on your network, you need to keep a close eye on the hard disk space of the print servers. The spooling process involves sending files from the print user to the print server. Remember that the print server can also be your Windows NT Server. In either case, if your network has a high volume of print activity, it's possible to fill up a hard disk quickly with the spooling process.

After files are spooled to the print server, they remain on the hard disk in the queue until an available print device is ready. If there's a problem with the print device, jobs can get backed up quickly. Remember that queues take up space on the hard disk, so if the queues back up, more and more space is needed. Be careful you don't run low on disk space!

- **Memory in the print device:** Anytime your users print graphics on the network, memory becomes an issue on the print devices. Large graphics files require more memory to print. You can find out how much memory is in a print device by performing a self-test on the print device. Some organizations don't have a large budget for adding extra memory to all of their networked print devices, so they select one or more in strategic locations and then define logical print device setups that point to the loaded print devices.
- **Configuring the Printer's Properties:** Figure 11-3 shows the various settings you can alter for any print device on your network. We go through the each of the tabs here so you understand what you can change on the print device's properties:
  - ***General tab:*** Here's where you add information about this print device, such as comments, location, whether to use a banner page, and more. We recommend that you add some comments and the print device's location. In medium- to large-sized operations, adding a separator page so print jobs are more easily distinguished from one another is a good idea. Here you can also find the current print driver information. Only change this if you want to install a new driver.
  - ***Ports tab:*** This is where you tell the system the port that your print device is attached to. If it's a network-attached print device, you define it here using the MAC address; if it's a TCP/IP print device, you define it here using the IP address.
  - ***Scheduling tab:*** You may opt to have print jobs run at night for this print device. This is where you can schedule the print device's availability, priority, and spooling options.
  - ***Sharing tab:*** If this print device is to be seen by users on the network, you define the share name here (and make it meaningful). This is also the location where you tell Windows NT which client operating systems you have on your network that you want print drivers automatically downloaded to.
  - ***Security tab:*** This is the where you set up auditing of your print devices, which enables you to gather information should something go wrong with the print device. You may want to use the Security tab for charge-back purposes on a departmental basis (where you audit the usage and charge users or departments for that use), or you can use it to limit this print device's availability.
  - ***Device Settings tab:*** This is where you define specific properties of the print device, such as paper size, dots per inch, paper bin, and more.

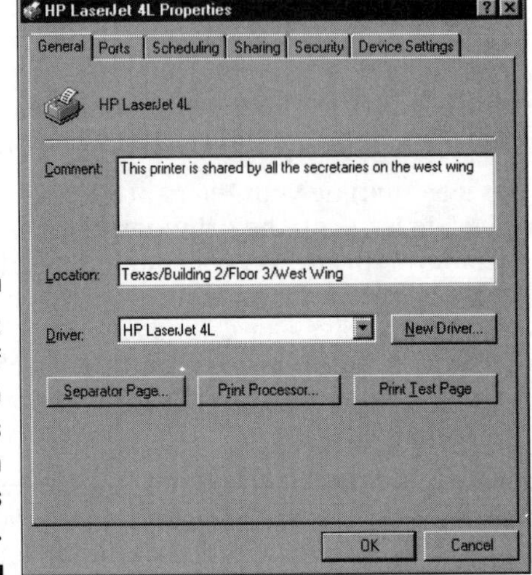

Figure 11-3: View of print device Properties tabs within the Printers folder.

Preventing Printer Problems

Printing problems on a network can wreak havoc. Here are a few pointers we can pass along to help you head off this kind of trouble before it starts. If you do experience problems, refer to Chapter 20 for some troubleshooting help.

- **Purchase HCL-compatible devices:** Only purchase network print devices listed in the HCL. Otherwise, you don't know if the print device will work on the network and you may spend hours trying to get it to work. And remember to always check Microsoft's site for the latest version of the HCL.
- **Get the latest printer drivers:** Make sure you obtain the latest print device driver associated with each print device on your network. Newer drivers fix bugs found in older drivers. If you use an older driver, you sometimes end up troubleshooting a known bug and one that is already fixed in the newer driver.
- **Purchase name brand:** We hope that your organization can afford to purchase name brand print devices for your network, such as Hewlett-Packard and Epson. We find that the biggest printing problems on networks stem from cheaper models. Even if you are able to hook up these cheaper print devices, sometimes it takes so long to get all the pieces working that you may have done better to have invested in the more popular brand name print device.

- **Purchase from one manufacturer:** We like to stick with one type (brand name) of print device where possible. Notice we said brand and not model. We realize that some organizations have black and white printing needs and color printing needs. However, if you can purchase all of your print devices from one manufacturer (for example, Hewlett-Packard), your life, and that of your users, will be easier. If you have all Hewlett-Packard laser print devices on your network, don't buy another manufacturer's laser print device just because it's on sale that day at your local computer superstore. You can save time by working with one vendor on their equipment and drivers, rather then having to hunt all over the Internet for various manufacturers' Web sites. Allow your users to become familiar with the one brand and they won't have to relearn new equipment all the time.
- **Buy enough memory:** The influx in graphics software has placed a strain on memory usage in print devices to produce the desired output. Don't wait until print jobs start fouling up before adding more memory. If your budget is too low to do this up front, then find a local vendor that stocks memory for your computer and keep their telephone number handy.
- **Join a Windows NT–related Internet mailing list:** You can find some very valuable information on these. For a detailed description, turn to Chapter 10's sidebar entitled: "What's in a mailing list and newsgroup?" Remember though that some mailing lists are very active, so if you sign up, be prepared to receive at least 50 e-mails per day in some cases.
- **Look for Windows NT Frequently Asked Questions (FAQs) on the Internet:** There are a few good sites where you can find Windows NT–related information and FAQs: `www.ntfaq.com` and `www.bhs.com` are two of the more familiar locations. You can also go to one of the main search engines like `www.search.com` and type in **NT FAQ**. Sometimes just looking at these FAQs provides insight into problems, questions, and answers that others have pioneered.

Chapter 12

Next on Montel — IP Addresses and the Nerds Who Love Them

In This Chapter

- Working with TCP/IP and NetBIOS names
- Understanding IP addressing, nets, and subnets
- Obtaining Internet-ready IP addresses
- Using private IP addresses
- Using proxy servers and address translation
- Working with DHCP
- Knowing when to use WINS
- Working with DNS

TCP/IP drives the Internet and makes it accessible around the world. TCP/IP, however, is a lot more than just a collection of protocols: Many elements in the TCP/IP marry protocols to related services to provide more complete capabilities. Important examples include dynamic address allocation and management, known as DHCP, plus domain name to address resolution services, known as DNS. You find out about TCP/IP names, addresses, and related standard services in this chapter, as well as some other services that are unique to Windows NT.

Name-Calling with TCP/IP and NetBIOS

Whenever you issue a command in Windows NT, you're expected to use the proper syntax. Otherwise, your efforts might not produce the desired results. For example, when you issue a NET USE command from a command prompt, you must enter the server name and a share name, as well as the drive you wish to map. Thus, a simple command like `NET USE G: \\LANWRIGHTS\APPS` associates the drive letter G: with a share named APPS on the LANWRIGHTS server. If you're using the TCP/IP protocol to convey the data involved, the protocol doesn't know how to interpret the name LANWRIGHTS as the server. Instead, it understands IP addresses, such as 172.16.1.7.

If you use TCP/IP on your network, you need some way to convert IP addresses into names, and vice versa. Just as the United Nations requires translators so everyone can communicate, so does Windows NT! That's why understanding naming conventions and name-to-address resolution is such an important part of working with TCP/IP on Windows NT.

NetBIOS names

If you're like most folks, you freeze like a deer in the headlights when you hear the word NetBIOS. Don't worry. Only a small number of people really understand NetBIOS in detail, but figuring out what you need to know without stressing out is easy.

A NetBIOS name is often called a computer name. When you install Windows NT onto a network, each computer that runs Windows NT requires a unique computer name. This permits all NetBIOS-based utilities to identify each machine by its name. Any time you enter a command that includes a computer name, Windows NT knows which computer you're talking about.

If you try to give two devices the same name, you run into trouble — like trying to use the same Social Security number for two people. Each time a computer joins the network, it registers its name with a browser service that keeps track of such things. When the second computer with the same name tries to register, it is rejected because that name is already "taken." In fact, that machine will be unable to join the network until its name is changed to something unique.

When creating NetBIOS names, you need to work within their limitations:

- NetBIOS names must be between 1 and 15 characters long. (If you have DOS or Windows 3.x machines on your network, they can't recognize NetBIOS names with more than 8 characters.)
- NetBIOS names may not contain any of the following characters: " (double quotation mark), / (right slash), \ (left slash), [(left square bracket),] (right square bracket), : (colon), ; (semicolon), | (vertical slash), = (equal sign), + (plus sign), * (asterisk), ? (question mark), < (left angle bracket), and > (right angle bracket). Dollar signs are not recommended because they have a special meaning. (A NetBIOS name that ends in $ does not display in a browse list.)

- Don't use lengthy names, or put spaces in names. Windows NT doesn't care if you use longer names or include embedded spaces, but other networking clients or systems may not be able to handle such usages.
- Pick names that make sense to users that are short and to the point. Don't name machines after their users or locations, especially if users come and go regularly, or if machines move around a lot. When it comes to servers, name them to indicate organizational role or affiliation (for example, Sales).

What's in a NetBIOS name, you ask? A short, clear indication of what's being named so that users can recognize what they see. At best, this kind of naming convention will make sense without requiring further explanation. At the least, you can do what we do and put a sticker with the machine's name on each monitor for self-identification purposes. Figure 12-1 shows a list of NetBIOS names in our network's Network Neighborhood (names that begin with Nts indicate Windows NT Servers, Ntw indicates Windows NT Workstations, and Win98 . . . well, you see what we mean; we also add numbers to identify each machine's IP address).

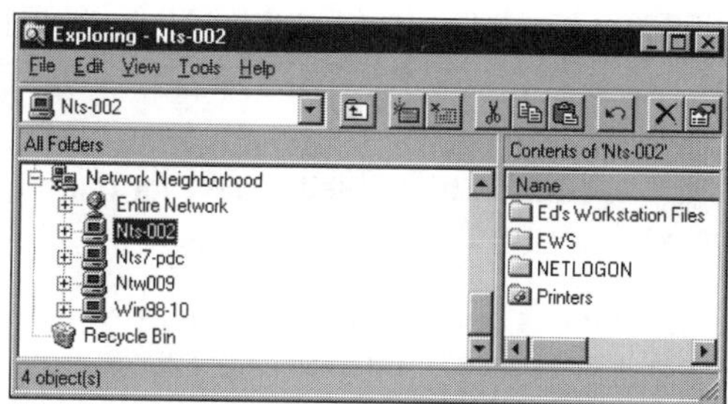

Figure 12-1: NetBIOS computer names show up for machines under the NT Explorer Network Neighborhood.

TCP/IP names and addresses

TCP/IP uses a different scheme for names than does NetBIOS. TCP/IP uses 32-bit numbers to construct IP addresses (for example, 172.16.1.11). Each host or node on a TCP/IP network must have a unique IP address.

IP addresses are not meaningful to most humans and are difficult to remember. Thus, it's helpful to have some way to convert IP addresses into meaningful names. On an Windows NT network, you use computer names (also known as NetBIOS names). The Internet community uses a different naming convention called domain names. Translation methods, such as WINS and DNS maintain databases for converting an IP address to a computer name (WINS) or a domain name (DNS).

If you've ever used a Web browser on the Internet, you know that you can type a URL (Uniform Resource Locator) such as `http://206.224.65.194/` or `http://www.lanw.com/` to obtain access to a Web page. You can do so because the Internet uses the Domain Name Service, also known as DNS, to resolve IP addresses to domain names and vice versa. If you type the IP address, the Web browser jumps straight to the named address; if you type a domain name, your request goes through a DNS server that resolves the name to an IP address, and then the browser jumps to the named address thereafter.

In the IP world, the naming scheme you can use is limited if you plan to connect your network directly to the Internet. An organization known as the Internet Network Information Center, or InterNIC, is in charge of approving and maintaining the database of "legal" Internet domain names. You can request any domain name you want, but if someone else is using it or has a legitimate claim to a trade or brand name, you won't be able to use it. For example, you probably won't be able to use `mcdonalds.com` or `cocacola.com` as domain names; likewise, if somebody else has already registered `xyzcorp.com`, you wouldn't be able to use that name, even if your company is named XYZ Corporation.

The format for a typical IP name is host.domainname.suffix. The domain name is something you can't guarantee, but typically represents your organization. The suffix sometimes identifies the country of origin (for example, .ca is Canada, .de is Germany) or the type of organization (.gov is government, .edu is education, .com is a commercial business, .org is a nonprofit organization, and so forth).

Some domain names are more complex; they can take a form like host.subdomain.domainname.suffix, as in `jello.eng.sun.com`, where the host name is `jello`, the subdomain is `eng` (for engineering), and the domain name is `sun` (the domain name for Sun Microsystems, Inc.) which is a commercial (.com) entity. The only part of the name that's under control of the InterNIC is the domain name part, and the suffix, but every domain name must be unique in its entirety to be recognized properly.

Names that include the host part and the domain name and suffix (plus any other subdomain information that may apply) are called Fully Qualified Domain Names or FQDNs. To be valid, any FQDN must have a corresponding entry in some DNS server's database that permits it to be translated into a unique numeric TCP/IP address. For example, your authors' Web server is named `http://www.lanw.com`, which resolves into a numeric address of 206.224.65.194.

As long as you're completely isolated from the Internet and intend to stay that way, you can assign any names and IP addresses you might like on your network. But if you ever connect your network to the Internet, you'll have to go back and change everything! If your network will be — or simply *might be* — connecting to the Internet, you have one of two options for assigning addresses:

1. **You can obtain and install valid public IP addresses and domain names now.**

   You can obtain these directly from the InterNIC at some difficulty and expense, or you can pay your Internet Service Provider (ISP) to do this for you. We recommend the latter course. When you obtain a range of IP addresses for your network — remember, each computer needs its own unique address, and some computers or devices need multiple addresses (one for each interface) — make sure you get enough to leave some room to grow.

2. **You can (and should) obtain a valid domain name from the InterNIC, but you can use any of a range of reserved IP addresses called private IP addresses to number your networks.**

   These addresses may not be used directly on the Internet, but have been set aside for private use. When used in concert with a type of software called Network Address Translation (or NAT for short), this approach requires you to obtain only a small number of public IP addresses but still permits Internet access for every computer on your network. This topic is discussed in more detail later in this chapter in the section "The magic of proxy servers and address translation."

To find out more about the process of obtaining a domain name, visit the InterNIC's Web site at `http://internic.net` and click the hyperlink that reads "domain name registration services." You'll find details on name registration services and well as the directory and database services that support the Internet's distributed collection of DNS servers.

If you're thinking about registering a domain name, check the existing name database at the InterNIC Web site to make sure that name's not already assigned to somebody else. Why ask for something you can't have?

An Address for Every Node

A unique numeric identification tag, called an *IP address,* is assigned to each interface on a TCP/IP network. Every IP address within a TCP/IP network must be unique. Each device on a TCP/IP network is known as a *host.* Each host has at least one network interface with an assigned IP address. However, a host can have multiple network interface cards (NICs), and even multiple IP addresses assigned to each NIC.

Of network and host IDs

An IP address consists of two components: a *network ID* and a *host ID.* The network ID identifies the network segment to which the host belongs. The host ID identifies an individual host on some specific network segment. A host can only communicate directly with other hosts on the same network segment. A network segment is a logical division of a network into unique numeric network Ids called *subnets.* A host must use a router to communicate with hosts on other subnets.

A *router* moves packets from one subnet to another. A router reads the network ID for a packet's destination address and determines if that packet should remain on the current subnet or be routed to a different subnet. When a router delivers a packet to the correct subnet, the router then uses the host ID portion of the destination address to deliver the packet to its final destination.

A typical IP address looks like 207.46.131.137 (which matches the domain name `http://www.microsoft.com`). This numeric IP address format is known as *dotted-decimal notation.* But computers "see" IP addresses as binary numbers. This same IP address is 11001111 00101110 10000011 10001001 in binary form and written in collections of eight bits called *octets.* Each octet is converted to a decimal number and then separated by periods to form the dotted-decimal notation format shown at the beginning of this paragraph. The decimal version of IP addresses is more human friendly than binary. As you may already know, domain names and NetBIOS names are still more friendly because they use symbolic names that make sense to humans.

An IP address requires 32 binary digits and defines a 32-bit address space that supports nearly 4.3 billion unique addresses. Although this seems like a lot of addresses, the number of available IP addresses is dwindling. Consequently, several plans exist to expand or change the IP addressing scheme to open up many more addresses. For more information on such plans please visit the Web site at: `http://www.6bone.net/ngtrans.html`.

IP designers carved the entire galaxy of IP addresses into classes, to meet different addressing needs. Today, there are five IP address classes labeled by the letters A through E. Classes A, B, and C are assigned to organizations to allow their networks to connect to the Internet, and Classes D and E are reserved for special uses.

The first three classes of addresses differ by how their network ID is defined:

- Class A addresses use the first octet for the network ID.
- Class B uses the first two octets.
- Class C uses the first three.

Class A addresses support a relatively small number of networks, each with a huge number of possible hosts. Class C addresses support a large number of networks, each with a relatively small number of hosts as shown in Table 12-1 (Class B falls in the middle). Thus, branches of the military, government agencies, and large corporations are likely to need Class A addresses, medium-sized organizations and companies Class B addresses, and small companies and organizations Class C addresses.

When it comes to recognizing address classes A through C, the network ID for Class A addresses always starts its first octet with a zero. Each Class B network ID always starts with 10, while Class C network IDs always start with 110. Consequently, you can determine address class by examining an address, either in binary or decimal form. (See Tables 12-1 and 12-2.)

Table 12-1 Address Classes and Corresponding Network and Host IDs

Class	*High-Order Bits*	*First Octet Range*	*#Networks*	*#Hosts*
Class A	0xxxxxxx	1-126.x.y.z	126	16,777,214
Class B	10xxxxxx	128-191.x.y.z	16,384	65,534
Class C	110xxxxx	192-223.x.y.z	2,097,152	254

Table 12-2 Division of IP Address Component Octets According to Class

Class	*IP Address*	*Network ID*	*Host ID*
A	10.1.1.10	10	1.1.10
B	172.16.1.10	172.16	1.10
C	192.168.1.10	192.168.1	10

Note: Network ID 127 is missing from Table 12-1. That's because 127 is a loopback address (when testing IP transmission, it transmits to itself).

No valid IP address may include an octet that consists entirely of ones or zeros (0 or 255 in decimal), because these addresses are reserved for broadcast addresses (255) and subnet identification (0).

Subnetting IP addresses

Subnets represent divisions of a single TCP/IP network address into logical subsets. The motivation for subnetting is twofold. First, subnetting reduces the amount of overall traffic on any network segment by collecting systems that communicate often into groups. Second, subnetting makes is easier for networks to grow and expand, and adds an extra layer of security controls. Subnets work by "stealing" bits from the host part of an IP address and using those bits to subdivide a single IP network address into two or more subnets.

Subnet masks are typically used to divide IP address blocks into smaller subnetworks. The base subnet masks for Class A, B, and C networks are 255.0.0.0, 255.255.0.0, and 255.255.255.0 respectively. By adding extra bits set to 1 in the space occupied by the 0 that appears next to the rightmost 255 in any such number, additional subnet masks may be created. This transformation is illustrated in Table 12-3, which shows the some typical values for usable subnet masks.

Routers move packets among subnets and networks

Only *routers* can transfer packets from one subnet to another, or from one network ID to another, in the TCP/IP world. Routers may be specialized devices that include high-end, high-speed devices from companies like Cisco Systems or Bay Networks. But any computer with two or more NICs installed, where each NIC resides on a different subnet, can be a router, provided that the computer can forward packets from one NIC to another (and thus, from one subnet to another). Right out of the box, in fact, Windows NT Server includes the software and built-in capabilities to function in this way. Computer nerds like to call such machines *multi-homed computers* because the machines are "at home" on two or more subnets.

Table 12-3 Subnet Masks and Results

Binary Mask	*Decimal Equivalent*	*Number of New Subnets*	*Number of Hosts*
00000000	A: 255.0.0.0 B: 255.255.0.0 C: 255.255.255.0	A: 16,777,214 B: 65,534 C: 254	1
10000000	A: 255.128.0.0 B: 255.255.128.0 C: 255.255.255.128	A: Not valid B: Not valid C: Not valid	Not valid
11000000	A: 255.192.0.0 B: 255.255.192.0 C: 255.255.255.192	A: 4,194,302 B: 16,382 C: 62	2
11100000	A: 255.224.0.0 B: 255.255.224.0 C: 255.255.255.224	A: 2,097,150 B: 8,190 C: 30	6
11110000	A: 255.240.0.0 B: 255.255.240.0 C: 255.255.255.240	A: 1,048,574 B: 4,094 C: 14	14
11111000	A: 255.248.0.0 B: 255.255.248.0 C: 255.255.255.248	A: 524,286 B: 2,046 C: 6	30
11111100	A: 255.252.0.0 B: 255.255.252.0 C: 255.255.255.252	A: 262,142 B: 1022 C: 2	62
11111110	A: 255.254.0.0 B: 255.255.254.0 C: 255.255.255.254	A: 131,070 B: 510 C: Not valid	126

Because routers are required to communicate across IP subnets, some router's IP address on each subnet must be known to every client on that subnet. This address is called the *default gateway*, because it is where all out-of-subnet transmissions are directed by default (it's the gateway to the world outside each local subnet, in other words). If no default gateway is defined, clients can't communicate outside their subnet.

Going public: Obtaining Internet-ready IP addresses

Deploying your own network or using a stand-alone system with NAT to connect to the Internet requires that you obtain one or more valid IP addresses. For some uses, you may simply contract with an ISP to use a dial-up connection. Each time you connect you'll be assigned an IP address automatically from a pool of available addresses. Once you disconnect from the ISP, that IP address will return to the pool for re-use. This works equally well for stand-alone machines and for the servers that might dial into an ISP to provide an on-demand connection for users who have private IP addresses but can attach to the Internet using NAT software.

One way to attach an entire network to the Internet, is to lease a block or subnet of IP addresses from an ISP. Leasing IP addresses can be expensive and can limit your growth. Also, many ISPs can no longer lease large blocks of IP addresses so you may have to limit Internet access to specific machines or subnets.

For more information about taking this approach, you need to contact your ISP to find out what it can offer by way of available addresses and contiguous subnets. For some uses, public IP addresses are required because security needs dictate a true "end-to-end" connection between clients and servers across the Internet. In plain English, a true end-to-end connection means that the IP address that a client advertises to the Internet is the same one it uses in reality. In the section "The magic of proxy servers and address translation," you discover an alternate approach where the IP address advertised to the Internet is different from the private IP address that a client uses on its home subnet.

For some applications, particularly where secure IP-based protocols like IPSec (IP Secure) or particular Secure Sockets Layer (SSL) implementations are required, network address translation techniques may not work! Make sure you understand your application requirements in detail before you decide whether to lease public IP addresses or use private IP addresses with network address translation.

The magic of proxy servers and address translation

If you don't want to pay to lease a range of IP addresses, and your application requirements permit you to use private IP addresses, you can employ the IP addresses reserved for private use in RFC 1918 on your networks. When used in combination with network address translation software to connect to an ISP, a single public IP address (or one for each Internet connection) is all you need to service an entire network.

RFC 1918 (`http://www.faqs.org/rfcs/rfc1918.html`) defines special IP addresses for use on private intranets. These addresses, which appear in Table 12-4, will not be routed on the Internet by design. This approach actually provides improved security for your network as a fringe benefit, because it means that any impostor who wants to break into your network cannot easily masquerade as a local workstation. (Doing so would require routing a private IP address packet across the Internet.) Because all of these addresses are up for grabs, you can use whatever address class makes sense for your organization (and for Class B and Class C addresses, you can use as many as you need within the legal range of such addresses).

Table 12-4 Private IP Address Ranges from RFC 1918

Class	*Address Range*	*# Networks*
A	10.0.0.0 - 10.255.255.255	1
B	172.16.0.0 - 172.31.255.255	16
C	192.168.0.0 - 192.168.255.255	254

Thus, using address translation software to offer Internet access reduces your costs and allows nearly unlimited growth. If you think private IP addresses combined with NAT software makes sense for your situation, consult with your ISP for specific details and recommendations on how to use this technology on your network.

You've probably heard the terms *firewall* and *proxy* thrown about often when reading or talking about Internet access. Firewalls and proxy servers are networking tools that are little more than special-purpose routers. A firewall may be used to filter traffic, both inbound or outbound.

Firewall filters can be based on source or destination address, a specific protocol, or port address, or even on patterns that appear in the content or a data packet. A proxy server is an enhanced firewall, and its primary purpose is to manage communications between an in-house network and external networks such as the Internet. Proxies hide the identity of internal clients and can keep local copies of resources that are accessed frequently (this is called *caching*, and improves response time for users).

You can check out several great online resources for firewalls, but online information on proxies is limited to product documentation. In addition to consulting the Windows NT Server Resource Kit and TechNet, here are several online resources you might want to check to discover more about these technologies:

- Zeuros Firewall Resource: `www.zeuros.co.uk/`
- Firewall Overview: `www.access.digex.net/~bdboyle/firewall.vendor.html`
- Great Circle Associates: `www.greatcircle.com/`
- 4 Firewalls: `www.4firewalls.com/`
- Microsoft's Proxy Server 2.0: `www.microsoft.com/proxy/`

- Aventail VPN: `www.aventail.com/`
- Netscape's Proxy Server: `www.netscape.com/`
- Ositis Software's WinProxy: `www.ositis.com/`
- Deerfield Communication's WinGate Pro: `www.deerfield.com/`

For example, your authors use Ositis Software's WinProxy product, which acts as a proxy and provides NAT services, to link their networks to an ISP across an ISDN connection. We allow the ISP to assign us an IP address each time we log onto their host for an Internet connection. This doesn't matter because the NAT services translate between whatever address they assign us and the internal addresses each machine uses on the other side of the WinProxy software. We only pay for the temporary use of a single IP address, but we can handle up to eight connections to the Internet at a time!

Go Figure: Configuring IP Addresses for Windows NT Server

Configuring TCP/IP on Windows NT Server can range from simple to complex. We review the simple process and discuss a few advanced items, but for complex configurations, you should consult a reference such as the Windows NT Server Resource Kit or TechNet.

Three basic items are always required for configuring TCP/IP:

- IP address
- Subnet mask
- Default gateway

With just these three items, you can connect a client or server to a network. The protocol is configured on the Protocol tab of the Network applet. If the protocol isn't installed already, click the Add button to display a list of installable protocols. If it's already installed, select TCP/IP in the list and click Properties.

The TCP/IP Properties dialog box has five tabs. The first tab, Microsoft TCP/IP Properties dialog box (see Figure 12-2), is where the three IP configuration basics are defined. Notice there's a selection to obtain an IP address from a DHCP server. Because most servers don't work well using dynamic IP addresses, you should define a static IP address for your Windows NT Server instead of using DHCP. You will either obtain a public IP address from your ISP, or use a private IP address from one of the reserved address ranges defined in RFC 1918.

Likewise, you must calculate a subnet mask for your network. Here again, you may obtain this from your ISP if you're using public IP addresses, or calculate your own if you're using private IP addresses. In most cases where private IP addresses are used, the default subnet mask for the address class should work without alteration or additional calculations.

Finally, you must also provide a default gateway address for your server. The default gateway should be the address of the router on the local subnet to which the server is attached that can forward outbound traffic to other network segments. On networks using public IP addresses, this will probably be a router, firewall, or proxy server that connects the local subnet to other subnets or the Internet. On networks using private IP addresses, this will usually be the machine where the proxy and NAT software resides, that mediates between the local subnet and an Internet connection.

Once you define an IP address, a subnet mask, and a default gateway, click OK, then close the Network applet, and reboot. That's all there is to basic TCP/IP configuration on Windows NT!

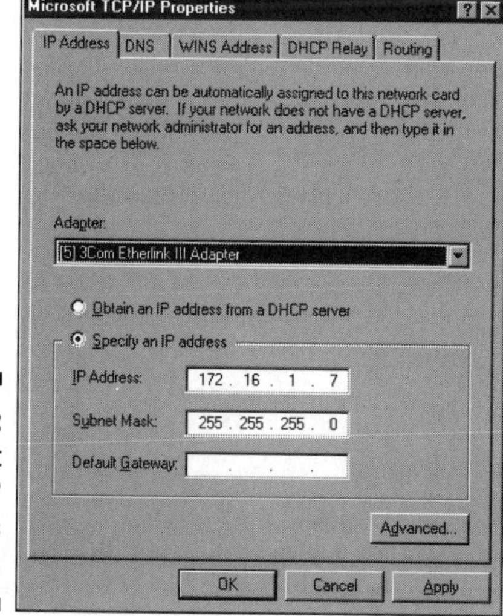

Figure 12-2: Microsoft TCP/IP Properties dialog box.

More complex configurations become necessary when your network is larger, and therefore, more complicated. The DNS tab is where you can define IP addresses for one or more Domain Name System (DNS) servers. DNS servers resolve domain names into IP addresses. For more information about DNS, please consult the section on DNS later this chapter.

The WINS Address tab is where IP addresses for Windows Internet Name Services (WINS) servers are defined. WINS servers resolve NetBIOS names into IP addresses. WINS is convenient for Windows NT networks with multiple servers and network segments. For more information about WINS, please consult the section on WINS later this chapter.

The DHCP Relay tab is where Dynamic Host Configuration Protocol (DHCP) server addresses may be defined. Using a Windows NT Server computer to relay DHCP messages permits clients on multiple cable segments to access a single DHCP server; otherwise, a DHCP server must be present on each network segment for DHCP to work. A DHCP server simplifies managing IP-based networks by assigning IP addresses and configurations to DHCP client systems on demand. For more information about DHCP, please consult the section on DHCP later this chapter.

The Routing tab is used only on Windows NT computers that include two or more NICs, where each NIC is connected to a separate subnet. If you check the "Enable IP Forwarding" box on this tab, it allows traffic from one subnet to travel through the server to another subnet. This capability is what allows Windows NT to act like a router. For more information on routing, please consult the Windows NT Server Resource Kit and TechNet.

Automating IP Addressing with DHCP

DHCP, the Dynamic Host Control Protocol, is used to dynamically assign IP addresses and other configuration settings to systems as they boot, which allows clients to be automatically configured each time they boot, thus reducing installation administration. DHCP also allows a large group of clients to share a smaller pool of IP addresses, if only a fraction of those clients need to be connected to the Internet at any given time.

What's DHCP?

DHCP is a service that Windows NT Server can deliver. In other words, a Windows NT Server can run DHCP server software to manage IP addresses and configuration information for just about any kind of TCP/IP client.

DHCP manages IP address distribution using leases. When a new system configured to use DHCP comes online and requests configuration data, an IP address is leased to that system (by default, each lease lasts three days). When the duration of the lease is half expired, that client can request a lease renewal for another three days. If that request is denied or goes unanswered, the renewal request is repeated when 87.5% and 100% of the lease duration has expired. If a lease expires and is not renewed, that client can't access the network until it obtains a new IP address lease. You can initiate manual lease renewals or releases by executing `ipconfig /renew` or `ipconfig /release` at the Windows NT Command Prompt.

You can view the current state of IP configuration using the `ipconfig` command. Issuing the command `ipconfig /all |more` at the Command Prompt displays all a machine's IP configuration information one screen at a time.

Configuring DHCP (Not for the timid!)

To install DHCP, use the Services tab in the Network Control Panel applet. (Click the Add button, select Microsoft DHCP Server from the Select Network Service window, then supply the Windows NT Server 4.0 CD when prompted.) When DHCP is installed, a new entry named DHCP Manager appears in the Administrative Tools (Common) menu.

To configure a DHCP server, use the DHCP Manager's Create Scope (Local) window, which appears in the figure. Here, you manage a single collection of IP addresses and lease properties, known as a DHCP scope.

The Start Address and End Address that appear in the upper-left corner of the Create Scope window define the range of addresses that the DHCP server will manage. This list is inclusive, so the values supplied for Start and End will also be used as part of the pool.

To the right, a list of Excluded Addresses may appear. This window shows any IP addresses you instruct the DHCP server to ignore within the range defined by the Start and End addresses. Normally, you need to exclude addresses that are already allocated to servers, routers, and other devices that require fixed IP addresses.

The Subnet Mask field simply defines the subnet mask for the pool of addresses in the current DHCP scope.

The Exclusion Range fields let you define a range of addresses to exclude from the IP address pool. To exclude a single address from the pool, use the same IP address for the Start Address and End Address fields. To exclude a range of contiguous addresses in the pool from use, enter the first address to be excluded in the Start Address field, and then enter the final address to be excluded in the

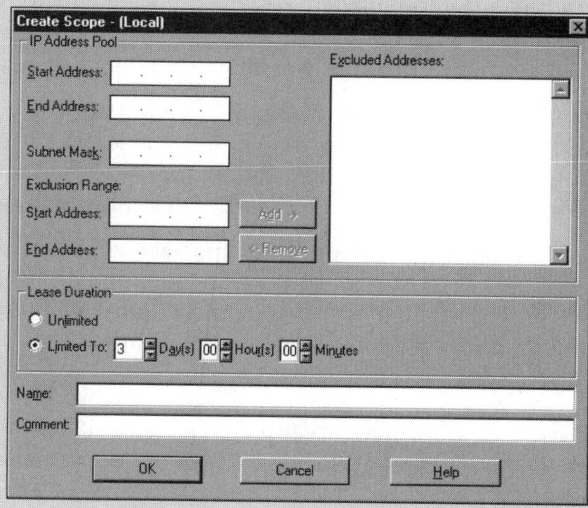

(continued)

(continued)

Stop Address field. You can use the Add button as many times as you must, so that you can exclude as many individual addresses, or ranges of addresses from the address pool as you must.

The Lease Duration can be set to unlimited, which means that the lease works just like a static allocation except it's managed by a DHCP server. Or, you can set a more limited duration for IP address leases. Notice that the default lease duration is set to three days.

You can also give a DHCP scope a name, and associate a comment with that name. This kind of information will come in handy if you work on a large, complex network with multiple DHCP scopes, and need to be able to tell them apart easily.

Is DHCP in your future?

We can think of two profound reasons why DHCP is a real godsend to Windows NT administrators like you:

1. DHCP allows you to manage an entire collection of IP addresses in one place, on a single server, with little effort beyond the initial configuration of the address pool. In the bad old days before DHCP, managing IP addresses usually required walking from machine to machine on a far too frequent basis.
2. DHCP automates delivery of IP addresses and configuration information (including subnet mask and the default gateway addresses) to end-user machines. This makes it astonishingly easy to set up IP clients, and to handle configuration changes when they must occur.

   To configure IP on a new client, all an end user (or you) must do on Windows NT, Windows 95, or Windows 98 is click the single radio button on the IP Properties window that says "Obtain an IP address from a DHCP server." DHCP does the rest automatically.

   When configuration changes occur, these changes will be automatically introduced when IP leases are renewed. You can even cancel all existing leases and force clients to renew their leases whenever major renumbering or configuration changes require immediate updates to their IP configurations.

The ultimate reason for using DHCP is because it makes your job much easier. DHCP is recommended for all networks that use TCP/IP with ten or more clients.

Some You WINS, Some You Don't

Within a Microsoft Windows network, TCP/IP hosts can called by NetBIOS names instead of IP addresses or domain names. Because NetBIOS names are more or less unique to Microsoft Networks, there is no current standard for associating NetBIOS names with IP addresses. On a Microsoft Network that uses TCP/IP as its only networking protocol, it is essential to be able to resolve NetBIOS names to IP addresses.

Understanding WINS

Because resolving NetBIOS names to IP addresses is the key to providing access to many of Windows NT's built-in services and facilities, Microsoft provides two methods to handle this process:

1. Using a file named LMHOSTS (here, LM stands for LAN Manager, and points to the network operating system that preceded Windows NT in the Microsoft product world), you can create a static table that associates specific NetBIOS names with specific IP addresses. Such a file must be present on every machine to provide the necessary name to address resolution capabilities.

   For small, simple networks, using LMHOSTS files is an acceptable method. On large, complex networks, the busy work involved in maintaining a large number of such files can quickly get out of hand.

2. Larger, more complex networks are where WINS comes into play. WINS stands for Windows Internet Name Service. WINS runs on Windows NT Server machines as a service that automatically discovers NetBIOS names and manages a dynamic database that associates NetBIOS names with TCP/IP addresses as networks grow in size, multiple WINS servers sometimes become necessary to help speed up the time it takes to handle name resolution requests.

   A single WINS server can handle an entire network. But on networks that include multiple sites, or with many thousands of users, multiple WINS servers can distribute the load involved in providing name resolution, and speed users' access to NetBIOS-based resources.

WINS has several advantages over LMHOSTS files. For one thing, it's built on a dynamic database, which means that as networks change and names and addresses come and go, the database changes as the WINS server detects new name and address relationships, or finds old names with new addresses. WINS can be especially important on networks where DHCP is in use, if clients also share files or printers on their machines. Also, WINS is something like a multilingual Spanish-English dictionary that's constantly updated as new words are added. You give it a Spanish word, and out pops an English word or a translation that means the same thing!

WINS servers

A WINS server maintains a database that maps computer names to their respective IP addresses and vice-versa. Rather than sending out broadcasts for address information, which eats excess network bandwidth, a workstation that needs a NetBIOS name resolved makes a request directly to a designated WINS server (that's the real purpose of the WINS tab in the TCP/IP Properties window, in fact).

This approach lets workstations take advantage of a well-defined service and obtain address information quickly and efficiently. Also, when workstations with NetBIOS names log onto the network, they provide information about themselves and their resources to the WINS server, that that any changes will automatically appear in the WINS server's database.

WINS clients

When configuring workstations or servers (at least, those servers that don't play host to the WINS server software) on your network, you'll provide an IP address for one or more WINS servers on your network. When those machines boot, they provide the WINS server with their computer names, share names, and IP addresses. The WINS server handles everything else. If a workstation needs an IP address that corresponds to a NetBIOS name, it asks the WINS server to supply that information.

DNS

One way to simplify TCP/IP host identification is to use Fully Qualified Domain Names (FQDNs) instead of IP addresses. An FQDN is the type of name that's used to identify resources on the Internet to make access easier for humans (such as `http://www.microsoft.com`). Resolving domain names and FQDNs to IP addresses is a crucial service on TCP/IP networks in general — especially on the Internet, where hundreds of millions of names and addresses may be found. This is where the Domain Name System, sometimes called the Domain Name Service, always abbreviated as DNS, comes into play.

As with NetBIOS names and IP addresses, the association between FQDNs and IP addresses can also be maintained in two ways:

1. A HOSTS file can be created on each system. The HOSTS file maintains a local table that associates specific FQDNs with specific IP addresses. Whenever such associations change, the HOSTS file must be updated manually and copied to all machines on a network.

   HOSTS files are not well-suited for interaction with large IP-based networks, especially the Internet. This explains why HOSTS files are mostly a historical relic of an earlier, simpler era of IP networking. Except as a fallback should access to DNS fail, nobody uses HOSTS files anymore.

2. Access to a DNS server permits network machines to request name resolution services from that server instead of maintaining name to address associations themselves. Although DNS servers must be configured manually, a DNS server can handle the name resolution needs of an entire network with ease. DNS servers can also communicate with one another, so that a name resolution request that the local server cannot handle can be passed up the FQDN name hierarchy until it reaches a server that can resolve the name into an address, or indicate that the name is invalid.

The Internet includes tens of thousands of DNS servers. ISPs manage many of these DNS servers; others fall under the control of special top-level domain authorities. To stake out an Internet presence, you must obtain a unique FQDN through the InterNIC (or let your ISP do it for you). After you obtain this name, it will be associated with a special root IP address in some DNS server (probably at your ISP, unless you decide to set up a DNS server of your own).

DNS: No or yes?

Unless you're managing a large, complex network, chances are better than average that you will be working with somebody else's DNS server — probably, your ISP's — rather than managing your own. But if you have a large network with over 1,000 computers, or your network spans multiple sites using private wide-area links, a DNS server may be just the thing to help you stake out the right kind of Internet presence.

If you think you may be interested in setting up a DNS server, you need to consult a technical resource, such as the Windows NT Server Resource Kit or TechNet. We also highly recommend *DNS on Windows NT,* a book by Paul Albitz, Matt Larson, and Cricket Liu (O'Reilly & Associates, Sebastopol, CA, 1998, ISBN 1-56592-511-4) as the ultimate resource for using Windows NT as a DNS Server. Albitz and Liu also wrote a general book called *DNS and BIND,* now in its third edition (O'Reilly & Associates, Sebastopol, CA, 1998, ISBN 1-56592-512-2) that is widely regarded as the best general reference on DNS.

Dealing with Difficulties

Problems occurring on TCP/IP networks are almost always associated with incorrect configurations. The wrong IP address, subnet mask, default gateway, DNS, WINS, or DHCP server can bring a system, if not a whole network, to its knees. Therefore, you need to take extra caution to double check your settings and changes before putting them into effect.

If you are connecting to an ISP, you should contact the ISP's technical support personnel early on to eliminate as much "wheel-spinning" as possible. You may discover the problem is not on your end, but theirs. If so, your only recourse is to wait it out, then complain. If problems occur too often for your comfort at an ISP, take your business elsewhere.

Windows NT includes a few TCP/IP tools you can employ to help track down problems. We already mentioned ipconfig, so here are the others:

- **PING:** This tool tests the communication path between your system and another remote system. If a ping returns, you know the link is traversal and the remote system online. If the ping times out, then either the link is down or the remote system offline.
- **TRACERT:** This tool reveals the hops (systems encountered) between your system and a remote system. The results inform you if your trace route packets are getting through and at what system is a failure occurring.
- **ROUTE:** This tool is used to view and modify the routing table of a multi-homed system.
- **NETSTAT:** This tool displays information about the status of the current TCP/IP connections.
- **TELNET:** This tool is used to establish a text-based terminal emulation with a remote system. Telnet gives you access to remote systems as if you were sitting at its keyboard. Windows NT Server does not include an inbound Telnet server.

Complete details on these tools are included in the Windows help files, the Windows NT Server Resource Kit, and TechNet.

Enough TCP/IP to Choke a Hippo

If this chapter has whetted your whistle for TCP/IP, there are lots of great resources where you can obtain more details and information:

- Bisaillon, Teresa and Brad Werner. *TCP/IP with Windows NT Illustrated.* McGraw-Hill, 1998. ISBN: 0079136486.
- Stevens, W. Richard. *TCP/IP Illustrated Volumes 1,2 & 3.* Addison-Wesley, 1994. ISBN: 0201633469, 020163354X, 0201634953.
- Comer, Douglas E. *Internetworking with TCP/IP, Vol. I-III.* Prentice Hall ESM, 1995, 1996, 1997. ISBN: 0132169878, 0139738436, 0138487146.
- Wilensky, Marshall and Candace Leiden. *TCP/IP For Dummies,* 3rd Edition. IDG Books Worldwide, Inc., 1999. ISBN: 0764504738.

Chapter 13

Just Trust Me — Setting Up Domains and Trusts

In This Chapter

- Mastering the domain concept
- Modeling domain structures
- Trusting and trusted domains
- Managing multiple trusts
- Applying SP3 does the trick!
- Using domains effectively

Administering a Windows NT Server network generally means managing one or more domains, which roughly equates to maintaining centralized repositories of information about computers, users, groups, and other resources under lock and key. Even before you get Windows NT up and running, Windows asks you to make decisions concerning your domain configuration. (See the section titled "Down and dirty: Primary versus Backup Domain Controllers" for a description of the roles of these entities.) And after you have Windows NT installed, your choices about domain configuration are important factors in how much day-to-day upkeep your network requires.

In this chapter, we shed some light on Windows NT domains. We explain what a domain is, how you set it up, and how to make domains work together to allow access to material in other domains.

Master of Your Domain

An extremely simple definition of a Windows NT *domain* is the collection of data and services that a Windows NT domain controller provides. Although this definition is clearly circular, it does contain one essential and fundamental truth: You can't have a Windows NT domain without at least one domain controller.

So understanding domains and domain controllers are two sides of the same sheet of music (or something like that). In the following sections, we try to clarify how you can understand what a domain *is* by understanding what a domain controller *does*.

Understanding domain controllers

As it turns out, understanding what a domain controller does also gives you a better idea of what a domain is. Following is a list of the most important items and activities that a domain controller handles (and for now, it doesn't matter whether the domain controller involved is a Primary Domain Controller, aka PDC, or a Backup Domain Controller, aka BDC; we cover those differences in the section titled "Down and dirty: Primary versus Backup Domain Controllers"):

- **Managing Logins:** When a user attempts to log onto a domain by supplying a valid domain name, a domain controller for the specified domain checks the user's account name and password against a database of such information. If the account name is valid and a hashed value of the password matches the hashed value stored in its database, the domain controller grants the user permission to log onto the domain. If the account name is invalid or disabled, or the password hash doesn't match what's stored in the database, the logon request is denied.

  In some circumstances, a logon denial locks the user out of access to anything and everything; in other circumstances, that user is logged on as a low-level default user known as a *Guest* or a *Domain Guest* account. The process of checking a valid domain name, account name, and password combination against the database is called *user authentication*, in NT-speak.

- **Assigning access rights to users:** While the logon process is under way, the domain controller generates a special numeric value called an *access token*. An access token represents the user's collected set of explicit and implicit access rights; a new one is created for one-time use each time a user logs onto a Windows NT domain.

  Explicit rights are set up specifically for each user's account, and implicit rights come from the network groups to which an account belongs. The best analogy we've heard for the access token is that it represents a ring of keys, any of which can unlock access to some specific resource or object in a Windows NT domain.

- **Keeping track of permissions assigned to resources:** The operating system recognizes all services, tasks, printers, users, drive volumes, and so on — in fact, any network component that can be named — as various objects. Every object has a set of attributes. This set includes it's the object's access permissions in an access control list (ACL) and a set of associated services that define what kind of operations may be applied against the object (delete, create, read, write, and so on). Access controls in Windows NT not only indicate whether access to an object is permitted or denied, but also specify whether specific groups or users can perform given operations on that object. By default, if a name (either a user name or a group name) does not appear in an ACL, its level of permissions is assumed to be No Access. (See Chapter 15 for a discussion of user rights and object permissions.)
- **Mediating user requests for resources:** Whenever a logged-on user requests access to any specific domain object, the domain controller checks each key in the user's key ring (access token) against the permissions set for that object. If a match is found, the request is granted; if no match is found or access is explicitly denied, then the request is also denied. Thus, we can safely say that the domain controller also controls access to all objects and resources in its scope.
- **Managing group membership:** Users can be organized into named groups in a Windows NT domain. As with individual users, each such group has its own key ring that matches its set of access rights for objects in the domain. You can use the domain controller (and associated administrative utilities) to add or remove users from default groups, and to add, delete, or rename new groups and default groups.

Group membership is an important concept in the domain environment because it supports efficiency. That is, controlling user access to resources by adding them to or removing them from groups — which already have assigned access rights — is easier than managing all resource access separately for all users.

When new computers join a network, they may want to join a domain too!

Computers may or may not belong to a specific Windows NT domain; those computers that do belong can access domain resources, those that don't, can't. When a computer wishes to join a domain, it's necessary to provide a valid administrator account and password for that domain. Any computer that incorporates the Windows NT Security model — which is to say, any Windows NT Workstation, member server, or BDC — must be explicitly added to a domain to participate in that domain. Windows 95 and Windows 98 can also apply domain-based security controls to shares that they publish, but they don't have to formally join the domain the way NT machines must.

Users have rights; objects have permissions

The access token that is generated during logon can be likened to a ring of keys used to unlock access to specific objects. Therefore, user rights correspond to the key ring's individual keys on an object-by-object basis.

Following this same analogy, object permissions represent the locks that control access to objects when an access request is made. That is, the access token (the keys) is matched against the object permissions (the lock).

If a key fits a lock, the corresponding set of services or operations is unlocked (access is granted). Windows NT uses all-or-nothing-access control: either all requested services or operations are granted, or all are denied. There is no in-between access in Windows NT.

The domain database contains information about users and groups. It also contains information about computers and a whole host of other resources — printers, directory volumes, network shares, modems, and so forth — that belong to the domain. In most cases, users belong to a domain so that they can use the domain's resources.

What are domains good for?

First, foremost, and last, a Windows NT domain is intended to provide centralized control over a group of resources associated with that domain. The key concepts that make domains attractive are *centralized administration* and *centralized security*. Users need to log onto the domain only once by supplying a valid domain name, user name, and password. After this logon, all users' subsequent requests for resources are handled in the background by a domain controller. The controller checks the users' rights against the permissions for those resources to grant or deny the access requests. This centralized security makes it easy for users to work in a domain; centralized controls make it easy for administrators to set up and manage a domain.

The answers to the question "What are domains good for?" are as follows:

- Imposing a consistent, regular security policy on network users
- Imposing centralized control over users and resources
- Tracking access to certain resources (called *auditing* or *resource auditing*)
- Implementing client/server computing or widespread distributed computing

Domains aren't all champagne and roses, however; we'd also like to point out the downsides of using Windows NT domains:

- Any domain-based network must include at least one (preferably, at least two) servers to take on the role of a domain controller. This costs money and imposes additional overhead on the network (domain controllers have to talk to each other, and every object access request has to get a "security check" on some domain controller before it can proceed).
- Setting up and managing domains requires planning, discipline, and maintenance. Such requirements may not be a good thing for ad hoc organizations, or for organizations too small or poor to afford a server and the talent required to manage a domain.

Nevertheless, the Windows NT domain concept is appealing enough. The vast majority of organizations that use Windows NT Server also use domains to manage users, resources, and computers.

Down and dirty: Primary versus Backup Domain Controllers

During the GUI phase of installing Windows NT Server 4, Setup asks whether you want the machine to be a domain controller or a standalone server (also called a *member server* in other Microsoft documentation). If you answer "Yes," Setup asks whether you want the machine to be a *Primary Domain Controller (PDC)* or a *Backup Domain Controller (BDC)*. In this section, we give you the fine points for making this determination.

You can easily switch a machine that's acting as a BDC to act as a PDC, and vice-versa. But you cannot switch a machine's role from member server to domain controller, or vice-versa, without reinstalling Windows NT Server!

If you have only one domain controller in any Windows NT domain, it must be a PDC, because declaring any server to be a controller for a new domain during installation automatically makes that computer a PDC. Another way to state this is as follows: The first domain controller in any new domain is always a PDC. Only when you're adding additional servers to an already-defined domain can you declare a Windows NT Server computer to be a BDC.

Playing the part: The roles of the PDC and BCD

The PDC takes the role of master in a *master-slave relationship* with all the BDCs that belong to the same domain. Although this sounds like a form of subjugation, a master-slave relationship is computerese for "everything that changes on the master is copied to all slaves" and "only a master can accept changes, and copies all changes to its slaves."

Consequently, when you change the contents of the database for a domain, all such changes are applied to the PDC's database first. Over time, all changes to the PDC's database appear in the copies of that database that reside on the BDCs, because part of the PDC's job is to copy those changes to all BDCs on a regular basis.

The BDC's role in a domain has two primary facets:

- **Balancing processing load:** Each BDC helps to reduce the processing load in a Windows NT domain by handling logon and access requests offloaded from the PDC. This facet is especially useful when a BDC is available on a local network segment, and the PDC resides on another segment — or at another site altogether. That's because the BDC can respond to a request for information locally, without requiring users to wait for the PDC to respond. Likewise, BDCs become increasingly necessary as the number of users in a domain grows. In both cases, BDCs mean faster response time for users on a network.
- **Filling in for an unavailable PDC:** Although a BDC cannot accept changes to a domain database directly (even if the PDC fails), each BDC can provide authentication services and answer access requests indefinitely even if the PDC remains unavailable. That is, BDCs offer a certain amount of fault tolerance in the face of PDC failure (or failure of all working links from part of the domain to the PDC, as long as a BDC is available in that temporarily isolated part of the network).

Recovery from a failed PDC involves promoting some BDC to become the new PDC, or restoring the original PDC to normal operation.

Domain controller database limits

Microsoft hedges its bets in a number of interesting ways when setting upper bounds on the size of a domain controller's database:

- Microsoft recommends that the size of the Security Account Manager (SAM) database not exceed 40 MB. Microsoft also acknowledges that reading a 40 MB SAM increases a PDC's boot time by 15 minutes! Most non-Microsoft experts recommend keeping the database at or under 10 MB.
- Microsoft recommends trying to accommodate no more than 25,000 to 26,000 users in a single domain. Most non-Microsoft experts recommend 7,000 to 10,000 users as a more serviceable ceiling for a single domain.
- Microsoft recommends adding another BDC for every 2,500 to 3,000 users to help distribute processing for logons and object access requests.

On a domain controller, the entire SAM database resides in virtual memory (ideally, in physical RAM). That's why adding extra RAM to a domain controller is important, especially if your SAM is large (10 MB or bigger). Extra RAM is important whether you're dealing with a PDC or a BDC because all domain controllers in a single domain must be able to accommodate the same database (whatever its size).

When Trust Becomes Necessary

The Windows NT domain concept leads to other, more complex relationships when multiple domains coexist on a single network. In this case, each domain operates more or less independently, and users in one domain may or may not be interested in resources that belong to another domain.

When users in one domain require access to resources in another domain, you must define a special inter-domain access arrangement called a *trust relationship*. This inter-domain access may be as simple as using the high-speed line printer in the accounting department to occasionally print code listings. Or that access may be as complex as sharing an HR database with managers in all departments so that they can update employee records following their annual performance reviews.

Whatever causes the need for a trust relationship, the results are invariable. After one domain (we'll call it Domain A) trusts another domain (we'll call it Domain B), the existence of a trust relationship permits users in Domain B (the trusted domain) to access resources in Domain A (the trusting domain). Figure 13-1 depicts this relationship by an arrow pointing from Domain B (trusted domain) to Domain A (trusting domain). Although the direction of the arrow may seem backward at first, it shows where users come from (Domain B) and where resources reside (Domain A).

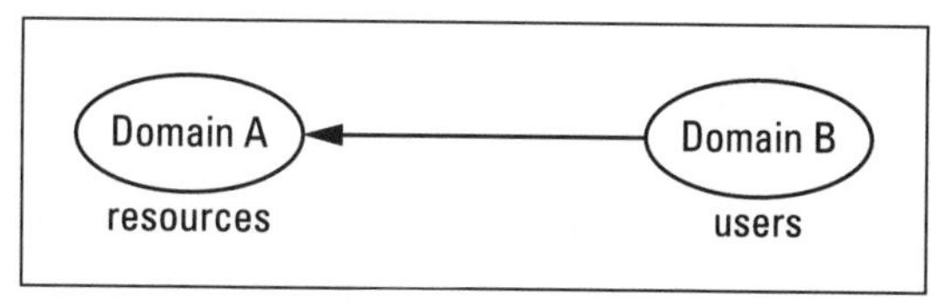

Figure 13-1: When Domain A trusts Domain B, users from B can access resources in A.

Here's an analogy you might find illuminating for trust relationships: Jane has a car. Her son Mike would like to borrow the car for the night. Jane hands the keys to Mike, points at him and says she is trusting him with the car for the night. That is the exact way a domain trust works. Jane has the resource. Mike wants to use the resource. Therefore, Jane must trust Mike with that resource.

Interesting trust trivia

Trust relationships among Windows NT domains are subject to some interesting limitations, as follows:

- Although a trust relationship may exist between Domain A (trusting) and Domain B (trusted), users from Domain B may not access any resources in Domain A until a Domain A administrator adds a user or a global group to some local group in Domain B. (We cover global and local groups in the section entitled "Groping for groupthink" later in this chapter.)
- You may occasionally hear about "two-way trusts" among Windows NT domains. Actually, there is no such thing: Any two-way trust between two domains is actually two one-way trusts (A trusts B, and B trusts A) between those domains.
- Trust relationships are not transitive in Windows NT 4.0 (however, this may change with the next release of Windows NT, known as Windows 2000, sometimes called Win2K). Thus, if A trusts B and B trusts C, A does not automatically trust C. For A to trust C, you must establish an explicit trust relationship between A and C.

Typically, users from a trusted domain are added to global groups in their own domain, and then that global group is added to a local group in the trusting domain. This grouping allows users from the trusted domain to access resources in a trusting domain. Whew! The next section clarifies this arrangement by covering the distinction between local and global groups.

Groping for groupthink

In a Windows NT domain, users and groups may have access rights for specific objects. Managing users in groups and associating groups with resources is a lot easier than managing all resources for each individual user. In essence, the principle that underlies this approach may be succinctly stated as "It's easier to manage users in bulk." At least, that's what our favorite Windows NT Wizards tell us, anyway. . . .

When crossing domain boundaries, the concept of *local* versus *global* groups comes into play.

- **Global groups** exist across an entire domain, primarily to let domain users access resources within the domain but also to let them access resources across multiple domains (with appropriate trust relationships defined, of course). Only users may be members of a global group. That is, no other global groups or local groups may appear within a global group, only users.
- **Local groups** are groups of users that you associate with specific machines in a domain. This is a good thing, because any resource of interest — be it a printer, a file directory, or whatever — ultimately resides on one and only one computer within a domain. You can assign users and global groups to local groups, but no local group may appear within another local group. You can also associate access to resources with local groups.

The four fundamental principles of managing user access to resources in other domains may be stated as follows:

- **Users belong to global groups on a per-domain basis.** This means that assigning users to global groups within a domain is the first step to providing them with access to resources — both inside and outside the domain to which they belong.
- **Global groups belong to local groups within or across domains.** If a global group from outside the local domain is assigned to a local group, the name of the group must be stated as *DomainA\Groupname,* where *DomainA* is the name of the foreign domain, and *Groupname* is the name of the global group within that domain.
- **A trust relationship must exist between the domain where the resources reside (the trusting domain) and the domain where the global group resides (the trusted domain).**
- **Local groups connect global groups to resources.** Thus, a global group from another domain can obtain access to that domain's resources if it's added to one or more local groups within that domain.

Enough principles and theory, already! In the following section, we describe exactly how to set up a trust relationship and how to add a global group from one domain into a local group in another — which should put some substance behind the principles!

Creating and using a trust relationship

A trust relationship between two Windows NT domains relies on what's called a *two-way handshake*. In English, this means that an administrator in the trusted domain indicates which domain is permitted to be trusting AND that an administrator in the trusting domain indicates its intention to trust the other domain.

Therefore, each domain has to explicitly acknowledge the other domain's role (trusted names trusting, and trusting names trusted) before the relationship can proceed. You can even create a one-time-use password so that both administrators must know the same password to set up the relationship correctly.

For the sake of this example, assume that Domain A intends to trust Domain B, making Domain A the trusting domain and Domain B the trusted domain. This relationship means that users in Domain B will be able to access resources in Domain A. Furthermore, be aware that a default global group named Domain Users is always set up for all users in any given Windows NT domain. When you assign rights to users from Domain B to access a resource in a local group in Domain A, the name of the global group to use is Domain B\Domain Users.

Following are the steps involved in assigning resource access rights. Please note that you need administrative access to the User Manager for Domains utility in both Domain A and Domain B to make this work:

1. **Log in as an administrative domain user for Domain B.**

   Domain B is the trusted domain, so you must specify that Domain A is permitted to trust Domain B.

2. **Select Start⇨Programs⇨Administrative Utilities (Common)⇨User Manager for Domains to start the utility.**

3. **Choose Policies⇨Trust Relationships.**

   The Trust Relationships dialog box appears, as shown in Figure 13-2.

4. **Select the Add button next to the Trusting Domains box.**

   The Add Trusting Domain dialog box appears. In the dialog box, enter Domain A in the Trusting Domain field. If you want to put a password on the trust setup for Domain A, enter a password in the Initial password field and re-enter that password in the Confirm password field. If you leave the Confirm password field blank, it will work, but it's less secure.

   Next, reverse the process to indicate that Domain B is trusted within Domain A.

5. **Login as an administrative user for Domain A and start the User Manager for Domains utility in that domain.**

6. **Choose Policies⇨Trust Relationships, but this time select the Add button next to the Trusted domains box.**

   In the Add Trusted Domain dialog box, enter Domain B in the Trusted Domain field. If you specified a password when you set up the Trusting Domain in step 4, you'll be prompted to enter that password now.

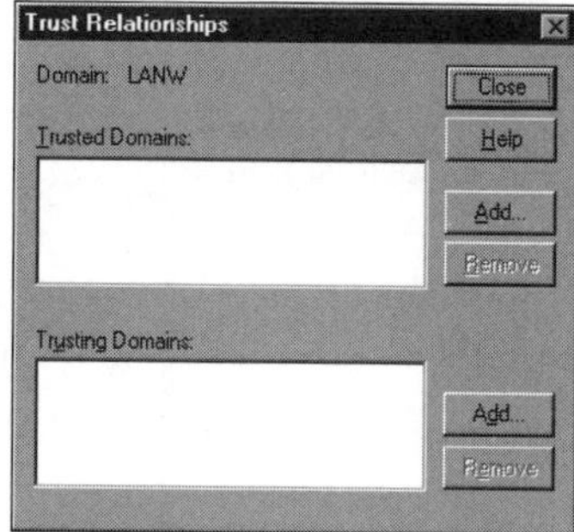

Figure 13-2: The Trust Relationships dialog box is where trusts are made (and broken).

That's all you do to set up the trust relationship so that Domain A trusts Domain B. But until you add members of a global group from Domain B (Domain B\Domain Users) to a local group in Domain A, that trust won't actually mean anything.

The process of setting up a two-way trust between two domains requires that you follow the previous steps (1 through 6). Then reverse the order of trusting and trusted, and repeat those steps again. So, Domain A not only trusts Domain B, but Domain B also trusts Domain A. Users from both domains will ultimately be able to access resources in the other domain (after a global group from one domain is added to a local group in the other domain, and vice-versa).

For example, assume that you log onto a Server named Server 1 in Domain A. If you launch the User Manager for Domains utility (by choosing Start⇨Programs⇨Administrative Utilities (Common)⇨User Manager for Domains), you see the dialog box shown in Figure 13-3. Notice the lower pane is labeled Groups. Global groups appear at the top of the list and include a globe symbol along with the user symbol on the left-hand side. Local groups show a terminal and a user symbol (also on the left-hand side) and occur beneath the global groups.

What's in a domain designation?

When global groups start moving across domain boundaries, as they will when trust relationships are in use, you'll see a new naming convention for such groups appear in User Manager for Domains when assigning permissions to trusted groups. Such names take the form <domain-name>\<global group-name> or <domain-name>\<account-name>. Thus in the preceding example, this name looks like "Domain B\Domain Users" and indicates that it names the default Domain Users global group in Domain B.

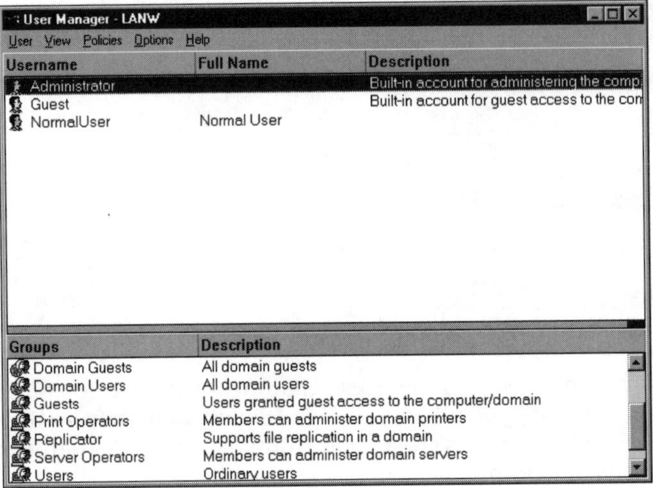

Figure 13-3: Global groups appear above local groups in User Manager for Domain's Group display area.

To add a global group from another domain to a local group, here's what you must do:

1. **Select a local group — for example, select Print Operators — double click this entry to produce the Add Users and Group dialog box.**
2. **Select the Domain B from the** `List Names From` **field at the top of this dialog box; then select Domain Admins from the list that appears next.**

   Notice that the name DomainB\Domain Admins appears in the text box labeled Add Names at the bottom of the dialog box.

3. **To make your selection official, click the OK button at the bottom of the Add Users and Groups dialog box.**

   Congratulations! You've just allowed the Domain Admins in Domain B to administer printers in Domain A. If you don't really want to do this, click the Cancel button instead.

Creating trust relationships is really is quite simple after you get all that theory under your belt!

To get the best out of trust relationships, keep track of how those trusts are used. If you ever need to break a trust, remove the two-way handshake on both sides (that is, you must remove the trust from both the trusted domain and the trusting domain). The result of breaking a trust is that some things (like access to printers) no longer work the way they did while the trust was still in effect. If you keep track of how trusts are used, you can inform those users who will be affected by these changes. You can call such notification common courtesy!

When One Domain Isn't Enough

Whether you believe Microsoft or the outside experts about the maximum capacity for a single domain, any organization with fewer than 5,000 users can clearly fit within the confines of a single domain. But some such organizations may choose to implement multiple domains, even if they aren't bumping into capacity ceilings. Why?

The answer is that domains often fall within political boundaries, as well as technological ones. No one can dispute that using one domain for an organization is easier than using several domains. However, in a decentralized organization, different departments may have different Information Technology (IT) staffs. That is, the folks in manufacturing may have their own Information Technology (IT) staff while the people in accounting have one, too. Neither department wants administrators from the "other camp" mucking around with "their Servers." When this kind of mentality prevails, organizations may order their domains around political boundaries (or a combination of political boundaries and sites, for larger companies).

No matter what drives a company to implement multiple domains, Microsoft describes several useful models that help to organize multi-domain environments. For convenience, we also list the simplest of all domain models — known as the Single Domain model — along with the others here:

- **Single Domain:** This model includes all users and groups within a single domain managed by a centralized group of administrators who handle users and resources alike. A single domain requires no trust relationships because only one domain exists.
- **Single Master Domain:** This model includes all ordinary users and groups within a single user domain managed by a centralized user management group. Each significant group of resources operates as a separate domain so that individual sites or departmental resources can be controlled separately. All resource domains trust the master domain, which lets users access resources (for which they have access rights) in any domain. The Single Master Domain, depicted in Figure 13-4, requires R trusts, where R is the number of resource domains.
- **Multiple Master Domain:** This model becomes necessary when a Single Master Domain can't contain all the users in organizations with 10,000 or more users. In this case, the organization is similar to a single master, except that all master domains must have two-way trusts established between them, and all resource domains must have one-way trusts with all master domains. The Multiple Master Domain model, depicted in Figure 13-5, requires M(M-1)/2 + R*M trusts where M is the number of master domains and R is the number of resource domains.

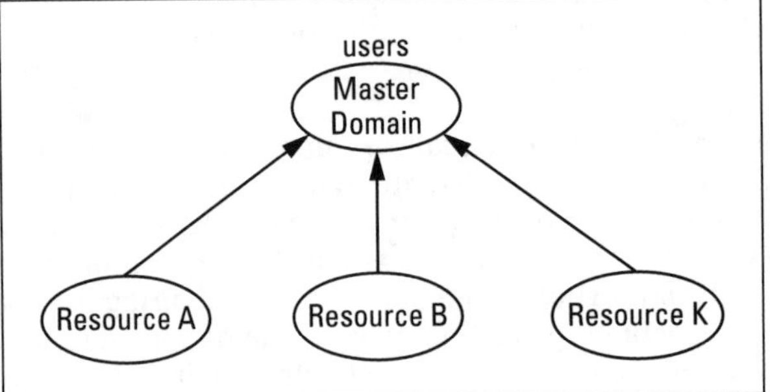

Figure 13-4: The Single Master Domain model separates users from resources, and permits centralized management of up to 10,000 users, plus departmental or site level management of resources.

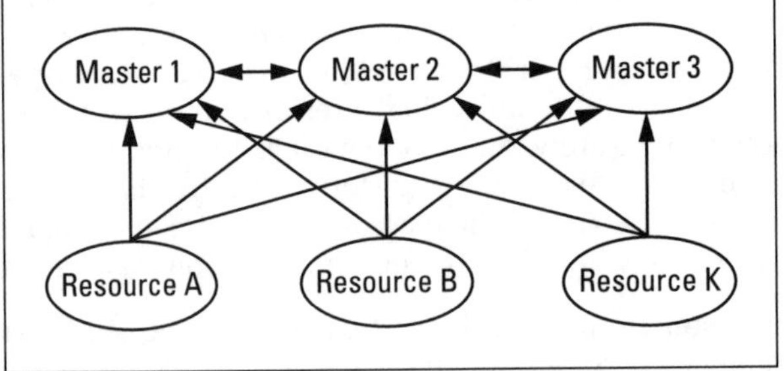

Figure 13-5: The Multiple Master Domain model separates users from resources, but organizes users into multiple master domains, plus departmental or site level management of resources.

- **Complete Trust:** This model is a free-for-all arrangement that requires every domain to have a two-way trust with all other domains so that anyone can get anywhere on any domain in the collection. A Complete Trust model, depicted in Figure 13-6, requires D(D-1) trusts where D is number of domains. ***Note***: Don't divide by two here, because two-way trusts require two trusts for each domain. Complete Trust is the most complex and difficult of all the models — 10 domains require managing 90 trusts; 100 domains require 9900 trusts!

Most organizations that use Windows NT domains use either the Single Domain model or the Single Master Domain model. Only a few organizations are big enough to require a Multiple Master Domain model. Microsoft no longer recommends using the Complete Trust model; owing to its complexity, we don't recommend it, either!

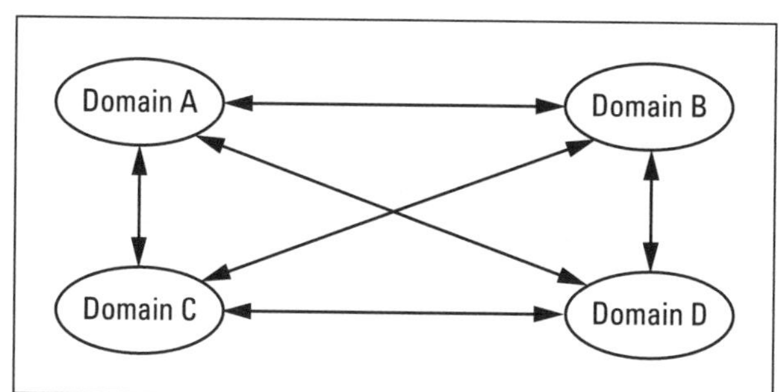

Figure 13-6: The Complete Trust model creates a two-way trust between every pair of domains in any collection of domains; this model gets ugly in a hurry as the number of domains increases.

Domain Secrets from the School of Hard Knocks

If you're going to use Windows NT domains, especially multiple domains, we'd like to close this chapter with a few well-chosen recommendations, based on hard-won experience:

- Keep the number of domains, and the number of trust relationships between domains, to an absolute minimum. More of either means more work for the NT administrator. And we're not sure, but we think this means you!
- Be judicious when creating global groups for inter-domain access. The whole idea behind using global groups is letting you handle users in bulk, rather than individually. The more global groups you create, the more you defeat the need to simplify what you must manage.

- Be careful when assigning users to multiple global groups, especially if some groups have the No Access right to certain objects. No Access always trumps other access rights, and certain users may be peeved when they can't access resources they need to use. (You can find out more about user rights and how to calculate them in Chapter 14.)

In general, less is more. This applies when setting up Windows NT domains and the global groups that are your most useful vehicle for providing users with access to resources outside their own local domain. Elaborate on your domain schemes with care and only after much thought!

Part IV
Managing Your Network

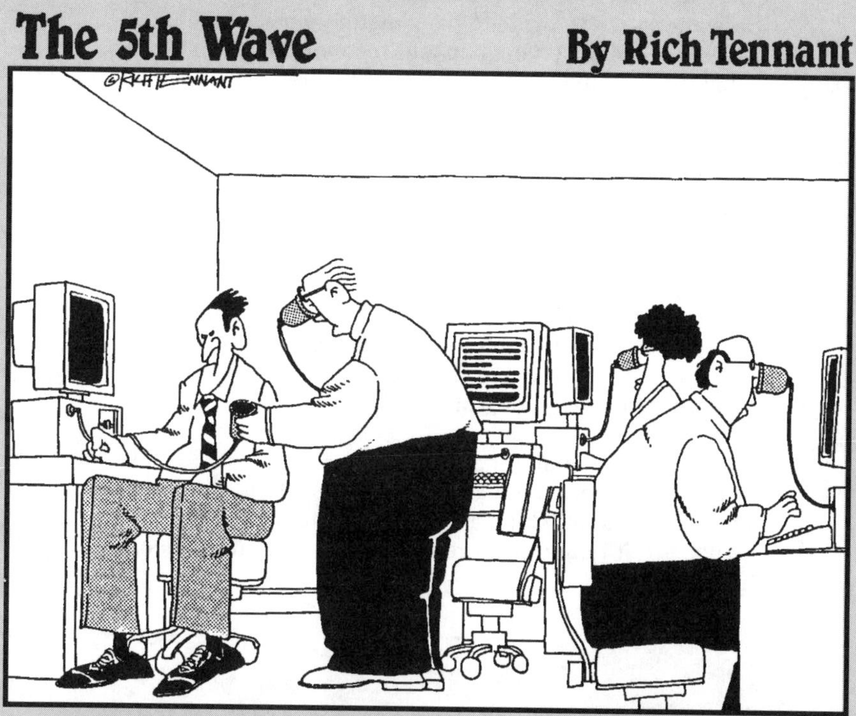

"C'MON BRICKMAN, YOU KNOW AS WELL AS I DO THAT 'NOSE-SCANNING' IS OUR BEST DEFENSE AGAINST UNAUTHORIZED ACCESS TO PERSONAL FILES."

In this part . . .

After you have your server up and running, then the real work — namely, maintenance — begins. Or at least so goes the conventional wisdom on the subject. In a very real sense, therefore, Part IV begins where Part III left off. You begin with setting up and managing user and group accounts in the User Manager for Domains utility, and then move on to handle NTFS and share permissions to control access to files and directories. Once you've got data and users to protect, backing up your system is no longer an option, so backup and recovery define a key topic for system maintenance. Part IV closes out with a discussion of computer and network security that ranges over this landscape from physical security all the way to the details of constructing solid passwords.

Thus, Part IV covers all the important topics related to maintaining a Windows NT Server–based network, to prepare you to live with one of your own (or somebody else's) making. Use these chapters to help establish a round of systematic maintenance at regular intervals — your users will not only thank you, but you'll actually wind up reducing your work load!

Just remember, maintenance activities and costs usually represent 90 percent of any computer system's life cycle. That's why establishing a solid maintenance routine, and sticking to it religiously, are the keys to running a successful network.

Chapter 14

Managing Users with the User Manager

In This Chapter

- Defining user properties
- Creating new users and groups
- Managing user accounts
- Understanding groups
- Assigning profiles
- Governing activities with policies
- Solving problems

User accounts are an indispensable element in the environment of Windows NT. User accounts are the central management and control tool used by the operating system to authenticate users, provide access, and enforce control. If you don't have a defined user account on a Windows NT stand-alone system or a Windows NT hosted network, you can't gain access. This chapter looks at user accounts and policies managed through the User Manager for Domains.

Users Have Properties

Computers are typically used by more than one person. Even systems that workers use exclusively on their desktops enable system administrators to log on. The computer distinguishes between one person and another by employing a security device — the *user account*. Each user on a computer or a network has a unique user account, which contains details about the user, his or her rights and restrictions to access resources, and more.

Thus, a Windows NT-based user account contains, is linked to, or is associated with the following items:

- **Password security:** User accounts are protected by a password so that only the authorized person can gain access to the system.
- **Permissions:** Permissions are the access privileges granted to a user account. This includes group memberships and user-specific settings to access resources.
- **Identification:** User accounts identify a person to the computer system and/or a network.
- **User rights:** A user right is a high-level privilege that can be granted to users or groups to define or limit their actions on a computer system.
- **Roaming:** You can define user accounts so that a person can log on to a system by any means, including local logon, RAS, or over a gateway.
- **Environment layout:** Profiles are user specific and store information about the layout, desktop, and user environment in general. You can define profiles so that they follow the user no matter where they gain access.
- **Auditing:** Windows NT can track access and usage by user accounts.

Access to Windows NT requires that users successfully authenticate themselves with their user accounts, which means that, when users sit down at a Windows NT system, they must press Ctrl+Alt+Del to start the logon process. Then, they must provide a valid username and password. Once the system verifies this information, they are granted access. After users complete their computing tasks, they can log out and leave the system available for the next user to log on.

When Windows NT (Server or Workstation) is installed, two user accounts are automatically created. One of these accounts, the Administrator account, is the account used to initially configure the system and to create other user accounts. The second account, the Guest account, is a quick method to grant low-level access to any user.

Administrators rule!

The Administrator account is the primary means by which you initially configure Windows NT. It's also the most powerful account within the Windows NT environment; therefore, you should make sure that the password for the Administrator account is complex and secret. The Administrator account has unrestricted access to everything within Windows NT, including managing user accounts, manipulating shares, and granting access privileges.

The Administrator account boasts the following features:

- You can't delete it.
- You can't lock it out or disable it.
- You can rename it (User➪Rename from the tool menu).
- Although you can define a blank password, some services don't function properly if you do; therefore, you should provide a valid password for this account.

Renaming this account is a good idea. Would-be hackers (that is, people who want to gain unauthorized access to your system) need only two items of information to gain access to your system: a user account name and password. Unless you rename this account, they already have half the information they need to gain access to the most powerful account on your system.

Guests can wear out their welcome

The Guest account is the second default account created by Windows NT. You can use this account as a temporary public access method. It has minimal access rights and restricted privileges to resources.

The Guest account boasts the following features:

- You can't delete it.
- You can disable it and lock it out.
- It can have a blank password. (It has a blank password by default.)
- You can rename it.
- Changes to the environment aren't retained by this user account. (That is, the user profile is mandatory because user changes to the environment are not retained.)

The Guest account can be a security hole, so plugging it is important. We suggest that you keep this account disabled, rename it, and assign it a valid password.

Creating New Users

Creating new users is a common and simple task. You use the User Manager for Domains (see Figure 14-1) on Windows NT Server to create and manage user accounts and groups. (Note: Windows NT Workstation has a similar tool called User Manager, which can manage only local users and groups, not domain users and groups.) You can also define account policies, set user rights, configure auditing, and establish trust relationships (discussed in Chapter 13).

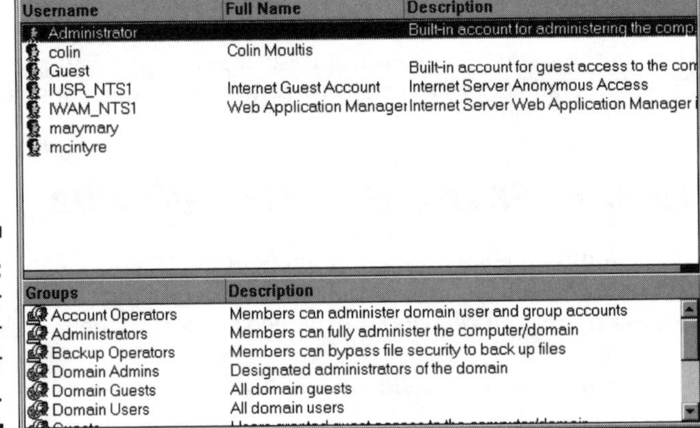

Figure 14-1: User Manager for Domains.

Creating users isn't difficult, but you need to pay attention to lots of details. First, we walk you through creating a quick-and-dirty user account. Then, we talk about all the fine tuning you can perform.

To get to the User Manager for Domains, choose Start➪Programs➪Administrative Tools (Common)➪User Manager for Domains. Initially, you see only the Administrator and Guest accounts. You can create a new user from scratch by choosing User➪New User from the menu. This reveals the New User dialog box (see Figure 14-2).

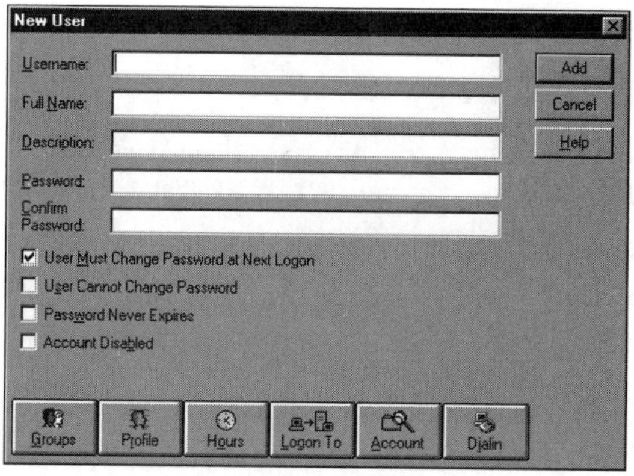

Figure 14-2: New User dialog box.

When you create a user from scratch, you should pay attention to every detail of that account, including the following:

- User name, full name (optional), description (optional), password, and confirmation
- User Must Change Password at Next Logon check box — forces users to change their passwords
- User Cannot Change Password check box — prevents users from changing their passwords
- Password Never Expires check box — exempts this account from the account policy that can require a password change after a specified time period
- Account Disabled check box — ensures that this account can't be used to gain access to the system

In addition to the items defined in the main New User dialog box, six other buttons reveal more detailed properties for user accounts. We discuss these buttons in the subsections that follow.

What's in a name?

Windows NT actually uses a SID, or Security Identifier, to recognize and track user accounts. Windows NT doesn't actually use or even care about the human-friendly name assigned to a user account. But, because you are human, you should employ human-friendly names whenever possible. This not only causes you less stress and makes user management easier, but it also improves your odds at winning the lottery.

What we are trying to say is that you should employ a naming convention. A *naming convention* is just a predetermined method for creating names for users, computers, resources, and other objects. The two key features of a naming convention are its ability to always create new names and that the names created provide descriptive information about the named object.

Small networks rarely need complex or even predefined naming conventions. But once the number of named items on your network exceeds about 100 or so, you may find it increasingly difficult to remember what "jackal," "herbie," and "8675309" actually are. So, starting a small network with a naming convention can ease the growth process later.

Windows NT doesn't impose or suggest a naming scheme. It just lets you define names as you please. So, if you decide to use a naming convention, you need to be diligent in enforcing and employing that scheme on your own.

The naming convention you choose or create doesn't matter ultimately. As long as it always provides new names and those names indicate information about the objects they label. Here are some general rules for naming conventions:

- The names need to be consistent across all element types (user names, computer names, share names, directory names, and so on).
- The names should be easy to understand. (If they're too complex or difficult, they won't be used.)
- The name should somehow identify the type of object.

You can create new names by mimicking the structure of existing names. Here are some examples of partial naming conventions that you can customize for your system:

- Create user names by combining the first and last name of a user (for example, JohnSmith and Jsmith).
- Create user names by combining the last name and a department code (for example, SmithAcct and SmithSales5).
- Create computer names by combining the user name, a computer type code, and room number (for example, SmithW98 and JS102).
- Create group names by combining resource descriptor, location, project, or department names (for example, Tower12, Planning2, and Conference12).
- Create share or directory names by combining the content or purpose descriptor with a group or project name (for example, Documents, SalesDocs, and AcctSheets).
- Create printer names by combining the model type, location, department, and group names (for example, HP5Sales, CLJRm202, and HP4Acct).

As you can see, each of these suggested partial naming schemes always create new names and provide enough information about the named object to determine where it is and whether it's a user account, computer, share, or printer.

Group memberships

Clicking the Groups button in the New Users dialog box reveals the Group Memberships dialog box (see Figure 14-3). In this dialog box, you can manage the group memberships for the account. As we discussed in Chapter 15, group membership determines the resources to which you grant a user account access.

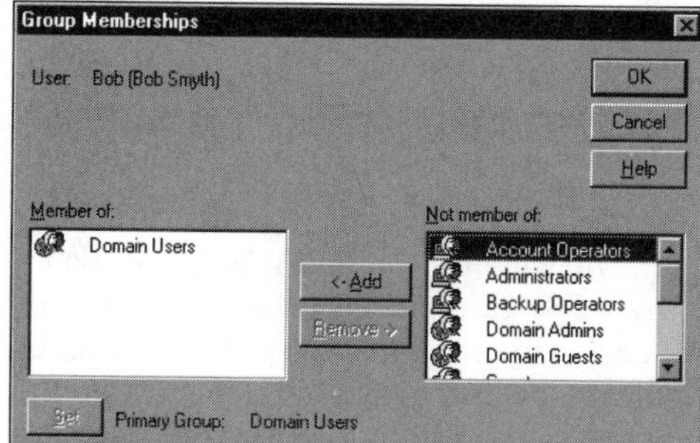

Figure 14-3: Group Memberships dialog box.

Environment profile

Clicking the Profile button in the New Users dialog box reveals the User Environment Profile dialog box (see Figure 14-4). In this dialog box, you can define the following:

- **User profile path:** The location where the roaming profile (which makes a user's working environment available to them on any workstation on the network) for this user is stored. (See User Profile section later this chapter.)
- **Logon script name:** The filename of the script file to be executed at logon. Logon scripts are usually batch files that define paths, set environmental variables, map drives, or execute applications. You typically only use logon scripts in Windows NT for compatibility purposes with older servers or DOS applications, or to automatically configure settings for NetWare server access.
- **Home directory:** The default storage location for this profile as a local path or as a mapped drive letter to a network drive.

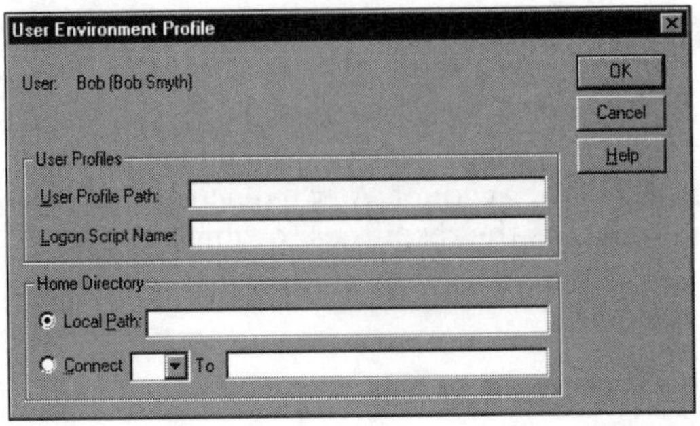

Figure 14-4: User Environment Profile dialog box.

Access hours

Clicking the Hours button in the New Users dialog box reveals the Logon Hours dialog box (see Figure 14-5). In this dialog box, you can define the hours during which a user can gain entry to the system. If this user account attempts to log on during off hours, the logon fails. If the user is already online when the hours expire, the user remains online but can't establish any new network connections (that is, the user can't send a document to a printer or open a new file). You define hours by selecting the day/hour sections and clicking the Allow or Disallow button.

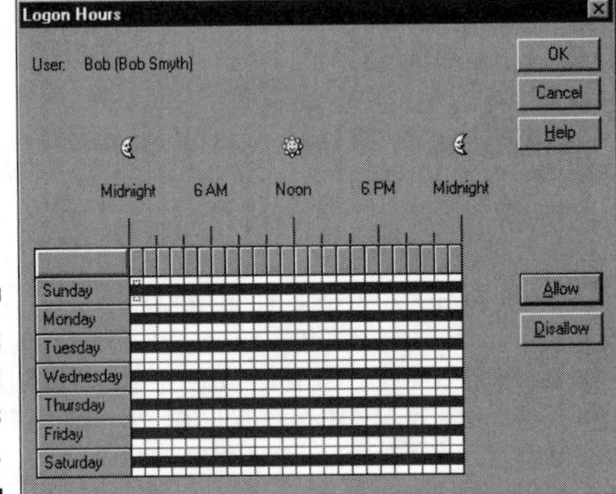

Figure 14-5: Logon Hours dialog box.

Logon locations

Clicking the Logon To button in the New Users dialog box reveals the Logon Workstations dialog box. In this dialog box, you can define whether to enable the account to log on to any workstation or log on to up to eight defined workstations. Workstations are listed by their NetBIOS name.

Account expiration

Clicking the Account To button in the New Users dialog box reveals the Account Information dialog box. In this dialog box, you can define when (if ever) the account expires and whether the account is a global (network) account or a local (this computer only) account.

Dial-in information

Clicking the Dialin To button in the New Users dialog box reveals the Dialin information dialog box. In this dialog box, you can define whether the account can connect to the network using a RAS dial-up link. You can also set whether to use call-back security.

Copying Users

As we show you in the previous section, several dialog boxes contain important information about user accounts. You must properly define each dialog box for every user account on your network. Doing all that from scratch for every user could take decades. Fortunately, you have a simpler way to do this — copying.

You can copy a user account simply by selecting it in the list of user accounts in the main User Manager for Domain's window and choosing User⇨Copy. This creates a duplicate account with the same settings as the original. You need to redefine only these items:

- User name, full name, password, and confirmation.
- User Must Change Password at Next Logon check box — this box is cleared in the new account.
- Account Disabled check box — this box is cleared in the new account.

When you have to create lots of users with the same or similar settings, you can create a template user account. The template account should have all of the details required, but should be disabled. Use this account to create all the account copies.

Getting Pushy with Users

At some point during your management lifetime, you may need to disable, rename, and delete user accounts.

Disabling a user account is when you "turn off" the account so that it can't be used to gain entry to the system. To disable an account, select the Account Disabled check box in that account's Properties dialog box. When a user account is "locked out," it's disabled — the automatic feature from the Account Policy enables the Disabled checkbox.

Renaming a user account changes the human friendly name of the account. Just select the user account and choose User⇨Rename from the menu. A dialog box prompts you for the new name. A name change doesn't change the Security Identifier (SID) of the account, just the user name.

Deleting a user account completely removes the user account from the system. Select a user account and choose User⇨Delete from the menu. You're prompted to confirm the deletion. When you delete an account, it's gone for good. The SID used by the deleted account is never reused. Creating a new account with exactly the same configuration as the deleted account still results in a different account.

When users leave your organization, you need to decide whether you want to retain their old user accounts. You have a couple of options:

- Copy the old account for the new employee, and then delete or disable the old account.
- Rename the old account for the new employee (and of course change the password).

If your organization performs security audits, you should always make a copy of an account for a new employee instead of just renaming an existing account. This provides a unique SID for each person so that the security tracking system can provide accurate use-or-abuse information.

What about Groups?

A *group* is a collection of users who need similar levels of access to a resource. Groups are the primary means by which Windows NT grants users access to resources. Groups simplify the administration process by reducing the number of relationships that you have to manage. Instead of managing how each individual user relates to each resource, you only need to manage how the smaller number of groups relate to resources and to which groups each user belongs. This reduces the workload by 40 to 90 percent.

A group is nothing more than a named collection of users. Two types of groups exist: global and local. *Global groups* exist on a domain level. They are present on every computer throughout a domain and are managed by any User Manager for Domains tool hosted by Windows NT Server. *Local groups* exist only within a single computer. They aren't present throughout a domain and are managed by User Manager or User Manager for Domains on a Windows NT Workstation or Windows NT Server computer.

The two group types simplify the user-to-resource relationship. Although it may seem a bit complicated for a small network, using groups greatly reduces the management overhead for medium and large networks. You can use groups like this:

- Local groups are assigned access levels to resources.
- Users are assigned membership to a global group.
- A global group is assigned as a member of a local group.

Thus, users are granted access to resources by means of their global group membership and in turn that group's membership to a local group that has access to the resource. Whew, now it's time for a drink!

Take a look at a few important items to keep in mind about groups:

- A user can be a member of multiple global groups.
- A global group can be a member of multiple local groups.
- A resource can have multiple local groups assigned access to it. By using multiple local groups, you can define multiple levels of access to a resource from Read/Print to Change/Manage to Full Control.

Although you can assign a user direct membership to a local group or even direct access to a resource, doing so subverts the neat little scheme that Microsoft developed to simplify your life. So, just follow this prescription and you'll be vacationing on the beach in no time.

While any other group can be a member of a local group, a local group cannot be a member of any other group.

Windows NT Server and Windows NT Workstation both come with tools for using groups, but the tool that comes with Windows NT Server has more capability. You can use the User Manager for Domains on Windows NT Server to create and maintain both local and global groups. You can only use the User Manager on Windows NT Workstation to create and manage local groups. (You can add global groups to local groups, but that's it.)

To create a new group, choose User⇨New Global Group or User⇨New Local Group from the menu. Then you provide a name and add members. That's it. After you create a group, it appears in the list of groups in the bottom pane of the User Manager for Domains dialog box. Global groups appear with a globe icon, and local groups have a client/computer icon.

You don't have to create your own groups; Windows NT Server has several built-in local groups that you can use. Here they are, with default members in parentheses:

- Administrators (Administrator, Domain Admin group)
- Server Operators
- Account Operators
- Print Operators
- Backup Operators
- Users (Domain Users group)
- Guest (Domain Guests group)

These groups have both predefined built-in abilities and default user rights. You can modify the user rights of these groups (see this chapter's section titled "Users have the rights"), but not the built-in abilities. Figure 14-6 displays the abilities of these accounts.

Windows NT Server includes these three default global groups as well (default members are in parentheses):

- Domain Admins (Administrator)
- Domain Users (Administrator)
- Domain Guests (Guest)

▲ Local group has right or ability △ Local group does not have right or ability	Administrators	Server Operators	Account Operators	Print Operators	Back-up Operators	Everyone	Users	Guests
Rights:								
Log on locally	▲	▲	▲	▲	▲	△	△	△
Access this computer from network	▲	△	△	△	△	▲	△	△
Take ownership of files	▲	△	△	△	△	△	△	△
Manage auditing and security log	▲	△	△	△	△	△	△	△
Change the system time	▲	▲	△	△	△	△	△	△
Shut down the system	▲	▲	▲	▲	▲	△	△	△
Force shutdown from a remote system	▲	▲	△	△	△	△	△	△
Back up files and directories	▲	▲	△	△	▲	△	△	△
Restore files and directories	▲	▲	△	△	▲	△	△	△
Load and unload device drivers	▲	△	△	△	△	△	△	△
Add workstations to domain 1	△	△	△	△	△	△	△	△
Built-in abilities:								
Add workstation to domain	▲	△	▲	△	△	△	△	△
Create and manage user accounts	▲	△	▲	△	△	△	△	△
Create and manage global groups	▲	△	▲	△	△	△	△	△
Create and manage local groups	▲	△	▲	△	△	△	▲	△
Assign user rights	▲	△	△	△	△	△	△	△
Manage auditing of system events	▲	△	△	△	△	△	△	△
Lock the sever	▲	▲	△	△	△	▲	△	△
Override the lock of the sever	▲	△	△	△	△	△	△	△
Format server's hard disk	▲	△	△	△	△	△	△	△
Create common groups	▲	▲	△	△	△	△	△	△
Share and stop sharing directories	▲	▲	△	△	△	△	△	△
Share and stop sharing printers	▲	▲	△	▲	△	△	△	△

Figure 14-6: The default properties of Windows NT Server groups.

You can also use yet another group that isn't listed in the User Manager for Domains. The Everyone group is a catch-all group that has every single user as a member. If you grant access to the Everyone group, you grant access to everyone.

You should create groups that make sense to your organizational pattern, method of operations, or just common sense. Groups should be meaningful, and their names should reflect their purpose. Naming a group Sales isn't very useful, but a name of SalesPrintOnly is very informative. You should create groups so that users are divided by purpose, access levels, tasks, departments, or anything else you consider important. Remember, groups exist for your benefit, so try to get the most out of them.

Give Your Users Nice Profiles

A *user profile* is the collection of desktop, environment, network, and other settings that define and control the look, feel, and operation of the workstation. Windows NT records profile information automatically for each user. However, unless you make them roaming profiles (which you find out about later in this chapter), these profiles are only accessible locally and are stored by default in the \Winnt\Profiles*<username>*\ directory (where username is the actual name of the user to which the profile is associated). A user profile records lots of information about the user's environment and activities, including the following:

- Start menu configuration
- Screensaver and wallpaper settings
- List of recently accessed documents
- Favorites list from Internet Explorer
- Network mapped drives
- Installed network printers
- Desktop layout

In addition, a profile includes a compressed copy of the HKEY_CURRENT_USER Registry key in a file named NTUSER.DAT. To find definitions for all the various Registry keys, access the *Windows NT 4.0 Resource Kit* Registry tools Utility and access Regentry.hlp.

You can turn profiles into *roaming profiles.* (Note that a nonroaming profile is called a *local profile.*) A roaming profile is a profile that's stored on a network accessible drive so that no matter which workstation is used to gain access, the user's profile is available. Therefore, the user's working environment follows him or her from one computer to the next. To create and enable a roaming profile for a specific user, follow these steps:

1. **On the primary domain controller (PDC), create and share a directory named Users (or whatever name you like best).**
2. **On the workstation where the existing local profile resides, choose System from the Control Panel.**
3. **Select the User Profiles tab.**
4. **Select the profile that you want to make into a roaming profile.**
5. **Click Copy To.**

6. **Define a network accessible path for the new storage location for the profile in the dialog box that appears.**

   For example, `\\PDC\users\<username>`, where PDC is the primary domain controller's name, users is a share name, and username is the name of the user who belongs to the profile.

7. **On the PDC (or any Windows NT Server in the domain), launch the User Manager for Domains.**

   To do this, choose Start➪Programs➪Administrative Tools (Common)➪User Manager for Domains.

8. **Select a user, then choose User➪Properties from the menu bar.**

   This opens the Properties dialog box for the user.

9. **Click the Profile button to open the Profile dialog box.**

10. **In the User Profile Path field, type in the same path from Step 6 (that is, \\PDC\users\\<*username*>).**

11. **Click OK twice to return to the User Manager for Domains.**

The profile for the selected user is now a roaming profile. Once a user has a roaming profile, the local profile is no longer used. It remains on the system but the user account is now associated with the roaming profile.

By default, each time a user logs out, all changes made to his or her profile during that logon session (no matter what workstation he or she uses) are saved to the profile on the PDC. The next time the user logs on, the work environment is exactly the same as when he or she logged off. Local and roaming profiles should be used only by a single user. If multiple users need to use a single profile, you should employ a *mandatory profile*.

A mandatory profile doesn't save environmental changes when a user logs out. Instead, the profile retains the same configuration at all times. You create a mandatory profile by simply renaming the NTUSER.DAT file to NTUSER.MAN in either a local or roaming profile. Once this change is made, the profile remains consistent no matter who uses it. You can always reverse this process by renaming the NTUSER.MAN file back to NTUSER.DAT.

Where You Find Profiles, Policies Are Never Far Away

System policies are the collections of rules governing, controlling, or watching over the activities of users. Windows NT uses four types of policies: account, user rights, auditing, and system.

Account policies

The Account Policy defines the password restrictions and lockout regulations. You access the Account Policy dialog box (see Figure 14-7) by choosing Policy⇨Account from the menu bar of the User Manager for Domains. Changes made to this dialog box affect all users in the domain. Users currently logged in aren't affected by the changes until their next logon. Table 14-1 shows the possible settings for this dialog box.

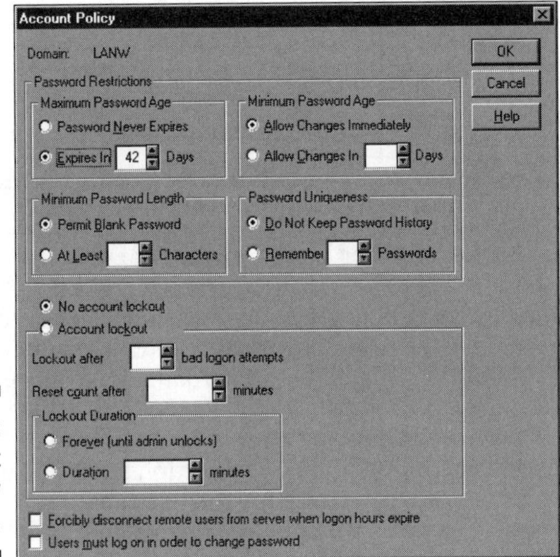

Figure 14-7: Account Policy dialog box.

Table 14-1 The Account Policy Settings

Policy	*Action*	*Settings*	*Default*
Maximum password age	Length of time before required password change	1–999 days or never	42 days
Minimum password age	Length of time password change is prevented	1–999 days or immediately	Immediately
Minimum password length	Smallest length of passwords	1–14 characters or blank	Permit blank
Password uniqueness	Maintain list of passwords to prevent re-use	1–24 history list or none	No history

Policy	Action	Settings	Default
Account lockout	Enables failed logon account lockout	Selected or not	No lockout
Lockout after	Number of attempts before lockout	1–999	Blank
Reset count after	Auto bad-logon counter reset time interval	1–99,999 minutes	Blank
Lockout duration	How long an account is locked out	1–99,999 minutes or forever	Blank
Forcibly disconnect remote users from server when logon hours expire	Disconnects remote users when logon hours expire	Selected or not	Not selected
Users must login to change password	Requires users to logon to change password	Selected or not	Not selected

If you're concerned about security, you should employ an accounts policy that requires regular password changes (a new password every 30 days or so) and locks out accounts that fail to logon successfully after three tries.

Users have the rights

You manage some capabilities within Windows NT as user rights. To call up the User Rights Policy dialog box, choose Policy⇨User Rights from the menu bar of the User Manager for Domains. You can grant user rights on a user or group basis. Table 14-2 shows you the 11 standard user rights.

Programmers and system developers use advanced user rights. We caution against working with advanced user rights unless you're well informed about their use and function. We encourage you to seek detailed information about advanced user rights in the Resource Kit or on Microsoft TechNet (`www.microsoft.com/technet/`).

Table 14-2 Group Default User Rights on Windows NT Server and NT Workstation

User rights	*Comments*	*Windows NT Server*	*NT Workstations*
Manage auditing and security log	Specify what types of file and object access are to be audited. View and clear the security log.	Administrators	Administrators
Back up files and directories	Administrators, Server Operators, Backup Operators	Administrators, Backup Operators	
Restore files and directories	This right supersedes file permissions; a user with the Restore right can overwrite files for which he or she has no permissions, when performing a restore.	Administrators, Server Operators, Backup Operators	Administrators, Backup Operators
Change system time	Administrators, Server Operators	Administrators, Power Users	
Access this computer from network	Access the computer from another workstation on the network.	Administrators, Everyone	Administrators, Power Users, Everyone
Log on locally	Ability to log on at the computer itself on the computer's keyboard.	Administrators, Server Operators, Account Operators, Print Operators, Backup Operators	Administrators, Backup Operators, Power Users, Users, Guests
Shut down the system	Administrators, Server Operators, Account Operators, Print Operators, Backup Operators	Administrators, Backup Operators, Power Users, Users, Guests	

User rights	*Comments*	*Windows NT Server*	*NT Workstations*
Add workstations and member servers to domain	Allows a user who is not a member of the domain's Administrators group to add computers running Windows NT Workstation or computers running Windows NT Server as member servers to the domain.	None	N/A
Take ownership of files and other objects	Take ownership of files and directories on the computer.	Administrators	Administrators
Load and unload device drivers		Administrators	Administrators
Force shutdown from a remote system	This right gives a user no abilities in this version of Windows NT but will be supported in future upgrades of the operating system.	Administrators, Server Operators	Administrators, Power Users

Auditing for trouble

The Audit Policy enables you to track the activities throughout your network. Auditing the goings on within your network can help you locate configuration problems, security breaches, improper activity, and misuse of the system. Auditing records the success and/or the failure of seven event types:

- **Logon and Logoff:** Records connections and disconnections to the network
- **File and Object Access:** Records connections to files, directories, printers, and other NTFS objects
- **Use of User Rights:** Records employment or activation of user rights
- **User and Group Management:** Watches for changes made to users and groups

- **Security Policy Changes:** Watches for alterations of user rights and audit polices
- **Restart, Shutdown, and System:** Watches system power ups and downs, as well as other security compromising occurrences
- **Process Tracking:** Monitors the activity of processes

The information obtained through auditing is recorded in the Event View's Security Log (choose Start⇨Programs⇨Administrative Tools (Common)⇨ Event Viewer, and then select Security from the Log menu). Figure 14-8 shows a sample audit event listing all the information about the event, including time, user, computer, source, and even description details. With this information and good resources (such as TechNet), you can track down the cause of the audit event.

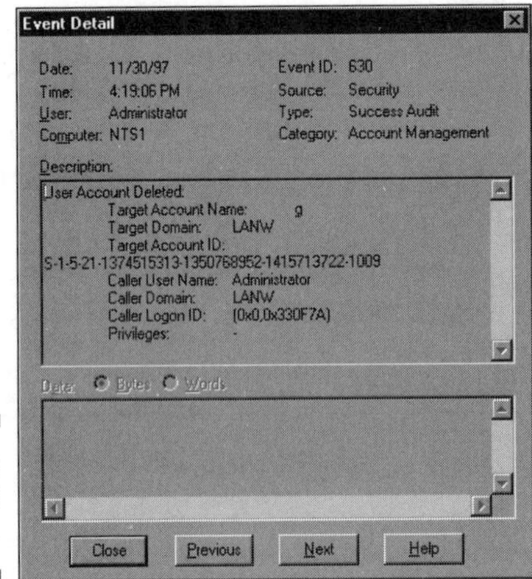

Figure 14-8: Event Detail dialog box.

You enable the auditing system of Windows NT through a series of switches. You access the main Audit Policy dialog box (see Figure 14-9) by choosing Policies⇨Audit from the menu bar of the User Manager for Domains. You can enable or disable auditing by using the Do Not Audit/Audit These Events radio button. When you enable auditing, the seven types of events are revealed each with a success and failure check box. By selecting from these fourteen check boxes, you determine which events are recorded by the audit system.

All events are controlled in this dialog box except for the File and Object Access types, which you find in another configuration box located at the object level. To access this dialog box, select any Windows NT File System (NTFS) object (such as a file, directory, or printer) and open its Properties

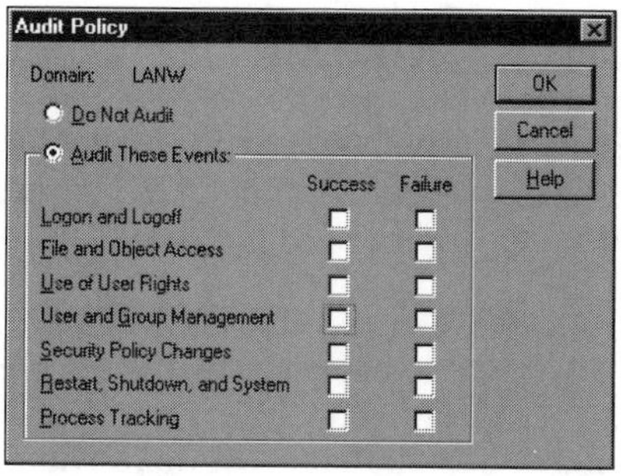

Figure 14-9: Audit Policy dialog box.

(typically by right-clicking and selecting Properties from the pop-up menu). Then, select the Security tab and click the Auditing button. You use the Object-type Auditing dialog box (see Figure 14-10) to set the types of activities to be audited on an object-by-object basis for selected users and/or groups. The dialog box you see in Figure 14-10 is for a directory; it offers audit events of Read, Write, Execute, Delete, Change Permissions, and Take Ownership. You can audit these for success (completed action) and/or failure (incomplete action) for all users and groups listed in the Name field. Users and groups are added to the Name field using the Add button.

Figure 14-10: A Directory Auditing dialog box. (Note: The Everyone group was added to this dialog box so that the Events list at the bottom would be readable instead of near-invisible gray.)

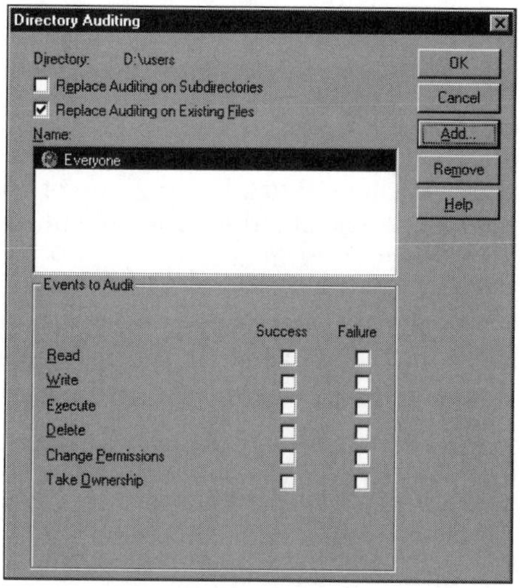

When Access Problems Loom. . . .

User accounts govern who can access a computer system and what level of access that person enjoys. However, users sometimes run into problems that prevent the normal operation of the logon process.

Most logon problems center around an incorrectly typed password. Therefore, users should take the time to type in their passwords correctly. This is good advice only if their accounts haven't been locked out due to failed logon attempts. If your user's account is locked out, it must be re-enabled. This occurs in one of two ways. If the lockout policy is set with a duration, you only need wait until the time expires and try again. But if the lockout policy requires administrative intervention, you have to reset that user's account.

When a user can't log on or communication with the network seems weird, here are some things to check:

- Make sure the NIC and other physical network connections are solid.
- If on a Windows NT Workstation computer, ensure that the computer is a member of the domain.
- If using IP, check the IP protocol settings to ensure that the computer is using the correct IP address and subnet mask.
- If the PDC is offline, you should be able to logon if a BDC (backup domain controller) is on the network.
- If no PDC or BDC is online, then you can't join the network until one of them returns.
- If your network employs Dynamic Host Configuration Protocol (DHCP) to assign IP settings from a small pool to a larger group of computers, you may be stuck as the last person standing when the music stops and all available connection addresses are in use.

If you can log on but not access all the resources you think you should, you need to verify (sometimes with the help of an administrator) several items:

- Group memberships
- Physical network connections to resource hosts (that is, check to see that a server's network cable isn't disconnected)
- Presence of system policies restricting your action

If everything we mention checks out, then you may have a fairly esoteric problem. Consult a Microsoft resource (online or via TechNet) to search for a solution. Yeah, that's a bit of weak advice, but it's the most valuable thing we can tell you. The Microsoft information database is expansive, and most often, someone else has had the same problem and you can find information posted about its resolution.

Chapter 15

Managing Shares and Permissions

In This Chapter

- Understanding how permissions apply to NTFS objects
- Understanding how permissions apply to file shares
- Exploring special access rights
- Distinguishing between creation and inheritance
- Determining actual permissions
- Undoing the NTFS and share defaults
- Making access controls work

To a large extent, working with Windows NT Server means using the *Windows NT File System,* usually known as NTFS. This file system's advanced features include object-level *Access Control Lists* (ACLs), so that you can control not only which users or groups may access a volume, directory, or file, but also control which operations users or groups can perform against a volume, directory, or file.

Windows NT also supports the *FAT file system,* which doesn't include object-level access controls. However, FAT does support so-called *file shares* (shared directories with the files they contain), that do support access controls. Understanding how shares work and how NTFS permissions combine with share permissions is a major focus of this chapter. Here, we show you how to figure out what a user can (and can't) do to your files based on their account permissions, the groups to which they belong, and the underlying defaults that apply to Windows NT Server itself.

Of Objects, Rights, and Permissions

Before you can revel in the details of the rights and permissions that apply to Windows NT, you should ponder some technical terminology. That's why we take a brief detour to dictionary-ville — right here, right now.

An object lesson . . .

Windows NT treats all user-accessible system resources — which includes users, groups, files, directories, printers, processes, and lots more — as *objects*. Objects have a special meaning to programmers and tech-heads: This term refers to a named collection of *attributes* and *values,* plus a named collection of *methods,* which Microsoft calls *services*.

For example, a file object has a variety of attributes that you already know about, if you've spent any time at all around computers: Files have names, types, lengths, owners, plus creation and modification dates. For an object, each attribute also has an associated value, so the attributes of an object of type "file" might be:

- **Name:** BOOT.INI
- **Type:** Configuration settings
- **Contents:** Information on how to boot Windows NT (Windows NT can locate and read the contents by using the drive's file directory.)
- **Size:** About 1KB

Attributes, in short, identify individual objects of some specific type — in this case, of type file — and define what they contain, where they're located, and so on.

On the other hand, it may not be so readily apparent why methods or services are important for objects. But if you examine an object of type file, you can see that the methods that apply to it describe operations that you would want to apply to a file. Thus, the methods that apply to objects of type file include things like read, write, execute, delete, and so on. In short, methods define the operations that can be applied to the objects to which they belong. Among other things, this makes objects pretty much self-defining, because they not only include complete descriptions of themselves in their attributes, but they also contain complete descriptions of what you can do to them in their methods or services. Thus, the methods or services that apply to a file are things like read, write, delete, rename, and other typical file operations. Other object types have different associated methods or services that reflect the object's capabilities and the data it contains.

When you examine the attributes for specific objects in Windows NT, things start getting pretty interesting. Every object in the Windows NT environment has an associated attribute called an Access Control List, otherwise known as an ACL (this is sometimes pronounced *ackle,* to rhyme with *cackle*). ACLs identify those individual user accounts or groups that may access a particular object, and also indicate which services each individual user or group may apply to that object. Administrators use ACLs to control access to objects, giving themselves free reign to troubleshoot objects while limiting ordinary users' abilities to accidentally (or purposefully) harm the system.

When is a file NOT an object?

Windows NT uses objects for just about anything in its operating environment that users can access. In fact, NTFS volumes, directories, and files are NT objects with associated attributes and a set of well-defined services that may be applied to those objects. But because the older File Allocation Table (FAT) file system does not include built-in support for ACLs, FAT files are *not* objects. Thus, even though FAT volumes, directories, and files still have attributes similar to those for NTFS files — namely, name, type, creation date, modification date, and so forth — FAT volumes, directories, and files are not NT objects, per se. This explains why FAT volumes and their contents are inherently insecure (because normal permissions don't apply to them).

More important, this also explains why the default logon behavior for Windows NT Server is to deny everyone but administrators, server operators, backup operators, and printer operators the "right to log on locally." That's because anyone who can access a FAT volume can do anything they want to it. By denying ordinary users the right to log onto an NT server at its keyboard, and requiring them to log on only through the network, NT can control access to FAT volumes through shares, which do function as NT objects, and therefore have built-in access controls.

Users have rights; objects have permissions

In Windows NT, the standard terminology is to refer to *user rights* and *object permissions*. Because object permissions is rather vague, you usually hear permissions used in reference to a specific object, such as *file permissions, printer permissions,* and so on.

A user's rights define what he or she can do to objects in the Windows NT environment. A user obtains rights to objects in one of three ways:

- Explicit assignments of the rights to an individual user account
- The rights that pertain to the groups to which the user belongs
- The User Rights controls in the Policies menu in the User Manager for Domains administration tool, which is where rights to log on locally, or to access a computer from the network, are set

When a user logs on to a Windows NT domain (or a stand-alone system), part of what happens during logon is the generation of special key called an *access token*. The access token represents the user's explicit individual rights and the groups to which the user belongs. It takes some time to generate an access token, which is one reason why logging on to Windows NT isn't instantaneous.

Every object in the Windows NT environment includes an attribute called *permissions,* which includes an ACL that identifies all the users and groups permitted to access the object as well as the services that each user or group may apply to the object. Each time a user requests an object, Windows NT uses a built-in facility called the *Security Reference Monitor* (SRM) to check the user's access token against the permissions for that object. If the SRM finds that the user has permission, Windows NT fulfills the request; otherwise, the user is out of luck.

Of NTFS and Permissions

NTFS (the New Technology File System) is a file system just like FAT (File Allocation Table) and FAT32 (the 32-bit File Allocation Table used in Windows 98) are also file systems. The difference between NTFS and these other file systems is that NTFS is an *object-oriented file system.* Unlike FAT and FAT32, NTFS sees everything in NTFS partitions as objects of some specific type that have attributes and to which methods and services can be applied. The benefit of using NTFS is that you can set permissions for the volumes, files, and directories that use NTFS.

In fact, NTFS recognizes three types of objects:

- **Volumes** are the NTFS-formatted drive partitions that show up as disk drive icons in Windows NT Explorer. A volume object may contain files and directories.
- **Directories** are named containers for files that occur in a volume or within some other directory. In fact, Windows NT enables you to nest directories however deep you want, which means that you can put as many directories within directories within directories as you like (although nested directories reach a point of diminishing returns fairly quickly).
- **Files** are named containers for data that include type, size, dates, and contents among their attributes. Files are where information actually resides in NTFS.

To examine the permissions for any object within NTFS, right-click that object in the left-hand pane of Windows NT Explorer. In the pop-up menu (see Figure 15-1), select Properties and then select the Security tab in the Properties dialog box. Then click the Permissions button to call up the Permissions dialog box (see Figure 15-2). From here, you can investigate the list of available permissions for this object (volume E: on our hard drive in this case) through the list that appears beneath the Type of Access text entry box in the lower-right corner.

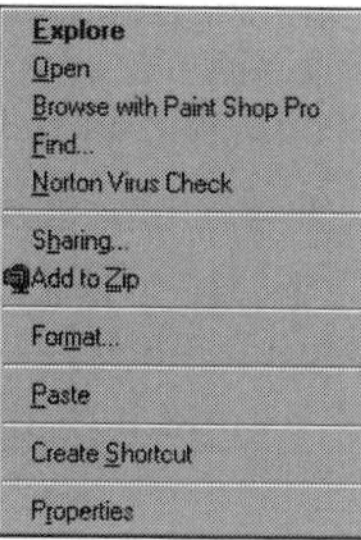

Figure 15-1: Right-click any object in Windows NT Explorer to call up this pop-up menu, and then select Properties.

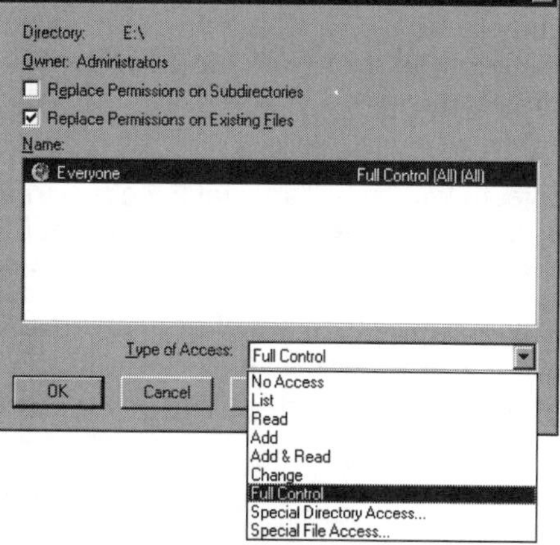

Figure 15-2: The Type of Access list shows you all the permissions that apply to the object.

Volume and directory permissions

The Type of Access list in the Permissions dialog box shows permissions for files, volumes, and directory objects in NTFS (see Figure 15-2). We use the generic term *container* to refer to volumes and directories, because other than how they're displayed in NT Explorer and differences in a few hidden attributes, volumes and directories use the same permissions. Here are the permissions that apply to containers:

- **No Access** means what it sounds like — if you apply this permission to a user or a group, that user or group can't access the directory. They may still be able to see the container name itself, but they won't be able to examine its contents.
- **List** means that users can inspect the contents of the container, usually by double-clicking its icon in either the left- or right-hand panes in Windows NT Explorer. The List permission only allows users to read file names, not their contents.

- **Read** means that any files created within this container may be read by users who have this permission. Users can open files and read their contents; if the file is a program of some kind, users can execute it. But users can't do anything else, such as write to or delete the file.
- **Add** means that users can add files or directories to the container, but doesn't let them read or execute files within the container.
- **Add and Read** combines the Read and Add rights so that users can read and execute files in the container, as well as add files or directories to the container.
- **Change** adds delete capability to Add and Read items within the container. (However, the user can't delete the container itself.)
- **Full Control** adds the ability to take ownership of any object. Once ownership is taken, the new owner can assign permissions to the object, plus do anything else that's associated with the Change permission. See the sidebar called "Taking ownership of objects in NTFS" for more about these permissions.
- **Special Directory Access** provides access to a set of permissions related to directory objects known as "special access permissions." See the section titled "Special Access Rights" later in this chapter for more on this topic.
- **Special File Access** provides access to set of permissions related to file objects known as "special access permissions." See the section titled "Special Access Rights" later in this chapter for more on this topic.

Taking ownership of objects in NTFS

An owner of an object can always modify its permissions, no matter what permissions may already be set for that object. This permission exists, at least in part, to sidestep the "No Access" trap that can occur when an object's owner mistakenly sets permissions for a general group, such as Everyone or Authenticated Users (these two default groups are discussed further in Chapter 14).

If Everyone has No Access to an object, that includes anyone who may want to access that object. Unless an administrator or the object's creator (its owner by default) can reset permissions to be a little less restrictive, nobody can access that object — or any objects it contains.

Full Control is important because it grants administrators and the object's owner the power to change access to that object and to change services that apply to the object. In essence, full control is your get-out-of-jail-free card!

File permissions

File permissions in NTFS have some similarity to directory and volume permissions, but remember that the meaning may be a shade different when applied to files rather than directories and volumes. NTFS file permissions consist of the following items:

- **No Access** means that any user with this permission can't access the file object at all.
- **Read** means that any user with this permission can read and execute the file, but can't request any other services from it, such as writing to or deleting.
- **Change** means that any user can read, write to, execute, or delete the file, but can't take ownership or change permissions.
- **Full Control** adds the ability to take ownership of a file or to change permissions for a file to the abilities already established by the Change permission.
- **Special File Access** provides access to a set of permissions related to file objects called "special access permissions." See the section titled "Special Access Rights" later in this chapter for more on this topic.

Special Access Rights

Directories have Special Directory Access and Special File Access entries, and files have a Special File Access entry in their Permissions dialog boxes. As it turns out, what you get under the heading of Special Access for files and directories includes two types of permissions: *basic permissions* that define specific individual operations and *advanced permissions* that only systems programmers and other propeller-heads ever mess with. You should probably familiarize yourself with the basic permissions, but we only discuss the most useful of the advanced permissions.

Basic permissions

The permission levels that we describe in the previous sections are actually combinations of the basic permissions that we describe in this section. Microsoft created access levels like No Access, Read Access, and so on as a convenience to users and administrators. Table 15-1 summarizes the basic permissions from which these access levels are derived. These basic permissions apply to both files and directories.

Table 15-1 Basic File and Directory Permissions

Name	*How it applies to a file*	*How it applies to a directory*
Read	View a file's contents, attributes, permissions, and owner's name	View file and directory names within the container, plus access to attributes, permissions, and owner's name for the directory itself
Write	View permissions, and permits changes to file's contents and attributes	View permissions, and permits creation of files and sub-directories within the directory, plus allows changes to attributes
Execute	Permits programs to be executed, and viewing of a file's attributes, permissions, and owner's name (doesn't imply Read permission)	Permits viewing of attributes, permissions, and owner, plus navigation to subdirectories
Delete	Permits the file to be deleted	Permits the directory to be deleted
Change Permission	Permits a file's permissions to be altered	Permits a directory's permissions to be altered
Take Ownership	Permits the user who exercises this permission to become the file's owner	Permits the user who exercises his permission to become the directory's owner

Table 15-2 shows what basic permissions (see Table 15-1) are included in each type of directory permission.

Table 15-2 Directory Permissions and Basic Permissions

File	*Read*	*Write*	*Execute*	*Delete*	*Change*	*Take*
No Access						
List	X					
Read	X		X			
Add		X				
Add and Read	X	X	X			
Change	X	X	X	X		
Full Control	X	X	X	X	X	X

Table 15-3 shows the basic permissions (see Table 15-1) that are included in each general kind of file permission.

Table 15-3 File Permissions and Basic Permissions

File	*Read*	*Write*	*Execute*	*Delete*	*Change*	*Take*
No Access						
Read	X		X			
Change	X	X	X	X		
Full Control	X	X	X	X	X	X

These tables tell you exactly what's included in the various file and directory permissions. Use them if you're ever in doubt about what's going on regarding permissions.

Advanced permissions

Advanced permission entries produce additional lists of often arcane special access rights that are seldom used (nor often needed) under ordinary conditions. For example, a system programmer might use one of these advanced permissions called "act as part of the operating system" for a system extension she wrote. This would permit that application to execute as if it were part of the Windows NT operating system, and to take on other system attributes, instead of running as an ordinary application outside the NT operating system kernel.

One special directory access that may occasionally come in handy is called "Bypass traverse checking." This right permits users with No Access to a particular directory to navigate through that directory to get to subdirectories beneath it, where they *are* permitted to access files. Most experts agree that bypass traverse checking is a workaround to overcome weird file system designs and that you shouldn't need it in a well-designed file system. We hope you never need it, but it's nice to know it's there!

If you really must dig up all the details on special access rights, please consult Microsoft's TechNet CD. If you search for a Technical Note called "Securing Windows NT 4.0 Installation," you will find them explained fully there.

FAT Has No Permissions

Because the FAT file system that Windows NT supports along with NTFS includes no object mechanisms for associating attributes with files and directories, files stored in a FAT-formatted volume have no associated permissions. Anybody who's allowed to log onto a Windows NT server with a FAT partition can access any of the files in that partition. This helps explain why you may want to restrict who's allowed to work on your servers, as well as lock up your servers.

There are two extremely good reason why FAT partitions are still around, however:

1. A dual-boot machine that runs Windows 95 or 98 and Windows NT together must include a FAT partition from which the other operating system can boot. This might be a FAT32 partition for Windows 98, but we recommend FAT because NT will be able to read that partition when it is running. (NT can't read FAT32 partitions without extra software help.)
2. More operating systems can read FAT partitions than any other kind of file system. That's why FAT remains popular — and present — on multi-boot computers that run Windows NT along with other operating systems: because files on the FAT partition should be readable no matter which operating system may be running at any given moment.

Only Windows NT can read NTFS partitions, so be careful when reformatting partitions on dual- or multi-boot machines!

Share Permissions

When users access files on a Windows NT server, they usually do so across the network, especially if you restrict who's allowed to log on to the server and limit physical access to the machine. Thus, most users who access files on a Windows NT server do so through a network share, which is a directory on a Windows NT server that you've shared to the network for public access.

Shares are also objects for Windows NT, so permissions do apply. The list of applicable permissions consists of the following four entries:

- **No Access** prevents access to the shared directory no matter what other permissions may apply.
- **Read** permits viewing of files in the share, loading of files across the network, and program execution.

- **Change** includes all Read permissions, plus creating, deleting, or changing directories and files within the share.
- **Full Control** includes all Change permissions plus changing permissions for and taking ownership of the share.

No Special Access exists for shares. Table 15-4 summarizes the basic permissions for shares (notice the complete overlap with Table 15-3).

Table 15-4 Share Permissions and Basic Permissions

File	*Read*	*Write*	*Execute*	*Delete*	*Change*	*Take*
No Access						
Read	X		X			
Change	X	X	X	X		
Full Control	X	X	X	X	X	X

If you want to expose contents of a FAT partition on a Windows NT server to network users, doing so through a share automatically gives you some degree of access control. Yet another advantage to using a network!

To create a share, select a directory in My Computer or NT Explorer, then right click. Select the Sharing entry in the resulting pop up menu, to produce the Properties window for that directory, with the Sharing tab on top. This is shown in Figure 15-3.

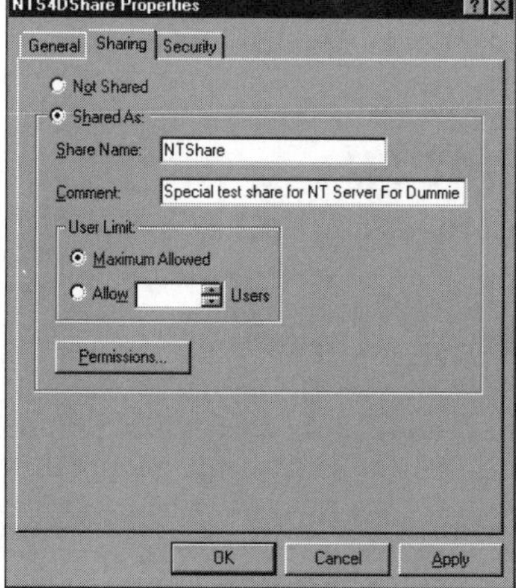

Figure 15-3: The Sharing tab in the Properties window provides easy access to a share's name, user limits, and permissions information.

There are four important areas in this window that relate to creating and managing shares:

1. You must click the radio button that reads "Shared As:" to enable sharing on a directory.
2. By default a share's name is the same as the directory from which it comes. When creating shares, remember that DOS and Windows 3.*x* users can only access shares with names that are a maximum of 8 characters long.
3. The User Limit pane lets you limit how many users can access a share simultaneously. This will usually be a concern only on heavily loaded NT servers; in most cases you'll leave it set to the "Maximum Allowed" default.
4. You control share permissions through the Permissions button at the bottom left of the Shared As pane. These work the same way as NTFS permissions.

Calculating Actual Permissions

Users have rights as a result of the NTFS permissions explicitly assigned to specific files or directories for their accounts, but also by virtue of the groups to which they belong. Because NTFS shares exist, figuring out permissions can get pretty interesting when you have to combine NTFS and share permissions for a particular file or directory, while also taking user settings and group memberships into account. To help you figure out what's what, we give you a recipe for calculation, plus a few rules to use, and then walk you through an example to show you how things work.

The rules of calculation

To figure out which permissions apply to a share on an NTFS object, you must first determine what permissions apply to the NTFS object by itself. Next, you must determine the permissions that apply to the share. The rules for this process appear in the following section. Whichever of the two results is most restrictive wins and defines the actual permissions that apply to the file or directory in question. This process isn't difficult, but it may produce some counter-intuitive results. You must apply these rules exactly as they're stated, or we can't guarantee the results. Here goes:

1. **Determine the permissions on the NT object.**

   If No Access appears anywhere in a collection of permissions, the result is No Access.

If No Access doesn't appear in the user's explicit permissions, the user gets to add up the permissions for each group to which the user belongs. (Thus Read from one group and Add from another group for the \DataFiles directory combine, and result in Read and Add.)

2. **Determine the permissions on the share.**

   Use the same instructions as for the NT object: Namely, if the user has No Access — sorry, Charlie, no permission. Otherwise, the user gets to add all the permissions for all the groups he or she belongs to together. The user has all these permissions.

3. **Compare the permissions between the share and the NT object. The *more restrictive* permission is the permission that applies.**

Figure this!

This formal explanation may not completely illuminate this process, so we give you a couple of examples to show you how it's done.

No Access rears its ugly head

Actually, when No Access appears in a collection of permissions, it means you can skip straight to the final result — namely, No Access. We've heard this rule succinctly summarized as "No Access means no access," but we can do the calculation work anyway.

Bob is a member of the Domain Administrators, Domain Users, and Log Files groups. His individual and group NTFS and share permissions for a file named Test.txt appear in Table 15-5.

Table 15-5 Bob's NTFS and Share Permissions

Type	*Membership*	*Name*	*Permissions*
NTFS	User Account	BobS	Read
	Group	Domain Administrators	Full Control
	Group	Domain Users	Change
	Group	Log Files	Change
Share	User Account	BobS	Change
	Group	Domain Administrators	Full Control
	Group	Domain Users	Change
	Group	Log Files	No Access

Even though you already know the result is No Access, you can work through the calculation process anyway, just for practice. On the NTFS side, Read (from Bob's account) plus Full Control (from the Domain Administrators group) equals Full Control (permissions accumulate, but Full Control already covers the whole gamut of basic access permissions). Full Control plus Change equals Full Control, so the result of the accumulation for the NTFS side is Full Control.

On the share side, change plus Full Control is Full Control, so that takes care of the first three entries. Then No Access appears, so the result is No Access.

Now, compare the NTFS result with the share result. Because No Access (from the share side) is more restrictive than Full Control (from the NTFS side), the result is No Access. Bob doesn't pass Go or collect $200!

Whenever you or your users can't obtain access to some file system object through a share (or NTFS by itself, for that matter), always check group memberships and their associated permissions.

When No Access doesn't apply

The next example doesn't include No Access. Betty belongs to the Marketing Dept, Domain Users, and Film Critics groups. She wants to delete the file in an NTFS share named Rosebud.doc. Can she do it? Table 15-6 shows her individual and group permissions.

Table 15-6 Betty's NTFS and Share Permissions

Type	*Membership*	*Name*	*Permissions*
NTFS	User Account	BettyB	Read
	Group	Marketing Dept	Read
	Group	Domain Users	Change
	Group	Film Critics	Change
Share	User Account	BettyB	Read
	Group	Marketing Dept	Read
	Group	Domain Users	Read
	Group	Film Critics	Read

On the NTFS side, Read plus Change equals Change; on the share side Read is the only game in town. The most restrictive of Read and Change is Read. Read won't allow Betty to delete a file, so Betty's out of luck! Maybe next time. . . .

Undo the Default!

We'd like to warn you about a gaping hole in Windows NT file security: The default is to grant Full Control access to files and directories to a default group named Everyone (to which every user in the domain belongs). This means that anyone and Everyone can read, write, execute, delete, change permissions, and take ownership of anything and everything in any new directory or volume that you create on your server. Delete the entire drive? Sure, no problem. Read any file you like? Whatever you say. Most workplace networks can't tolerate such lax security.

Here are two ways to fix this problem:

- **You can reset the permissions for Everyone to Read each time you create a new volume.** Don't go all the way to No Access or no one will have access to the volume, including you, because every user is a member of the Everyone group. This is a safe base-level permission for NTFS volumes.
- **You can apply the security fix in Service Pack 3 (and later Service Packs) to your Windows NT server.** Go ahead — we think it's a good idea for all kinds of reasons. SP3 (and SP4) replaces the Everyone group with a more restrictive group called Authenticated Users — only users with valid domain accounts belong to this group, and only they can access domain resources. Even so, we still recommend that you also set the base-level permission for new volumes to Read for Authenticated Users.

When you reset base-level permissions, make sure you also grant the Domain Administrators or Administrators group Full Control. That way, you can always take ownership and reset permissions if something funky happens.

Chapter 16

Backing Up for a Rainy Day

In This Chapter

- Understanding why backing up data is important
- Looking at Windows NT backup methods
- Discovering third-party alternatives
- Getting familiar with the terminology
- Making backup a habit
- Securing the backup delegates

Having a backup recovery scheme for your organization's data is very important because of the critical business applications and functions that reside on networks. Without a plan in place to protect data, disruptions to an entire organization's data and workflow process can occur, resulting in loss of revenue. Unfortunately, many organizations place little emphasis on protecting their data until an actual loss occurs. In this chapter, you find out about different methods for protecting your organization's data to prevent losses.

Why Bother Backing Up?

Backing up is the process of copying data from one location to another — either manually or unattended. Copying data from one directory on a hard disk to another directory on that same hard disk is effective until the hard disk crashes and both copies of the data are inaccessible. In addition, by copying the data to the same drive, you neglect to copy any of the security or account information. This means you have to re-enter that information manually. Don't you think it's a better idea to back up all files, such as system, application, and user data, to another physical medium, such as a tape or other backup device, and then rotate that device off-site periodically?

Many organizations today place critical business functions and data on a network, for example e-mail, accounting, payroll, personnel records, and operations. Loss of just one segment of that information hinders an organization's operations, even if it's just for a short time. Imagine if the payroll information disappeared from the system, and all or some of the employees did not receive their checks on time. We wouldn't want to be there!

Organizations can avoid data loss problems almost entirely by backing up their networks on a regular basis. Data loss occurrences can be as simple as one corrupt file, or as complex as the entire contents of a server's hard disk becoming unreadable.

All types of threats pose danger to data. Everything from fires to computer viruses can obliterate data on a network. Planning for each type of possible disaster can help you completely secure and restore your organization's data should that disaster occur.

Data loss on a network can occur in many ways. If you know what the potential threats are and you plan for them, you can prevent both serious damage to your network and loss of data. We want to urge you to back up your network always and to rotate a recent copy off site.

Following are some of the potential threats you and your network can encounter:

- **Hard disk crash:** Even if you've built in fault tolerance to your server, such as mirroring or duplexing, don't rely on those methods working 100 percent. We've seen mirrored drives going out of synch without notice until the hard disk crashes. Without backups, you can lose all of your data or segments of it. Complementing mirroring and duplexing with regular backups is a good idea.
- **Ungraceful shutdown:** Every once in a while, you get a smart-aleck employee who hits the on/off switch to the server, causing it to shut down improperly. Most servers today come right back up, but not always. Shutting the server down in this manner can render the hard disks unreadable. You should put your servers in a secure location away from end users. And don't forget, back up on a regular basis!
- **Viruses:** Many organizations connect to the Internet, permitting employees to download all types of data to the LAN that could introduce viruses. Viruses pose a real threat to organizations. One virus can ruin an entire computer and render it useless in a very short amount of time. If this computer happens to be a server on your network, someone's going to be reading the employment classifieds. Installing virus protection software on the server allows you to check for viruses before they're stored on the server. Put a backup plan in place that permits you to restore data to your network prior to the introduction of the virus.

- **Environmental disasters:** We've seen many organizations lose data during environmental disturbances, such as a bad storm. If lightning can zap the electronics in your home, imagine what it can do to the data on a network.

  Some environmental disasters you should plan for include

  - ***Fire:*** One fire in a building or on a floor can annihilate an entire organization. If your organization loses everything in a fire, you'll be the savior if you produce a recent tape of the network that was sitting safely offsite somewhere. However, if you store your backup tapes on top of your server in the computer room, you'll be the one pounding the pavement.
  - ***Floods:*** Placing a computer room, server, or backup equipment in the basement or first floor of a building is a bad idea, particularly in flood-prone areas. One flood can obliterate an entire organization. Even if a flood does occur, you're safe with your backup tapes offsite — away from the flood zone.
  - ***Hurricanes:*** Hurricanes bring high winds with them. Don't put your server or backup equipment in a computer room with outside windows. You could just come back and find everything strewn around the computer room and sopping wet and have no backup tapes to restore.
  - ***Temperature:*** Something as simple as placing a server or backup machine in an enclosed room without proper air conditioning and ventilation can cause problems. Don't put a server or backup equipment in a small room with other heavy heat equipment, such as a copier, without cool air flowing through it. Buildings do shut down their air systems on weekends and holidays and the heat can kill servers.

Some viruses have a gestation period; therefore, they can be inserted onto your network but go unnoticed until after a set number of days. We've seen disgruntled employees place viruses on networks and then leave a company — 30 days later, a virus appears. Incorporate this thought into your backup plan by always backing up on a 30-day rotation scheme. If a virus like this is introduced onto your network, you can go back at least 30 days in your backup tapes to try to restore the network prior to the virus' introduction. If you only have a week's worth of backup, then all the backup you have contains the virus. Virus software from Norton (`www.symantec.com`) and McAfee (`www.mcafeemall.com/`) tend to have less conflicts with Windows NT than other brands of virus software.

The Windows NT Built-in Backup Facility

Windows NT ships with NTBACKUP, which includes two methods for backing up your server: a GUI interface (Start⇨Programs⇨Administrative Tools⇨Backup) and a command line execution (\WINNT\system32 directory\ntbackup). We prefer the GUI interface (as shown in Figure 16-1) for quick manual backups, and the command line interface for batched and scheduled backups. These methods are not exactly unattended because you have to start them to run manually — unless you set them up with a scheduler task to run automatically at a preset time. Although somewhat crude and not so fancy, NTBACKUP is better than nothing. If your budget is low and you can't afford to purchase a third-party vendor that specializes in backup software, then this is the way to go. And, the best part is that it's free (it's included in the price of Windows NT Server)!

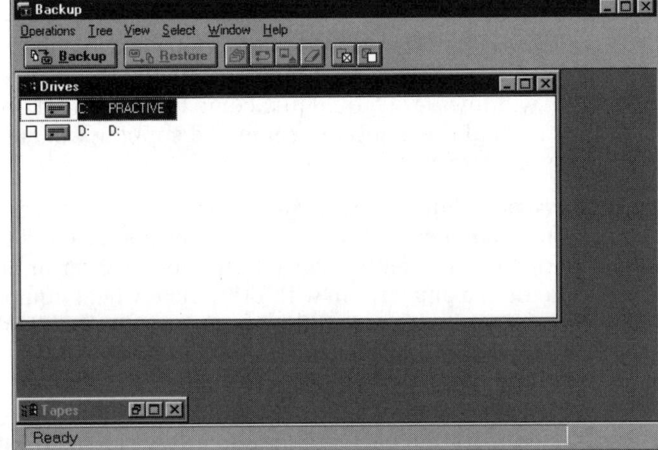

Figure 16-1: NT's built-in GUI backup.

Before purchasing a third-party backup product or using the Windows NT built-in backup program, search Microsoft Knowledgebase (`support.microsoft.com/support`) for known bugs and problems regarding backup issues. Be specific in the search (for example, **NT Server 4.0 ntbackup**). Also, always install the latest Service Pack on your Windows NT Server, which fixes most minor bugs known to Microsoft.

You can choose from several different approaches to backing up data: full (also called normal), copy, daily, incremental, and differential:

- **Full:** Backs up all of the files from the server, and each file gets an archive bit set to denote the file was archived.
- **Copy:** The same as full, but no archive bit is set on the file to indicate it was backed up.

- **Incremental:** Looks at the last full or incremental backup and determines which files have changed. After it does that, it backs up only those files and sets the archive bit.
- **Differential:** Grabs only the files that have changed since the last full backup and does not change the archive bit.
- **Daily:** Specifies to back up those files modified today or on the day specified.

What's the difference between an incremental and differential backup? When restoring data to a server that used the incremental method to back up, you first restore the full tape set, then restore as many as incremental tape sets as it takes to bring you to the current date. With differential restore, you need to restore only the full tape set plus the differential tape.

Before backing up, run the repair disk utility (START⇨RUN, then type in: `\WINNT\SYSTEM32\RDISK /S` to back up the Registry to the `\REPAIR` directory, have all users log out, and stop all services in the Control Panel that have databases open, such as WINS and DHCP. The /s switch backs up the security and Security Account Manager (SAM) Registry hives.

Command line backups

You execute NTBACKUP from the command prompt using the following syntax:

```
ntbackup operation pathname [/a][/v][/r][/d "text"][/b]
         [/hc:{on | off}] [/t{option}][/l"filename"][/e]
         [/tape:{n}]
```

The / parameters options in the syntax above are defined as follows:

- **Operation:** Values = *backup* or *eject*
- **Backup:** If you specify *backup* as the operation, the following parameters apply:
  - **path:** Insert all directory paths you intend to back up.
  - **/a:** Appends the current backup data to the end of the tape. Omitting the /a means you want to overwrite the previous data on the tape.
  - **/v:** Verifies the backup and requires twice the amount of time.
  - **/r:** Restricts to only the owner of the file(s) or administrators.
  - **/d "text":** Tape set description.
  - **/b:** Backs up the local Registry.

- **/hc:on or /hc:off:** Turns hardware compression on or off.
- **/t {option}:** Backup type where option = *normal, copy, incremental, differential,* or *daily.*
- **/l "filename":** Name and path for the backup log file.
- **/e:** Writes exceptions to only the backup log file you specified.
- **/tape:{n}:** Tape drive and number (0 to 9) of unit to back up to.

The following command line example is executed from the \WINNT\SYSTEM32 subdirectory and backs up all of the files the C drive, overwrites the tape with the new backup data, labels the tape as "Monday", backs up the R, and creates a log file named C:\TAPES\MONDAY.LOG:

```
NTBACKUP backup c: /D "MONDAY" /B /L "C:\TAPES\MONDAY.LOG"
```

Obviously, this task can become tedious to perform by hand. You can try to automate some of your backups using batch files, but a few exceptions do exist:

- **User input:** Some of the commands like /nopoll and /missingtape require you to input keystrokes. Therefore, if your backups don't require those specific commands, you can run batch files to perform unattended backups.
- **Backup scope:** You may back up directories by using batch files only, but not files by themselves.
- **Backup syntax:** You may not use wildcards in batch files.

Some files that are hard-coded into NTBACKUP don't get backed up, and you can't change or alter this:

- **Open files:** Users can't have files open while the backup is running, or those files won't be backed up. Have the users log off the system and disconnect them from any shares.
- **Temporary files:** No temporary files like PAGEFILE.SYS are backed up.
- **Permissions:** The account used to perform the backup must have permission to read files.
- **Registry:** Only the local Registry is backed up. Registries on other servers are not backed up.

Scheduling a backup

Now that you have all the syntax down for the command line backup, you can schedule your backups to run at a preset time using the Windows NT built-in scheduling service. You have a little work to do, however, to schedule this preset time:

1. **Create a user account:** Name the account anything that makes sense, like MrBackup. Choose Start➪Programs➪Administrative Tools➪User Admin.
2. **Set password information:** From the User Admin window, select User, New User, and type in a user name. Make sure that you don't give it a password, and that the Password Never Expires option is checked. Uncheck the User Must Change Password at Next Login option.
3. **Set security access:** Click the Groups button and add this user as a member of the Administrator account. Click the OK button, then click the Add button to add this user. Then click the Close button.
4. **Permit service and batch job logon:** Give this user account rights to log on as a service and a batch job: Highlight the new user you just created, Select Policies➪User Rights and mark the Show Advanced User Rights box. Scroll down through the list and find Log On As A Batch Job, highlight it and click the Add button. Do the same for Log On As A Service.
5. **Set to run as service:** Choose Start➪Settings➪Control Panel and double-click the Services icon. Scroll down the list of services to find the scheduler service and change the startup to use this account. Set the service to log on automatically. Stop and restart the service.
6. **Create the command file:** Open Notepad (Choose Start➪Programs ➪ Accessories) to create the command file. Name the file *ANYTHING*.CMD and type in the command line syntax of the backup you want to perform. Save the file.
7. **Execute the command file:** Insert your information in the following command line by using the example below as a guideline. Type

```
AT hour / interactive / every:days cmd.exe /c
       "DRIVE:\DIRECTORY\SCHEDULE.CMD
```

The following AT example schedules the text file BACKUP.CMD found in the C:\TAPES subdirectory to run every Monday and Friday at 6:00 p.m.:

```
AT 18:00 /interactive /every:M,F cmd.exe /c
       "C:\TAPES\BACKUP.CMD"
```

Type **AT/ ?** to get a list of all commands and their syntax.

Running NTBACKUP in the background

Hopefully, you're not backing up during the daytime when users are most likely to be on the system and have files open. However, if you need to, there's a way to run NTBACKUP in background mode:

1. **Create a shortcut to ntbackup.exe by choosing Start⇨Programs ⇨Windows NT Explorer. Find NTBACKUP.EXE in the \winnt\system32 directory and right-click on the file. Choose Create Shortcut.**

   You have created a shortcut icon.

2. **Drag the shortcut icon to your desktop.**
3. **Right-click the NTBACKUP.EXE shortcut icon and select Properties.**
4. **Choose the Shortcut tab and, in the Target box, type in your backup information using syntax you would use from the command line.**
5. **Click the arrow next to the Run List box and choose Minimized.**

   Click on the OK button to close.

To start the backup in background mode, insert a tape and double-click on the NTBACKUP shortcut icon you created.

Third-Party Backup Alternatives

If NTBACKUP doesn't provide enough features for you, third-party alternatives are a good way to go — and you have a plethora of choices. With third-party alternatives, you can find a variety of price ranges to select from, depending on your budget.

We always recommend going with the well-recognized, name brand, third-party companies to ensure good compatibility with Windows NT and other network operating systems. Most of the popular packages support the ability to back up several different network operating systems at one time, plus contain easy-to-use interfaces for backup and restore options.

One easy way to find other third-party backup software is to visit popular search engines on the Internet, such as `www.search.com` and enter the keywords `NT Server Backup`. Discount Internet shops, such as CDW (`www.cdw.com`), provide information about various backup devices in one handy location where fact sheets and information are at your fingertips. On the CDW Web site, click the Disk Storage option and look at how much information you have.

Two types of vendors are in the backup market: small-business backup solutions and enterprise backup solutions. We list the top several in each category to get your search started:

- **Small business:** Arcada (the original developers of NTBACKUP, now Seagate), `www.arcada.com`; Exabyte, `www.exabyte.com`; ADIC (Advanced Digital Information Corporation), `www.adic.com`; Hewlett-Packard's Colorado, `www.hp.com`.

- **Enterprise business:** Computer Associate's Cheyenne, `www.cai.com`; Palindrome, `www.palindrome.com`; or Legato, `www.legato.com`.

Search some of the backup vendors' Web sites for white papers and cost of ownership documents. This information is free and a lot of research has been compiled. You can use this information to convince management of your backup requirements.

Regardless of which vendor you choose, the following checklist provides some helpful criteria in evaluating tape systems. Choose the requirements for your organization and query the vendor as to whether their product has the features you desire, or if you have to pay extra for some add on modules.

You may not need all of the following criteria, but this list should give you a good idea of what you need when choosing a tape backup system:

- **Critical System Files:** An essential feature in any tape system that you purchase is that it can back up Windows NT's system files, such as the Registry and event logs, security information, user accounts, and access control lists, in addition to the actual data.
- **Fast tape index:** When backing up large amounts of data, it's critical during the restore process that you're able to obtain a catalog of the tape's contents within a minute or two. You won't want to wait 30 minutes each time you need to see the contents of a particular tape.
- **Multiplatform support:** Networks that support multiple networks, such as Novell, Microsoft, Unix and others, are easier to backup if one backup system can support more than one platform.
- **Client backups:** Some users simply refuse to store files on the network. In this case, look for a package that automates client workstation backups across the network to your tape backup system. Some popular systems already include this option. Ask which client operating systems it supports — for example, Macintosh, UNIX, Windows 98, and OS/2.
- **Unattended operation:** Some tape systems work like jukeboxes and have a mechanical arm that inserts and removes tapes, so you can go home while the backup runs. These systems are expensive, but if you have a lot of data to back up and don't wish to insert tapes all night, look for this feature.
- **Scheduling features:** If you want to perform incremental and full backups on different days, look for a system that is flexible, allowing you to automate the scheduling features based on day of the week.
- **Open files:** Does the system back up open files on the network? These are files that are in use during the backup operation. Not all backup systems are designed to back up open files, and some even halt when they get to one that's open. Most systems skip over the file and write an exception to a log file. You will want one that backs up open files, though.

- **Security and encryption:** For small operations, this feature might not be as critical, but for larger environments, ask the vendor how their system handles passing information through the network, such as passwords and account information.
- **Hierarchical Storage Management (HSM):** Does the vendor's product support online, nearline, and offline storage and management of using all three at one time?
- **Data storage size:** How much data can you backup to the system (MB or GB)? What size tapes does the system use (4mm, 8mm, DLT, or others)? Does it compress data?
- **Remote management:** Getting to monitor backup status and progress remotely instead of being in front of the console is a handy feature.
- **Scalability:** Is this system one that can be scaled up to a larger environment should your network grow?
- **Year 2000 compliant:** We're only one year away from the year 2000, so you probably aren't going to find a vendor that isn't compliant, but it's always best to check.
- **Security access:** Running an unattended backup means that a device must either log in to the network while you're gone or remain logged in with the keyboard locked. Check with the vendor as to how the product logs into the network and maintains security.

Understanding the Technology

Regardless of which vendor you choose, and regardless of how often you decide to back up, you need to understand some terminology and technology about the equipment used in backup systems and different methods.

Online, nearline, offline

You hear a lot of buzz about online, nearline, and offline storage options. Of these three backup types, choose the method that suits your organization's retrieval time and effort, depending on how often you find yourself restoring data and how fast you want data retrieved.

- **Online:** This type of backup is done typically on your server, usually in the form of a second hard disk purchased that is mirrored or duplexed. Data is readily available to users through their desktop with no intervention from you except that you must regularly check the status of this fault tolerance. Drives can go out of synch without notice unless you monitor the drives manually or through software.

- **Nearline:** These backups are performed on a device attached to the network and require some intervention from you to perform backups or restores. This type of backup requires some work on your part because it usually uses some method unknown to the user when backing up files, such as compression techniques. The data is there, but your users won't know how to perform functions like decompressing the files to access them.
- **Offline:** This type of backup involves separate devices from the server that include their own software and hardware. You'll need to know how to operate these devices because the users won't know how or might not have security access to do so. These devices are typically the slowest because data must go from the server to another device. Many organizations place these devices on the network backbone and connect them via fiber-optic cabling for higher transmission rates.

As you progress downward in the preceding bulleted list, options become less expensive and slower to retrieve information and require more interaction on your part.

What's in the hardware?

Backup systems are composed of backup units, backup medium, and software components (oh, and you the operator). The systems come in all sizes, shapes, and dollar signs, depending on your needs. In the following sections, we describe the most common ones you encounter so that you can talk with your vendor about meeting your network needs.

Backup units

A backup unit is hardware that can be as simple as a tape device with one slot, or as complex as a jukebox platter system that has mechanical arms. If you have small data-storage requirements, a simple tape backup unit that has more capacity than your server will suffice. These units are not that expensive and available at local computer stores. Some of these units can be daisy-chained together if you need more space and don't want to be present to change the tapes.

If your organization has lots of data to back up, then you might consider one of the jukebox approaches. A *jukebox* is a device that looks like a little computer tower with a door. Inside, it has several slots plus a mechanical arm that can insert and move around tapes or CDs. With this type of system, you typically can insert a week's worth of backup tapes and let the system back up unattended.

Another option is *magneto-optical (MO) drives*. These units use a combination of magnetic and optical technologies for rewritable backups. The advantage of this technology is that it performs random access retrievals, which is faster than sequential retrievals. The units are not expensive, but the medium is. If you have large data requirements and need fast retrieval, look into this technology.

Each type of backup unit will have some sort of slot where the medium is placed. The size of this slot depends on the unit. Some come in 4mm, 8mm, 1/4 inch, 1/2 inch, and more. You must purchase the correct size medium for the backup unit because you can't fit a 1/2-inch tape in a 1/4-inch drive!

Backup media

Backup media means tape, cartridge, CD-WORM (write once read many), erasable CD-ROMs diskettes, and more. Any device the backup unit stores data on becomes the medium. Backup media comes in many shapes, sizes, and thicknesses. You want to make sure that you follow the manufacturer's recommendation for purchasing the right medium for your unit.

Don't buy video-grade tape cartridges at your local discount store for your backup purposes. Purchase data-grade tapes, which cost more but are designed for more rugged use.

Backup media comes not only in different physical sizes, but also in capacity. Some little tapes store as much as 5GB of data. Erasable CD-ROMs store as much as 650MB in uncompressed mode and GBs in compressed mode. Regardless of which unit and medium you select for your needs, get plenty of them so you can work on a rotational scheme without continually using the same medium. We've seen folks who buy just one tape and use that tape over and over until it's time to restore from that tape. And guess what, the tape was defective and so there was no backup! Spread out your backups over multiple tapes to minimize putting all your eggs in one tape basket!

Software

You can use the Windows NT built-in back up software on a third-party backup device or you can use the software that comes with the device. We prefer to use third-party software because it's designed to work with certain manufactured devices and the drivers are always readily available. Installation of the devices goes much smoother when you use the recommended software. Always keep a copy of the backup software off site somewhere in case of fire or other disaster. If you lose all of your equipment, you'll need to reload this software on another machine before you can restore data.

Getting Back Up from Your Backup

Backing up your data is only half the picture. The other half involves restoring files on the network. We hope that you only have to restore a few files for users from time to time. Making regular backups along the way makes this task friendly and easy. You can run into occasions, however, when you lose your data and computer equipment, including the server you need to restore to. We really hope this never happens, but in a fire or other disaster, it's entirely possible. Hopefully, you heed our advice when we say to rotate tapes off site each week to plan for this catastrophe. If you also lose the server, we hope that you have a good working relationship with your local vendors so you can get equipment in a hurry.

The most important thing to remember in restoring is to practice the restoration process when you are not under the gun. This not only gives you confidence in performing the task, but also tests the integrity of your backup periodically. Although you can examine log files each morning, it's better to perform real restore tests just like a dress rehearsal. When disaster does strike and you need to perform a real restore, there are typically all sorts of people looking over your shoulder asking you when things will be up and running. If you confidently know your backup system, you can perform this task under extreme pressure. Don't wait until the last minute to test and learn the system.

Always restore the system files (\SYSTEM32\CONFIG and registry files) first, reboot, and take a peek at the system to make sure everything looks like it's in place. Then restore the data files. If you plan your network directory and volume structure to segment the system and data files, this task is much easier. Know ahead of time if certain business departments require that their data be restored first. Sometimes this is not necessary, but in instances where a customer service department exists, they usually want the network back up right away with immediate access to their data. Why? Because they are servicing the external customers that generate the revenue for your organization! Before restores become necessary, try to devise a restoration order plan for your network and practice it.

Note that sometimes you can't restore system files in Windows NT and may have to first reinstall Windows NT, then restore the system files.

Setting up mirrored disk drives for the system and boot volumes of the server (covered in Chapter 10) builds in fault tolerance for system files, and you can avoid reinstalling Windows NT during an outage.

The Backup Operator: Maven or Mystery?

Within Windows NT's account management, you can specify users to be members of the Backup Operator's group. If you determine that you don't have time to perform daily backups, and want to off load this task to another individual, you can make them a member of the Backup Operator group. Although this gives them access to perform backup tasks and permissions, such that all files can be backed up, it does not give them Administrator privileges where they can change or modify user accounts. Being a member of the Backup Operator's group only permits them to perform backup and restore functions on the network, log on locally to the server, and shut the server down. Okay, anyone can hit the on/off switch to the server, but we mean shut the server down gracefully.

The security problem is that the backup operator can restore files anywhere on the network. If you don't want your backup operator accidentally over-writing files on the network while restoring data, assign them with permission to only back up data, but not restore. You can accomplish this three ways:

- **Alter the Backup Operator built-in group by removing the right to restore files. We don't like this method because it means tinkering with Microsoft's stuff.**

  To modify the Backup Operator group, choose Start⇨Programs⇨Administrative Tools⇨User Manager⇨Policies⇨User Rights. Use the down arrow to select the "Restore Files and Directories" option and you'll see names appear in the window — particularly the Backup Operator name. Highlight the name and click the remove button.

- **Give a user account rights to backup files and directories on the network (without adding them as a member to the Backup Operator group) by modifying their user account policy information.**

  To do so, select Policies⇨User Rights and use the down arrow to highlight the "Back up Files and Directories" option. Then click Add to add the username. If you don't see usernames in the window, click the Show Users button and then highlight the user name. Click the Add button and then the OK button to close.

- **Create a new group entirely and give the group permission to back up files. Then in the future, if you have more than one person you'd like to designate as a backup operator, you can just add them to the group. (This is our favorite method.)**

  If you want to create a group, first create a new local group (Start⇨Programs⇨Administrative Tools⇨User Manager and select User then New Local Group). Follow the same steps in the preceding paragraph and give the group rights to "Back up Files and Directories."

Chapter 17

Managing Network Security

In This Chapter

- Finding out about basic network security
- Understanding how Windows NT Server handles security
- Finding and filling Windows NT security holes
- Developing the right security attitude
- Examining security resources

In the advancing world of information technology, protecting private data from prying eyes is becoming more and more important. Maintaining security to prevent access to internal information is often critical to sustaining a competitive edge. In this chapter, we discuss how to impose tight security on Windows NT.

Just Because You're Paranoid, Doesn't Mean They Aren't Out to Get You

Windows NT Server right out of the box is not a secure environment; in fact, you'll find almost no effective security measures. You must impose security on Windows NT. This process involves several steps, careful planning, double-checking your settings, and a few non-computer activities. But if you don't care about your data, you can skip this discussion entirely.

The goal of security is not to create a system that is impossible for a hacker or misguided user to compromise. Instead, the goal is to maintain a sufficient barrier against intruders so the difficulty encountered while attempting to access your system is significantly more than someone else's system. Your goal is to convince the hacker to attack an easier target. By following the prescriptions in this chapter, you can deploy a Windows NT Server system that is not just harder to crack than your neighbors, but is nearly watertight!

Protecting proprietary and private electronic property is not just a defense against outside attackers, but also involves erecting a barrier against inside assaults and taking precautions against other threats to your data.

Basics of Network Security

The basics of network security are to keep unauthorized people out of your network, to keep unwanted data out, and to keep wanted data in. Leave it to us to point out the obvious.

Creating a secure environment requires you to pay attention to three key areas:

- Understanding the operating system (or systems)
- Controlling physical access to the computer
- Educating the human users

These three areas are like legs on a bar stool. If any one of the legs is weak, the person on the stool will hit the floor.

In the following two subsections, we briefly discuss the issues involved with maintaining physical control and education of users. The third leg, the operating system itself, is the subject matter of the remainder of the chapter.

Physical access

Controlling physical access means preventing unauthorized people from coming into close proximity of your computers, network devices, communication pathways, peripherals, and even power sources. A computer system can be compromised in several ways. Physical access is always the first step in breaking into a system. Remember that physical access does not always mean a person must be physically present in your office building. If your network has dial-up access, they can gain access remotely.

Controlling physical access means not only preventing access to keyboards or other input devices, but also blocking all other means of transmitting to or extracting signals from your computer system.

Some physical access controls are obvious to everyone:

- Locking doors
- Using security badges
- Employing armed guards
- Using locking cases and racks

But just addressing these items will leave several access methods wide open. You need to think about the architecture, structure, and construction of your building. Can ceiling or floor tiles be removed so access can be gained over or under walls? Do ventilation shafts or windows allow entrance into locked rooms?

A person getting into your computer room is not the only issue to concern yourself with. You also need to think about the environment in which the computers operate. Most computers have a limited range of temperatures within which they operate properly. Thus, can intruders gain access to thermostat controls? What is the one thing that all computers need? Electricity. Is your power supply secure? Can it be switched off outside of your security barriers? Do you have uninterruptible power supplies (UPS) attached to each critical system?

Even after preventing entrance into the computer room and protecting the operating environment, you still have not secured your computers physically. You need to think about your trash. Yes, the trash. You would be amazed at what private investigators and criminals can learn about you and your network from the information discarded in your trash. If you don't shred or incinerate all printouts and handwritten materials, you may be offering passwords, user names, computer names, configuration settings, drive paths, and other key elements of information.

Do you think we've covered everything now? *Wrong!* Ponder the following issues:

- Does the nightly cleaning crew vacuum and dust your computer closet?
- Is that crew bonded?
- How often do they unplug computer systems to plug in cleaning machines?
- Is the same key that unlocks your front door also the key that unlocks the computer room?
- How do you know that the cleaning crew is not playing with your computer system?
- How do you know that the members of the cleaning crew are who you think they are?
- Are floppy drives installed on servers and other critical systems?
- Can systems be rebooted without passwords or other authentication controls (i.e., smart cards)?
- Do servers have extra ports ready to accept new attachments?
- Are your backup tapes stacked beside the tape drive?
- Are your backup tapes protected by encryption and passwords?

- Are all of your backup tapes accounted for? Where are the missing ones? What information was stored on them?
- What really happens in your office building after business hours? Are the doors actually locked?

If you can still sleep at night, you probably have most of these items under control. If you can't answer some of these questions with a solid and reassuring response, you have some work to do.

So far, the physical access issues we've discussed have dealt with a computer system that was stationary. But what about the workstation that is mobile? Remember that expensive notebook system you purchased for the boss or that manager or that system administrator so they could work while traveling and connect to the network over the phone line. Well, if that notebook were to fall into the wrong hands, they would have an open door to walk right into your network and take or destroy whatever they pleased.

Notebook theft is becoming the number one method of gaining access to a company's network. Most notebooks are stolen at the airport. (We bet you could have guessed that one!) Although most travelers are smart enough not to check their notebooks in as luggage, there's a common location where a notebook and its owner are often separated — the metal detector. All it takes is a few moments of delay while waiting to walk through the metal detector after you've placed the notebook on the x-ray treadmill, and *poof!* The notebook is gone by the time you reach the other end.

Controlling physical access is important because without interaction with a computer system, a hacker cannot break in. Just like you can't swim if you can't get to the water. If you fail to prevent physical access to your network, you'll be relying on your operating system supported software security to protect your data. However, there is one problem — if you have failed to properly educate the network users, your security may already be compromised.

User education and a security policy

The most secure networking environment is completely useless if the human users don't respect the need for security. In fact, if left to their own druthers, most humans will find the easiest path of least resistance when performing regular activities. In other words, they'll do anything to make traversing the security simple. Such as automating the entry of passwords, writing down passwords in plain view, mapping unauthorized drives, installing unapproved software, transferring data to and from work and home on floppies, attaching modems to bypass the firewall or proxy servers, and more. If you put a software/operating system-based security measure in place, a human can often find a way to get around it, or at least reduce its effectiveness.

User education is a two-fold process. First, the users of your network must be thoroughly taught what security is, why it's important, and what security measures are in place on your network. Second, violations of the security system must be dealt with swiftly and strictly.

In most cases, educating your network users requires that an official organization document detailing the security restrictions, requirements, and punishments be created. This document, called a *security policy,* serves as your network's constitution. It's the governing body of regulations. This document allows your network security to remain intact while violators of the law are terminated.

So what does a user need to know about the security imposed on the organization's network? Here is a brief list of the highlights:

- Use passwords properly and choose them wisely. (Don't use an obvious name or number such as a pet's name or birth date.)
- Never write down or share passwords.
- Never share security badges and smart cards or leave them unattended.
- Restrict network access to only authorized employees.
- Do not share user accounts with other employees or with anyone outside of the organization.
- Do not distribute data from the network in any form outside of the organization.
- Users should not step away from their workstations while they are logged into the system.
- Understand the various levels of security in place on the network and the purpose of the stratification.
- Do not install unapproved software.
- Make clear to all employees that tampering, subverting, or bypassing security measures is grounds for termination of employment.
- Respect the privacy of the organization and other users.
- Deal with violations of the security policy in a swift and severe manner without reservation or exemption.

This brings up the issue of punishment. If a user violates a significant issue in the security policy, a severe punishment must be applied. In most cases, firing the individual is the only form of punishment that will effectively control the situation and prevent that user and all others from making the same mistake. The repercussions of violating the security policy must be detailed in the policy itself. But, if you spell out the punishment, you must follow through. Even if your top programmer is the culprit, he must receive the same severity of punishment as the temporary mail person.

Most analysts have discovered that the deployment of a severe security policy results in a common occurrence — a short-term improvement in security, followed by a brief period of laxness, which results in violations causing several users to be fired, which immediately results in an overall sustained improvement in security. Companies have reported that the loss of manpower due to violations was negligible in comparison with the prevention of security breaches.

You should create your own security policy that includes details about physical control, user education, and operating system level security measures. Remember the old adage about the ounce of prevention . . . ?

How Windows NT Server Handles Security

Windows NT security centers around access control. Access control is dependant on user identity. A user's identity is their user account. To gain access to a Windows NT Server computer or network, you must provide a valid username and password associated with a user account. Anyone who knows a valid username and password combination can gain access. Thus, both the usernames and passwords of user accounts need to be protected.

Protecting usernames

Protecting usernames is not always that easy, but a little effort here can subvert several "easy" attacks. First, don't create usernames that employ just the first or last name of a person. Combine two or more elements to create the name, such as first name, last name, initials, department code, or division name. You should also avoid using the same name for log on that is used as your email address. This will make guessing usernames a bit more difficult. Even if a hacker knows your naming convention (covered later in this chapter), making usernames complicated can make brute force attacks more difficult.

You should also rename the common accounts. These include administrator, guest, and the IUSR_<servername> (created by IIS). Rename these to something descriptive but not easily guessed. Then, create new dummy accounts with the original name that have absolutely no access. This will provide a decoy for hackers, effectively wasting their time and giving you more opportunity to discover who they are.

In your security policy, you should include a restriction to prevent users from employing their network logon username as a logon name anywhere else. In other words, their network logon name should not be used as a logon name for Web sites, FTP sites, or other external systems. If they don't use the same logon name everywhere, they'll be less tempted to use the same password everywhere as well.

Even with these precautions, usernames are often discoverable. The important issue here is to make obtaining any data item needed to log into your network as difficult to get as possible. Once a username is known, the responsibility of protecting your network rests on the strength of the account's password.

Password controls

Passwords are the primary method by which unauthorized access to a system is prevented. The stronger the password, the more likely security will remain intact. As part of your security policy, you need to require that strong passwords be used by each and every user. (See the end of this section for guidelines that lead to strong passwords.) A single account compromised can result in the entire system being accessed.

Strong passwords can be enforced using the built-in controls of Windows NT, through add-ons from Service Packs and the Resource Kit, and via security policy elements. (NT Service Pack 4 contains enhanced security features, including the Security Configuration Editor. Visit the Microsoft site at `www.microsoft.com/ntserver` for more on this. See also the section "Service Packs and Security," later in this chapter.) By employing all of the system level controls that force passwords, little additional effort will be required to ensure users comply with the security policy.

The Account policy (Figure 17-1), defined through the User Manager for Domains (accessed using the Policy⇨Account command from the menu bar), is used to force some elements of strong passwords and prevent brute force cracking attempts. The Account policy options are as follows:

- **Maximum Password Age:** Defines when, if ever, passwords expire and must be changed. A frequency of 30, 45, or 60 days is recommended.
- **Minimum Password Age:** Defines how quickly passwords can be changed. A time frame of 1, 3, or 5 days is recommended.
- **Minimum Password Length:** Sets the smallest number of characters for a password. Six or more characters is recommended.
- **Password Uniqueness:** Defines the number of previous passwords recorded to prevent reuse. A setting of five or greater is recommended.
- **Account Lockout:** Enables the lockout capabilities of Windows NT. If a user account is unable to log in successfully, it can be locked out (that is, disabled).

- **Logout after ? bad logon attempts:** Sets the number of failed logins allowed before locking out the account. A value of 3 is typical.
- **Reset counter after:** Sets the number of minutes the lockout counter is reset. A value of 30 minutes is typical.
- **Lockout Duration:** Sets the length of time an account is locked out. A setting of Forever requires an admin to re-enable the account. A value of 60–360 minutes is recommended.

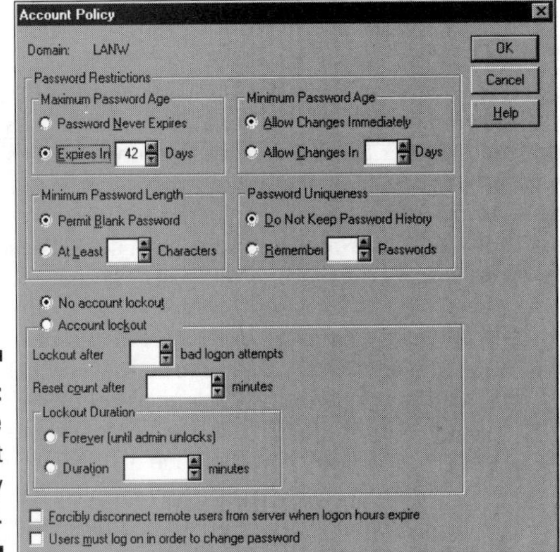

Figure 17-1: The Account Policy dialog box.

In addition to the built in Account policy controls, additional strong password restrictions can be added by installing the PASSFILT.DLL from Service Pack 2 or later, or by using the PASSPROP tool from the Resource Kit (see their distributions for installation instructions). Both of these tools add the following criteria to passwords:

- Minimum of six characters.
- At least three out of four types of characters must be used: uppercase, lowercase, numerals, non-alphanumeric (symbols, punctuation).
- Prevents the e-mail address, account name, or real name from being part of the password.

If these software-enforced password restrictions are not enough, you can deploy further requirements through your security policy. However, these requirements will need to be enforced by some other means than through the software.

- Don't use common words, slang, terms from the dictionary, or other real words.
- Don't write passwords down, except to place them in a vault or safety deposit box.
- Don't use words, names, or phrases that can be associated with you, such as family, friends, hobbies, pets, interests, books, movies, car, or workspace.
- If real words are used, split them with capitalization, numbers, and/or non-alphanumeric characters, for example, Go7Ril-la.
- Use numbers or non-alphanumeric characters to replace letters, for example, 13TT3r (letter with a one and three's).
- Create acronyms to use as passwords from sentences, for example, Fifty-five dollars will pay a parking ticket = 55$wPaPt.

Through the combination of Windows NT–enforced password restrictions and strong recommendations in a company security policy, you can improve the security of your system through the use of strong passwords.

Service Packs and Security

Microsoft has been releasing updates and fixes for Windows NT since the day it hit the streets back in 1996. To maintain a secure deployment of Windows NT, you need to keep your system current on the latest releases of these fixes. The fixes come in two types: Service Packs and hotfixes.

A *hotfix* is a patch for a single problem. A *Service Pack* is many hotfixes combined into a single "Band-Aid." But there are more significant differences as well. Hotfixes are not fully tested nor are they supported by Microsoft. A hotfix should only be applied if you are actually experiencing the problem it fixes, because they sometimes cause other problems. Service Packs are thoroughly tested and should be applied when they are released.

Service Packs are cumulative, meaning that each new release of a Service Pack includes the previous Service Pack plus all hotfixes and other improvements since. You only need to apply the most current Service Pack and any required hotfixes.

Before you apply any patch to Windows NT, you should read the documentation included with the patches. Then make the following preparations:

- Backup the system, or at least your data and the Registry.
- Execute "rdisk /s" from a Command Prompt to update your Emergency Repair Disk.

- Reboot the system.
- Close all applications and stop any unnecessary services.

After you apply a Service Pack, you may not be able to install items from the original distribution CD successfully. Many core device drivers and system files are updated by the Service Packs. To prevent problems, always install everything off the CD before you apply a Service Pack. If you install new applications after installing a Service Pack, it's a good idea to reapply the Service Pack. If the new application fails to operate afterward, contact the application's vendor for a solution.

If you don't know what level of Service Pack you've already applied, you can check by looking at the Help⇨About page from any native Windows NT application (such as Windows NT Explorer, Control Panel, or My Computer).

The Microsoft Web site is often very secretive about the location of Service Packs and hotfixes. You can attempt to locate the link on your own starting from `www.microsoft.com/ntserver/`, or you can jump directly to the FTP site at `ftp://ftp.microsoft.com/bussys/winnt/winnt-public/fixes/usa/nt40/`. The Service Packs are in a subdirectory labeled "ussp#" (where # is the number of the Service Pack). The hotfixes are found in the "hotfixes-postsp#" directories.

Although Microsoft is still too quiet about Service Pack issues, there are several other online repositories of excellent information. We recommend keeping an eye on the following sites:

- **NT Bug Traq Web site:** `www.ntbugtraq.com`
- **Paperbits Web site:** `www.paperbits.com`

Security Is an Attitude

To maintain a secure networking environment, you must be a pessimist. View every user as a potential security leak. With this attitude, you're more likely to deploy a meaningful security structure, than if you are too trusting. The key to this philosophy is to grant only the exact level of access a user or group needs to perform their work tasks and absolutely nothing more.

To take this to its logical end, you need to deal with the Everyone group and User Rights.

The Everyone group

The Everyone group is a default group created by the system that includes absolutely everyone in the entire universe. This is a security problem, especially since Windows NT defaults to grant Full Control to the Everyone group on new partitions and shares. The Everyone group does not appear in the User Manager for Domains. The Everyone group cannot be removed from the system, but it can be effectively managed with a little effort.

First, apply Service Pack 3 or later. This creates a new group named Authenticated Users that should be used in place of the Everyone group when you need to assign blanket access.

Second, remove the Everyone group from all non-essential locations. The document entitled "Securing Windows NT 4.0 Installation" from the Windows NT Server 4.0 Technical Notes (TechNet and Online support) details the files and directories where the Everyone group must remain. If you use a sweeping CACLS command to completely remove the Everyone group, you'll end up with a system that won't boot. (CACLS is a command line utility used to control Access Control Lists for directories and files.)

Don't set the Everyone group to No Access, because this will prevent anyone from accessing a resource. Instead, just remove the Everyone group from the list of users/groups granted access.

If you want a graphical interface to the CACLS command, try the Security Explorer from Small Wonders of Orlando at `www.smalwonders.com/` ($349, demo available).

Each time you create a new drive or a share, always remove the Everyone group, then add in only those users or groups that need access to the resource.

Just as you don't want anyone gaining access to your computer, neither should the Everyone group be used anywhere when its not required by the system.

User rights

User rights are system level privileges that control what types of activities can occur or can be performed. The default setting of user rights is reasonably secure, but there are a few improvements you can make. The User Manager's Policy|User Rights command reveals the dialog box where user rights are granted or revoked. Here are several changes you should consider making:

- **Remove the Everyone and Guests groups from the "Log on Locally" right.** Making this change inhibits non-authenticated users from gaining unauthorized access.
- **Remove the Everyone group from the "Shut Down the System" right.** Making this change inhibits non-authenticated users from powering down the computer.
- **Remove the Everyone group from the "Access This Computer from the Network" right.** Making this change inhibits non-authenticated users from gaining access to hosted resources over the network.
- **Remove the Everyone group from the "Bypass Traverse Checking" right.** Making this change inhibits non-authenticated users from jumping into subdirectories for which they do not have access to parent directories.
- **Remove the Backup operators group from the "Restore Files and Directories" right.** Making this change inhibits non-administrators from restoring files from backup tapes. Since files can be restored to FAT partitions where ACLs are lost, this is an important security modification.

After you make these changes, double check that regular users still have the capabilities they need to perform their required tasks. If not, you may need to grant a few users or groups these user rights. For example, if you want users to access resources on a server from across the network, you should add a group, such as the Users group, to the "Access this computer from the network user" right.

Don't Be Insecure (Common NT Security Holes and How to Fill Them)

Windows NT has a handful of common security holes you need to look for and fill. Fortunately, we have crawled around on our hands and knees so you don't have to. Just follow our friendly advice and you'll be all snug and secure.

Hidden Admin Shares

Each time Windows NT boots, a hidden administrative share is created for every drive. These shares are a backup path for the system just in case direct access to system files is somehow interrupted. In other words, it's a redundancy you don't need! The administrative shares are disabled by adding AutoShareServer (Windows NT Server) or AutoShareWks (Windows NT Workstation) to the following Registry key:

HKEY_LOCAL_MACHINE\System\CurrentControlSet\Services\LanManServer\Parameters. A value of 0 turns the administrative shares off, and a value of 1 turns them back on.

A hidden share is just like any other share, except is has a dollar sign as the last character in its name. This tells the system not to display the hidden share in standard browser listings of shares. You can view hidden shares by using the System Manager. You can create your own hidden shares just by adding a dollar sign to the end of the share name.

The problem with administrative shares is they offer unrestricted access to every file on a drive. If the username and password of an administrator account is ever compromised, this share can be used by anyone to map to any administrative share on the network. Thus, it's a good idea to turn these off just as a precaution.

Decoys

Everyone knows the name of the most important user account on your system. Because the administrator account is created by Windows NT when Windows NT is installed, everyone already knows that you have such an account and exactly what its name is. Therefore, you need to change it!

But don't just change the name, do one better and create a new dummy account that has absolutely no access or privileges at all and give it the name "administrator." This dummy account will serve as a decoy to lure hackers away from real access.

Creating decoys for other common accounts, such as the Guest and IUSR (the one created by IIS) accounts, is also a good idea.

Broadcasting internal information

Microsoft chose to employ NetBIOS communications to support system activity. Most system level functions and network activities use NetBIOS for naming conventions, instructions, commands, and more. Microsoft conveniently added NetBIOS to all of its network protocols — NBT (NetBIOS over TCP/IP), NWLink (NetBIOS over IPX/SPX), and NBF (NetBIOS Frame). We think this is a bit sloppy and adds to network overhead. In addition, it can pose a security problem if this information is transmitted over external links.

You can seal off most of the problem by unbinding the NetBIOS interface on each external network adapter. If you are really paranoid about it, you can deploy a firewall or proxy server that supports port filtering. Then you can block all communications over TCP ports 135–139. That's one way to shut Microsoft up.

Last logged on username

By default, when Ctrl+Alt+Del is pressed, the logon dialog box displays the username of the last person to successfully log on. This is not the most secure setting. To prevent the dialog box from appearing, change the DontDisplayLastUserName value to 1. This value appears in the `HKEY_LOCAL_MACHINE\Software\Microsoft\WindowsNT\CurrentVersion\WinLogon` Registry key.

Bad Floppy, bad!

A nifty tool from System Internals (`www.sysinternals.com/`) enables anyone to read NTFS files after booting from a DOS floppy. The NTFSDOS drivers make possible what Microsoft claimed was impossible. Now, anyone who has physical access to your system can reboot with a floppy and copy files right off of your NTFS protected drives. If you value your data (and your job), remove the floppy drives from critical systems.

Password crackers

Password cracking is the art of extracting passwords from a protected security database. Password crackers exist for Windows NT, but they all require that a copy of the Security Accounts Manager (SAM) database be directly accessible. Microsoft uses a one-way hash function to encrypt passwords before storing them in the security database. But the hash formula is well known and can be used to discover passwords by hash-comparison. It's a long and tedious process, but not impossible.

Before a hacker gets the chance to use a password cracker against you, use the tool to improve your own security. Any discovered passwords should be changed immediately.

Most of the password cracking tools use a dictionary attack. A long list of words is generated, which the tool uses to compare hash results to the contents of the SAM. If matches are found, passwords are known. Other tools sequentially work through all possible characters. This second type of tool is more thorough, but requires significantly more time to execute. A dictionary crack is typically complete within a day or so; a brute force attack can last hundreds of years or longer.

Your SAM database is often easy to obtain. It exists on all Emergency Boot Disks, a copy is stored in the Winnt\Repair directory, it may be stored on backup tapes, and any administrator can extract if from the Registry with REGEDT32.

Following are a few popular password-cracking tools you can use to test your own passwords:

- **L0phtCrack:** www.l0pht.com/ (***Note:*** the second letter is a zero.)
- **ScanPro:** www.ntsecurity.com/Products/ScanPro/index.html
- **NT Crack:** www.secnet.com/

Eternal Vigilance Is the Price of Freedom

Maintaining a secure environment is an ongoing process. Keeping up with security fixes, system changes, user activity, and a security policy is often a timely task. In your efforts to maintain a protected deployment of Windows NT, take the time to review the contents of the following Web sites, newsgroups, and print and other resources:

- Microsoft Security Advisor & Notification Service: www.microsoft.com/security/
- Microsoft Security Partners: www.microsoft.com/security/partners/
- Windows NT Magazine: www.winntmag.com/
- Windows NT Systems Magazine: www.ntsystems.com/
- Windows NT Enterprise Computing: www.entmag.com/
- NTsecurity.com: www.ntsecurity.com/
- NT Shop, NT Security News: www.ntshop.net/
- Security Bugware: http://oliver.efri.hr/~crv/security/bugs/NT/nt.html
- Robert Malmgren's NT Security FAQ: www.it.kth.se/~rom/ntsec.html
- Bill Stout's Known NT Exploits: www.emf.net/~ddonahue/NThacks/ntexploits.htm
- TISC Security Web site: http://tisc.corecom.com/
- Somarsoft: www.somarsoft.com/
- Security Mailing lists: http://oliver.efri.hr/~crv/security/mlist/mlist.html
- l0pht: www.l0pht.com/
- BHS Software: www.bhs.com/

- SERVERxtras, Inc.: `www.serverxtras.com/`
- Microsoft KnowledgeBase: `www.microsoft.com/kb/`
- MSNEWS.MICROSOFT.COM - NNTP server:
  `microsoft.public.inetexplorer.ie4.security`
  `microsoft.public.java.security`
  `microsoft.public.windowsnt`
- Microsoft Security reporting email: `secure@microsoft.com`
- NTSecurity mailing list: `Majordomo@iss.net` - subscribe ntsecurity
- *Windows NT Security Handbook,* by Tom Sheldon. Osborne McGraw-Hill, 1997. ISBN: 0078822408
- *Maximum Security,* anonymous. Sams.net, 1997. ISBN: 1575212684
- *Internet Security with Windows NT,* by Mark Joseph Edwards. Duke Press, 1998. ISBN: 1882419626
- *Windows NT Security Guide,* by Stephen A. Sutton. Addison-Wesley Pub Co, 1996. ISBN: 0201419696
- *Windows NT Security: A Practical Guide to Securing Windows NT Servers and Workstations,* by Charles B. Rutstein. Computing McGraw-Hill, 1997. ISBN: 0070578338
- *Firewalls and Internet Security: Repelling the Wily Hacker.* William R. Cheswick and Steven M. Bellovin. Addison-Wesley, Reading, MA, 1994. ISBN: 0201633574. New edition announced for 1999.
- *Building Internet Firewalls.* D. Brent Chapman and Elizabeth D. Zwicky. O'Reilly & Associates, Sebastopol, CA, 1995. ISBN: 1565921240.

Part V

Troubleshooting Network Snafus

"This is what happens when good networks go bad."

In this part . . .

Despite your best efforts and all the prevention in the world, networks occasionally will go south or get weird. That's when troubleshooting comes into play. What you discover in Part V is that troubleshooting is as much a state of mind as it is a set of tried and tested tools, tricks, and techniques for solving problems when they affect your systems.

Part V kicks off with a review of some key NT utilities for troubleshooting system problems, and then continues on with a similar review to help you troubleshoot network problems. After that, you tackle problems with printing and conclude with a concise guide to troubleshooting hardware problems in the NT environment.

Part V consciously covers all the important bases when it comes to troubleshooting a Windows NT Server, and the networks to which it is usually attached. Although we can't address every conceivable problem you might encounter, we do our best to point out all the well-known potholes, cracks, fissures, and bumpy spots on the road to networking success.

Troubleshooting is something we all have to do from time to time. Remember not to panic and to perform a systematic survey of the symptoms through which problems manifest themselves. Also, document recent changes to your systems and record previous successful fixes. If you do all these things, you'll not only be able to solve most problems yourself, you will build a knowledge base that will stand you in good stead for the rest of your networking career!

Chapter 18

Using NT Troubleshooting Utilities

In This Chapter

- Using Event Viewer
- Dealing with crash dumps
- Working with Windows NT Diagnostics
- Plotting performance with PerfMon
- Investigating the Resource Kit Utilities

Although it's not necessarily the case that "where there's NT, there's trouble," trouble with an NT Server system is certainly not unimaginable, either. As you survey the contents of this chapter, you have a chance to delve into some of the better-known — and more obscure — troubleshooting tools that Windows NT offers to savvy users.

And if that's not enough to satisfy your appetite, we mention some worthwhile Resource Kit troubleshooting utilities at the end of this chapter.

Special Events with Event Viewer

Event Viewer is an essential troubleshooting tool for Windows NT. This tool has at least one valuable characteristic, however — namely, when drivers or services fail to load during system startup, you can always count on Event Viewer to give you more details about what's going on. Event Viewer is also your entry point into analyzing what's going on with your system, whether you're auditing specific events by design, or whether you're trying to figure out where problems and errors might be coming from.

To begin with, you'll see a warning window show up after startup completes, like the one shown in Figure 18-1. This is your clue to launch Event Viewer and start poking around.

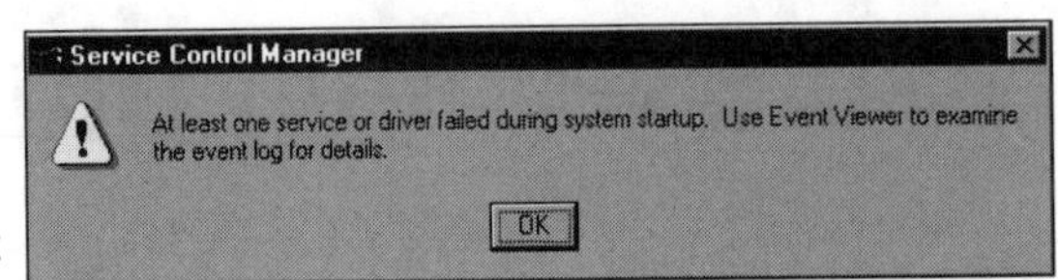

Figure 18-1: When a service or driver fails during startup, Event Viewer catches all the details.

To launch Event Viewer, follow this menu sequence: Start⇨Programs⇨Administrative Tools (Common)⇨Event Viewer. This produces the Event Viewer window shown in Figure 18-2.

Event Viewer - System Log on \\NTS-NBK1

Log View Options Help

Date	Time	Source	Category	Event	User	Co
12/16/98	6:05:40 PM	Service Control Mar	None	7026	N/A	
12/16/98	6:03:58 PM	EventLog	None	6005	N/A	
12/16/98	6:05:27 PM	BROWSER	None	8015	N/A	
12/10/98	12:38:42 AM	Srv	None	2013	N/A	
12/10/98	12:33:30 AM	EventLog	None	6005	N/A	
12/10/98	12:34:50 AM	Service Control Mar	None	7026	N/A	
12/7/98	6:25:51 PM	Dhcp	None	1003	N/A	
12/7/98	6:19:47 PM	Dhcp	None	1003	N/A	
12/7/98	6:18:45 PM	Srv	None	2013	N/A	
12/7/98	6:14:46 PM	Service Control Mar	None	7026	N/A	
12/7/98	6:12:31 PM	EventLog	None	6005	N/A	
12/7/98	6:13:41 PM	Dhcp	None	1003	N/A	
12/7/98	6:10:04 PM	Dhcp	None	1003	N/A	
12/7/98	6:04:00 PM	Dhcp	None	1003	N/A	
12/7/98	5:57:56 PM	Dhcp	None	1003	N/A	
12/7/98	5:56:57 PM	Srv	None	2013	N/A	
12/7/98	5:52:49 PM	Service Control Mar	None	7026	N/A	
12/7/98	5:50:41 PM	EventLog	None	6005	N/A	
12/7/98	5:51:53 PM	Dhcp	None	1003	N/A	
11/21/98	4:39:39 PM	Service Control Mar	None	7026	N/A	
11/21/98	4:37:19 PM	EventLog	None	6005	N/A	
11/21/98	4:38:29 PM	Dhcp	None	1003	N/A	
11/21/98	4:28:06 PM	Dhcp	None	1003	N/A	

Figure 18-2: The Event Viewer, System Log.

The small icons in the left column of the Event Viewer's various logs represent the following:

- **Small red stop sign:** Known as the error icon, identifies an error report that may be worth investigating.
- **Blue circle enclosing a lower-case *i*:** Called the information icon, indicates an event that describes successful operation of a major server service.
- **Yellow exclamation point:** Known as the warning icon, indicates that an event occurred that wasn't necessarily serious, but might indicate potential problems lie ahead. This may be worth investigating, too.

To investigate any log entry, double-click the line where it appears. Double-clicking the top stop sign in Figure 18-2 produces the Event Detail report shown in Figure 18-3. This report indicates that a serial mouse driver failed to load, because we deliberately neglected to attach that device to our laptop when we booted this machine so that we'd have something juicy to show you!

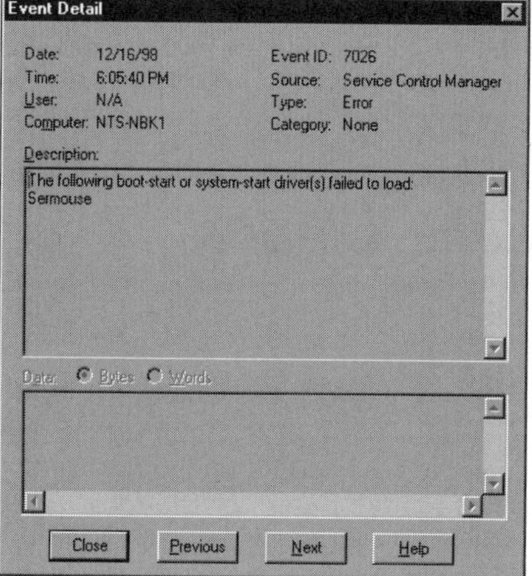

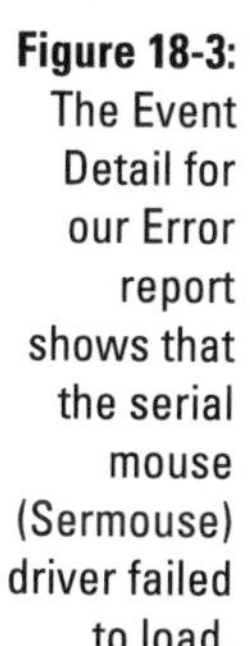

Figure 18-3: The Event Detail for our Error report shows that the serial mouse (Sermouse) driver failed to load.

The system log is what shows up by default in Event Viewer, but the utility includes three log files (accessible using Log on the program's menu bar):

- **System log:** This log all records events logged by Windows NT system components and appears by default the first time you run Event Viewer. By default, the System log records all system-related hardware and operating system errors, warnings, and information messages.
- **Security log:** This log records security-related events, such as changes to a machine's security policy, failed attempts to log on or access files or directories, and so on. This is where security audit information, covered in Chapter 17, is recorded. The security log uses two special icons: A yellow key indicates an audited security event completed successfully, and a gray lock indicates an audited security event failed.
- **Application log:** This log records events logged by some system services, such as the Replicator service, which Windows NT can use to copy key configuration files from PDCs to BDCs on a network. Likewise, when developers build applications they can instruct those applications to send event information to the Event Viewer as part of their installation. The icons that appear in the application log are the same as those for the system log.

Working with Event Viewer should become part of your regular system maintenance routine. Check the System and Application logs at least once a week to see if anything untoward has happened. If you audit security events, check the Security log as often as makes sense.

Whenever you troubleshoot, the Event Viewer should be an early stop along your path. Count on this tool to keep you informed about most system problems, and any application or service problems that know how to use this facility to report warnings and errors. Unfortunately, this does not include all applications, but does include most server services and important applications, such as database managers, e-mail packages, and the like.

After the Train Wrecks Comes the Crash Dump!

Should you ever be unfortunate enough to uncover a bug in Windows NT itself — a painful process that begins with mysterious server failures and progresses to long, arduous calls to Microsoft's technical support staff — you will probably have to create a crash dump for their use.

Reading crash dumps is well beyond the ken of ordinary system or network administrators. All you need is to recognize the term and to know how to create a crash dump for some expert to peruse at his leisure.

Thus, we begin with a definition: A *crash dump* is a snapshot of everything in memory when a Windows NT system configured to capture a crash dump actually crashes. It includes information about the operating system, the hardware, applications, and all kinds of other information that NT usually keeps hidden from view that it uses to manage its own operations.

Experts can pick through a crash dump to pinpoint causes of a crash, and use their knowledge to start formulating fixes or workarounds. This is one of the things that drive the patches and fixes that eventually show up in the Windows NT Service Packs — in case you wondered where that stuff comes from.

To enable a crash dump, your computer must first meet the following criteria:

- Your paging file must reside on the same partition where the Windows NT system files reside. (This is called the *boot partition* in Windows NT–speak; the paging file contributes to the bulk of the crash dump and must be accessible after the system quits working — that means it must be on the same drive where the crash dump utility resides.)

- You must have sufficient free space on the boot partition to capture everything in RAM plus everything in the paging file, which means free space equal to the sum of those values. To find out how big this value should be, look at the number reported in the Limit field in the Commit Charge pane on the Windows NT Task Manager (to launch task manager, right-click on any open area on the start menu, then select Task Manager from the resulting pop up menu). This represents the number of kilobytes of free space you'll need (to convert to MB, divide this number by 1,024).

After you meet these criteria, you can enable crash dumps through the Recovery pane on the Startup/Shutdown tab in the System Control Panel applet. Click the check box next to the item that reads "Write debugging information to:" next to the default filename (%systemroot%\MEMORY.DMP). You don't need to change this default, either. This pane is shown in Figure 18-4, with the proper box checked.

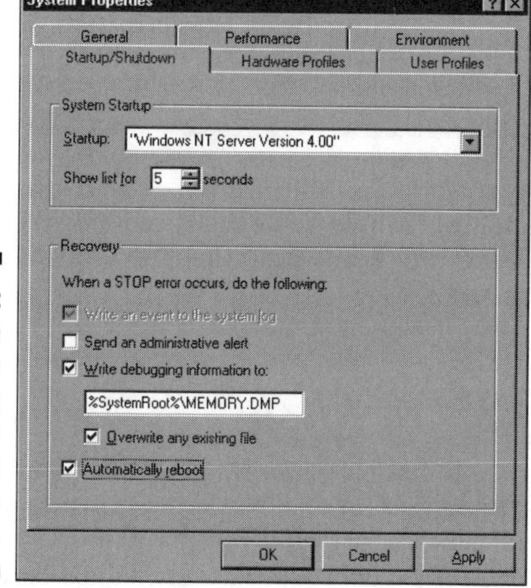

Figure 18-4: Check the "Write debugging information . . . " box to capture a crash dump.

After you check this check box, the next time your system experiences a STOP error, it writes the MEMORY.DMP file to your Windows NT system directory. By default, the value of the symbol %systemroot% equals C:\WINNT, assuming you installed Windows NT Server on the C: drive.

A crash dump creates two interesting problems. First, because the sum of RAM and the paging file is probably 200MB or more, you must find a way to get a copy to technical support (you'd better have a fast Internet link). Second, you must remember to delete that file once it's copied, or your server is likely to run out of space on the boot partition.

When applications go bad . . . call Dr. Watson!

Throughout this book, you encounter loads of tools and utilities for troubleshooting Windows NT Server hardware, networks, and the operating system itself. But what to do when applications go awry?

The answer to this question is "Nothing!" Not because you can't *do* anything about application problems, but because such problems in the Windows NT environment automatically provoke error reports from the Dr. Watson utility. In fact, Dr. Watson's job is to report on application difficulties whenever they occur.

Although you probably won't know what to make of Dr. Watson's contents — unless you've got extensive Windows programming experience and are familiar with debuggers — rest assured that there are plenty of people out there for whom this is old hat. Your entire involvement with Dr. Watson will be to check where the crash dump resides — it's noted in the "Crash Dump" text box at the top of the Dr. Watson application window that you can produce by entering `drwtsn32` in the text entry box of the Run command — to make a copy of that dump, and e-mail it to someone who can make heads or tails of this stuff!

But when applications get weird, Dr. Watson can be good for the tech support folks who will try to cure what ails your system.

We've learned that compressing crash dumps usually reduces them by 70 percent or more, so we recommend that you zip them up before you send them out (using a utility such as WinZip).

Diagnosing Difficulties with Windows NT Diagnostics

As its name implies, Windows NT Diagnostics is purely a diagnostic tool. That is, it can tell you an awful lot about your system, but you can't change anything using this tool. It only reports the situation — you'll need recourse to other utilities such as the System, Network, and Services applets in Control panel, among others, to fix whatever problems it finds.

To launch Windows NT Diagnostics, you can follow this menu sequence: Start⇨Programs⇨Administrative Utilities (Common)⇨Windows NT Diagnostics. Or, if you're lazy like we are, you can simply choose Start⇨Run, and then enter **WINMSD** in the Run command's text box. We've tested both methods, and the Run method is definitely faster!

We like speed so much, in fact, that we call the program WinMSD from here on. The default display for WinMSD appears in Figure 18-5.

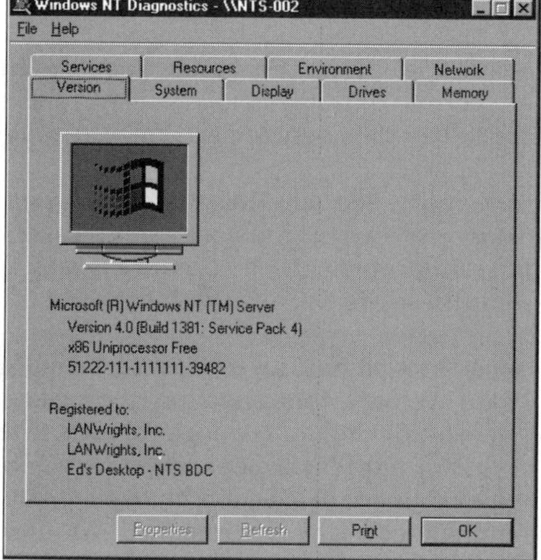

Figure 18-5: The Windows NT Diagnostics provide a plethora of system information.

As with so many other Windows NT utilities, using WinMSD effectively means understanding what's on the various tabs in this tool, so we'll cover them in order of appearance:

- **Version:** Shows which version of Windows you're running, including the build number and the latest service pack you've applied.
- **System:** Identifies the type of system, CPU, and system BIOS in use.
- **Display:** Shows information about your graphics card settings, including its BIOS information, current adapter settings and drivers in use, and driver hardware and components.
- **Drives:** Produces a hierarchical list of floppy drives, hard disks, CD-ROM drives, and other storage devices, with information about their file systems and configuration settings.
- **Memory:** Shows the same information about memory that appears on the Performance tab in Task Manager. In addition, this tab also tells you how large your page file is, how much of that space is currently in use, and what peak usage has been since the last time the system booted. It also indicates where the page file resides, and what it's named.
- **Services:** Shows all services currently loaded on the machine, and their status. (Running means the service is operational, Paused means it's installed but not in use, and Stopped means it's been disabled and must be re-enabled to resume operation.)
- **Resources:** Use the buttons on the bottom of this tab to list all interrupts (IRQs), I/O Ports, DMA, memory locations, and devices currently in use on your system.

- **Environment:** Lists environment variable defined for the system (System button) and for the user who's currently logged in (Local User button).
- **Network:** Provides invaluable information about your current logon data (access level, workgroup or domain, logon server, and so on), network transports installed, plus network settings and statistics.

In practice, you'll find the Memory, Services, Resources, Drives, and Network tabs to be of greatest interest when troubleshooting (especially the Resources tab for configuration problems). The other tabs may come in handy from time to time, but these are the ones with the most to tell you.

WinMSD is a great all-purpose tool, almost as good as seasoned salt in the kitchen. Use it to document a system's configuration, to check configuration settings before installing new hardware, to look for problems when hardware acts funky, and to check for hard disk, memory, and environment problems. WinMSD is not quite "one tool fixes all" but it's a great place to start fixing just about anything that might go wrong with Windows NT!

Plotting Performance with PerfMon

Windows NT's Performance Monitor utility (PerfMon for short) is an underappreciated work of inspired genius. We say that not only because it's true, but also because we've come to rely on this outstanding tool to help us with all kinds of troubleshooting over the past few years.

PerfMon is another utility you can launch from the Administrative Tools (Common) menu (Start⇨Programs⇨Administrative Tools (Common)⇨Performance Monitor). But it's faster to enter PerfMon in the Run command's text entry box (Start⇨Run) instead!

When you first launch PerfMon, it presents an entirely bland exterior, as Figure 18-6 indicates. It takes some work to get PerfMon to do anything, but the results make the effort worthwhile.

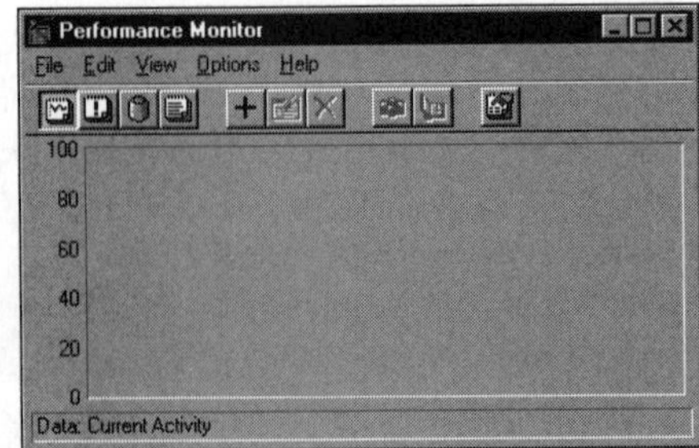

Figure 18-6: PerfMon shows nothing interesting when it's first launched.

The four faces of PerfMon

A close look at Figure 18-6 reveals some of the capabilities in the PerfMon program. The four buttons on left side of the toolbar (underneath the standard menus) stand for the following capabilities (reading from left to right):

- **Chart:** Displays a real-time view of selected performance data as the system gathers this data, based on the update time settings in the Chart, Options menu (the default update is once every second). This is the most common view for PerfMon, which explains why it's also the default view. You discover more about the Chart view later in this chapter.
- **Alert:** Allows administrators to instruct PerfMon to watch certain counters, and to send a message when pre-set values are reached. Administrators use the Alert view to issue warnings when disk space is running low, or when network or CPU utilization becomes dangerously high. Think of the Alert view as a kind of "system alarm" capability. The Alert view is worth investigating further on your own, even though we don't cover it further in this book.
- **Log:** Gives PerfMon a sense of history. Logging performance data is the only way that PerfMon can record the data that it displays over time. Administrators use this function to capture performance statistics, but typically import these logs into other programs (such as spreadsheets or statistical analysis tools) to plot trends or to establish the typical patterns of system usage that performance wizards call a "baseline." Logs produce no viewable output (just log files), so we don't cover them any further in this book.

Basically, a *baseline* defines what's "normal" for a system, so you can compare what you see when you're troubleshooting to something else, to see if significant deviations in certain areas might indicate potential problems. Logs are an essential tool for analyzing changes in system behavior over time, usually called "trending" or "trend analysis" — as such, they help to plan for system upgrade, expansion, and growth. For more information on using PerfMon to create a baseline, see Chapter 19.

- **Report:** Report provides a non-graphical way to list the data that PerfMon gathers in textual form. Administrators use this view to gather numbers or values to import into other reports, or to create reports for management that summarize key aspects of system activity. The Report view is another of PerfMon's functions that you should explore on your own, because we don't discuss it further in this book.

Of objects and counters

When you click the big plus sign on the toolbar in PerfMon, it permits you to add a counter for a specific system object to your chart, alert, log, or report. Figure 18-7 shows the dialog box that appears when you add a counter to the Chart view in PerfMon.

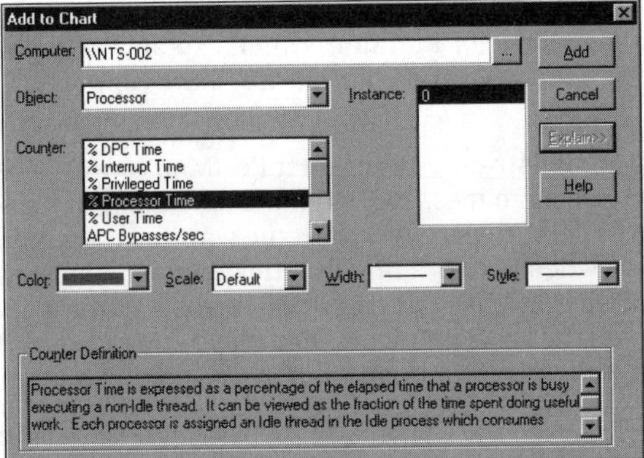

Figure 18-7: The Add to Chart dialog box permits you to select objects and associated counters for PerfMon to track and add to your current chart.

Chapter 15 goes into some detail about Windows NT object orientation. Here, it suffices to say that Windows NT has a built-in capability to gather statistics about objects that it recognizes, and that PerfMon provides a way to capture that data on demand. The default object that PerfMon selects is the Processor object, which has a large number of associated counters. The counter that's selected by default is called %Processor Time; choosing to display this counter, therefore, shows you what percent of the time your computer's CPU is busy performing useful work. This counter almost always shows up in PerfMon charts because it's a key indicator of system health and overall usage.

On systems with more than one CPU, PerfMon maintains a processor object, with separate counters for each CPU on the machine.

Other key Windows NT system object/counter pairs include the following (in the following list the object name appears to the left, followed by a backward slash, followed by the counter name):

- **Server\Bytes Total/sec:** Shows how much data your server is handling over time for a basic measure of how busy your system is. Other counters for the Server object, such as Sessions Errored Out, Work Item Shortages, Errors System, and Blocking Requests Rejected can all indicate potential system bottlenecks.

- **Memory\Pages/sec:** Shows how frequently the server is moving data from memory to disk, and vice-versa. If this number gets large (over 2,500 pages per second on an average server), it can indicate a shortage of RAM on your server.
- **PhysicalDisk\Avg. Disk Queue Length:** Indicates how many disk requests are pending service. If this number stays over 2.0 for long, it can indicate a disk drive that's too slow to handle its load, or one that's overwhelmed by current disk activity. Sometimes, this indicates a need for a faster drive, disk controller, or even, a faster disk subsystem altogether.

To enable counters for your physical disk, which will otherwise show up only with zero values, enter **DISKPERF -y** at the command line, then reboot the machine. This turns on physical disk monitoring in PerfMon, which is ordinarily disabled. To turn these counters off, enter DISKPERF -n at the command line, then reboot again.

- **Network segment\%Network utilization:** Indicates the level of usage on the network segment to which a server NIC is attached (in machines with multiple NICs, you must choose which NIC to monitor).

To enable counters for the network object, you must install the Network Monitor Agent on your server. You can do this by using the Add button on the Services tab in the Network applet in the Windows NT Control Panel. (Choose Start⇨Settings⇨Control Panel. Double-click the Network icon, click the Services tab, and then click the Add button.) In the ensuing dialog box, you must select either Network Monitor Tools and Agent or Network Monitor Agent to access these counters. If you choose to add the former item, you'll also be able to run the Network Monitor utility on your Server. If not, you'll still be able to access these counters, but you won't be able to run Network Monitor on that machine.

Figure 18-8 shows a PerfMon Chart with most of these counters enabled. A complete listing of all the objects and counters available in PerfMon runs to more than 30 pages of single-spaced text. Obviously, this program takes some time to get to know.

If you click the Explain button in the Add Counters dialog boxes, it produces a brief explanation of the counter in a text box at the bottom of the window. Simply browsing through the counters and objects with this display turned on is a great way to learn more about PerfMon (and Windows NT).

Entire books about this PerfMon are available. They can teach you how to use PerfMon to troubleshoot performance problems with Windows NT. At the same time, you won't be able to help learning a lot more about how Windows NT itself works as well. We strongly recommend these books to help you learn more about PerfMon:

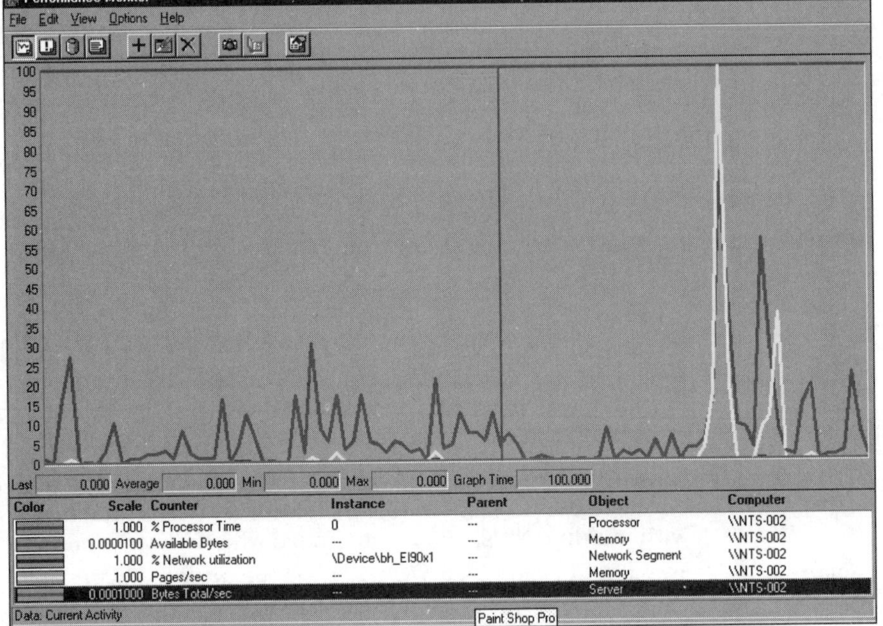

Figure 18-8: A typical PerfMon chart includes numerous objects and counters.

- *Windows NT Performance Tuning & Optimization,* by Kenton Gardinier, Osborne/McGraw-Hill, Berkeley, CA, 1998. ISBN: 0-07-882496-6. This book includes a great overview of Windows NT architecture and performance, and terrific coverage of PerfMon.
- *Windows NT Server 4.0 Secrets,* by Valda Hilley, IDG Books Worldwide, Indianapolis, IN, 1996. ISBN: 1-5688-4717-3. Although it's not as in-depth as Gardinier's book, Hilley's book includes the best discussion of key PerfMon objects and counters, and how to use them for handling bottlenecks, that we've ever seen in print.

On the other hand, if you visit your favorite online bookstore and use a search string like **"Windows NT" AND performance**, you'll find several other titles on this topic.

Windows NT ResKit Utilities

Microsoft Press publishes an excellent book/CD collection called the *Windows NT Server Resource Kit* (ISBN 1-57231-344-7). Since its release in 1996, Microsoft Press has also released three supplements for the Resource Kit, or ResKit as it's affectionately known. On the other hand, the entire contents of the work, up through the latest supplement, appear in searchable electronic form on TechNet, which is a lot less bulky and easier to access. TechNet even includes a special *Windows NT 4.0 Resource Kit Utilities* CD, which could become your launching point for further investigation.

Whichever way you gain access to the ResKit, you'll find that it contains tons of troubleshooting utilities. Here, we provide a brief list of the categories, and encourage you to explore this resource further for yourself:

- **Batch tools:** Includes several scripting tools and languages, plus executable batch commands
- **Computer Administration/Configuration tools:** Includes all kinds of configuration and setup utilities, such as the policy editor (policies are covered in Chapter 14; this is a tool that lets you edit them) and a tool that permits applications to run as server services
- **Computer and Network Setup Tools:** A setup manager, a Help version of the Hardware Compatibility List (HCL), plus automated install and setup utilities, such as SYSDIFF
- **Computer Diagnostic Tools:** All kinds of useful add-ins for PerfMon, plus a variety of system load and test utilities
- **Desktop Tools:** Numerous GUI tweaks, system add-ins, and desktop widgets
- **Disk/Fault Tolerance Tools:** Key disk exploration, management, and repair utilities, including DiskProbe (repairs MBR and partition table faults)
- **File Tools:** All kinds of file copy, file reporting, and file comparison tools
- **Internet and TCP/IP Services/Tools:** A grab bag of IP tools, including Telnet, a Web capacity analyzer, Web-based admin tools, and more
- **Network Diagnostic Tools:** A variety of network analysis tools, including monitors for the browser service, domain controllers, and more
- **Network/Server Administration Tools:** Password security management, domain checks, remote access tools, policy audits, and more
- **Registry Tools:** Reams of Registry tools, including REGBACK and REGRESTORE (back up and restore entire Registries), plus Regentry.hlp (explains all known Registry keys and values)
- **Tools for Developers:** Programming interfaces, tools, and documentation
- **User Account Administration Tools:** All kinds of tools to manage users and groups within NT domains

For troubleshooting purposes, any category that includes Diagnostics in its name, plus the Computer/Configuration Tools, Disk/Fault Tolerance Tools, Network/Server Administration Tools, Registry Tools, and User Account Administration tools are probably the most worth digging into. Enjoy!

To find out more about these utilities, search for the file named RKTOOLS.HLP on the *Resource Kit Utilities* CD. It includes an explanation for each and every one of them!

Chapter 19

Nixing Network Problems

In This Chapter

- Knowing what happens when networks go bad
- Understanding the symptoms
- Nosing about with NetMon
- Double-checking network settings
- Finding a missing server
- Dealing with a slow network
- Beating the blackout blues
- Fixing intermittent problems

Even with the best planning and equipment, network administrators have their networks crash from time to time. Spotting trouble before it happens is best, but knowing how to quickly remedy trouble after it happens can be a lifesaver. Because of today's heterogeneous networking environments, so many things can go wrong. In this chapter, we discuss some of the common network problems you may encounter, and we tell you how to solve them.

What Happens When Networks Go Bad?

Believe us when we say that you'll know when something goes wrong on your network! Your pager beeps (or vibrates), your phones ring, and people stand in your doorway tapping their feet. To help you lessen the chance of network problems, you should learn the warning signs associated with network problems and add preventative measures to your network.

Because networks consist of so many resources, when the network goes down, so could the Internet, e-mail, fax, and printing services. Whoops, that sounds like the business could come to a crashing halt! That's right, a broken network today could cause a lot of problems for many organizations.

What's healthy? Creating a baseline

One way to watch and monitor your network for trouble is to create a baseline report of what your network looks like on a day when it's healthy (that is, working properly). When you think the network is functioning poorly, you can compare the snapshot of the network on a good day with a snapshot of your network on a bad day. Some administrators like to take a baseline snapshot and then take weekly snapshots so that they can keep a continuous eye on the network. You should monitor the network's memory, processor, logins, and utilization, because these areas usually contain the warning signs when something goes wrong.

You can monitor these functions using the Performance Monitor tool (Start⇨Programs⇨Administrative Tools⇨Performance Monitor) that comes with Windows NT Server. Once Performance Monitor (affectionately called PerfMon) is running, you tell it what you want to look at by selecting various objects and counters. To add counters and objects, select Edit⇨Add to Chart. Tell PerfMon which server you wish to monitor (if you're running this from another workstation), and then add the following objects and counters. Use Figure 19-1 as a guideline. Click Add after each object you add, and then click Done.

You can check out the server, processor, and memory for issues such as the total number of logons, how many logons your system is experiencing per second, how much memory is being used, and how much of the available bandwidth of the server is being used. If you don't understand a particular object or counter, you can click Explain for more information.

You must install the Network Monitor agent and have the service running before the Network Segment object appears.

You can add as many objects and counters as you want. As you add each counter, it takes on a color that appears on the graph and in the legend at the bottom of the chart. Figure 19-2 shows PerfMon in action after we added several counters and began monitoring. Notice the real-time (one-second intervals) moving lines on the graph.

Because you want to monitor your server on a regular basis, save the configuration settings (File⇨Save Chart Settings As) and give it a filename like Perfset.pmc. Then, each time you monitor the server you can pull up your configured settings.

If you save the previous performance configuration settings to your desktop, Windows NT creates an icon for you that you double-click the next time you want to monitor the server with these settings.

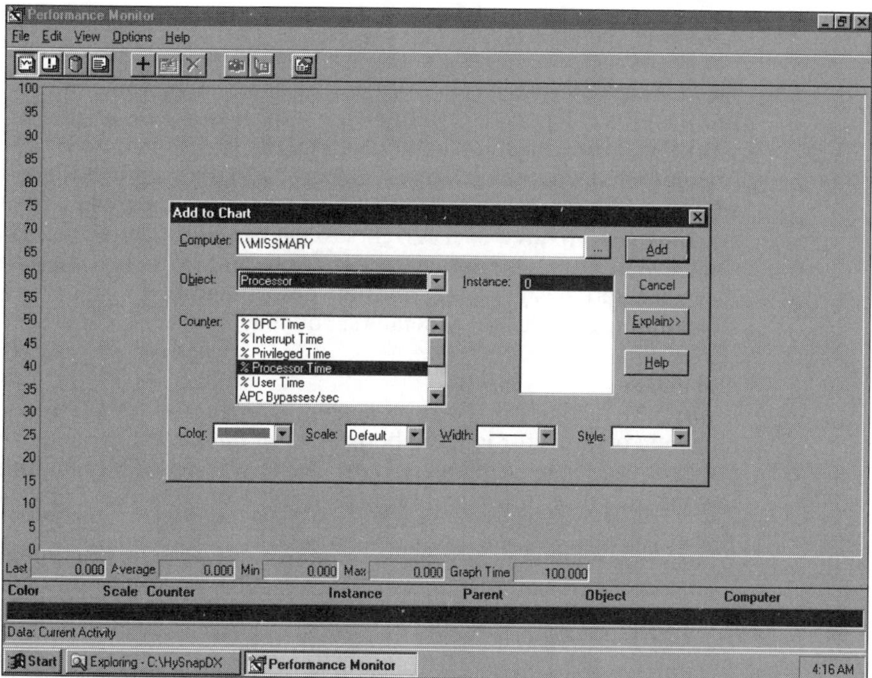

Figure 19-1: Configuring baseline settings in PerfMon.

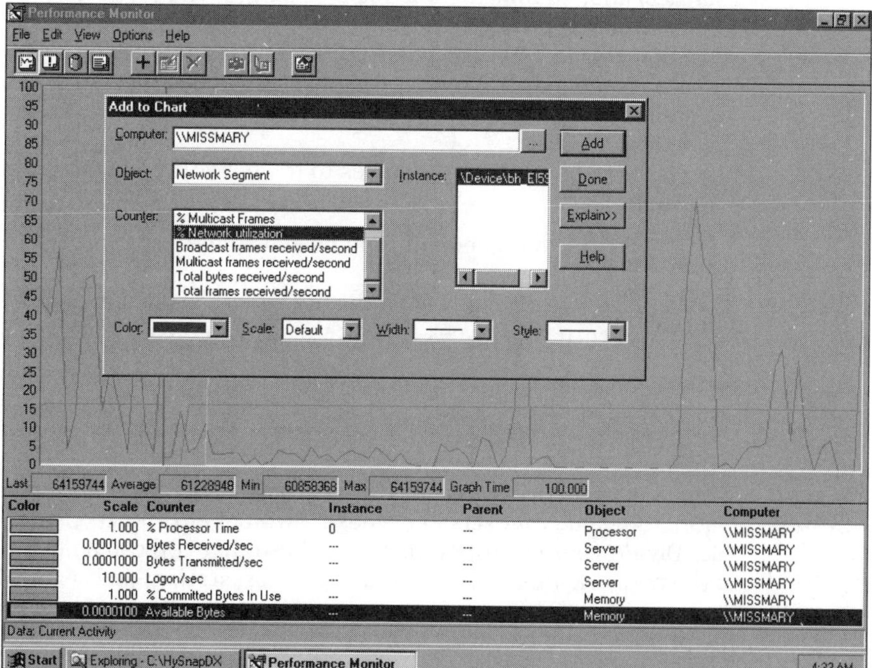

Figure 19-2: A graph of PerfMon doing its thing.

Documenting problems

We recommend that you grab a notebook and begin to document all network problems as they occur or immediately thereafter. You should record the symptoms, the items you changed to fix the problem, and the date and time. Documenting what you changed can give you a leg up if, a week later, something else breaks that's related to a change you made. For example, you may need to give User A rights to get to a spreadsheet application, and then a week later, you notice the master template file has been altered by that user, and everyone on your network is complaining that their spreadsheet application has new defaults. You may have given that user too many rights.

If you have a computer room, you should lock the door and require visitors to sign in on a visitor log notebook — even the person who comes to change the light bulb in the ceiling, because the ladder could bump into some wires in your computer room and bring a segment of your network down.

What we've seen in organizations that have several network administrators is that while one administrator works on one problem, another lets the maintenance person into the computer room. When something on the network goes down, network administrators start looking for the problem, but didn't know there was someone in the computer room. If you keep access to all of your equipment as restricted as possible, know exactly who goes near that equipment, and log all changes, you stand a better chance of troubleshooting problems quickly.

When a problem does occur, if you have more than one network administrator, gather everyone together and ask these questions:

- Has anyone made any changes to the network today that don't appear on the log?
- Has anyone outside our group been inside the computer room?

Then, check your change log on the network to see if any changes to the network over the past week could be related to the current problem.

30,000-foot view

When your network breaks, try to step back and look at it from a distance. Ignore the panic that sets in because it won't help you keep your wits about you. Divide your network into segments so that you can analyze which parts of the network are broken. Is it just one workstation, one segment, one server, one application, one service, and so on? After you begin to isolate the problem, you can start to fix it.

If this network is connected to a wide area network (WAN), you have more work to do. Someone could have made changes on the WAN that affect your network. If you're connected to a WAN, be sure to use unique naming and addressing schemes. If everyone names their Windows NT Servers and domains the same, things stop working well. For example, you can install a Windows NT Server in an isolated manner (not connected to any network) and then later connect it to a WAN. If no naming scheme is in place, duplicate names and address assignments can really foul up the network. It's possible that WAN links can go down and if you don't build redundant paths or links in your WAN, you can find that remote offices are not available until the link is restored. The link can go down due to a carrier problem, or because of faulty equipment on your end.

See Chapter 20 for more information on naming a device.

Flowcharts can help diagnose problems because they force you to think in a logical pattern (if the flowchart is logical). Draw a flowchart of your troubleshooting technique and have it handy so that when trouble arises, you can look at your flowchart for quick determination.

Understand the Symptoms?

Just as a runny nose can tell you that you're coming down with a cold, symptoms on a network can indicate when problems are about to occur. Not only do you want to monitor your server and network for its general health, but you should also walk around the building and talk to your users. We find that a lot of users don't report problems as often as we would like. Sometimes you bump into a user who casually tells you about a problem they have that forces them to reboot three times a day. They just accept this instead of reporting it. We like to consider "walking the floors" as part of our general network-monitoring scheme.

Gradual slowdown of network

Any time the networks begins to slow down, suspect trouble right away and start poking around at the disk space and memory on the Windows NT Server. Bad NICs in workstations can cause a real slowdown as the network tries to work around the malfunctioning board. You can use PerfMon and Network Monitor (NetMon) to poke around and gather information about what's fouling up.

Nosing about with NetMon

NetMon is a Windows NT Server utility that enables you to poke around the data on the network in a fashion similar to the way a protocol analyzer works. You can capture data from the network and analyze what's going on at an error level, protocol level, and more. It's not that fancy because you can't view your entire network, just the computer on which you install the agent and tools. If you want a broader tool to view the entire network, you have to go with NetMon for Service Management System (SMS), simply because it's more robust and includes more features.

The Windows NT Server installation doesn't install NetMon automatically. It's a service that you install separately and access via the Control Panel. Follow these steps to install NetMon on your server:

1. **Choose Start⇨Settings⇨Control Panel⇨Network.**

   The Network dialog box appears.

2. **Click on Services tab and click Add.**

   A list of services appears.

3. **Highlight Network Monitor Tools and Agent, and then click OK. Setup prompts you for the location of your Windows NT installation files.**

4. **Type in the path where your Windows NT installation files reside (that is, c:/i386) and click Continue.**

   You see the new service appear in the Services tab.

5. **Click Close.**

   Windows NT will prompt you to reboot your system.

To start the NetMon service:

1. **Choose Start⇨Settings⇨Control Panel⇨Services.**

   A list of services and their status (started/not started) appears.

2. **Highlight "Network Monitor Agent" and click the Start button.**

   The service starts.

3. **If you want to have this service start automatically each time the system boots, click the Startup button and select the radio button Automatic.**

After you have everything running, you can start NetMon through the Administrative Tools area (Start⇨Programs⇨Administrative Tools⇨ Network Monitor). Your screen should look similar to Figure 19-3:

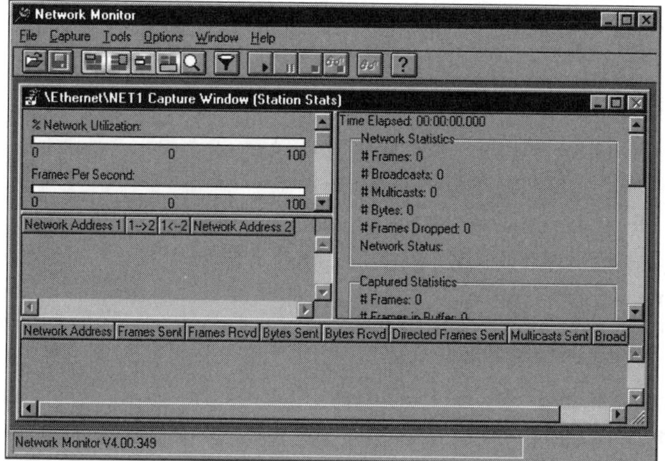

Figure 19-3: NT Server's NetMon screen.

Once inside NetMon, you can set up filters so that you only capture certain information. For example, you may not care about NetBIOS multicast information, but may want to hone in on IP information. By setting filters, you separate what's captured and what's not.

You can set triggers on events so that "when this happens, take this action." For example, you may not want to capture all the data coming and going on the server. You may be looking for a certain pattern and when that pattern occurs, then you want to begin the capture. This helps you to further define what you're looking at in the capture trace.

Double-Checking Network Settings

A host of things can be configured improperly or changed that affect network operation. The following list can help you sleuth about:

- **Proper addressing set (no duplicate addresses)?** Each node on the network (including servers) must have a unique address and computer name. If you can't ping (ping is an IP utility discussed in Chapter 12) or see the computer in the browser, check to make sure its identifiers are correct.
- **Proper IP ranges?** If you're using in-house IP numbering scheme and then connect to the Internet, your scheme may conflict with another registered set of numbers. Before connecting to the Internet, be sure to check with your ISP about setting up your network so that you don't use someone else's numbers.

- **Services on server running?** Sometimes the service you need stops running on the server. Check the Control Panel⇨Services icon to make sure the service is installed and running. Sometimes you need to start and stop a service again.
- **Event Viewer information?** Look in the Event Viewer to see if any errors have been logged.
- **Devices conflicting?** Use the Windows NT Diagnostics utility to see if any devices are conflicting with IRQs or memory.
- **Domain availability?** Check if the primary domain controller (PDC) is up and running. If you're adding a new user, verify that the proper domain name is inserted.
- **Access rights assigned correctly?** Check that users have the proper rights to the groups and resources they require.
- **Shares set?** Check to make sure that the resource in question has been shared on the server for all or some to see. Sometimes devices don't appear because they haven't been told to.

Whoa! "Server Unavailable"

When clients can't find the server, they get antsy. Check to see if only one user has the problem, or several. If just one user can't find the server, then the problem is probably at their workstation. If several users can't, chances are that you have a segment problem, such as a downed bridge or router.

If one user has the problem, ask the following questions:

- **Is the user logged in?** Don't laugh, but sometimes users call you about not getting services on a network and they haven't logged in yet.
- **Has the user ever accessed the network before?** If this is a new user who is logging in for the first time, the account may not be set up yet. Or if the user recently transferred from another department, you may need to reassign the user to another group with User Manager.
- **Has the user tried to reboot the workstation?** Sometimes, if the user reboots his or her workstation, the one-time glitch disappears.
- **Does the user have the proper rights?** Check in User Manager to make sure the user has the proper access rights on the network to access the needed resource.
- **Has anyone made changes to the workstation?** If any new devices were added to this workstation, the new device may have a conflicting IRQ or memory address problem. Take a look at the root directory on the workstation and sort the files by date and time to see when the latest changes were made. If a new NIC was added, check to see if it was set to the proper speed of the network.

- **Can you ping the user's workstation?** If TCP/IP is installed on the workstation, try pinging the workstation from your desktop. Try pinging the server from their workstation. Try to find the server in the browser listing. For more information on how to ping, see Chapter 12. If you can ping the server but can't see the server in the browser, you can force a browser election on the network to reset the master browser.
- **Does the user have a bad satin cable?** This is the silver-colored cable sometimes used for the network connection between the user's NIC and the wall plate. Sometimes housekeeping vacuums over the cables on a network and damages them. You can easily change out a cable to see if it's bad. If not, try the NIC.
- **Does the user have a bad NIC?** NICs go bad sometimes. You can replace the card with a known working card.

You may also want to check the following:

- **Login time restrictions:** If the user can log in to the network at specific times only, check the user's configuration in User Manager to make sure no restrictions apply.
- **Remote Access Service (RAS):** If the unavailable server is a RAS server, you must grant users a dial-in privilege to connect to it. Grant them rights as necessary in User Manager.
- **Dynamic Host Configuration Protocol (DHCP):** If the unavailable server is a DHCP server, make sure that the DHCP service is installed and running in Control Panel⇨Services. If users can't see the DHCP server, then they can't obtain an IP address if they depend on DHCP services.

Suddenly, Slow Networking

When services on a network start to slow down, trouble is surely just around the corner. When this happens, it's possible that disk space on the server is running low, memory needs to be reconfigured, or a token ring board has gone bad and broken the ring. Hopefully, you're using NICs in the server that are capable of handling a lot of traffic. If not, think about upgrading to higher performance NICs in the server.

Board beaconing?

Token ring is a funny creature because it forms a ring, and the data travels around the ring in a circular fashion. When a break in the ring occurs, data travels in a "U" shape instead. People located at the bottom of the U won't notice the slowdown as much, but those located at the tops see a tremendous slowdown. A token ring break typically happens when wiring gets out of whack or when one NIC starts beaconing. (This means the NIC is sending out a signal that something is wrong with it.) If you use hubs that aren't intelligent, or Multistation Access Units (MAUs), you have to isolate the bad token ring board or port on the MAU by a process of elimination. We've had to take an entire ring and unplug one MAU at a time, then unplug one port at a time. The older MAUs are actually relays, and you have to use a MAU tool to reset the relay. Other times, you need to replace the faulty NIC.

Hogging the bandwidth with large database or printing

You should check to see if an application is running on the network that's consuming a lot of bandwidth. Applications consuming a lot of bandwidth occurs frequently in Ethernet 10MB/s (10MB per second) environments in which you have a lot of network activity and database applications. Some database applications aren't designed well, and therefore, when a user makes a database query, the entire contents of the database are downloaded to the user's workstation for processing. This creates a lot of extraneous traffic. To help alleviate this problem, you can upgrade to database software that has a database engine to do the record crunching. Therefore, the user gets only the results. Or you can upgrade your network wiring scheme to a faster scheme, such as 100MB/s.

High-volume printing can also cause this problem. If certain users or groups of users are printing volumes of data during the day, see about switching them to print at night if possible to alleviate the network congestion. You can set up a print definition that only prints between certain hours.

Some organizations elect to upgrade their existing network backbone to help relieve bandwidth congestion problems, but this has a high cost associated with it. Organizations that have remote offices sometimes place an extra Windows NT Server in the remote office and install it as a backup domain controller (BDC). This allows user authentication to be performed locally at the remote office, thus conserving WAN bandwidths. Other organizations elect to upgrade their current network backbone to 100MB while leaving the users connected to the hubs at 10MB. This involves upgrading the devices connected to the backbone to include 100MB NICs and cables, plus adding a switch capable of changing between the workstation speed of 10MB to the backbone speed of 100MB. With this arrangement, even if users are going full throttle, the server still has 90 percent bandwidth available for other clients.

Congestion on the network due to lots of collisions and errors

Is the network experiencing a lot of collisions and errors? This can happen on Ethernet networks especially due to the CSMA/CD media access method. If you have intelligent hubs on the network, you can view information about the network either through a graphical interface or by looking at the LEDs on the hubs. High collision rate is usually an indication of faulty wiring or bad boards. It can also mean the bandwidth utilization is high. Ethernet has a lower utilization than token ring. Sometimes you need to segment off certain users that are high volume users.

Disk space on server low?

This problem should be obvious, but it never is! If your server's disk space is low, you're in for a fair amount of trouble, because servers can contain print queues, as well as user's data and applications. When disk space begins to run low, all sorts of strange problems appear. You should buy a lot of RAM up front, but if you can't, Windows NT uses disk space to swap recently used information back and forth from RAM. Low disk space causes Windows NT to encounter difficulties when trying to write to the PAGEFILE.SYS file. You can view and change the minimum and maximum size of this file. Go into Control Panel⇨System⇨Performance⇨Change. You see a screen similar to that shown in Figure 19-4.

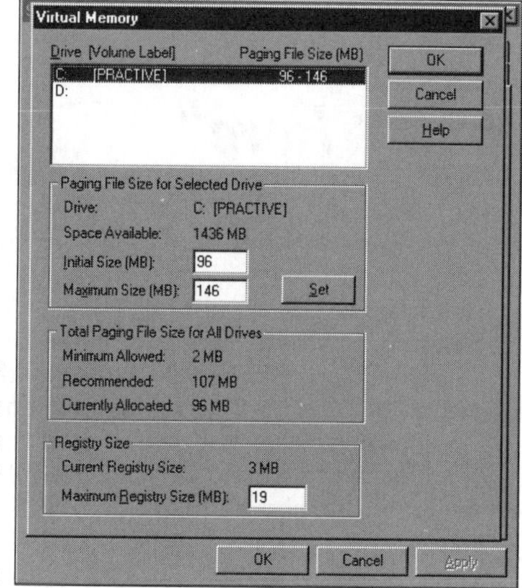

Figure 19-4: NT Server's memory paging file information.

You should have at least the same minimum and maximum numbers that Windows NT recommends or you may encounter problems. You can also move the PAGEFILE.SYS to a separate location other than the Windows NT boot partition and make sure the boot partition has plenty of disk space.

Also note the size of your Registry at the bottom of the screen in Figure 19-4. Keep an eye on this number so that when your Registry begins to grow, you can allocate more memory space for it. Remember that the Registry contains settings for applications, hardware, and more. As you add items to the server, your Registry grows.

Is someone performing network tasks that should be done off hours?

Is someone performing a network task that's transferring a large amount of data, such as restoring a lot of files? Or is someone performing a function such as remirroring drives? If a network has large storage drives that are mirrored, and the mirroring breaks, you can remirror the drives, but doing it during working hours isn't a good idea. Check to see if anyone is performing some sort of maintenance — either on the network or the server. If a large restoration of files is required across the network, try to do it during nonpeak hours — if possible.

If you check in PerfMon and see a heavy resource load, you can get a better handle on who's placing that load by going into Server Manager (Start➪Programs➪Administrative Tools➪Server Manager) and checking the resource usage per share, per person.

Can't Get "There" from "Here"

When a segment of your network is down, getting "there" is impossible. Several factors can cause this, depending on how you configure your network. Try to ping different nodes of the network to pinpoint what's down. For example, if you can ping one interface of a router, but not the other interface, chances are the problem is inside the router. You can also perform a TRACERT (as discussed in Chapter 12) on TCP/IP to determine the time intervals between the current and final destination. A slow response between two destinations could point you to the exact location of the problem. Try pinging and TRACERT from different locations on your network to further define what can be seen and from where.

Use more than one utility to determine where your network failure may be. For example, ping works with the TCP/IP protocol: Try using another utility, such as NBTSTAT, which works with NetBIOS and TCP/IP.

Also, the following problems could prevent you from accessing portions of the network:

- **Router problem:** Routers connect different networks together. If you've defined it improperly, you can't see what's on the other side. Routers can also experience congestion and drop packets. Sometimes more memory is required in these cases.
- **Bridge problem:** If your network contains bridges, sometimes you need to reboot the bridge. Depending on the software and hardware in use, you may find this occurring frequently. Remember that bridges need high-end NICs because they pass a lot of packets between them.
- **WAN link problem:** If a T1 or 56KB line goes down, you don't see anything on the other side. Sometimes, you may have to call a telecom company to resolve this problem. You need to have circuit information plus the customer support number handy.
- **Hub problem:** If you lose an entire segment of the network, check the hub that connects that. Hubs usually have power supplies that can go bad, plus ports that can go bad. Sometimes, just plugging a node into a different port on the hub fixes a problem. Make sure you mark the port as bad so that someone else doesn't plug a device into that port.
- **Wiring problem:** Wiring can degrade over time or can be moved around enough that the wires can go bad. Use a Time Domain Reflectometer (TDR) tool to check the cable for breaks. You may have to pull a new cable to the desktop or server. Replace satin cables if you suspect that housekeeping has vacuumed over one!
- **Server problem:** Check that the server in question is up and running. This seems obvious, but check it anyway.
- **Name resolution problem:** You may need to install WINs, DHCP, or a host file depending on the protocols in use on your network. (See Chapter 12 on TCP/IP for more information.)

Beating the Blackout Blues

If you haven't already experienced the blue screen of death (BSOD) on a Windows NT Server, you probably will at some point in your career. When Windows NT crashes, you get a blue screen with a dump of error messages on it that look pretty frightening to most people.

Microsoft dedicated an entire manual that ships with the Windows NT product just to help you decode the messages. Seems that whenever we get an error message though, the number isn't in the book. Isn't that the way it always works!

Windows NT allows for two modes of operation: *user mode* and *kernel mode*. Programs running in user mode cannot directly access the memory (they are assigned their own virtual address space) of the server or its hardware. Therefore, when a program running in user mode encounters an error, it does not crash the system. However, items running in kernel mode do have this access and this is where the crashes occur. Printer and video drivers operate in the kernel mode and can crash the system, leaving you no alternative but to reboot the system.

The BSOD provides cryptic information that, when decoded, gives you a good idea of which device caused the problem. But you have to do some detective work to decode the message; it doesn't just tell you that the printer driver went awry.

The BSOD has five sections, depending on the problem you encounter. Section 2 (BugCheck Information) is the most useful section because it tells you which device (if applicable) crashed the server. Section 3 (Driver Information) also helps because it tells you the driver information (if applicable). Sometimes just looking at the device and driver information tells you exactly what's going on. If not, you have to break out the Windows NT Error Messages manual to understand all the STOP codes.

You can go into Control Panel⇨System⇨Startup/Shutdown to change the startup of your server, to write the error information to a file, and automatically reboot the server upon crash, as shown in Figure 19-5.

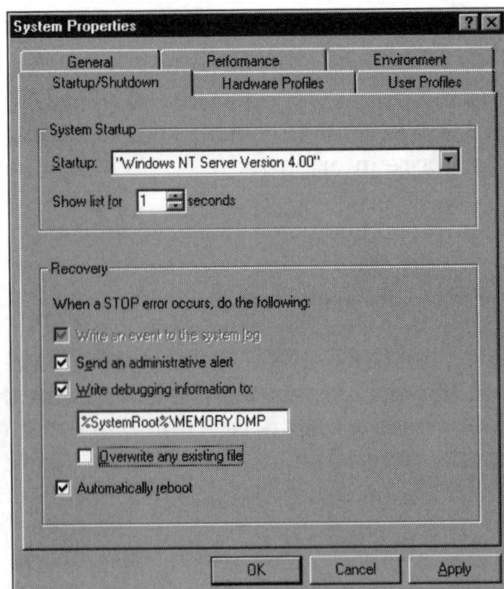

Figure 19-5: Configuring Windows NT Server to write crash information to a file.

Tracking Down Intermittent Problems

Intermittent problems are by far the most difficult to solve because they don't happen when you want them to. Because you can't always reproduce intermittent problems, you often have a difficult time figuring them out. These types of problems occur after a sequence of events, usually in a particular order unbeknownst to you. Your work is to figure out the sequence of events. Impossible you say — not really!

Record the following items in your system error log to help you eliminate possible causes of the problem:

- **Note the time and day of the problem:** For example, does the problem only seem to occur at 10 a.m. on Wednesday? Perhaps a particular activity in one of the departments happens every week, such as a departmental meeting, during which everyone is trying to access or print reports. This extra activity could place a load on the server or network depending on the nature of the activity. Look for trends in dates and time. Use PerfMon if you suspect this.
- **Note the equipment in use:** Does the problem occur only on a particular workstation or server? Does the problem occur when only a particular user logs into the network?
- **Note the application in use:** Does the problem occur only when a certain application is used? Reinstall the application. An application file can become corrupted, and the corruption can go unnoticed until a user performs particular function of that application.
- **Note the environment in use:** Does the problem occur only on a certain floor, near a certain area like an elevator? If so, you may get some wiring conflicts near heavy motors or fluorescent lighting.
- **Check the visitor's log:** Look at the log of visitors to your computer room. Does the problem occur every time the maintenance person enters a wiring closet or the computer room? If so, follow this person in the next time and see what they're doing. (Don't forget the overcoat and sunglasses!)
- **Viruses:** Always an obvious possibility, viruses are often the last thing checked. Viruses introduce random oddities onto networks. If you suspect one, immediately disconnect the server from the rest of the network and WAN, and scan it.
- **Known bugs:** Sometimes, you pound your head into the wall trying to solve a problem that is really a known bug. Check the Microsoft Web site regularly and check for new Service Packs. Remember to check other organizations' Web sites as well. For example, if you use Microsoft Office, check Microsoft's site for Service Packs for that suite. If you use all 3Com Ethernet cards, check the 3Com Web site for driver updates that fix bugs. Staying on top of known problems can save you oodles of time.

Chapter 20
Solving Printing Problems

In This Chapter

- Getting cozy with troubleshooting procedures
- Finding out about lots of ways network printing can fail
- Locating the right printer driver
- Spooling print jobs
- Naming print devices to make sense
- Using logical and physical printer definitions to ease output congestion
- Testing network printing by printing to the client's parallel port
- Aborting a print job

Printing problems occur frequently on a network because different components must work as a team for the printing process to work properly. Any of the components along the path can (and usually do) go awry at times. In this chapter, you find out about some of the common problems you may encounter while printing on a network and some of the ways you can avert those troubles or prevent them altogether.

Throughout this chapter, we use the Microsoft terminology "print device" and "printer," which may be confusing in the real world. Microsoft defines "print device" as the physical printer, such as an HP LaserJet 4Si, and they define "printer" as the spooler. We use their terms here to be technically accurate. However, if this is your first time working with NT, this may be confusing.

Taking Printer (Print Device) Problems a Step at a Time

To aid you in troubleshooting, Windows NT has an entire troubleshooting section dedicated to printing. On the server desktop, choose Start⇨Help⇨Content⇨Troubleshooting if you have trouble printing. The help menu asks you a series of questions and then pulls up a list of suggestions on what to do depending on your answer. This wizard can help you with many printing problems.

Why the paperless office remains a myth

The late '80s brought the advent of document-management software and hardware that promised to create the "paperless office." The premise was that all information contained on paper or microfiche could be incorporated into networked databases to be retrieved. The "paperless office" foretold of getting rid of network print devices and viewing all information online. The idea came at an appropriate time: conservation issues, such as recycling and saving trees, were springing up right and left.

But if you believe that myth, we have some property to sell you. Even with paperless office software and hardware, paperless offices virtually haven't developed. Reality dictates that paper will be around for a long time — as long as people have a print-media mind-set. Some people don't find it handy to view data on a screen. Even before computers arrived, people were used to viewing data on paper. This method is simply ingrained in us, just as driving on the right side of the road is in the United States. Try going to another country and driving on the left side of the road. It just doesn't feel right.

The following factors also play into the print-media mind-set of humans:

- **Paper is more permanent.** A document filed neatly in a file drawer gives people a greater sense of security than a document on a hard disk, even if it's backed up.
- **Paper is more trusted.** Look at how many people believe the outrageous lies perpetrated in supermarket rags. Could you imagine being served a summons to appear in court in an e-mail? You'd probably think it was a joke.
- **Paper is more final.** Documents on paper have the air of something "published." In electronic form, documents are easily revised, so many people see electronic documents as less formal or less important.
- **Paper is more mobile.** Try throwing your desktop into your briefcase and reading it on an airplane if you don't have a laptop. For absorbing documents at your leisure, nothing beats paper.

The paperless office isn't coming anytime soon. People get some kind of warm and fuzzy feeling when they see the printed results of all their hard work. So for now, you're going to have to make sure your organization has a well laid out plan for network printing and troubleshooting.

Don't be too dependent on the troubleshooting wizard, however, because you're sure to run into problems that are beyond its powers. For those times, you must do some detective work.

Troubleshooting printing problems is fairly simple — if you approach the problem logically. Starting at one end of the problem is best — change one thing, and then test to see if the problem still exists. If you make five changes and solve the problem, you'll never know which change fixed the problem. Then, if the same problem occurs, you have to make the same five changes to get the same result. This just isn't logical.

We prefer to use a process of elimination to help isolate the problem. The printing process begins at the client PC then traverses the network to the print device. So, check the client PC first, then the network, then the print device. If there's nothing wrong with the client PC or the network, you know there's something wrong with the print device itself. Simple as pie!

If you use a systematic approach to all of your network troubleshooting and keep a log of how you fix problems, you can reference your notes if the problem occurs again.

The Many, Many Ways That Printing Can Fail

Use the process of elimination to your advantage when performing network troubleshooting tasks.

In the following sections, we separate the types of printing problems you may encounter into three areas: the client PC, network, and print device.

When clients can't print

When your users can't print, what do you do? Obviously, you have to solve their immediate problem and in this section, we give you some pointers. At the end of this section, we give you some tips on how to help the clients help themselves before they call you. Here are some questions to ask yourself (and the user) when you're trying to figure out what the problem is:

- **Is the user logged on to the network?** You may think this question sounds silly, but this should be among the first things you check! It never fails: The user calls and reports a printing problem, you go through numerous troubleshooting loops, scratch your head, and later find out that the user only *thought* he or she had logged on to the network that morning. Save yourself the trouble. Try to print from your workstation and if that works, visit the user and perform a quick test to make sure that he or she really did log on.
- **Is the user at the right print device?** Sometimes users send their printer output to a different print device without realizing it. The user may be standing at Print Device A when in fact, the output is on Print Device B.
- **Is user intervention needed?** Maybe your user is trying to print envelopes or a certain size of paper that requires the user to physically go to the print device and insert the proper paper or envelope in the proper bin or slot. Ask the user what he or she is trying to print and then figure out if the print device is waiting on the user to do something, such as insert an envelope.
- **Is this user the only one unable to print?** It's possible there is a printing problem at this workstation only, or within a segment of the network, or possibly throughout the network. Check with other users to see who can print and who can't. If more than one user can't print, see if a print device is down or if any access rights were altered in the device's share. If this user is the only one who can't print, check if any changes were recently made to their account or workstation.
- **Has anyone made changes to this user's workstation?** In medium to large organizations, there may be more than one technical person supporting end users. Sometimes, the left hand doesn't notify the right hand. Ask the user if anyone has been to his or her workstation from your group. Check the help desk ticket log, if one exists, to verify any changes made to this workstation. Sometimes users make changes themselves without realizing the impact on other programs. Ask the user first, but sometimes going to the workstation and examining the dates and times of files in the root directory (for example, C:\) on their workstation plus any system subdirectories gives you a better idea of recent changes.
- **Has this user ever printed successfully?** Is this a new user that was recently added to the network? If so, perhaps they never printed on the network successfully. Has this user recently switched to a new department and needs to print to a new print device but isn't aware of it? If this is their first attempt at printing, first check their user account setup.

If users complain that the printing is taking too long and they can't perform other tasks on the computer, someone possibly could have altered the device's spooling settings on the server. Choose Control Panel⇨Printers.

Right-click on the device in question and choose Properties. Select the Scheduling tab and make sure that the "Spool print documents so program finishing printing faster" button is selected (see Figure 20-1).

There are two options to choose from in printing: EMF (spooling) or RAW (no spooling). If you enable the RAW setting, NT doesn't enable spooling and users must wait until their document is finished printing before performing other workstation tasks.

Now that you know how to solve the immediate print problem, take a few minutes to determine what types of problems the user could have handled before calling you. The more educated your users are on the fundamentals of printing, the more they can solve their own problems. Remember that some users have mastered the copy machine simply because they had to — there was no technician available to get rid of the paper jam or change the toner cartridge. Consider sending your users an e-mail containing the following tips on solving simple network printing problems to save you some time:

- **Resetting the print device:** Users can easily turn an on/off switch on the print device or take a look at LED lights on the front panel. If the device is out of paper, a "paper out" light often is available, or the user can simply slide out the paper tray to reveal this.
- **Rebooting the client PC:** Users can save their data and then reboot their workstations to determine if the application is hung in a spool that never ends.
- **Verifying network logon:** If the user isn't sure whether he or she is logged onto the network, the user can do one of two things to test it: reboot and log on, or try to send a test e-mail to you.

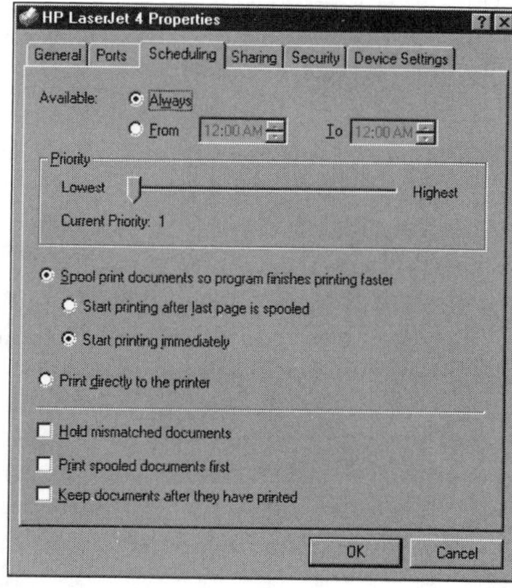

Figure 20-1: The Printer Properties Scheduling tab.

The network is amok

After ensuring that the problem isn't on the client computer, you can check the network for a problem. The following are factors you should check at the network end:

- **Is the NT Server up?** We always check our NT Servers to make sure they are up and functioning! Sometimes servers crash and it may be a little while before you catch wind of it. Look out for little things like several users calling about printing problems. Then, perform a quick test to make sure you can access the NT Server yourself. One possibility is that a bridge is down, which can affect an entire floor or just a segment of the LAN.
- **Is there a wiring closet snafu?** If your network is running through hubs in wiring closets, check to see if someone unplugged the connection to the print device in the closet. If you're the only network administrator, you usually don't have this problem, but if you have a separate wiring contractor, check to make sure the contractor hasn't removed any devices from their respective network ports.
- **Does your NT Server have enough memory?** If you're running all your network printing off the NT Server, don't forget to leave enough memory and disk space to manage the print queues and spooling. Now may be the time to offload your print service functions to a separate PC and designate it as the print server.
- **Are the permissions set properly?** In NT Server, you can restrict users or groups from printing to certain print devices, or you can give a particular user higher priority when printing. Check the device's definition to determine if any user or group has been blocked for accessing that print device. (See Chapter 11 for more information.)
- **Is the print device configured properly?** Check the printer-port settings in the device's configuration in case all the printout is going to LPT2 but the device is connected to LPT1, in which case the data is spilling out onto the floor.
- **Is there enough hard disk space on the server?** If you enabled spooling, did you allow for enough hard disk space on the server where the spooling takes place? This could be the NT Server, the print server, or the user's workstation, depending on the spooling in question.
- **Can the user browse the server in Network Neighborhood?** If the user is unable to browse portions of the network, they will be unable to print to those areas. Is the server down? Sometimes it takes 15 minutes for browsers to force an election if the master browser malfunctions and some portions, or all of the network, do not appear during this time. Try pinging the server to see if the server is available but just not showing up in the browser. If you need assistance troubleshooting your network, turn to Chapter 19.

- **Do you have the same IP address assigned to the print device and the server's printer definition for that print device?** It's possible, when connecting a network-attached print device, to define the device as one IP address, but connect it to the server's LPT port using another IP address. Check the device's port properties to make sure that both addresses match.

The print device is the culprit

As we stated in the two previous sections, you should check the client PC first, then the network, and then, if neither of those is the source of the printing problem, you should check the print device. Check the following on the print device to see if this is where the problem is:

- **Is the print device offline?** This is our favorite one! Sometimes, the problem is so easy to solve that we never check the obvious until hours of head-scratching have passed. Always check to make sure the device is online. You can check it through the printer manager on NT or go physically to the print device and look at the LED lights on its panel. Sometimes, pushing a button on the print device is all it takes. We've found that some users need the electrical outlet and unplug the print device!
- **Is the print device out of paper?** Thanks to copying machines that often run out of paper, your users are used to this phenomenon occurring. You'll rarely get a call for a print device not working only to find out that it's out of paper. Users are pretty good about checking the bin and keeping it full. The trick is to never run out of paper. Have someone be in charge of monitoring the paper supply so when it's low, there's ample time to order paper.
- **Is the cable damaged?** Always check the cables. If the print device is attached directly to the network via a Network Interface Card (NIC) and a cable, the cable could be damaged. (The NIC could also be faulty, which you can determine by trying a good NIC.) We've found cables that looked okay, but were damaged by getting rolled over with cleaning equipment or the user's chair. In one case, a crew came in and rebuilt cubicles, which they built on top of the network cabling. The cable looked fine, but it was actually damaged.
- **Is the cable unplugged?** Not all cables to the print device stay snapped in. A good idea is to unplug the cable and plug it back in. Is the cable from the device to the network still connected? Sometimes users unplug cables not realizing the cables actually perform a function on the network.

- **Does the print device display an error message?** Typically, most modern print devices provide operational and status LEDs that blink or turn a particular color if something is not functioning properly. These functions are usually off-line, paper jam, buffer overflow, low or no toner in cartridge, or plotter pens or color in cartridges low (in a color print device). We've seen some pretty strange-looking graphs when one color is off! If the print device is a dot matrix model (and we sure hope not), perhaps the ribbon cartridge needs changing.
- **Is the print device driver outdated or incorrect?** This is probably the most common problem you'll encounter while setting up your network print devices. Luckily, this is terribly easy to solve by going to the manufacturer's Web site and downloading the proper Windows NT driver. If you're installing a device that's not on the Hardware Compatibility List (HCL), and the printer manufacturer is a small organization, it's possible that a new driver isn't available yet, in which case you're stuck. The word of advice here is to always buy print devices that are popular models instead of trying to save a few dollars with the cheaper print device models.

You've Gotta Have Drivers

One advantage of printing through a network is that you install the *printer drivers* or *print device drivers* (discussed more in Chapter 11), which are the programs that format documents from your software applications into a language that the print device can understand, on the NT Server itself rather than on each client. The advantage is that you only have to install each driver once, as opposed to many times (as would be the case if you had to install the driver on each client computer). Also, when it comes time to upgrade the printer driver or operating system, you can save tons of time by having to install the upgraded printer driver only once. That's good news!

Check Microsoft's HCL before implementing your network to determine which print devices are supported and compatible with Windows NT. Microsoft has a testing lab that certifies drivers and print devices for compatibility with NT. Those devices passing certification get to display a Microsoft logo to that effect, so you can also look for the logo. Some print devices were never designed to be a network print device, so they have no associated driver.

You should install printer drivers for each manufacturer and model of print device on the network. If you have print devices by different manufacturers, then, of course, you need to obtain the correct printer drivers from each manufacturer. Even if one manufacturer produces all your print devices, you probably need drivers for each different model. For example, Hewlett-Packard's (HP) LaserJet II print devices use a different driver than the HP LaserJet 4Si print device, because the HP LaserJet 4Si has more features (such as duplex printing) than the HP II does.

Popular printer drivers are usually bundled with the operating system or supplied by the printer manufacturer and designed to work with specific operating systems. Because the release of the software and hardware isn't coordinated, however, you may not have the most recent driver.

Typically, you can download the latest printer driver for the Windows NT 4 operating system from the printer manufacturer's Web site.

Of Spoolers, Queues, and Logical Printers

When everyone has a print device on his or her desktop, there's no need to worry about who will print when and how. However, even small companies that share print devices need some organization to make sure everyone gets an even chance at the device — except the president of the company — the president's stuff always has priority over the underlings'. Remember to give priority to print jobs initiated by people who may be able to increase your salary.

Spooling jobs can get fouled up if the network is running slowly or if a print device is tied up for a long time. Looking at a print server's queues will tell you immediately if the print device has a bottleneck. The longer the queue, the more likely a problem exists. Hopefully, you've named your print servers and queues in a fashion that allows you to easily find which print device is not servicing jobs properly.

The spooling process on a network

All of the following happens behind the scenes. You and the user don't have to get involved — unless there's a problem.

1. The client PC application issues a request to print to a specific device. (The printer driver typically resides on the NT Server.)
2. The NT Server then ships the driver over to the client PC and the request is formatted and sent back to the NT Server.
3. The NT Server then offloads this request by spooling it to the print server.
4. The print server coordinates printing with the print device.

Here are some things you can investigate if you suspect spooling trouble:

- **Stuck print job:** Sometimes a print job gets stuck in the spooling process and never actually prints. In this case, you can delete the job from the queue or simply pause it. Either way, you can access these functions through Start➪Control Panel➪Printers. Double-click on the print definition in question to view a list of print jobs in the queue. Pausing the print job allows other jobs to be serviced. After all the jobs clear from the queue, you can resume printing the job to see if it begins printing. Sometimes, clearing the job from the queue and asking the user to submit the job again is just as efficient as pausing.
- **Insufficient disk space:** Spooling works by sending print jobs to a disk for storage until a print device is available to service the job. If the disk space is reaching capacity, spooling may not function properly because there's no room to store jobs.
- **Spooler service halted:** When you install Windows NT, the spooler service is set to start automatically. As with other services, it's possible that the service halts itself, in which case you need to restart the service on the NT Server. Choose Start➪Settings➪Control Panel➪ Services, and then scroll down to the Spooler service setting. Make sure the service is started. If not, highlight the service and then click Start.

If you create a baseline of your network's regular printing patterns, then when something is out of whack, you should be able to spot it right away. If you know that the users on the second floor print large jobs overnight, and you pass by the print device in the morning and there's no output in the bin, you should suspect trouble and take a quick look at the print server.

What's in a Name?

Ever had to track down a print device named Fred, Barney, Wilma, or BamBam? Don't laugh, network administrators really do name their devices and servers after their favorite cartoon characters. Although these names may be cute in a small office, it becomes a troubleshooting nightmare in medium to large organizations. And, many small LANs sometimes grow up and get connected to WANs, so it's best to plan your print names as if you might one day hook up to other LANs.

We prefer to name print devices using a scheme that allows your users to know the devices' locations. Your naming scheme should make sense to both you and your users. As you plan your naming scheme, remember to think globally because your LAN may get attached to another LAN or a WAN. You don't want to name your print devices something common, such as Printer 1, P1, Printer 2, P2, Printer 3, or P3. Instead, when you name your print devices, try to include some or all of the following information:

- Floor and/or wing (for example, FL2WEST for second floor West wing)
- Printer make and model (for example, HP4SI for HP4SI)
- Function (for example, ENV for device set up to print envelopes)

Using the previous information, you can have a print device named HP LaserJet 4Si_FL2West_ENV. Users looking at this can easily identify this device as an HP LaserJet 4Si print device located on the west wing of the second floor that is set up to print envelopes only. In addition, if you hookup your LAN to another LAN or WAN, the chances of someone else having this same naming scheme is unlikely (unless that person is reading this book too). Don't be frightened because you're using lots of letters. NT allows you up to 127 characters. We don't advise that you use all 127 characters, but don't shorten the names to the point that no one can understand them.

You want to be careful with long share names. Operating systems such as Windows For Workgroups and DOS don't support long share names. So, if you have any of these types of clients, you want to stick to an 8.3 naming convention for file names and an eight character limit on share names. In those cases, each letter in the share name should be meaningful.

Mixing the Logical and the Physical

NT Server's print manager allows you to logically group print devices (what you and I call physical printers) under one umbrella or to group one print device under several logical printer definitions. This is also known as print pooling, and its functionality enables you to optimize your networking printing so jobs can be serviced based on function or based on high volume output. In the following section, we take a closer look at why you'd want to set up print pooling.

Logically speaking

A logical print definition is not a physical print device (see Chapter 11). A *logical printer definition,* or print pooling, manages the print requests for a group of print devices on an NT network. Print pooling finds an available print device, and sends print jobs to that device. This arrangement frees up the user from having to determine which print devices are not tied up and are free to print to. The only caveat to this arrangement is that you'd want to have the print devices in the same general area so the users aren't running all over the building looking for their print jobs. The print devices must be identical in this case, meaning the same make and model, same RAM installed, same printer driver, and the like.

The main reason you'd want to set up print pooling is if users on your network are complaining that one user or group is printing a lot of high-volume documents. If you simply add more print devices to the network, then the burden is still placed on the users to determine which devices are not busy.

Physically speaking

If you have a print device that allows you to print different sizes of paper, envelopes, letterhead, and more, you know that manual intervention is required. The user has to go to the print device and put the paper in a special bin, or maybe put the envelope in the correct slot. Well, if the user does this without pausing the existing print job, someone's going to get upset. Therefore, whoever is managing this print device needs to know to pause the device and wait for manual intervention.

The easiest way to solve this dilemma is to set up multiple logical printer definitions that then print to the one print device. In the section entitled "What's in a Name" in this chapter, we suggest that you add the function of the printer to the naming scheme. Well, here's a perfect example where you would add the function to the name of the logical printer definition. The users would know to print all envelopes to the print device shared with the word "ENV" at the end of the name.

If you happen to have a budget that allows you to buy just one jiffy print device but not several devices, then you can avoid setting up any logical printer definitions by purchasing a print device that has multiple tray slots and built-in functions that require no user intervention.

Direct Printing

After you set up your network print devices and definitions, you won't normally want to go back to printing directly to a print device — that is, physically hooking up a print device to a PC. However, if a user is having difficulty printing, you may need to troubleshoot the problem to determine if it's a network setup problem or the print device or definition itself.

If the print device isn't functioning on the network, you can quickly determine whether the problem is in the device by following these steps:

1. **Disconnect the print device from the network.**
2. **Connect the print device directly to a working PC's parallel port and try to print a test page from that PC. Do so by choosing Start⇨Programs⇨Accessories⇨WordPad. Type a few words of text into WordPad, then select File⇨Print.**

If no local print device has been defined on this PC, depending on the operating system in use, you'll need to go into the Printer applet of Control Panel (for Windows applications) and add the print device under Add Printer.

Be sure to install the proper driver on that PC.

Here's what the test tells you:

- **If a test page prints, then the print device works and your problem lies either in the client PC or the network.** After you determine that the print device is okay, you can hook it back to the network.
- **If the print test doesn't print and you get the same problem as when the print device was connected to the network, then you have isolated your problem to that device.**

Sometimes, you may have users who need their own print device attached to their desktop, instead of printing to the network. It's also not uncommon to find people who have to answer the phone a lot and can't afford to leave their desk every time they print a document.

That Print Job Must Die!

Ever print a long document and then stroll over to the print device only to find that it's printing one strange symbol per page? This phenomenon is a common occurrence when printing a PostScript file to a print device that doesn't understand or interpret PostScript files. You're scratching your head thinking that if the document was 20 pages long and you're only seeing one symbol per page, then you'll be waiting all night for the job to finish (plus wasting a lot of paper). Well, the good news is that you can stop print jobs from printing. The bad news is if you have a lot of memory in the print device, the entire job may have already downloaded, in which case you have to turn off the device to clear its memory. If you don't time your move just right, you usually end up with a paper jam to clear.

You can kill a print job a few other ways:

- Users can kill print jobs from their client PC if their client operating system can talk to the NT Server print manager. Windows clients already have the proper print manager tools on their desktop to interact with NT Server's print manager tools. Users merely need to click on their printer folder, locate the job in the queue, and select the delete function and that job will stop spooling to the network print device. But the print device will continue to output what's in its memory. If nothing is in the print folder, that means it's already been spooled. You can't delete something that ain't there! For other clients, such as Macintosh and Unix users, you need to see what version the users are running, and whether or not those versions interact properly with NT Server's print manager function.

- You can permit your users to kill the print job from the NT Server's print folder. However, this approach can open a can of security worms. You have to give users rights to kill a job this way. If you don't plan the rights carefully — and name your network print queues and devices clearly — you could end up with users accidentally deleting other print jobs. We've seen users delete (or pause) other print jobs from a queue just so their print job would print faster. This practice can create an environment of hostility if the offending person is caught red-handed by coworkers.
- You can set the page limit to a specified number so print jobs don't print over that number. If most of your users print documents that are only a maximum of 20 pages, then set the page limit to 50 pages. However, if your users typically print documents of 50 pages or so, then set that number to something like 100. Doing so means users can print only 100 pages at a time without your intervention. A good idea is to train your users to print only the first few pages of a long document as a test to make sure the formatting is as expected before printing the entire document.

Chapter 21
Solving Hardware Problems

In This Chapter

- Booting up, alas, can be hard to do sometimes
- Going verbose with NTLDR
- Listening to NTDETECT
- Using the HCL
- Checking the Event Viewer

Although Windows NT Server is a reasonably stable operating system, hardware problems can rear their ugly heads nevertheless. When good systems go bad, you must resist the temptation to yield to panic and instead put on your troubleshooting helmet. Why a helmet? Because sometimes, trouble shoots back!

When NT Won't Boot

No matter what the cause, bootup failures can be disconcerting — primarily because the system doesn't run. Although this condition can result from problems with hardware or software, a boot failure leaves you with hardware that doesn't work (and that's why we cover this problem in this chapter).

Fortunately, you can deal with boot failure by the numbers. You can start out with easy fixes, and then try increasingly drastic repairs until you reach the point where restoring a backup of your server on another system is your last and best hope to resume operations. (You *do* have a recent backup of your NT Server, right? We cover backup and restore operations in Chapter 16.) The keys to solving most boot problems rely on four crucial ingredients:

- A set of Windows NT boot disks
- A current Emergency Repair Disk (ERD) for your sick NT Server
- A recent backup of your sick NT Server
- A Windows NT Server installation CD, plus the latest Service Pack (SP4 at the time of this writing)

Step 1: Repair the startup files

The first thing to try when you can't boot Windows NT is to repair the startup files. If you're lucky, this set of steps will solve your problems:

1. **Boot from the first Windows NT boot disk.**

   If this doesn't work, the system qualifies as "truly dead." In that case, see the Sidebar entitled "Resurrecting a truly dead server" later in this section. Otherwise, proceed to Step 2.

2. **When prompted, insert the second boot disk. Shortly after, you'll be prompted for a startup option. Select the option to repair by pressing the R key on the keyboard.**

   Note: All options are selected by default, so you have to clear those selections that you don't want to use. For this go-round, deselect the Inspect Registry Files entry; leave the other options selected.

   When you're finished, the display looks like this:

   ```
   [ ] Inspect Registry files
   [X] Inspect startup environment
   [X] Verify Windows NT system files
   [X] Inspect boot sector
       Continue (perform selected tasks)
   ```

3. **Click the option that reads** `Continue (perform selected tasks)`**.**

4. **You're prompted to insert disk 3 of the startup disk set, and then prompted to insert the Emergency Repair Disk.**

   Follow all on-screen instructions. The Setup program displays this message when it has finished its repairs:

   ```
   Setup has completed repairs.
   If there is a floppy disk inserted in drive A:, remove
       it.
   Press ENTER to restart your computer.
   ```

Most boot failures are related either to damage to key Windows NT startup files — namely BOOT.INI, NTDETECT.COM, NTLDR, or Ntoskrnl.exe — or to damage to the Master Boot Record (MBR) on the system drive. These repairs will fix such problems, and therefore restore the system to bootability. If the fixes described here in Step 1 don't get your machine back up and running, please proceed to Step 2 in the section that follows next.

Understanding the Windows NT repair options

As shown above, using the Repair option from the Windows NT startup disks presents you with four repair choices. These should be understood as follows:

- **The Inspect Registry Files option** provides a way to repair damaged Windows NT Registry keys (and reflects one reason why you should regularly refresh your ERD — namely, to keep the Registry snapshot as current as possible). This particular repair option can replace existing Registry keys; if you suspect problems with the Registry and you have a current version on your ERD, simply select all keys for replacement.
- **The Inspect Startup Environment option** makes sure that the Windows NT files in the system partition (where the PC boots from) are correct. If any of these files are missing or damaged, Repair replaces them from the Windows NT installation files, which must be available from the Windows NT Server CD or from a drive with a copy of the /i386 directory (for x86 PCs, that is; other CPU types require files from their related directories). This option repairs and replaces the BOOT.INI file.
- **The Verify Windows NT System Files option** checks that each file in the installation is valid and matches the file installed from the Windows NT Server CD. Repair uses the Setup.log file on the ERD to determine what files were loaded and to verify checksums. It also verifies that key startup files, such as NTDETECT.COM, NTLDR, and Ntoskrnl.exe are present and correct. If you've installed any Service Packs, you must check the file named Files.1st on that Service Pack to see if the Service Pack must also be reinstalled.
- **The Inspect Boot Sector option** applies only to x86 PCs (but because that's 95 percent or more of the NT installed base, including Pentium machines, we bet this means you). If the Partition Boot Sector on the system partition doesn't reference the NTLDR program, ERD replaces the Partition Boot Sector. The Repair process can also repair the Partition Boot Sector for the system partition on the startup disk, but only if you've saved the Partition Boot Sector as a part of your ERD (which we strongly recommend).

Step 2: Restore your Registry backup

If repairing your startup files doesn't allow your system to boot, your problems are more serious. The next step is to use the startup disks and the ERD to replace the Windows NT Registry (but only if you have a current copy of its contents). Follow these steps:

1. **Boot from the first Windows NT boot disk.**

   If this doesn't work, the system qualifies as "truly dead." In that case, see the Sidebar entitled "Resurrecting a truly dead server" later in this chapter. Otherwise, proceed to Step 2.

2. **When prompted, insert the second boot disk. Shortly after, you'll be prompted for a startup option. Select the option to repair by pressing the R key on the keyboard.**

   Note that all options are selected by default, so you have to clear those selections that you don't want to use. For this go-round, select only the Inspect Registry Files entry (do so by deselecting the bottom three options).

   When you're finished, the display looks like this:

   ```
   [X] Inspect Registry files
   [ ] Inspect startup environment
   [ ] Verify Windows NT system files
   [ ] Inspect boot sector
       Continue (perform selected tasks)
   ```

3. **Click the option that reads** `Continue (perform selected tasks)`.

4. **You're prompted to insert disk 3 of the startup disk set, and then prompted to insert the Emergency Repair Disk.**

   Follow all on-screen instructions. The Setup program displays a completion message when it has finished attempting its repairs to the registry. This message will either indicate success (hooray!) or failure (boo! hiss!).

If your repairs are successful, you're done. If not, it's time to consider tackling the recommendations in the section that follows next. But first, you may want to consider calling your system vendor's tech support operation, and asking for their input on your situation. The changes necessary in Step 3 (the next section) can't be undone, so ask for help and exhaust all other options first.

Step 3: Reformat or replace the hard drive

If replacing the Registry doesn't solve your problem, you may have to replace the hard drive that contains the system partition.

Reformatting or replacing a hard drive results in the COMPLETE LOSS of all data and programs on that drive. You can't contemplate this without tears unless you have a backup of that drive's contents to restore to the reformatted or new drive that takes the old drive's place. Before you do this, call your vendor or your favorite NT guru, and go over what you've tried so far, and ask for their recommendations on how to proceed. Don't reformat or replace a drive until you've tried everything else you and your panel of experts can think of to beat this problem!

If you're committed to performing this ritual, follow these steps:

1. **As a last-ditch effort before reformatting, try to rebuild your disk's Master Boot Record manually.** The Master Boot Record (MBR) is where your PC reads all its information about how the disk is partitioned, and where to look for boot information to start up an operating system.

   To replace the MBR manually, boot from a DOS floppy, then use the DOS `fdisk/mbr` command. If you do this, you'll also have to repeat the prescription in the Step 1 section that appears earlier in this chapter. This time, choose the Repair option and select the "Inspect Boot Sector" box so that it can rebuild your MBR to make it compatible with Windows NT. That's because rebuilding the MBR using DOS produces an MBR that Windows NT can't read. Don't ask us why, but we've learned the hard way that this trick sometimes resurrects apparently dead NT drives. Reboot your system after running the Repair option, and see what happens. If NT boots, thank your lucky starts; if not; proceed to the next step, with a heavy heart!

   Don't rebuild the MBR manually if you have a dual-boot setup or are using a third-party partition manager, such as Paragon Software's Partition Manager, PowerQuest's Partition Magic, or V Communications Partition Commander. If you're using a partition manager, use its built in MBR repair facilities instead; if you're running a dual boot machine, this trick probably won't work, so proceed to the next step. Sigh!

   If you haven't updated your Partition Table since the MBR was last saved, replacing the MBR also replaces that table as well. The *Windows NT Server Resource Kit* includes two utilities, DiskProbe and DiskSave, that you can use to save a copy of the MBR and partition tables for emergency use (this situation qualifies) — we suggest you use one of these tools to back up your hard drive setup. And please, do this right away — neither tool will work if your hard disk crashes!

2. **Reformat the drive — or should we say: "Reinstall Windows NT Server."** To do this, boot from the Windows NT Startup disks, and reinstall Windows NT from the CD. During the install process, you'll be able to repartition and reformat the drive anyway, so why not kill two birds with one stone? If this works, you'll have to restore your backup when the initial installation is complete. Plan to spend the better part of a day at this task. If it doesn't work, proceed to Step 3.

3. **Replace the drive.** To do this, you have to know something about rooting around inside a PC's innards and how to mess with ribbon cables, disk controllers, and whatnot. If this scares you in the slightest, pay somebody else to do the job for you. Then, if they screw up, you can make them do it over but you'll only have to pay for things once. If you do it yourself and screw up, you may have to pay for things twice. But if you know what you're doing go ahead and replace that drive with one that's compatible with its controller (you'll probably get twice as much space for half the price, so even this grim gray cloud has a silver lining).

4. **After your boot drive is operational, you must reinstall Windows NT** (and any Service Pack you may have added) and then reinstall your backup software.

5. **Restore your most recent backup to get your system back in operation.**

If this approach doesn't solve your problems, your server is well and truly dead. Serious repairs are now necessary (as if what you've been through isn't already serious and time-consuming enough). If you're still dead in the water, proceed to Step 4 (covered in the next section).

Step 4: Replace the server

If a drive repair followed by a backup restore fails, you may have to replace your entire server. If the replacement machine is identical to the machine that won't boot, follow Steps 4 and 5 in the list of action recommended in the preceding section, titled "Step 3: Reformat or replace the hard drive."

Resurrecting a truly dead server

Sometimes a server may fail because the motherboard has gone south, the power supply has given up the ghost, or any of a number of other causes that can kill your system dead, dead, dead. When this happens, an incredibly handy system utility called NTRecover, created by a couple of genuine NT Wizards at Sysinternals (`www.sysinternals.com`), might be able to save the day.

NTRecover can access a dead PC-based NT system's disks from a good system across a serial connection between the two machines. You can then salvage data from the dead machine's drives using native NT commands and utilities. With the write-version you can even run `chkdsk` on the dead system's drives, and attempt other repairs to bring that system back to life.

However, one word of warning is necessary here: If a drive fails, this utility can't do any good because it can access only operational hard disks. If you have to recover data from a failed drive (and no backup is available), you have no choice but to pay the high prices ($400 and up per drive) and wait for service from the various drive-recovery companies that specialize in such work. For more information about this option, visit your favorite search engine using "data recovery" as your search string. Be prepared to spend some money, too!

If the replacement machine uses different hardware components, you must install Windows NT Server (and the Service Pack) onto that machine. Next, you must reinstall any additional applications and services that were present on the old machine, and then restore *only* the data from the old machine onto the new machine.

The reason why you can't simply restore a backup on a machine that's not configured the same as the machine it's replacing is because all kinds of Registry and software settings are hardware-dependent. If the two machines aren't identical, you run the risk of creating a Windows NT installation that can't run on the hardware where it's installed! But before you take such drastic steps, or if you find yourself without a current backup for the dead machine, please read the sidebar titled "Resurrecting a truly dead server" in this chapter.

Going Verbose During Bootup

Sometimes, driver incompatibilities or device failures can cause Windows NT to fail even when the MBR is okay, the Partition Table is intact, the Windows system files are pristine, and the Registry's not too bad off. When this happens or when mysterious hardware failures plague a system, it's a good idea to edit your BOOT.INI file to make your system "go verbose" during startup. In plain English, this means that the Windows NT boot loader program, which is named NTLDR, will report Kernel and driver names while they are loaded during startup. Use this option if Windows NT does not start up correctly and if you think a device driver may be missing or damaged.

To make Windows NT "go verbose," you must edit the BOOT.INI file and add the `/sos` switch to the bootup command for Windows NT. Here's how you do this:

1. **BOOT.INI is a hidden, system, and read-only file. To find it, Windows Explorer must be configured to show such files. To do this, select the Options entry from the View menu in Explorer.**

   The resulting Options dialog box is shown in Figure 21-1. Make sure the Show All Files radio button labeled is selected and that the Hide File Extensions for Known File Types check box is deselected. After you've made these settings, you can find BOOT.INI in the root directory of the Server's system partition.

2. **Select BOOT.INI in Windows Explorer, and then right-click to call up the Properties dialog for that file. Deselect the Read-Only check box so that you can edit the file.**

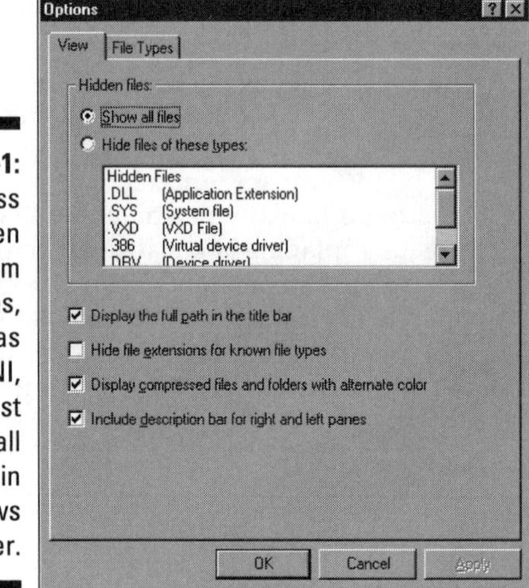

Figure 21-1: To access hidden system files, such as BOOT.INI, you must show all files in Windows Explorer.

A typical BOOT.INI file looks something like this:

```
[boot loader]
timeout=5
default=multi(0)disk(0)rdisk(0)partition(2)\WINNT
[operating systems]
multi(0)disk(0)rdisk(0)partition(2)\WINNT="Windows NT
       Server Version 4.00"
multi(0)disk(0)rdisk(0)partition(2)\WINNT="Windows NT
       Server Version 4.00 [VGA mode]" /basevideo /sos
C:\ = "MS-DOS"
```

Before you edit your BOOT.INI, copy it to a floppy or create a duplicate named BOOT.BAK in the same directory where BOOT.INI resides. Formatting or typing errors in BOOT.INI can make a failing NT system completely unusable, so you may want to take out insurance against your own human frailty!

3. **Open BOOT.INI in Notepad or some other ASCII editor, and add the string `/sos` after the line immediately following the `[operating systems]` entry in the file as shown. Save BOOT.INI with this change, then exit Notepad (or whatever).**

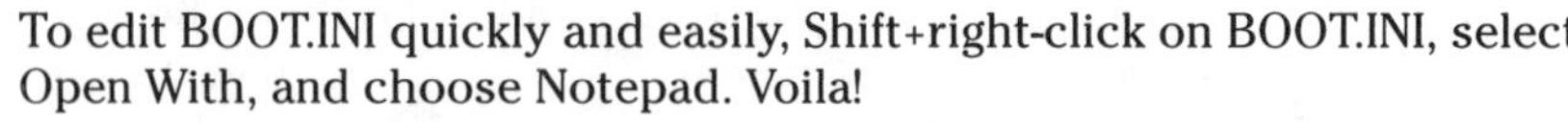
To edit BOOT.INI quickly and easily, Shift+right-click on BOOT.INI, select Open With, and choose Notepad. Voila!

Notice that the [VGA Mode] entry already includes the `/sos` option, so you can always elect to boot your system with this option to "go verbose" with Windows NT. This is the easy way out, and you'll pay for it by being forced to run in vanilla VGA mode at 640 x 480 resolution.

4. **Go back to Windows Explorer and right-click BOOT.INI to bring up the Properties dialog box again.**

   You must reset BOOT.INI to Read-only (check the box next to this entry) for Windows NT to boot properly.

5. **Reboot the system, and watch NTLDR on-screen as it tells you about its activities.**

   If a driver problem is halting the boot process, you should know the name of the offending element because it will be loading when the system hangs or fails. Your first move should be to replace that driver with a known working copy (and while you're at it, you may want to check the vendor's Web site for the hardware component involved to see if a newer or more stable version is available for that device).

After you find the offending driver and reboot the system successfully, replace the edited version of BOOT.INI with the original version to turn off verbose mode. That way, you won't have to watch the show any more — now that you've seen what you needed to see!

What NTDETECT Can Tell You

Part of what happens when Windows NT starts up is that a hardware detection program named NTDETECT.COM takes an inventory of what's in the system and compares what it finds with what the Registry recorded the last time the system booted successfully.

Like BOOT.INI, NTDETECT.COM is a system, hidden, read-only file. You must reset these attributes, or change your Windows Explorer configuration as explained in the preceding section to view this file. (Select the Options entry from the View menu in Explorer. The resulting Options dialog box is shown in Figure 21-1. Make sure the Show All Files radio button is selected and that the Hide File Extensions for Known File Types check box is deselected.)

When things get weird on an NT machine, you can replace the normal version of NTDETECT.COM with a special debugging version named NTDETECT.CHK. This file resides in the \SUPPORT\DEBUG\I386 directory on the Windows NT Server CD. Here's how you use this tool to help your troubleshooting activities:

1. **Copy NTDETECT.CHK to the root directory of the system partition on the Server.**
2. **Rename NTDETECT.COM to NTDETECT.BAK; then rename NTDETECT.CHK to NTDETECT.COM.**
3. **Reboot the system to use the debug version of NTDETECT.**

4. **When you finish with your testing, rename NTDETECT.COM back to NTDETECT.CHK (you might want to leave in the directory in case you need it again), then rename NTDETECT.BAK back to NTDETECT.COM.**

   The next time you reboot the system, the old version will take back over the hardware detection job during startup.

When the debug version of NTDETECT executes, it notes all its activities on the screen as they complete. Here's a small sample of the output you'll see this program produce on your system:

```
Detecting System Component...
Reading BIOS date...
Done reading BIOS date (2/5/1998)...
Detecting Bus/Adapter component...
Collecting Disk Geometry...
Detecting Keyboard Component...
```

After it completes its recounting of the components it finds, the debug version of NTDETECT requires you to press the Enter key before it continues. Then it displays information about the current status of controllers and peripherals on the system. You must press the Enter key each time the screen fills with information to go on to the next screen.

If something's wrong with your system, the debug version of NTDETECT halts on the component that's causing problems, and it might even give you an error message of some kind (but not always). Like the verbose mode of NTLDR, this can be a valuable diagnostic tool to tell you when (or where) your system is hanging during startup.

Don't forget to switch back to the "quiet" version of NTDETECT when you're finished with it. Otherwise, your system will take much longer to boot!

Check Out the HCL!

HCL stands for Hardware Compatibility List, which is a comprehensive list of all hardware and system components that have been tested with Windows NT and shown to work in a laboratory environment. If you come across a device in NTDETECT or NTLDR that's causing your system to hang, you should check the HCL to make sure that device is included (and of course, make sure you've got the latest and greatest driver for that sucker in your system).

Based on long, hard, bitter experience, if you find a device that's not on the HCL in your system, we strongly recommend that you replace that device, unless you can obtain a Windows NT driver for that device from the manufacturer (and even then, we'd be nervous). That's why we like to say it's better to switch to a device on the HCL than try to fight with Windows NT to accept a device that's not on the HCL.

For really, really new equipment, it might not have made it onto the HCL by the time you check it out. If you're using anything that's remotely "bleeding edge" in or on your system, don't give up on running Windows NT until you check with the vendor. They can not only tell you if it's compatible, but they'll also be able to give you information about drivers, if any special software elements are called for. Also be aware that vendors often provide two drivers: one that's optimized for maximum performance, and the other that meets all of Microsoft's HCL requirements. You may even get a performance boost by checking with the vendor!

Having tried to make such noncompliant devices work on NT systems and having failed dismally despite access to expert help, we think it's far more trouble than it's worth to try to stray from the large collection of devices on the HCL just to save a little money.

Although a version of the HCL is included on your Windows NT Server CD, that version is dated August 1996 (when the software was released). This list ignores everything that's happened, PC-wise, since then. Because of the rapid pace of change in the PC marketplace, we suggest you grab your version of the HCL from Microsoft's Web site:

```
www.microsoft.com/isapi/hwtest/hcl.idc
```

If it doesn't live here by the time you read this, use the Search function with **HCL** as your search string. That's how we found this URL, and how you can find its next home, too.

Don't Forget the Event Viewer

Sometimes, hardware or driver problems aren't enough to keep NT Server from booting. But boy, can they cause headaches. Any time a driver or a service fails to load, Event Viewer records an event in the System Log that tracks this occurrence. Also, an ominous error message like the one depicted in Figure 21-2 shows up on your server's screen.

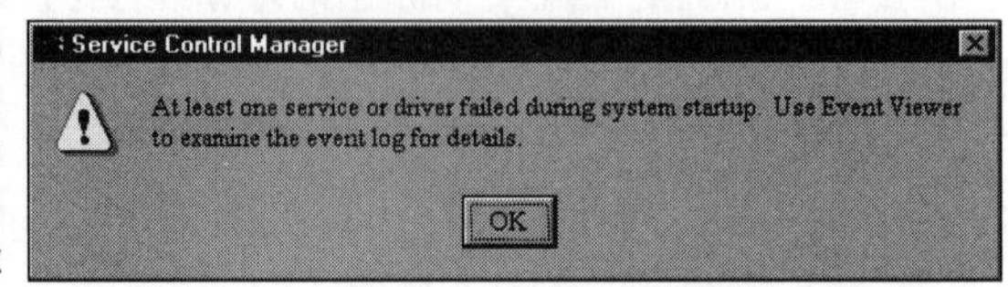

Figure 21-2: When a device or a driver fails during startup, the following dialog box appears after the first login.

Whenever this happens, don't fail to investigate. Launch Event Viewer from the Start menu (Start⇨Programs⇨Administrative Tools (Common)⇨ Event Viewer) and make sure you're looking at the System Log (Log⇨ System). You should see an event record marked with a small red Stop sign at the far left near the top of the log. Double-click this entry to read the details. They'll probably point you at whatever's causing your problems.

Regardless of whether hardware or software problems provoke your troubleshooting activities, always ask yourself this question, "What has changed most recently?" Except for outright device failures (which are rare, but do happen from time to time), the most common cause of troubleshooting is the most recent change to a system. You can always test this theory by rebooting your Windows NT system and hitting the space bar when the prompt that reads

```
Hit Space Bar NOW to Invoke Last Hardware Profile/
          Last Known Good Configuration
```

appears. Rebooting restores the Registry to its state during the last successful system startup and might be just the thing to fix your problems. But this also cancels out all changes you've made since that last bootup. So think hard about whether you want to go for this quick fix or not. If you choose it, you can't go back to where you were without repeating all that work, *unless* you back up your current (but possibly damaged or defective) Registry first!

Part VI
The Part of Tens

"You the guy having trouble staying connected to the network?"

In this part . . .

When Moses came down from the mountain, how many commandments did he carry? Ten. How many toes do most people have? Ten. How did Bo Derek rate in that old movie of the same name? Ten! We're not sure what the connection is here, but that number shows up everywhere, even on *Letterman.* Perhaps that's why the Part of Tens is a key ingredient of this and all other ...*For Dummies* books. Then again, it could just be a big coincidence. . . .

Each chapter in this part includes a list of tips, tricks, techniques, reminders, or sources for inspired information about your Windows NT Server system and its network. We'd like to claim the same source of inspiration that Moses had for his commandments but, alas, ours came from the "School of Hard Knocks" next door!

These chapters have been constructed to save you time, steer you around common networking potholes, and get you past common sources of chaos and confusion. The best part of tens, however, is one that doesn't appear directly in this part of the book — that's the part where you *count to ten* as you begin to lose your cool. If you try that part first, the other parts of ten will probably do you a lot more good.

Chapter 22

The Top Ten NT Server Installation and Configuration Tips

In This Chapter

- Exceeding the minimum requirements is the only way to go!
- Qualifying hardware helps avoid ugly rebuilds
- Using the network to simplify installation
- Automating installation
- Dealing with installation problems
- Using the VGA mode boot option
- Returning to the Last Known Good Configuration
- Building (and using) NT Startup disks
- Engaging the Emergency Repair Disk
- Planning a successful NT Server

If you spend enough time working with Windows NT Server, you undoubtedly will be required to install this software on multiple systems. This job can be more "interesting" than it has to be, not to mention that it can take more time than you may want it to.

This chapter provides you with some fact-filled sources of information, some tried and true guidelines, and some great repair tools and techniques to help you successfully survive the Windows NT Server installation process. Knowing these ten tips and not needing them is better than not knowing and needing them anyway.

Minimum NT Server Requirements and Recommendations

Table 22-1 offers a quick rundown of the minimum requirements to run Windows NT Server 4.0.

Table 22-1 Windows NT Server Minimum Requirements (Plus Realistic Recommendations)

Item	*Minimum Requirement*	*Recommended*
CD-ROM	None	CD-ROM or DVD player
CPU	Intel 486	Pentium 90 MHz or better
Disk Space	124MB free	At least 500MB free
Display	VGA	VGA or better
Floppy drive	3.5 inch or 5.25 inch	3.5 inch
NIC	At least one	PCI bus mastering NIC
Pointing device	MS-Mouse or compatible	MS-Mouse or compatible
RAM	16MB or more	64MB or more

To try to run a production server by meeting the minimum requirements is a recipe for disaster. The performance you'd be able to eke out from such a machine would have a lynch mob of users at your heels in no time at all.

When building an NT server, more of just about everything is better: This applies to more powerful CPUs, more RAM, and more powerful network interface cards (NICs). Servers do their thing in quiet obscurity in most circumstances, so you don't have to install an 8MB graphics adapter, a fancy monitor, or a top-dollar mouse or touchpad. You can opt to skip the CD-ROM or DVD player on the NT server as long as you can get access to the server across the network from another machine where the contents of the CD-ROM have been copied to a hard drive.

If you install Windows NT Server on a machine that doesn't include a NIC, you won't be able to install or configure any network-related aspects of the system. We're convinced that there's no point in installing a server that's not attached to a network, so don't install NT Server on a machine unless it has a NIC inside (even better is a NIC connected to a live network).

The NTHQ Is Not NT Galactic Headquarters

Before you even think about installing Windows NT Server on a machine, you'd best be sure that the hardware you're considering will make a good home for that software. Nevertheless, without a formal seal of approval or a guarantee from a vendor, how can you be sure that the software will work with your hardware?

Fortunately, you can be sure two ways:

- **The NTHQ method for old hardware:** NT shipped in August 1996 with a DOS-based analysis tool that could judge existing hardware for NT compatibility called NTHQ. Therefore, if the hardware you're considering was built before the August 1996 release date of NT, NTHQ can help. To install NTHQ, use the MAKEDISK utility in the \Support\Hqtool subdirectory on the NT Server 4.0 CD to create a diagnostic floppy disk that automatically assesses your hardware (the program creates a report saved in a file named NTHQ.TXT). Simply reboot your computer with the NTHQ disk in its floppy drive, and NTHQ assesses your hardware and produces a report of everything incompatible that it finds. If you can't boot to the floppy, be sure to reset your BIOS to permit the computer to boot from the floppy, if one is present.
- **The search online method for new hardware:** Microsoft maintains a comprehensive list of hardware that's been tested and certified to be compatible with Windows NT. This list is called the HCL, or Hardware Compatibility List. You can find the list online at

  ```
  www.microsoft.com/hwtest/hcl/default.htm
  ```

  in a form that you can search interactively by component category or by the company name of a component's manufacturer.

Of the two methods, the NTHQ is easier, but using the HCL is the only way to be absolutely sure that what you have will work with Windows NT.

Many hardware vendors offer server machines with Windows NT Server preinstalled. If NT is the network operating system of choice when you're buying new servers, price one that includes the operating system versus one that doesn't. You may be pleasantly surprised by the price breaks you can get when buying a preinstalled system.

Installing from Your Network

The following may seem counterintuitive, but here goes: Copying files from a hard drive elsewhere on a network is faster than copying files from a local CD-ROM player (even a 24x or 32x player). Why? Because hard disks are still as much as 100 times faster than CD-ROM drives.

Savvy network administrators create a set of directories on a network drive and install Windows NT (Server, Workstation, and so forth) across the network when they can. This tactic is fast, easy, and requires only that you load a CD once, no matter how many times you install. In fact, network installation is what makes the next topic feasible — namely, automated installations.

Let the Software Do the Work: Automating Installation

Normally, user input drives the Windows NT installation program: from character-based prompts during the text phase, and by user navigation of menus and input items during the GUI phase. As an alternative, text files may drive Windows NT installation instead, making it possible to automate installation more or less completely. Script-driven installation can be especially handy when you must install more than two or three copies of Windows NT at any given time. The key files that drive this process appear in Table 22-2.

Table 22-2 Windows NT Setup Files

Name	*Description*
TXTSETUP.SIF	Drives the text-mode portion during Windows NT installation.
DOSNET.INF	Names the list of files to be copied to a local hard disk from a network drive when using WINNT or WINNT32 to install Windows NT.
IPINFO.INF	Defines IP addresses for the default gateway, the adapter (or adapters) in the NT Server machine, and the subnet mask for each adapter.
LAYOUT.INF	Manages the text and GUI mode installation of Windows NT components.

Consult the *Windows NT Server Resource Kit (Microsoft Press)* or the TechNet CD to find out all you can about the various install files before starting any big jobs. You'd also be well advised to try a couple of trial runs using these tools before attempting to automate the installation of a production machine.

You will also find several excellent non-Microsoft software products for Windows NT that can help to automate bulk installations on identical or similar computers. Symantec Corporations Norton Ghost lets you build and clone generic installations quickly (visit `www.ghost.com` for more details). Likewise, PowerQuest's Drive Image Professional permits you to create drive images that contain a Server installation, and install it across a network quickly and easily (visit `www.powerquest.com` for more information).

When Installation Goes Awry

Despite your best efforts, and taking all the proper precautions, the occasional Windows NT installation will fail. I've seen causes of failure that range from defective media, to network congestion (trying to copy files to too many machines at once), to boot sector viruses.

When an installation fails, take a deep breath, and try any or all of the following potential fixes:

- **Restart the installation.** If you get past the initial parts of the character mode portion of the install, the software is often smart enough to pick up where it left off and carry on from there. If you're that lucky, count your blessings, then go out and buy a lottery ticket!
- **If installation won't pick up where it left off, look for a directory named WIN_NT.~LS.** (If you're doing a floppyless install with the /B parameter, also look for WIN_NT.~BT.) Delete one (or both) of these directories and their contents. The Windows NT install program looks for these directories and attempts to save time by picking up where it left off. This behavior works fine when copies are correct and pristine, but can get in the way when problems surface. We include the DOS DELTREE command in our emergency install disk tool kit, because it lets us dispatch these directories and their contents quickly and easily.
- If all else fails, repartition and reformat the boot drive to remove all prior vestiges of your failed attempt. You'll start over with a clean slate! Our emergency install disk tool kit also includes DOS Fdisk and a handy utility called Delpart.exe, which can remove even non-DOS partitions (like NTFS) from a PC hard drive. Delpart.exe is available for download in the Disk and File Utilities section at:

  `www.apricot.co.uk/ftp/bbs/atsbbs/allfiles.htm.`

If the final technique doesn't work, recheck the Windows NT Hardware Compatibility List for potential sources of difficulty (see the NTHQ section earlier in this chapter for the details on the HCL). Or look for guidance on your problems on Microsoft's TechNet CD or the NT-related newsgroups in USENET and the `msnews.microsoft.com` news server.

When [VGA Mode] Gets the Boot!

You will find out that NT doesn't care a bit if the display on your NT Server or Workstation machine is working or not. NT continues to chug along quite happily, even if you can't see what the system is doing because the screen is totally "confuzled" or if nothing is showing at all. The leading cause of this problem is loading a display driver that doesn't work with your graphics adapter or your monitor, or perhaps won't work with both of them!

When this problem happens (and it's a common post-installation problem), don't panic. Simply reboot the machine. When the boot menu shows up, you'll notice another option in that menu that reads:

```
Windows NT Server Version 4.00 [VGA Mode]
```

If you hit a key to halt the automatic boot countdown, you can use the arrow key to move the highlight to this option. Doing so boots Windows NT with a plain-vanilla VGA driver. Then, you can try a different driver (or trouble-shoot the hardware). This time, use the test button to make sure the driver works before you change your display over!

The LKGC Gets the Nod

After installation is complete, you must continue configuring your Server to add all kinds of information about system and user policies, account and group names, install additional software, and so forth. Every time you make a change to Windows NT, those changes are recorded in the Windows NT Registry. Sometimes, those changes can have unforeseen side effects — especially if you've been editing the Registry directly — and can make your machine falter, or even fail to boot.

When your machine does falter or fails to boot, always try reverting to the last working version of the Registry. Hit the space bar when the following message appears (after you have selected the boot OS):

```
Press Space Bar NOW to Invoke Hardware Profile/Last Known
        Good Configuration
```

You roll back to the version of the Registry that was in use the last time your machine booted successfully. The good news is that your machine will probably boot; the bad news is that you will lose all the changes you've made since the last time you rebooted the machine. Bummer!

When you make lots of changes, either back up the Registry frequently or reboot frequently. This keeps the amount of work you can lose — from an ill-advised Registry change, a bad driver selection, and so on — to a minimum.

Using the Windows NT Startup Disks

When the NT Server machine can't boot, use your Windows NT Startup disks to boot that machine. These disks often give you access to the hard drive where the operating system and boot files live, so you can attempt repairs before worrying about restoring a backup or rebuilding the machine.

You do have a set of NT Startup disks don't you? If not, build yourself a set by running the 32-bit version of the install program, WINNT32, from the NT Server CD right now. If you use the /O parameter, you build only the startup floppies, so take that approach and don't reinstall NT unnecessarily!

"ERD to Windows NT Server!"

The Emergency Repair Disk contains the important parts of your system's Registry files, plus other utilities, that you can use to perform system repairs when NT doesn't boot or run properly. Because Registry sizes vary from machine to machine, an ERD may actually consist of several floppies, especially when you create one for a domain controller.

Although you can create an ERD as part of NT installation, that version probably won't reflect all the changes you'll make to a typical NT Server afterwards. Go ahead and create one — you may need it if problems occur. Nevertheless, remember to run RDISK.EXE after you finish tweaking your machine to update or create an ERD that reflects your most recent changes. That way you can repair the system you painstakingly built, rather than repairing the naked version of a system that the install program creates.

A generic NT boot floppy saves systems!

The problem with the NT Startup disks is that it takes three of them to boot Windows NT. Using these disks also takes you through a time-consuming set of steps to get a machine running. Even worse, each set of boot floppies is specific to the machine on which it was created. This can be frustrating, and led creative minds to develop a generic NT boot floppy. It works on any system and kick-starts just about any balky Windows NT machine. Here's how to build one:

1. Format a floppy using the Windows NT Explorer (right-click on the floppy drive icon in the left-hand panel, then select Format from the pop-up menu).

   This floppy MUST be formatted inside Windows NT. A DOS-formatted floppy will not work as a generic NT boot floppy!

2. Check your NT Explorer settings to make sure you can see hidden files (View, Options, then click the Show all files radio button on the View tab in the resulting Options dialog box).

3. Copy these files from your server's root directory to the NT-formatted floppy disk:

   NTDLR

   NTDETECT.COM

   BOOT.INI

   NTBOOTDD.SYS (only if it appears)

This creates a boot floppy that can bring up an NT System without using all three startup disks. Make this part of your standard NT toolkit.

If this generic boot floppy won't produce a booting system, try the Startup floppies and attempt a full-fledged system repair!

Now for the Real Work!

Although installing Windows NT Server by itself is no mean feat, the real work begins when that job is over: You must translate your plans for domain structures, machine names, user names, group names, and disk structures from concept into reality. This is the real work that makes NT Server usable to your audience and able to deal with the demands they will put on your system. Remember to update your ERD on a regular basis!

Chapter 23

Ten Ways to Network NT Server — and Live to Tell the Tale!

In This Chapter

- Investigating the obvious often pays off
- Routing, from A to B
- Diagnosing IP troubles
- Choosing proper network interfaces
- Dividing to conquer network congestion
- Checking your services
- Addressing address issues
- Checking on changes
- Asking for help . . . and getting it!
- Preventing problems beats fixing them

Windows NT Server without a network is like ham without eggs or coffee without cream and sugar (our apologies in advance to the vegetarians, coffee purists, and caffeine-free members of our audience).

Because Windows NT Server and networking go together like gangbusters, the gang (of users) may try to bust you when the network stops working. Try as you may, this happens from time to time. When it does, read over these tips and tricks.

Always Investigate the Obvious

The number one cause of ailing networks is — you guessed it — loose connections. Always check the network interface card (NIC) to make sure that the cable is still plugged in or otherwise attached. Also be sure to check the hubs, the routers, the ISDN box, or the modem, and anywhere else the cables go.

Networking experts often talk about a troubleshooting pyramid that follows the progression of network capabilities up from the hardware and cables, through the protocol stack, to the applications that request network services. In this analogy, the base of the pyramid is far bigger than the top. This pyramid illustrates that problems are most likely to occur at the physical level of networking. Why? Because that's where the cables and connections are. Go ahead — check 'em again, Dano!

When NT Must Route Packets

Because Windows NT happily enables you to insert two or more NICs, or other devices that can carry network traffic — such as modems, ISDN boxes, or even CSU/DSUs for high-speed digital networking — Windows NT is also built to move traffic from one connection to another. This behavior is called *routing* and enables Windows NT to tie individual pieces of a network together.

The most exposed and important part of many networks is the link that ties a local network to the Internet (or at least, to your local Internet service provider). If Windows NT is filling that role on your network, be prepared to perform regular troubleshooting rituals to keep this all-important link to the outside world running.

Trying to isolate this function on a separate computer if you can is a good idea for two reasons: First, adding the burden of routing traffic and managing an Internet interface requires additional software and services that can tax a (possibly overburdened) Windows NT Server; and second, you should limit the impact of system failure to as few services as possible. Chances are that your users will be less unhappy if they lose only Internet access or access to shared files and applications rather than losing both at once.

If you do use a Windows NT system as a router, especially if an Internet link is involved, think about installing some kind of firewall software on that machine, such as Microsoft's Proxy Server 2.0 or Ositis Software's WinProxy. A firewall protects your network from interlopers and enables you to monitor and filter incoming (and outgoing) content and information.

Troubleshooting Tools for TCP/IP

If you're going to attach to the Internet (and who isn't, these days?), you want to build a TCP/IP toolkit to help with the inevitable troubleshooting chores involved in keeping a TCP/IP network working properly.

Fortunately, Windows NT includes a fine collection of TCP/IP tools and utilities that you can use immediately. Table 23-1 includes some prime candidates for your IP troubleshooting toolbox.

Table 23-1 TCP/IP Diagnostic Utilities

Utility	*Description*
ARP	Displays the address translation tables used by the IP Address Resolution Protocol (ARP); helps detect invalid entries and ensure proper resolution of numeric IP addresses to MAC addresses.
HOSTNAME	Displays your IP host name on-screen; use this to check your machine's current name.
IPCONFIG	Displays all current network configuration values for all interfaces; use this to check address assignments for your machine, the default gateway, and the subnet mask.
NBTSTAT	Shows protocol statistics and active connections using NetBIOS over TCP/IP; use this to troubleshoot Microsoft naming issues.
NETSTAT	Shows active TCP and UDP connections; use this to check TCP/IP network connections and statistics.
NSLOOKUP	Displays information about known DNS servers.
PING	Verifies basic connectivity to network computers; type PING loopback to check internal capabilities first, and then check local and remote machines to check overall connectivity.
ROUTE	Displays network routing tables and enables you to edit entries; useful primarily when static routing is in effect.
TRACERT	Determines the route from the sender to a destination by sending ICMP echo packets that cause all stations between sender and receiver to announce themselves.

Given this arsenal of tools, you should be well-prepared to shoot TCP/IP troubles before they shoot you!

Let Your NICs Take the Knocks

On a Windows NT Server, performance is the name of the game. In networking, because network traffic tends to congregate at the server, spending extra bucks on a fast, powerful NIC makes sense. At a bare minimum, you want a PCI-based NIC because it offers the best bus connection to the rest of the system. Other hardware enhancements worth purchasing for Windows NT Server NICs include the following:

- **Direct memory access (DMA)** enables the NIC to transfer data directly from its on-board memory to the computer's memory without requiring the CPU to mediate.
- **Shared adapter memory** means a NIC's on-board RAM maps into the computer's RAM. When the computer thinks it's writing *to* its own RAM, it's writing straight *to* the NIC, and when it thinks it's reading *from* its own RAM, it's reading straight *from* the NIC. Shared system memory works the same way, except the NIC reads from and writes from the computer's RAM instead of its own on-board RAM. Extra memory for NICs is almost as good as more RAM on Windows NT PCs!
- **Bus mastering** lets the NIC manage the computer's bus to coordinate data transfers to and from the computer's memory. Bus mastering enables the CPU concentrate on other activities and can improve performance by 20 to 70 percent. This is the most worthwhile of all the enhancements mentioned here.
- **On-board coprocessor** puts an additional CPU on a NIC and permits the NIC to process data that the CPU would otherwise have to handle. Many NICs today use such processors to speed operations.

The idea is to put the processing power and speed where it does the most good: on the NIC that all the users must interact with to obtain data from (or move packets through) a server.

When to Divide Up Your Network

When traffic reaches high levels on a network segment, traffic jams occur just like they do at rush hour on the highway. When this happens, you either need to build some new roads (switch to a faster networking technology) or add more roads (break up the existing network and put one subset of users on one new piece, another subset on another piece, and so on).

How can you figure out when the traffic is starting to choke your network? Easy! Windows NT Server includes a service called the Network Monitor (NetMon) that you can install on your server to monitor the traffic moving into and out of your server (and on the cable segment or segments to which that server is attached).

NetMon doesn't install on Windows NT Server by default, but it's easy to add. Just launch Network applet⇨Control Panel⇨Services⇨Add⇨ Network Monitor Tools and Agent. After you follow the instructions from there, NetMon shows up in the Administrative Tools (Common) entry in the Programs group under the Start menu.

Get to know NetMon, and you get to know your network much better!

When in Doubt, Check Your Services

What do network servers do? They provide network services. When things get weird on a Windows NT Server and you can't find anything wrong with the network, you want to visit the Services applet in Control Panel, as shown in Figure 23-1. Be sure to check the entries for key services like the Computer browser, the Server service, and the Workstation service. Make sure the Status field says "Started" and the Startup field is properly set. (It should read "Automatic" for services that are supposed to launch upon startup.) Many times when the network shows no obvious problems, you may find a key service has been paused or stopped or has simply quit for some reason. If the service has stopped, you should refer back to Event Viewer to find out why; a stopped service usually indicates a serious problem that will recur.

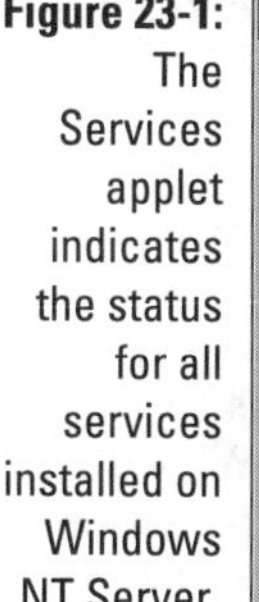

Figure 23-1: The Services applet indicates the status for all services installed on Windows NT Server.

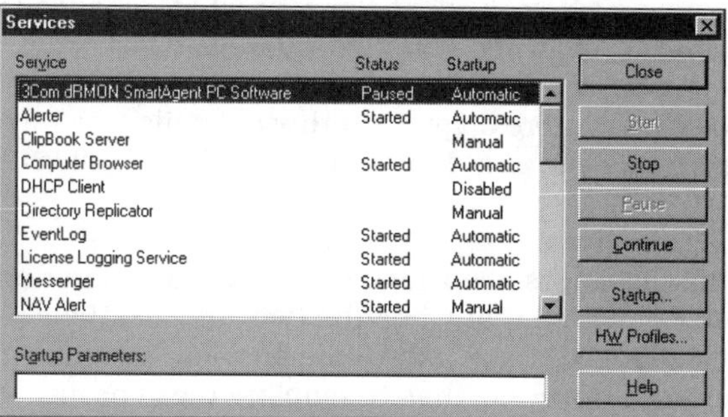

Managing Network Names and Addresses

The only way to find things on a network is to know their addresses. But alas, human beings are much better at remembering symbolic names than numeric addresses (or worse still, the arcane bit patterns that computers use to address one another).

This means many things when you operate a working network, but two primary concerns from a troubleshooting perspective exist:

- The services that provide name to address translation must be properly configured and working correctly for users to make effective use of a network.
- Network addresses, subnet masks, and related information (such as default gateways, router addresses, and so on) must be unique, properly specified, and in substantial agreement for computers to use a network properly.

Symptoms of trouble in this area are many and varied. Duplicate addresses usually cause all holders of the same address to lose their ability to access the network. Invalid names or addresses simply can't be reached and may require serious troubleshooting to fix. (Check the spelling of names carefully and the numeric values for addresses equally carefully.)

Fortunately, problems in this arena usually make themselves known during initial configuration or when settings change. If you can simply check your settings and assumptions against a known working set of values, you can usually fix these troubles quickly and painlessly.

What's New? What's Changed?

When troubleshooting a network, what's new or what's changed is often the source of the trouble. Thus, when you investigate network woes, be sure to ask yourself these questions right away, and then answer them in as much detail as possible. While you're digging up those details, you often uncover the source of the trouble and can determine the solution, all in one swift maneuver.

Savvy network administrators keep a log of changes and additions to the servers on their networks, so that when the two key questions ("What's new?" and "What's changed?") are asked, the answers are immediately forthcoming. You could do worse than to emulate these professionals!

Ask for Help When You Need It

Occasionally, when troubleshooting a system, you run into problems that are so mysterious or baffling that you won't have a clue about how to fix them. When that happens, don't tear out your hair — ask for help instead.

If you're having a problem with Windows NT, then paying $195 for a "Technical Support Incident" with Microsoft may be worth it. You can also check the TechNet CD (you can order it from `www.microsoft.com/technet`) or the Microsoft Developer Network (which you can join at `msdn.microsoft.com/developer/`).

If the problem's with a piece of hardware, check the manufacturer's Web site or bulletin board for a driver update. If that leads to no joy, you may have to pay their tech support operation for some advice, too. If you can determine the focus of the problem, you can often get help from those who know that focus best. Even if it costs you, think about the value of the time (and the aggravation) you save. Better to light a candle than curse the darkness!

Outfits like the Technical Support Alliance Network (`www.tsanet.org`) and even 1-900-787-7678, or the easy to remember version 1-900-SUPPORT (the phone number's also the name of the organization), can help with multivendor support issues. Don't be afraid to use them!

Prevention Always Beats Cure

The best way to shoot network trouble, and other kinds of system problems, is to stop them before they ever happen. The only way to prevent problems and keep your network running is to study your network environment closely and carefully and figure out where its weak points are. Do this before your network demonstrates its weaknesses to the world at large by breaking.

If you keep an eye on potential trouble spots and make sure to perform regular maintenance and upkeep activities (like scheduled backups, file system cleanups, keeping up with upgrades, Service Packs, and hotfixes), you can prevent problems. And believe us, preventing problems isn't only less work, but it's also the cause of far less unwanted notoriety than fixing things when they break.

Chapter 24

Ten Tips and Tricks for Troubleshooting Windows NT Server

In This Chapter

- Conquering common configuration problems
- Ensuring disk consistency
- Fixing file system errors
- Defragmenting files
- Cutting down on file overhead
- Preventing viruses beats curing them
- Perfecting system performance
- Beating the boot up blues
- Using the Task Manager
- Viewing events in Windows NT

Although Windows NT Server is a reasonably stable and efficient network operating system, it's not perfect. You can expect to encounter trouble on your server from time to time, and you should be prepared to deal with it.

That's why we've documented some of the most common causes of trouble along with well-known fixes, workarounds, and solutions. The ten tips in this chapter should help you tackle whatever NT Server trouble comes your way.

Common Configuration Confusions

A Member Server cannot become a domain controller unless you reinstall Windows NT Server. A Backup Domain Controller (BDC) can always become a Primary Domain Controller (PDC) and vice-versa, but changing roles between domain controller and Member Servers involves real work.

The Identification tab in the Network applet in Control Panel makes it seem like switching between domain and workgroup membership is a snap. Be painfully aware, however, that switching from domain to workgroup membership involves serious account changes and Registry activity, and that the switchover means lots of reconfiguration work — even under the best circumstances. Of course, if your server is a domain controller, switching to workgroup membership is pretty unlikely.

A Windows NT Server boot drive (which means, in Microsoft terminology, the drive partition where the NT system files reside) needs at least 500MB of disk space, especially if it is a print server. Windows NT stores spool files for print servers in this partition by default (you can move it by editing the Registry), and it's also a common site for lots of other temporary files. Remember to give Windows NT Server plenty of room to breathe on its boot drive!

When setting up a Windows NT Server, make sure to establish your naming conventions for machine names, user accounts, groups, printers, and file shares. Once established, changing names can be difficult under most circumstances and can even require reinstalling Windows NT in the worst cases. If you know what you're doing before you start, you probably won't have to do things over!

CHKDSK and Check DAT!

Although CHKDSK is a familiar utility to those with long-standing DOS or Windows backgrounds, for those who are unfamiliar with this venerable tool it's a Windows NT command line utility worth getting to know. Simply put, CHKDSK checks a specified disk — for both FAT and NTFS volumes — and provides a status report. Nevertheless, CHKDSK is prey to certain problems that you should know about:

- **Symptom:** CHKDSK won't run.

  Solution: CHKDSK can have problems when applications keep files open. To work around this, boot from NT floppies to check the NT boot partition itself, or make sure to shut down all applications before checking other drives.

- **Symptom:** CHKDSK runs, but doesn't complete.

  Solution: Because a memory shortage often causes this problem, adding more memory can help. See the Task Manager item later in this chapter for ways to check memory.

- **Symptom:** CHKDSK runs but reports odd errors.

  Solution: Unless you specify the /F (fix problems) parameter, CHDSK lets other applications write to the disk while it's running. This trait can cause all kinds of strange behavior. Close all applications and services before you run CHKDSK.

- **Symptom:** CHKDSK runs every time the machine boots.

  Solution: Often indicates that NT didn't shut down properly, encountered problems shutting down, or didn't fully flush the file buffers before the power went off. If you wait for NT to tell you it's safe to turn off the power before hitting the power switch on a machine, this problem goes away.

You can launch CHKDSK in a DOS Window by using the Run command (Start, Run) or with NT Explorer. To use NT Explorer to launch CHKDSK, right-click the drive icon in the left-hand NT Explorer pane that you want to inspect, then select the Properties entry from the pop-up menu that results. Next, click the tool tab in the Properties dialog box, then click the Check Now button in the Error-Checking pane in that Window. Sounds like a lot of work, but it's actually a quick and easy way to run Chkdsk.

Handling File System Errors

When a Windows NT drive becomes unavailable or files become inaccessible, a serious file system problem is usually at work. Here are some possible causes and solutions:

- **Symptom:** Disappearing or inaccessible drives.

  Cause: May indicate system files are loading improperly or have become corrupt.

  Solution: Replace file system driver files in the \System32\Drivers directory: FASTFAT.SYS (for FAT volumes), NTFS.SYS (for NTFS volumes), and FTDISK.SYS (if using stripe or volume sets) from the install CD.

- **Symptom:** System errors when accessing files.

  Cause: Corrupted files in the file system.

  Solution: Run CHKDSK /F to see if it can detect and fix problems. If not, back up the drive, wipe all partitions, repartition and reformat the drive; then restore the backed up files.

- **Symptom:** Corrupt FAT or NTFS volumes.

  Cause: FAT volumes can become corrupt due to system errors. NTFS fixes most such problems, but may still experience corruption.

  Solution: For FAT, run CHKDSK; for NTFS, consider replacing the drive because this may indicate a failing drive.

- **Symptom:** Strange but reproducible errors that don't fit the other descriptions.

  Potential cause: A bug in Windows NT! File corruption errors or system lockups while accessing certain files may indicate a pesky bug of some kind.

  Solution: Check with Microsoft technical support and verify that your problem is unique and reproducible. Your problem may lead to a fix for some application (more likely) or even to Windows NT itself (less likely, but not impossible).

Fixing Fragmented Files

When the FAT or NTFS file system write files to a hard disk, each has its own way of deciding where to put their contents. Although NTFS is a bit smarter about where it puts files, both FAT and NTFS volumes become fragmented over time. This condition is best described as one where larger files are broken up into smaller chunks, and those chunks are not stored next to each other on a drive platter's surface. An operation called *defragmentation* gathers up these pieces and figures out how to rewrite files so all the pieces of a file are stored contiguously, whenever possible.

Microsoft does not include a file defragmentation utility with Windows NT. The company recommends backing up a drive, wiping its contents, and then restoring the backup to eliminate fragmentation. Although this approach works, the process is often more trouble than it's worth. At least two vendors offer defragmentation utilities for Windows NT: Executive Software builds a utility called DisKeeper, and Symantec offers its Norton SpeedDisk. Each of these utilities cost around $300 (but Norton SpeedDisk in included with a bunch of other utilities, whereas DisKeeper stands more or less alone).

Regular defragmentation is a good idea, especially on drives that experience lots of write and delete activity (like e-mail systems, user application files, and so forth). Get a "defrag tool" and use it at least monthly, if not weekly!

The File System Clean-up

Over time, file systems can fill up with garbage if they're not regularly cleaned out. This includes temporary (.TMP) files, backup files (.BAK), outdated copies of documents, old applications and DLLs, and all kinds of other gross stuff. Cleaning out files is a nasty job, but somebody has to do it — and if you're running an NT Server system that provides shared file storage, that somebody is probably you!

You can tackle this problem in one of several ways. First, you can state a policy (or buy software for something called disk quotas) that limits users to specific amounts of server disk space. Then, you have to police their directories and warn those who go over their limits that they're going to have to reduce their holdings or you will do it for them. Alternatively, quota enforcement capabilities were just added to Windows NT Service Pack 4 as of this writing, so you can now let the operating system police and enforce these limits for you.

Likewise, you can observe the kinds of files that litter your drives and write some batch files to seek out and delete them, or you can look for third-party tools to handle this for you. No matter how you slice it, somebody has to find the trash and take it out — permanently!

Victory over Viruses

As operating systems go, Windows NT is pretty virus-resistant. However, it has become the target for numerous viruses and is prey to application-level viruses, such as the many Microsoft Word macro virus strains that infest our world. An infected NT boot disk drive may not boot properly, or it may be subject to terrible performance hits.

Be sure to scan all your hard drives — not just Windows NT drives, if you operate a multiboot system — on a regular basis for viruses of all kinds. We recommend that you obtain and use one of the many virus scan utilities designed for Windows NT.

If you do catch a boot sector virus, you may be able to eliminate it by booting from a DOS disk and running FDISK /MBR. This rebuilds the Master Boot Record (MBR), which may then require you to boot from NT Startup disks and use the ERD (Emergency Repair Disk — see Chapter 22) to repair the MBR further. Sometimes, this approach may render a drive unreadable. That's why we recommend that you install an antivirus utility on your NT Servers that scans all incoming files and that scans its own drives every time it boots.

Fixing Poor System Performance

Understanding computer performance in general, and Windows NT performance in particular, is a grand subject of its own. In fact, we've seen at least a dozen books on this subject.

But all of those books boil down to two essential observations:

- Any performance problem is the result of a bottleneck, which is some component or subsystem on a computer that limits the performance of a system because it's significantly slower than other components on that system. Common culprits are RAM (NT is quite memory hungry), disk space, CPU, and network interface cards (NICs).

  Fixing performance problems means identifying and correcting bottlenecks; the tool of choice for this task is Performance Monitor. Once you pinpoint a cause, use this tool to verify your suspicions before you change anything — sometimes, one problem masks a deeper, less obvious problem. You must find the real bottleneck before you can fix it!
- Every time you fix a bottleneck on a system, the next slowest component becomes the bottleneck. This means you can tweak and tune forever, and you'll never have a perfectly fast system. Good enough has to be just that! Don't spend the time and money that the last 2 percent gain in performance can cost; do spend the time and money that the first 10 percent can cost.

Ultimately, the bottleneck on any system should be its users. We mere humans are so much slower than computers that they should be waiting for us rather than the other way around. In the meantime, get to know the Windows NT Performance Monitor tool (PerfMon). Chapter 15 of the outstanding book *Windows NT Server 4.0 Secrets,* by Valda Hilley (IDG Books Worldwide, Inc.), provides the best short discussion of Windows NT tuning and performance issues we've ever seen, anywhere.

The easiest potential performance boost on a Windows NT system may be accessed on the Performance tab of the System applet in Control Panel. Click the Change button in the Virtual Memory pane. Then make sure the Paging File is at least twice the size of the RAM installed in your server. This large size is especially useful on systems that may sometimes experience heavy user loads. Another quick speedup technique is to relocate the paging file on another hard disk (preferably, one that's attached to a different controller than the NT boot drive). This distributes the hard disk load across multiple drives (and possibly, controllers) and can improve overall performance by as much as 10 percent.

When NT Server Won't Boot

When viruses mess with the boot sector on your boot drive or if the Registry has problems that prevent the device drivers from working, NT may be unable to boot itself. Before considering reinstallation or other major forms of repair, remember to try the following approaches to fix this problem:

- Always try booting to the Last Known Good Configuration first (see Chapter 22 for the details on this potentially life-saving technique).
- Boot from the Startup disks and use the Repair installation and the ERD to try to fix the drive. This action fixes most problems.
- If you ever catch a boot sector virus, or the Master Boot Record (MBR) becomes damaged, you may have to precede the previous step by booting from DOS, then running FDISK/MBR to repair the MBR. Finally, you'll need to apply the ERD so it can fix the MBR to work with Windows NT again.
- Sometimes, a damaged NTDETECT.COM file can also impede the boot process. NT may occasionally inform you that it has a problem with NTDETECT, but other times the symptoms may be more mysterious. If you can boot using the Generic boot floppy described in Chapter 22, you might want to copy NTDETECT from that floppy onto your NT system partition to see if it fixes your problems!
- If you suspect a damaged or deranged BOOT.INI file (which usually means you've been editing it by hand, haven't you?) verify that its file attributes are system, hidden, read-only. If it's not read-only, the file doesn't work properly. Otherwise, restore from your backup (which means you must get in the habit of creating a backup copy — we call ours BOOT.OLD) — *before* you start editing away.

This litany may not cover all potential boot problems, but it covers most of the ones we've seen, anyway!

Viewing the Evidence with Event Viewer

Windows NT's built-in Event Viewer utility appears in Figure 24-1. This is a premier troubleshooting tool that provides an audit trail of events that it detects on a Windows NT machine.

For each event it records, Event Viewer stores a detail record. To launch the Event Viewer, the sequence is Start⇨Programs⇨Administrative Tools (Common)⇨Event Viewer. To produce the detailed records, double-click any entry in the event log. Also, be aware that Event Viewer maintains three logs named System, Security, and Application. If you can't find an event reported

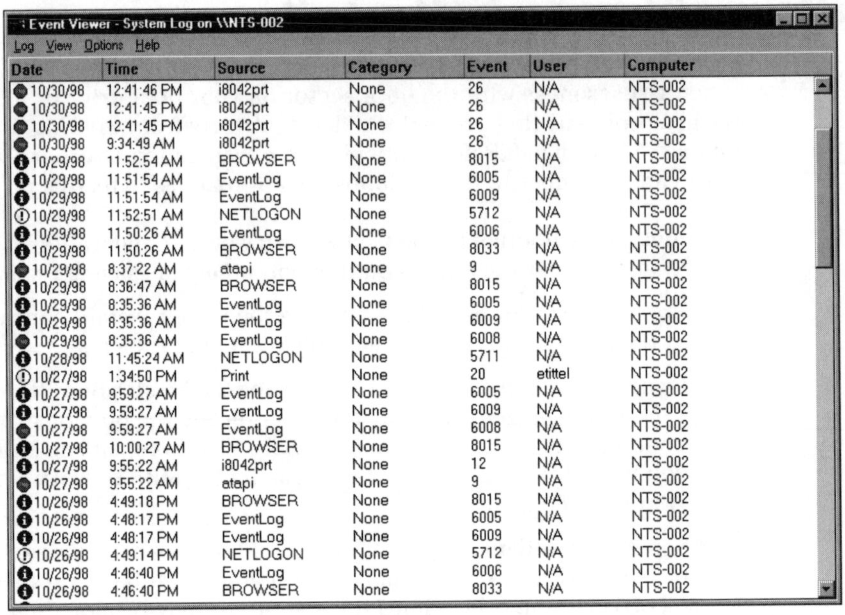

Event Viewer - System Log on \\NTS-002

Log View Options Help

Date	Time	Source	Category	Event	User	Computer
10/30/98	12:41:46 PM	i8042prt	None	26	N/A	NTS-002
10/30/98	12:41:45 PM	i8042prt	None	26	N/A	NTS-002
10/30/98	12:41:45 PM	i8042prt	None	26	N/A	NTS-002
10/30/98	9:34:49 AM	i8042prt	None	26	N/A	NTS-002
10/29/98	11:52:54 AM	BROWSER	None	8015	N/A	NTS-002
10/29/98	11:51:54 AM	EventLog	None	6005	N/A	NTS-002
10/29/98	11:51:54 AM	EventLog	None	6009	N/A	NTS-002
10/29/98	11:52:51 AM	NETLOGON	None	5712	N/A	NTS-002
10/29/98	11:50:26 AM	EventLog	None	6006	N/A	NTS-002
10/29/98	11:50:26 AM	BROWSER	None	8033	N/A	NTS-002
10/29/98	8:37:22 AM	atapi	None	9	N/A	NTS-002
10/29/98	8:36:47 AM	BROWSER	None	8015	N/A	NTS-002
10/29/98	8:35:36 AM	EventLog	None	6005	N/A	NTS-002
10/29/98	8:35:36 AM	EventLog	None	6009	N/A	NTS-002
10/29/98	8:35:36 AM	EventLog	None	6008	N/A	NTS-002
10/28/98	11:45:24 AM	NETLOGON	None	5711	N/A	NTS-002
10/27/98	1:34:50 PM	Print	None	20	etittel	NTS-002
10/27/98	9:59:27 AM	EventLog	None	6005	N/A	NTS-002
10/27/98	9:59:27 AM	EventLog	None	6009	N/A	NTS-002
10/27/98	9:59:27 AM	EventLog	None	6008	N/A	NTS-002
10/27/98	10:00:27 AM	BROWSER	None	8015	N/A	NTS-002
10/27/98	9:55:22 AM	i8042prt	None	12	N/A	NTS-002
10/27/98	9:55:22 AM	atapi	None	9	N/A	NTS-002
10/26/98	4:49:18 PM	BROWSER	None	8015	N/A	NTS-002
10/26/98	4:48:17 PM	EventLog	None	6005	N/A	NTS-002
10/26/98	4:48:17 PM	EventLog	None	6009	N/A	NTS-002
10/26/98	4:49:14 PM	NETLOGON	None	5712	N/A	NTS-002
10/26/98	4:46:40 PM	EventLog	None	6006	N/A	NTS-002
10/26/98	4:46:40 PM	BROWSER	None	8033	N/A	NTS-002

Figure 24-1: The Event Viewer is your viewport into the errors and behaviors of a Windows NT system.

in the System log, check the Application log because many NT services and applications write to that log instead.

Certainly, Event Viewer should be a stopping-off point when troubleshooting a Windows NT system that's experiencing difficulties. However, you should get in the habit of checking this log on a regular basis, even when a server may not be showing symptoms of trouble. This log can often forewarn you about impending difficulties because it can indicate untoward patterns of system use and behavior (such as outsiders trying to break in).

Using Task Manager

One of the best and most accessible utilities built into Windows NT is the Task Manager. The Task Manager's performance tab appears in Figure 24-2. To call up this display at any time, right-click on any blank area on the Windows NT toolbar (the portion of the screen where the Start button appears), or press Ctrl+Alt+Delete and click the Task Manager button on the Windows NT Security window that pops up.

Task Manager's Performance tab lets you take your system's temperature

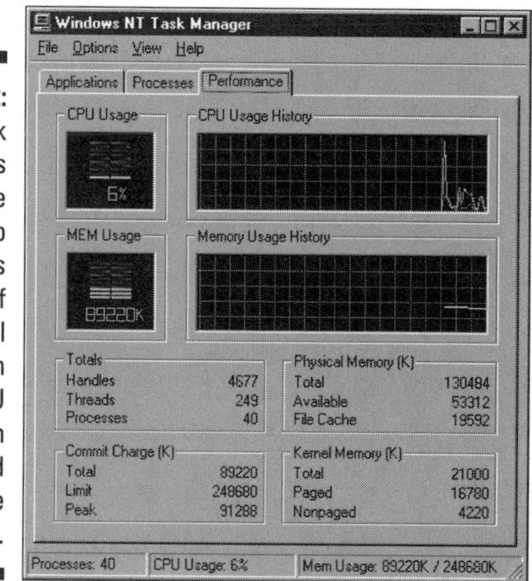

Figure 24-2: The Task Manager's Performance tab provides lots of useful information about CPU utilization and available memory.

quickly and accurately. Pay special attention to sustained high levels of CPU utilization, and check the relationship between the Peak and Limit values reported in the Commit Charge pane (if Peak comes within 10 percent of Limit, this may indicate an overloaded or memory-constrained machine).

You can use the other eponymous tabs in Task Manager to control or terminate Windows NT processes and applications. You also can use these tabs to change process priorities, to switch between applications, and to get a good sense of which processes are consuming the bulk of a system's resources over time.

Get to know the Task Manager. This tool should be among the first diagnostic tools you use any time you suspect performance or application problems on a Windows NT machine.

Index

• Numbers •

• A •

• B •

• D •

• E •

• F •

• G •

• H •

• I •

(continued)

• J •

• K •

• L •

• M •

• N •

(continued)

• O •

• P •

(continued)

• T •

(continued)

• U •

• V •

• W •

• X •

• Y •

• Z •

Notes

Notes

Discover Dummies Online!

The Dummies Web Site is your fun and friendly online resource for the latest information about *...For Dummies®* books and your favorite topics. The Web site is the place to communicate with us, exchange ideas with other *...For Dummies* readers, chat with authors, and have fun!

Ten Fun and Useful Things You Can Do at www.dummies.com

1. Win free *...For Dummies* books and more!
2. Register your book and be entered in a prize drawing.
3. Meet your favorite authors through the IDG Books Author Chat Series.
4. Exchange helpful information with other *...For Dummies* readers.
5. Discover other great *...For Dummies* books you must have!
6. Purchase Dummieswear™ exclusively from our Web site.
7. Buy *...For Dummies* books online.
8. Talk to us. Make comments, ask questions, get answers!
9. Download free software.
10. Find additional useful resources from authors.

Link directly to these ten fun and useful things at **http://www.dummies.com/10useful**

For other technology titles from IDG Books Worldwide, go to **www.idgbooks.com**

Not on the Web yet? It's easy to get started with *Dummies 101®: The Internet For Windows®98* or *The Internet For Dummies®*, 6th Edition, at local retailers everywhere.

Find other *...For Dummies* books on these topics:
Business • Career • Databases • Food & Beverage • Games • Gardening • Graphics • Hardware
Health & Fitness • Internet and the World Wide Web • Networking • Office Suites
Operating Systems • Personal Finance • Pets • Programming • Recreation • Sports
Spreadsheets • Teacher Resources • Test Prep • Word Processing

IDG BOOKS WORLDWIDE BOOK REGISTRATION

We want to hear from you!

Visit **http://my2cents.dummies.com** to register this book and tell us how you liked it!

- Get entered in our monthly prize giveaway.
- Give us feedback about this book — tell us what you like best, what you like least, or maybe what you'd like to ask the author and us to change!
- Let us know any other *...For Dummies*® topics that interest you.

Your feedback helps us determine what books to publish, tells us what coverage to add as we revise our books, and lets us know whether we're meeting your needs as a *...For Dummies* reader. You're our most valuable resource, and what you have to say is important to us!

Not on the Web yet? It's easy to get started with *Dummies 101*®*: The Internet For Windows*® *98* or *The Internet For Dummies*®, 6th Edition, at local retailers everywhere.

Or let us know what you think by sending us a letter at the following address:

...For Dummies Book Registration
Dummies Press
7260 Shadeland Station, Suite 100
Indianapolis, IN 46256-3917
Fax 317-596-5498